Brazil and Africa

Brazil and Africa

José Honório Rodrigues

Translated by
Richard A. Mazzara and Sam Hileman

UNIVERSITY OF CALIFORNIA PRESS

Berkeley and Los Angeles   1965

University of California Press
Berkeley and Los Angeles
California
Cambridge University Press
London, England
© 1965 by The Regents of the University of California
Translated from *Brasil e África: outro horizonte*
(Rio de Janeiro: Editôra Civilização Brasileira, S. A.
1961; Second Edition, revised and augmented, 1964)
Published with the assistance of a grant
from The Rockefeller Foundation
Library of Congress Catalog Card Number: 65-23155
Designed by Jorn B. Jorgensen
Printed in the United States of America

To Lêda, as ever

Foreword

José Honório Rodrigues is one of the most articulate and thoughtful of the Brazilian scholars who are seeking to understand and interpret contemporary Brazil and to assess its role in international affairs. In this volume his focus is on Afro-Brazilian relations, but in developing this theme he presents a comprehensive analysis of the interaction of African and Brazilian cultures and a forthright statement on a reorientation of Brazilian foreign policy.

He divides the work into two parts. In Part I he provides the background for his analysis of the contemporary situation by a review of Afro-Brazilian relations from 1500 to 1960. The review consists of a brief narrative of Afro-Brazilian relations during the colonial period to 1800, a more intensive study of the contributions of African and Portuguese cultures to modern Brazilian culture, an analysis of the racial democracy which has stemmed from miscegenation and the interaction of the two transplanted cultures, and a detailed history of what he terms modern relations from 1800 to 1960.

A clear, unequivocal thesis emerges from these pages. The Brazilians of today, Professor Rodrigues insists, are neither European nor Latin American. Ethnically and culturally they are a mixed race in which the European-American strains have been Africanized through miscegenation. This does not mean that Brazilians have discarded their Western European heritage, as their persistent support of a constitutional regime, their insistence on the rights of the individual, and their adherence to the economic and technological system of the West demonstrate. It does mean, however, that through the historical process of cultural interaction Brazilians are singularly qualified to serve as an intermediary between the peoples of Western Europe and the emerging states of Africa.

In Part II Professor Rodrigues analyzes the current situation in the light of history and adduces specific policies for the conduct of Brazilian foreign relations. In the chapter devoted to the analysis he addresses himself to aspects of the international situation which relate to the South Atlantic as a geographic area. The marked shift of emphasis from the traditional East-West focus to a new North-South orientation has introduced a significant factor into Brazil's international position. The growing division of the world's wealth into an industrialized northern and an underdeveloped southern hemisphere provides a setting in which Brazil can play a vital role. As a leading, if not the leading power of the two continents which enclose the South Atlantic Ocean, it is in a strategic position to exercise, if it so desires, a pronounced influence over a large and critical area. Completely free of the taint of colonialism and intimately linked to the cultures of both hemispheres, Brazil admirably fulfills the need for an effective liaison between the two camps.

The political implications of this point of view are clarified in the final chapter of the volume. The situation, as Professor Rodrigues sees it, entails a fundamental reorientation of Brazilian policy toward Portugal, the United States, the OAS and hemispheric solidarity, NATO, the European Common Market, the East-West conflict, the UN and its blocs, and the Western European tradition. Brazil must discard its provincial attitude toward world affairs. It must liberate itself from its traditional solidarity with Latin America and from its subservience to Portugal, to European imperialism, and to North American hemispheric economic interests. By so doing it will free itself from restrictions imposed by an outworn past and enable itself to deal with all nations, all peoples as it, and it alone, sees fit.

In order to make certain that his meaning would not be misunderstood, Professor Rodrigues formulated his basic ideas into a set of numbered theses, seventeen for Part I and eleven for Part II. These are brief statements, most of them in single sentence form, of the conclusions which the author has drawn from his research and observation.

Some are factual summations, such as the first thesis of Part I in which he points out that from the seventeenth to the nineteenth centuries Brazil maintained closer relations with Angola, Dahomey, and sections of the coast of Mina and Guinea than did Portugal itself. Others are more general in their interpretation, such as the fifth thesis of Part II in which he insists that Brazil to be consistent in its anticolonialism must support the independence of Angola and that if blood and sentiment mean anything Africa, as well as Portugal, deserves the sympathy and support of the Brazilians. All of them, since they are theses, are debatable, and all of them somewhere in the course of the volume receive substantiation with appropriate documentation.

The procedure is most useful, as useful as it is unusual. The reader is informed in advance of the position which the author assumes relative to his data and the points of view to which he has committed himself. The result is a running argument between the reader and the author. Are the theses valid? Has the author substantiated his position? Is the documentation adequate? To what extent do the points of view reflect accurately the author's exposition of the facts in the case? These are questions which each reader must answer for himself, but he should be warned that in undertaking the debate he will encounter a formidable adversary. For the author is not a demagogue waving the flag of nationalism. On the contrary, the theses are the considered opinion of a scholar whose credentials are impressive.

Currently, Professor Rodrigues is Executive Director of the Brazilian Institute of International Relations and Professor of the Economic History of Brazil in the Faculty of Economic Sciences of the University of Guanabara. For eight years he was Director of the Division of Rare Books and Publications of the National Library. For ten years he was Professor of the History of Brazil and the Diplomatic History of Brazil in the Rio Branco Institute of the Ministry of Foreign Relations and for six years Director of the National Archives and a member of the National Council of Geography, of the Brazilian Institute of Geography and Statistics. He has been and still is a member of the Commission for the Study of the Texts of Brazilian History. He has been one of the Committee of Editors of the *Revista da Historia de America* of Mexico, Associate Editor of the *Hispanic American Historical Review,* Collaborator of the *Cahiers d'Histoire Mondiale* of UNESCO, and member of the Board of *Historical Abstracts*. He has served as Visiting Professor in the Department of History of the University of Texas.

He has published extensively in the fields of historiography, bibliography, and history. He is particularly noted for his works on colonial Brazil with special reference to the Northeast, for his contribution to the theory of historical investigation, and for his skill in unearthing sources of Brazilian history in the archives of Brazil and of Europe. He edited volumes 66 to 74 of the *Anais da Biblioteca Nacional,* volumes 71 to 110 of the collection *Documentos Históricos,* volumes 43 to 50 of the *Publicações do Arquivo Nacional,* and miscellaneous works such as the correspondence of Capistrano de Abreu, letters of the Visconde do Rio Branco, and others. And he has published numerous articles in the leading scholarly journals of North America and Europe as well as of Brazil.

The types of achievement and experience which are reflected in this biographical sketch have a special relevance to this volume, for the reader's evaluation of Professor Rodrigues' interpretation of his data will depend in no small part on his evaluation of Professor Rodrigues as an objective scholar. The remarkably broad and varied documentation which is presented in support of the theses will carry weight, obviously, but in the final analysis reaction to this volume will also be determined by the qualifications of the author. That a Brazilian of the stature and background of Professor Rodrigues should arrive at the conclusions stated in these pages is a fact of considerable importance to the English-reading public.

It is true that he does not represent the opinion of the controlling element of his country. This is obvious from the violent reaction to the program of similar views initiated by President Jânio Quadros and his Minister of Foreign Relations, Afonso Arinos de Melo Franco, and from the policies in force since the resignation of Quadros. But it is equally true that Professor Rodrigues is not alone in his advocacy of a new orientation in Brazil's foreign policy. In the unsettled state of affairs characteristic of contemporary Brazil, it is inevitable that there should be a diversity of viewpoints on the direction which the nation should follow in its dealings with other states. The orientation advanced by Professor Rodrigues is significant in that it is based on a scholarly investigation of the historical development of the country and an extensive analysis of the contemporary situation. The book, in effect, constitutes a reasoned declaration of Brazil's coming of age among the family of nations.

The title and the space allotted to the contemporary situation necessarily direct attention to the reorientation theme. But it would be unfortunate if this emphasis were to obscure other facets which lend additional merit to the volume. There are, for example, chapters of intrinsic interest to the reader who is attempting to understand the complexities of present-day Brazil. Particularly noteworthy in this connection are: the section which identifies the contribution of the Negro to Brazilian diet, dress, art and architecture, literature, music, folklore, engineering, journalism, and politics; the section which lists the reciprocal contribution of Portuguese America to sub-Sahara Africa; and the section on the process and effect of miscegenation. The scholarly-minded will find the copious footnotes a happy hunting ground for references. And throughout there are insights which illuminate the historical development of half a continent.

This is a significant piece of work. The University of California Press is to be commended for making it available to the English-reading public.

ALAN K. MANCHESTER

Preface to the English Edition

The first Brazilian edition of this book was well received by the public and honored by considerable national and foreign criticism. The second edition was a revision, brought up to date and augmented. This translation is of the second edition; the first two sections of chapter 7 and the first three of chapter 8 in the Brazilian edition have been omitted because they contain material already familiar to the English-reading public.

I repeat what I wrote in the Introduction to the first edition regarding my lack of party affiliation, my sympathy for all peoples, independent of race or religion, my conviction that priority must be given to national interests, and my recognition of Brazil alone as my mother country. In the sense that it is a defense of national interests above all others, this is a nationalistic book. Private hesitations, whether derived from blood ties or based—fallaciously—upon oversensitiveness, should not induce a writer to shirk his public obligations, especially the obligation to attempt to pass what he has learned on to the rising generation with, in the words of that honored, cogent, and lucid historian Diogo do Couto, "the freedom and sincerity of a veteran soldier who neither fears reprisal for what he may reprehend nor expects rewards from whom he may praise."

On my mother's side I am descended from another Diogo, Teles Barreto de Menezes, who fought with Salvador Correia de Sá e Benevides, and to whose grandsons the city is indebted for its Teles Arch, a part of our national heritage. Precisely because of my descent

I must not fail to speak clearly and in good faith to the Portuguese, neither confounding Portugal and its people with the dictatorship that oppresses them, nor thinking that I owe Portugal my allegiance.

It is my hope that this book will make historically evident the following propositions:

1. That from the seventeenth to the nineteenth century Brazil had more contact with and greater bonds to Angola, Dahomey, and parts of the coasts of Mina and Guinea than did Portugal itself.

2. That there existed in the eighteenth century a Brazilian–Afro-Asian community from which Portugal was not excluded but in which it had reduced participation.

3. That the Africanization of Brazil began in the sixteenth century with the arrival of the first slaves and continued until the cessation of the slave trade in 1856, and was in part a consequence of the fact that away from their native communities and homeland the Negroes could be controlled more easily than our Indians, who were simply decimated.

4. That the groups foreign in Brazil, the dominating Portuguese and the dominated Africans, developed modes of coexistence involving greater Portuguese influence in the class structure of society and greater Negro and Indian influence upon the socio-economic structure, so that from the beginning Brazil was more a Negro and Tupi product than a Western, Portuguese one.

5. That the African role in the evolution of Brazilian society was such that Brazil is, like Cuba, more Africanized than any of the American states except Haiti, which is the most purely African.

6. That de-Africanization began in 1808 with the arrival of Prince Regent Dom João, afterward Dom João VI, and was accelerated following the cessation of the slave trade in 1856. Martius himself in 1817 noted little European influence upon the tone of society and observed that the arrival of twenty-four thousand Portuguese, as well as a goodly number of Englishmen, Frenchmen, Dutchmen, Germans, and Italians, began to impose "a change upon the characteristics of the inhabitants such that the existing relative preponderance of Negroes and mulattoes over whites is reversing." Our Europeanization for a long time was a process of "whitewashing."

7. That in the beginning the Brazilian historical process was through the imposition of its ruling minority discriminatory racially, but that it

became racially democratic to the point that it is today if not a perfect at least an exemplary demonstration of racial coexistence.

8. That this development was more Brazilian than Portuguese, which explains the failure of Luso-African miscegenation.

9. That as Deputy Cunha Matos declared in 1827 and Senator Bernardo Pereira de Vasconcelos repeated in 1843, Brazil's Africans played a civilizing role.

10. That Brazil is therefore a Mestizo Republic, neither European nor Latin American, the synthesis of Tupi, African, Occidental, and Oriental antitheses, a unique and original creation.

11. That at the beginning of the last century most of our diplomatic energy was directed to reconciling our interests in importation of African slaves with the intentions of the British to end that practice and with it our involvement upon the African continent, for as Cunha Matos clearly saw in 1827 and declared in the Chamber of Deputies, Britain aspired to world domination including rule over Africa and would presently promote African agricultural competition with Brazil.

12. That Angola was more closely linked to Brazil than to Portugal, it having been Brazil that freed Angola from Dutch rule, with the consequence that at the time of Brazilian independence, two of Angola's three deputies to the Portuguese Cortes cast their lot with Brazil; and that it was in Rio in 1822 that the proclamations in favor of "despised Angola" were made, followed immediately by revolutionary movements in Luanda and Benguela.

13. That in Portuguese Guinea the men elected deputy and alternate to the *Cortes* in Lisbon were respectively a citizen living in Rio de Janeiro and the *Inconfidente* [member of a Brazilian revolutionary group] José de Rezende Costa; that the revolutionary movements in Mozambique had close relations with the liberal "rabble" of Rio de Janeiro; and that the Goan deputies were imprisoned in the fortress of Santa Cruz.

14. That in the agreement recognizing Brazil's independence, Dom Pedro accepted the clause prohibiting the Portuguese colonies from joining Brazil, with the consequence that Brazil as a nation was born free of taints of colonialism and imperialism. (I recognize that the Angolan rebellion of 1824 and the attempt to join Brazil were initiated by white Portuguese settlers without popular African support, as Roger

Bastide pointed out in his review of the first edition of this book,[1] and that their rejection by Brazil was owing to the fact that the Portuguese officials still controlling Brazil did not wish to move against Portuguese interests. No matter what the reaction of the minority ruling in 1831 might have been, the obviously liberal Brazilian popular spirit at that time was not colonialist.)

15. That the treaties entered into immediately after Independence gave birth to anti-European feeling expressed in the Chamber by outstanding conservatives, and to demands for real independence, the defense of our national interests, and the opening of new markets with "especially those nations that have no colonial interests," as Baron de Cairu was to say; that the repugnance toward our subjection to Europe, especially Great Britain, created a wave of nationalism throughout the Empire of Brazil that was summed up in the words of Bernardo Pereira de Vasconcelos in 1827: "America belongs to America; let Europe belong to Europe, and all will be for the best," a remark that reminds one of "Africa for the Africans."

16. That the break with Africa made around 1855 as a result of British pressure in which Portugal participated (refusing from 1847 to 1895 to permit a Brazilian consulate in Angola) resulted in the concentration of Brazilian policy in the Rio de la Plata, although that policy was still subject to British political and economic preëminence and French political and cultural influence, and later to American ascendancy.

17. That Great Britain despite its many commercial privileges was nevertheless of service to Brazil in warding off the enormous pressure and demands of other European powers.

I recognize that, as Professor Florestan Fernandes pointed out in his review of the Brazilian edition,[2] the Brazilian contribution to Africa is insignificant when compared with the enormous African contribution to Brazil. Precisely for this reason it is well that Jânio Quadros' *Message* to Congress admitted that "our effort in Africa, however intense, can constitute only a modest . . . repayment of the immense debt that Brazil owes the people of Africa." Our policy in regard to repaying that debt has been less than coherent, words have substituted for actions,

---

[1] "A Propos d'un livre bresilien sur l'Afrique," *Presence Africaine* (2d trimester, 1962), pp. 123–128.
[2] *Estado de São Paulo*, January 27, 1962.

and at that the words have generally concerned Brazilian sentimental feeling for Portugal rather than Africa. We forget our ties with Africa, what we owe our Negroes, who waited for their release from slavery until 1888 and are still waiting, the great majority of them, for their release from educational and economic deprivation. Our elitist policy seems to resemble that defended by Mr. Louw of the Union of South Africa, who attributes that nation's development exclusively to the white minority.

I have no apology to make for miscegenation. Professor Bastide speaks of it as an ideological tenet of the half-breed. But cultural miscegenation is fruitful and ethnic miscegenation was in Brazil a factor in easing race relations. If Africans today condemn miscegenation because of its weakening effect upon their revolutionary process, Brazilians know that it has positive as well as negative aspects. Positively, it has made Brazilian history less bloody. Negatively, it has delayed the political emancipation of Brazil's long-suffering people, as I try to show in my study *Aspirações Nacionais, Interpretação histórico-política*.[3] Negatively, through the "whitewash complex," its effect has been to hold mestizo elements of the population subservient to white elements.

Politically, I hope to make the following points clear:

1. Atlantic solidarity does not signify merely unity of the North Atlantic contrary or indifferent to the interests of the South Atlantic nations, nor must it remain in the service of European or United States hegemony. NATO, a military combination of Atlantic and non-Atlantic nations, has an antithetical character and can be converted into a threat, as almost occurred in the incident of the *Santa Maria* when the Organization was called upon to act in the South Atlantic by a European partner. Revision of Atlantic policy is necessary, and in it Brazil, Argentina, Uruguay, and the west African nations cannot be forgotten.

2. The fall in the world prices of raw materials, the constant and progressive deterioration of per capita income and living standards in the underdeveloped nations, and the accelerated progress of the industrialized nations, which are supported by the policies of interna-

---

[3] (São Paulo, Editôra Fulgor, 1963).

tional organizations such as G.A.T.T., justify the generalization that the underdeveloped are helping the developed to become still more developed.

3. The gates open to trade between the superdeveloped nations and western Europe are not open to the underdeveloped nations, except to certain ones chosen by the European Common Market. The loss in the purchasing power of Brazilian exports to the United States amounted to $1,486,000,000 during the period 1955–1961. It has been calculated that the renewal of United States restrictions on raw materials imported from Latin America would result in an increase in duties ranging from $850,000,000 to $1,700,000,000 annually. Internal pressures do not permit a nation to remain attached to traditional markets, to wait patiently for programs of commercial expansion to go into effect, or to expect favors from other nations. The opening of our foreign policy to the world at large is not provoked by ideological motivations but by real needs. Brazil, like Canada, has been obliged by the decline in its traditional markets to seek other outlets.

4. It is a mistake not to see that Brazil is committed only to its own national interests. To interpret the Brazilian position as unconditional involvement reveals lingering imperialistic feeling.

5. Brazil's anticolonialism must be consistent and support the independence of Angola, for otherwise we should compromise our international political destiny before the new African nations with which we shall have to maintain coöperation and understanding in the future. In the past Brazil's policy regarding colonialism vacillated but usually, until Jânio Quadros, it supported the colonial powers and those administering non-autonomous territories. Proclaiming itself anticolonialist, Brazil presented one face that frowned upon colonialism in general, and another that smiled upon, or at least averted itself from contemplating, Portuguese colonialism as it hangs on in the African colonies that Brazil has sometimes agreed are integral parts of the Portuguese empire, and sometimes has preferred to consider special colonial situations where independence should not be supported. It may be said that in respect to the Portuguese colonies, Brazil has maintained union with Portugal, serving the latter's interests more than its own. But if blood and sentiment mean something, then not only Portugal but also Africa deserves our sympathy and support.

6. Making is *modus operandi* legalistic fictions and constitutional dodges, Brazilian foreign policy has avoided stating clearly that the government of Portugal must recognize that independent of legal or constitutional principles the people of Angola are qualified to exercise the right of authentic self-determination, even if at some future date. So long as we fail to proclaim this, we compromise ourselves before emerging Africa; only by proclaiming it shall we reduce our policy to unity and coherency.

7. The Luso-Brazilian community may soundly be judged no longer to exist, because: (1) it has no economic basis; (2) the national interests of Brazil do not coincide with those of Portugal in the international sphere, and have not since 1822; (3) the blood-tie that joins us with Portugal, like the one that joins us with Africa, is insufficient justification for a role of dependency; (4) the fact that the pretended community was never allowed to include Portugal's overseas possessions proves its absurdity (this restriction prevented economic and political common interests from being regulated internationally on the basis of the interdependence of free and autonomous units).

8. The fact is that Brazil has not had and does not have an African policy, the beginnings of one that appeared when Quadros took office having progressed no farther than preliminary declarations. As our internal policy is indecisive, our foreign policy is hesitant, disguising vacillation as conciliation and compromise. Legalism is its essence, permitting it to advance or retreat whether it is directed by the conservative Raul Fernandes or the Labor Party member Hermes Lima, whose colonialist thinking unites them.

9. It is encouraging that the Portuguese opposition proposes to support self-determination (though with reservations as to its immediate practicality).

10. A sovereign and free nation reveals its freedom by its independence in international affairs, and in this respect the presidency of Jânio Quadros brought an about-face through its policy of respecting the regionalism of hemispheric interests without sacrificing international objectives. This policy broadened the horizons of our international life and set the roots of greater participation in the world scene.

11. The innocence of the Brazilian people before the frauds per-

petrated by their elite classes must not lead to the impression that we are a nation of lambs who always lose, are always deceived, may always be maneuvered, as, for example, by the attorneys of the great international economic interests. Brazil's love of peace and espousal of universal understanding come from the heart, but from the same heart comes the courage to begin the great struggle for development that will be made not for a few but for all.

I do not know Africa but I believe that this book, written from the Brazilian point of view and perhaps excessively parochial, represents an effort for understanding and a message of brotherhood.

J. H. R.

Contents

Mutual Relations and Contributions

Brazil has its body in America and its soul in Africa.

ANTÔNIO VIEIRA
(Second half of the XVII century)

Africa is civilizing America.

BERNARDO PEREIRA DE VASCONCELOS
Brazilian Senate, April 25, 1843

The Brazilian Image of Africa

From its birth Brazil had the most intimate relations with the continent of Africa or, at least, with certain parts of the continent. So close indeed were Brazil and Portuguese Africa that the latter, at that time already halted in its territorial expansion, was for a time a Brazilian administrative dependency. These relations—geographic, ethnic, and cultural —persisted for over three hundred years, but ended in 1850 with the abolition of the African slave trade. Thereafter Africa's image lived on vitally in Brazil only in those scattered parts of the country where the culture was Afro-Brazilian.

Only thorough research could determine what was our ancestors' image of Africa and Africans, what values, attitudes, and stereotypes it embodied. We know that the attitudes of one people toward other peoples express a shifting and confused mixture of the real and the mythical. If this is true even when the peoples involved are familiar with one another because of geographic proximity and cultural affinities, then the distortion is likely to be magnified when they are remote and isolated for a long time from one another. The Brazilian image of Africa was influenced by the European image of Africa, which in turn derived directly from the image of Africa held by the Portuguese. And the last was exotic before the discovery of the continent, formed from legend and myth, and afterward was constructed of startling reports: I refer not to the news that a habitable continent was to be found to the south, nor to the news of the voyages down the Atlantic, the Dark Sea, or of the existence of the antipodes, but precisely to the astonishing report of the crossing of the equinoctial line, for this, together with the discovery of the Congo, made it certain that there was a new world on the old earth, and a new man in that world.[1] Even in the time of Pedro Álvares Cabral (1467–1516), the discoverer of the coast of Brazil, Portuguese settlers in Sofala were still under the sway of the medieval imagination: they saw monsters in the form of men with four eyes. Dominating European and Portuguese thinking about Africa were two myths. The first was the myth of Prester John, the most Christian monarch who was said to reign in the interior of Africa. The other was the myth of the Empire of Monomotapa, the vast kingdom of the Congo. The Earthly Paradise was also searched for, for medieval tradition located it in Africa. Simão de Vasconcelos later imagined it to be in Brazil.

Following the voyages of Vasco da Gama and Cabral, and the discovery of the Congo, Portuguese consciousness of the Southern Hemisphere began to be more factual and to have a radical influence on European consciousness, correcting its myths and legends. Though the Portuguese position in Africa was always threatened, and great hostility was felt by the Portuguese toward the Negroes and Arabs, nevertheless a clearer idea of the continent began to implant itself. One realization was shocking: the human race was not basically Christian with a Mohammedan fringe; rather, there existed vast primitive societies in Africa and America which were totally ignorant of Christianity, as well as Asian societies where the number of Christians was insignificant. Islam, then, was not the great heretical aberration vis-à-vis a Christian world. To understand this was to be forced to reformulate the traditional medieval theory concerning positive and negative infidelity. How was the infidel to be distinguished from the merely non-Christian? The Portuguese, and Europeans in general, did not place infidel Moors and non-Christian Negroes on the same spiritual plane. They felt that the latter, from the religious point of view, should be regarded as neutral beings. Azurara, chronicling the settlement of Guinea, wrote in 1488: "I hear the prayers of the innocent souls of those barbarous nations,

---

[1] The following section is based upon the excellent study by W. G. L. Randles, *L'Image du Sud-Est Africain dans la Littérature Européenne au XVIe Siècle,* Centro de Estudos Históricos Ultramarinos, Lisbon, 1959.

whose forefathers from the beginning of the world have never seen the divine light." [2]

Despite this feeling for the souls of the Negroes, the Negroes' behavior still shocked. "Pagan and bestial folk," was Duarte Pacheco's phrase. Brutal, evil: with contact with the Hottentots, who in 1510 killed Viceroy Dom Francisco de Almeida and in 1554 sacked Sepulveda, that image became fixed. Camões evoked the latter tragedy in *Os Lusíadas:*

> They will see die of hunger
> Children the fruit of so much love;
> The vicious avaricious Savages
> Shall strip the woman of beauty,
> Reveal her crystal limbs naked
> To air both hot and bitter
> After her long and painful walk
> Over burning sand. [3]

And since that time the "vicious and avaricious Savages," advancing with complete lack of respect, have repeatedly dishonored and brutalized the "crystal limbs" of refined and superior Europeans—as witness, most recently, the accusations in 1961 by the noble, sensitive, and very white Belgians.

Dom Francisco de Almeida's punitive expedition to avenge black insults reminds us of the brutalities and crimes of Vasco da Gama and Pedro Álvares Cabral, which were vividly related by the great João de Barros, a chronicler held in such esteem in Europe that Pius IV placed his portrait alongside that of Ptolemy. Almeida was killed and the Portuguese came off badly in the bloody fighting, and the Hottentots continued to be "bestial Negroes." In Portugal there was intense debate as to whether the town where the disaster had taken place should not be destroyed in reprisal. It was decided to forego reprisal "because an

---

[2] Gomes Eannes de Azurara, *Crónica do Descobrimento e Conquista de Guiné,* Paris, 1841, p. 9. Augusto Meyer, commenting on the Portuguese expansion into Africa, writes that "Azurara's chronicle is at times impregnated with unconscious irony rather at odds with the stated high purposes of the actually miserable and predatory activities his narrative relates." "História," *Correio da Manhã,* February 10, 1962.

[3] Canto V (facsimile edition) Teófilo Braga, Lisbon, n.d. 87.

offense committed by such bestial men as those Negroes is to be overlooked."

Deformed, horrible, cruel, bestial, ferocious, these are the characteristics attributed to the Negroes by Barros, Castanheda, Góis, and Osório. The importance of their descriptions lies in the fact, which Randles has noted, that they served as the basis for the travel narratives and compendia so avidly read by the European public. Thus they set the tone for later judgments upon the Negroes.

The Negro stereotype was established well within the sixteenth century and thereafter developed variously in ways pleasing to Europeans, who were solicitous of the spiritual direction of the Negroes' poor souls, for, as Azurara observed, "supposing their bodies to be under some subjection, this were a small thing compared to their souls, which would possess true freedom eternally." [4] The Negro did not fare as did the Indian, considered the "good savage." All blacks suffered from the harsh opinion of them formed by the Portuguese and deformed by other Europeans: the Hottentots for example were beasts, kingless, lawless, faithless. And although Brazil's Indians were similarly described, yet here was also born the theory of the "noble savage."

Already the Portuguese view of the Negro, as it was developed by Europeans, was united with the Biblical accursed race of the sons of Ham, who looked on naked Noah. Randles stresses that neither classical nor Oriental tradition had favor for the "savage and ferocious" Ethiopians. But Europe disvalued Arabs, Negroes, and Indians in different degrees. The first were positive infidels who reciprocated that judgment, considering the Portuguese "accursed, one of the nations of the accursed Franks," as was stated by an Arab historian of the tenth century of the Mohammedan calendar (1495–1591). The Negroes were not in essence hostile to Christianity, but were barbarous and cruel. The Indians were the noble savages—praised by Montaigne [5] and from the beginning defended by Vitória, Bartolomeu de las Casas, and the Brazilian Jesuits. The Negroes were never protected as were the Indians. They were considered inferior and upon this image was

---

[4] Gomes Eannes de Azurara, *op. cit.,* 88.

[5] The most important work is by G. Chinard, especially *L'Exotisme Américain dans la littérature française au XVIᵉ siècle,* Paris, 1911, and *L'Amerique et le rêve exotique dans la littérature française au XVIIᵉ et au XVIII siècle,* Paris, 1913.

constructed the doctrine of white, dolicho-blond European superiority, an irrational myth like others—such as the doctrine of "just war"—that served to justify domination and enslavement.

Similarly, from the time of the reign of Dom Sebastião (1557–1578), Africa's reputed bad climate—the uninhabitable torrid zone where heat was so incredible that it carbonized both ships and military equipment—served to darken further the Dark Continent. A report to Sebastião stated that Africa was "a region where the climate, the geography, the ways of the people, and the characteristics of the land are the inhabitants' most powerful weapons against foreigners; for in such a burning climate, where water and provender are so scarce, it would not to be easy to maintain an army of men from well-watered and shady lands who are unaccustomed to suffering the thirst and barrenness into which Africans are born, by which they are sustained." [6]

So to human evil was added the wretchedness of sterile nature. And if these impressions of Africa, these stereotypes, were held by the Portuguese, among whom indeed they are still dominant, and were passed along to be further distorted by Europe, we must believe that they were also transplanted to Brazil and our ancestors. Here the evolution of the African image began with the importation and distribution throughout the country, but especially in the Northeast and East, of a constant stream of Africans that by the middle of the nineteenth century, that is, after three hundred years, had totalled more than three millions. Interracial hostility dominated Brazil and doubtless favored the formation of a pejorative image, which might or might not have been corrected by greater contacts with Africa itself. The enormous migration of Africans transformed Brazil, according to the *Diálogos das Grandezas do Brasil* (1618), into a second Guinea.

What was thought here, by whites and men of mixed blood, of the real Guinea and other parts of Africa? There is no doubt that during the nineteenth-century abolition movement feeling toward Brazil's own Negroes underwent a sentimental reversal; to the Negroes were attributed characteristics and sentiments that earlier had been denied them. Thus discrimination was overcome, tolerance furthered. But Africa and

---

[6] "Desenganos que Sidemuca deu a El Rey D. Sebastião sôbre as calidades de África . . . ," in *Studia,* Revista Semestral do Centro de Estudios Históricos Ultramarinos, Lisbon, V (1960), 234.

its native peoples remained more than ever remote and unknown, distant both culturally and geographically. The image of the continent as a whole, rather than that of a part or parts of the continent, had been that transmitted by slave traders and slaves. With the end of the slave trade, the image become one of a land and peoples as far away and unknown as the Poles. Few knew of the various political and administrative units that had been established in Africa by the colonial powers for their sole and exclusive benefit. And I believe that if we were to make an inquiry even today as to what Brazilians—not only the masses but the upper classes too—know about Africa, we would discover an ignorance that should not surprise us. Brazil's elite cultivated Europe—but not all of Europe; no one cared much about Eastern Europe, the Balkans, nor even Scandinavia; interest was concentrated upon the Iberian peninsula, the place of our origin, and especially France, which was the mirror in which we sought to see our own images, and to a lesser degree upon England and Germany. Recently, to the great distaste of the francophile elite, the United States has become better known. If today the average Brazilian knows, indeed, the names of a few "Latin" American countries, he usually does not know the names of their capitals; and his ignorance about Asia and Africa is limitless. Nor am I speaking of the illiterate fifty per cent, who at most have occasionally heard some mention or reference to Africa or Asia, but of the other half of our populace, including some upper class individuals, who are contemptuous of African and Asian affairs because they feel themselves utterly unlinked to them by any affiliation. Very recently, of course, immigration from Japan and Lebanon has brought a vague notion of the Far and Near East.

We should not be surprised that we think today of Africa as only a barren land explored by Europeans, from which our former slaves came. No more was known five years ago, except perhaps concerning Dakar, familiar to a small intellectual or wealthy elite from their flights to Europe. At that time, suddenly, one of history's most violent processes began to occur in Africa. Nothing could be more extraordinary, vital, and dynamic than the creation one after the other, as if by chain reaction, of a number of new sovereign states. Such an event took place in the Americas a century ago. Its happening in Africa today means that the Brazilian image of Africa is going to undergo a radical transformation that our newspapers will help to formulate without relating it, not to former ethnic ties nor to historical precedents, but to the reasons for the process of African liberation, a process that has not generated itself spontaneously.

For two types of Brazilians, the African revolution has meaning, deep significance. On the one hand, it is important to the officials who are charged with our diplomatic and international relations and are alert to events and must be alive to their consequences. It is important on the other hand to our teachers and the new generation of students, who, though they can know and do little or nothing firsthand in regard to Africa, need to be informed of the rationale and causes of the revolution.

Little, practically nothing, is today taught in Brazil concerning Africa. In the existing programs on the secondary and lower levels, non-European peoples, except indigenous Americans, receive slight treatment. All that is given in the third series of the *ginásio* is a summary review of the ancient Orient and the Arabs. In the *colégio,* the non-European world consists of ancient and medieval Oriental history, the near East, and colonial expansion. Only the last concerns itself with Africa, and only from the sixteenth through the nineteenth centuries. The study of Brazil's own history touches Africa merely through slaves and slavery.

The rigid school curriculum thus prevents immediate enlightenment, which can come only outside the school system or perhaps occasionally from a teacher of superior talents or one who dares to step outside the curriculum. Yet if such important subjects as the modern history of the United States and the Soviet Union, the nations that are really forging our present destiny, do not find an important place in our educational program, we must not be surprised if the Orient and Africa, strengthless regions empty of interest, are ignored. American history to us is the history of the Indians and the colonial period; Russian history is that of Europe. If our youth, among them our future professors, have no clear view of recent historical developments, we will never become better informed about the Orient and Africa. Only liberalization of curriculum and reform of the university, until today a sterile seedbed because of inadequate methods, can allow the formation of a national spirit prepared for the new tasks of the present world.

Traditionally the expression *é uma África* ("it's an Africa") signifies something heroic, a feat, a difficulty hard to overcome. In it is compressed the image of a land harsh because of its natural conditions, the barbarity of its people, and the numbers and ferocity of its wild animals.

Colonial Relations: 1500–1800

PORTUGUESE EXPANSION IN AFRICA

The conquest of Ceuta and other strongholds in Morocco and the movement toward Africa that culminated in the voyage of Vasco da Gama to India mark not only a spreading of the influence of the Portuguese people but also and especially the opening of new frontiers for the expansion of aggressive European power, which thereby outflanked and surrounded the Islamic world.[1] It is unnecessary to review the entire fantastic tale of Portuguese heroism, which has been claimed responsible for the emergence of the modern world, in order to reveal the relations existing from the sixteenth century between the African coast and Brazil. These relations, mutually influencing the lives and actions of Brazilians and Africans, began immediately with the establishment of the trade in slaves.

Prince Henry himself took part in no voyages, but he did everything in his power to make the maritime expeditions possible. He was not, as Alexander Humboldt wished to imply, a man of science who could have arrived at his plans for exploration from his study of ancient and medieval authors. Rather, the expansion was a state enterprise recommended by the Royal Treasury precisely because the state coffers were empty. The expeditions were paid for by coining all available gold and

---

[1] José Honório Rodrigues, *D. Henrique e a Abertura da Fronteira Mundial,* Coimbra, 1961 (reprint from the *Revista Portuguêsa de História*), and "Webb's Great Frontier and the Interpretation of Modern History," *The New World Looks at Its History,* eds. A. R. Lewis and T. F. McGann, Austin, University of Texas Press, 1963, 155–164.

silver and by using all the resources at the disposal of the state and the Order of Christ. This Order, inheriting the properties of the dissolved Order of the Templars, became a financial institution for the backing of state enterprises. Soon sugar from Madeira, gold, and African Negroes became the principal elements in the formation of Portuguese capital.[2]

Prince Henry's efforts were more successful out to sea than on the African coast: the islands of Porto Santo and Madeira and the archipelago of the Azores rose from the waves. On the coast, the effort was greater and the return slower. "Who goes beyond Cape No," it was said, "will either return or no." But the Prince did not allow himself to be intimidated. He thought, and quite naturally, that if he did not support the exploration of those regions, they would remain forever unknown, for seamen and merchants would venture only where profit was certain.

Hope for better times brightened in 1434 with the conquest of Cape Bojador, a barrier finally broken, after repeated disappointments and failures, by the persistence of Gil Eanes, one of the Prince's pages and a native of Lagos. Every year brought new progress. At Rio de Oro the temperate zone was left behind and the equatorial entered, the region that scholars had from Antiquity declared to be uninhabitable. The navigators did not at first go south of eight degrees north, but already the barren and inhospitable aspect of the cost, from which one could glimpse the great deserts, had been replaced by tropical vegetation, teeming fauna, and the vigorous populace of the Negro tribes.

From Cape Verde the African coast moves eastward until it forms the Gulf of Guinea. Thus was visible an approach to the lands of riches, commerce with which constituted the wealth of Egypt and the Italian republics. In the confusion reigning concerning African hydrography, it was considered possible to reach India by moving up one of the rivers that empties on the west coast. It was also thought that one could proceed by skirting the coast, for either Africa joined Asia in the south, and the Indian Ocean was an inland sea, or Africa was separated in the south from the Orient by only a narrow passage like the one linking the Mediterranean and the Atlantic.

---

[2] Richard Konetzke, "Der Weltgeschichtliche Moment der Entdeckung Americas," *Historische Zeitschrift* (Oct., 1956), 267–289.

But exploration of the African west coast and the establishment of trading posts at Arguim (1443: Cape Branco, in present-day Mauritania), at Mina (1481, on the Gold Coast, now Ghana), at Santiago (Cape Verde) and at São Tomé, fell far short of establishing the vast dominion that would have included, as some Portuguese historians conjecture, the present coasts of Ghana, Togo, Dahomey, Nigeria, the Cameroons, Spanish Guinea, Gabon, and the southern part of French Equatorial Africa, to say nothing of Mauritania, Senegal, and the present Portuguese Guinea and Angola. Control of this vast coast was never attained; there were only a few trading posts that devoted themselves to the commerce in gold and slaves. Until the discovery of America, Spain—and only Spain—shared in the west African commerce. Already in 1479, by the Peace of Alcáçovas, confirmed by the Toledo Accord of 1480, Spain recognized Portugal's exclusive rights in Guinea, at Cape Verde, and in Mina (Ghana). Then, as earlier in medieval times, the highest temporal authority was the prerogative of the Church, and various Papal Bulls from 1454 to 1539 granted Portugal the exclusive rights of discovery, conquest, navigation, and commerce from Africa to the Indies.

Exploration extended from Ceuta to Cape Padrão (now Cross, in Southwest Africa, a fideicommissum of the Union of South Africa). The west coast was known as Guinea and in 1486 gave John II the title of Lord of Guinea. Colonization, which at that time signified merely evangelization, was attempted only in the Congo, immediately after the discovery of the mouth of that river in 1483, and ended in failure. The Kingdom of the Congo, subject to Portugal as a dependency of São Tomé, became a center for the slave trade, but lasted little over fifty years (1491–1543); a small part of the region returned to Portuguese control in 1887. The experiment in Angola was associated with the activity in the Congo, especially the Congolese slave trade. Before the experiment could be firmly established, expansion inland from the coast was interrupted—following Diogo do Cão's second voyage, in 1486—because the coast of Angola was considered inhospitable and unpromising and also because Dom João insisted on swift search for the southern extremity of the continent. For the royal—and national—objective was not Africa, as later it was not Brazil: it was the Orient, India. The discovery of the Cape of Good Hope satisfied one of the chief Portuguese aspirations of the period.

Thereafter Portuguese advances were made on two fronts, western and eastern. Gold and slaves were the incentive in the west; in the east the dominant interest from the island of Mozambique to Melinde, in Kenya, was trade with India and in the west it was gold and slaves. The fortress of Sofala was built in 1505; in 1506 the Portuguese established themselves in Kilwa (Tanganyika); in 1508 they erected a fort on the Island of Mozambique. In 1593 they sacked Mobass (Kenya) and began to build Fort Jesus.[3] But after a few years the zones of influence became isolated from one another. Mozambique was left as the principal point of support in the south; from Cape Delgado northward the Arabs were dominant despite the Portuguese forts, which were always threatened and were finally lost, as Professor Boxer emphasizes, because of the incompetence of their commanders.

Thus nothing is more precarious than the allegation that a vast Portuguese province existed in Africa. On both sides of the continent the monopoly began from the seventeenth century to become fragmented by growing competition from other European powers. In the west, Angola, Guinea, the Islands of Cape Verde and the Gulf, São Tomé, and Principe represented the extent of Portuguese dominion. In the east Arab opposition was always increasing, wars were continual, and the Arabs controlled commerce with the Orient. The Portuguese worst enemies were always the Moslems. Between the followers of the two religions there was from the very first an instinctive, irrepressible, and inexorable struggle.

In western Africa the Portuguese could not consolidate their discoveries. In the east they saw themselves reduced to Mozambique, almost to the island itself. Only that was left, of the vast coast that had been navigated and explored. Following the Dutch conquest of Luanda (1641), Mozambique supplied Brazil with slaves. In 1651 the Dutch established themselves on the Cape of Good Hope, and the Portuguese lost their points of support along the coast. Until 1752 Mozambique was a dependency of Goa, as Angola was one of Brazil. With the fall of Mombasa in 1729, the loss of the mercantile empire in the east, and the

---

[3] Cf. C. F. Boxer and Carlos de Azevedo, *Fort Jesus and the Portuguese in Mombasa, 1593–1729*, London, 1960.

decrease in transoceanic and coastal commerce, Mozambique lost contact with both India and Portugal and from 1700 on, for two hundred years, was reduced to complete apathy.

The fact is that in Africa the Portuguese behaved as they did in Brazil in the sixteenth and seventeenth centuries, when, according to Friar Vicente do Salvador (in 1618), they were content to gain a clawhold along the sea, like crabs. The imperial objectives and national energies were directed toward Brazil rather than toward Africa, were concentrated in Brazil and those parts of Africa serving Brazil. That Mozambique remained in Portuguese hands was a miracle that each succeeding century saw repeated. As for Angola, the Portuguese government was never convinced of the possibility of the success in Angola of an economic system like that of Brazil, and fought against financing its implantation. Thence the monotonous course of Angolan history, which as James Duffy said,[4] for three centuries amounted to a chronology of small wars against tribes, military expeditions into the interior, and a dedicated commerce exporting slaves—mostly to Brazil, which received four-fifths of the total. A population promoting miscegenation and Westernization was never established.

The existence of a vast Portuguese province in Africa is only a conjecture by Portuguese historians, who in dealing with the Empire are not objective. The isolated strips of land on both sides of the continent that were controlled for greater or lesser periods caused historians' imaginations to be fired, to the detriment of quantitative precision. Obviously the Portuguese explored a far greater area than they now hold. For that very reason Brazil had social and economic intercourse with parts of Africa that by the seventeenth or eighteenth century were no longer controlled by Portugal, with the consequence that those areas still held by Portugal were actually more bound to Brazil than to Portugal itself.

Yet it is true that although not much was controlled, a large coastal zone reveals Portuguese influence. In Senegal, in Gambia, in Dahomey, in Gabon, one can even today find vestiges of the Portuguese presence.

Portuguese rule in Morocco ended in 1769. The inhabitants of

---

[4] *Portuguese Africa,* Cambridge, Harvard University Press, 1959.

Mazagão left that city to settle in Brazil, where they built the city of
Mazagão—now Mazagão and Mazagão Velho—in the territory of
Amapá.

Portugal's proverbial weakness is further revealed by the cession of
tracts and territories to other powers in order to avoid worse consequences. In 1777, by the Treaty of Santo Ildefonso, which demarcated
the frontiers between Portuguese and Spanish America, Portugal not
only ceded the Colônia do Sacramento without, as had been the case in
1750, the compensation of the Sete Povos das Missões, but she also gave
Spain the islands of Ano Bom and Fernando Pó on the African coast, so
that the Spanish could trade in Gabon and the Cameroons.[5] At Rio de
Janeiro in 1810, in the Treaty of Alliance and Friendship with Great
Britain, Portugal in the second secret article ceded Bissau and Cacheu
(Portuguese Guinea) to British sovereignty for fifty years. In the Treaty
of Commerce and Navigation of the same year, Britain was assured the
right of commerce on the east coast of Africa.

It may be said generally that in none of the Portuguese colonies in
Africa did miscegenation and Europeanization attain the degree attained in Brazil. The lack of success of the colonial policy and economic
planning in the areas that have remained under Portuguese rule is
proved by modern data on miscegenation. By the time colonial development was finally attempted, in this century, "the general conditions of
life had already ceased to be appropriate for the phenomena of social
and cultural symbiosis." What took place, and is taking place, was the
"growth and stabilization of the white European population," which
"in order to adapt to the tropics not only did not need to rely on
widespread miscegenation but did not even need to abandon the
European system of collective living and civilization." No effort was
made to create an original type with its own culture; rather the struggle
was to combat the native enemy and impose European forms by
assimilation.[6] Angola is an example.

The Portuguese failure has been well explained by Professor Pierre

---

[5] See the *Treaty,* secret articles III and IV, in José Carlos Macedo Soares, *Fron-
teiras do Brasil no Regime Colonial,* Rio de Janeiro, 1939, 187.
[6] Jofre A. Nogueira, "Aspectos fundamentais da miscigenação étnica na província
de Angola," in *Atas,* III Colóquio Internacional de Estudos Luso-Brasileiros, Lisbon, 1959, I, 188 and 195-197.

Gourou, who compares Amazônia and the Congo basin, physically similar regions both of which were colonized by the Portuguese.[7] In Brazil the result was the states of Pará and Amazonas, in Africa, the city of Cabinda and Angola. Despite their early appearance in the Congo (in 1482; they did not reach Pará on the other hand until 1616), the Portuguese did not penetrate the interior nor even hold on to the mouth of the river. The designs of Leopold II of Belgium upon the region in 1885 would have been as impossible to realize as were the equivalent various French, English, and Dutch attempts in Amazônia, if control of the mouth of the Zaire and occupation of its estuary had been maintained. As it was, Leopold had no difficulty.

Gourou shows that the Portuguese did not behave on the Atlantic coast of Africa as they did on the Atlantic coast of America. Although they colonized Madeira and the Cape Verde Islands, on the coast itself they achieved nothing comparable to Pernambuco and Bahia. Africa provided the slaves that made Brazilian plantations valuable, but no attempt was made to create African plantations worked by the same slaves. Gourou believes that it was easier to overcome the resistance of the Indians than that of the Negroes, and that to use slaves in the country of their origin would have been imprudent if not impractical. Slaves ran away even in Brazil. But in Amazônia Portuguese policy transformed the population and the civilization by interracial mixture, by the early imposition of the Portuguese language, and by the conversion of the natives to Catholicism and with it to the social, moral, and intellectual values that are characteristic of Brazil. Because of a common "Latin" background, Gourou felt himself to be a brother to the half breeds of the Amazon, to the gatherers of rubber he met in the narrow channels between the islands deep in the equatorial forest. His observations there measure the depth of the Luso-Brazilian civilizing action.

In the central Congo, on the other hand, the old African civilization remained intact until the end of the nineteenth century. From the end of that century there was evolution, but the native population never knew the racial and cultural transformation that Europeanized the Amazon. For a very long time the region was terra incognita; Stanley

---

[7] "Étude comparée de l'Amazonie et du Congo Central," *ibid*, 147–153.

was the first European to navigate the Congo, and he did so in 1877, while Orellana and Pedro Teixeira long before, in 1542 and 1639 respectively, crossed the Andes in both directions traversing the continent, the one crossing to the Atlantic, the other to the Pacific. Gourou notes the difference in demographic density between the two regions, the Amazon being much less thickly populated than the Congo; this may have been the result of the decimation of the Indians by the Europeans. The Congo also suffered depopulation following the coming of the Europeans. Gourou suggests that the hospitable aspects of the Amazon and the savagery of the Congo influenced Portuguese enterprise.

ANGOLA AND BRAZIL

Although it was known from the time of Diogo do Cão's second voyage, Angola was forgotten or ignored until Paulo Dias de Novais founded São Paulo de Luanda in 1575. By 1600, because of the decline of the Congo, it had become the most important area of Portuguese influence in western Africa. Like the Portuguese establishments on the Gulf of Guinea, Angola was a Brazilian dependency. Speaking of the success of colonization in America, Oliveira Martins, recently echoed by Jaime Cortesão, observed that "a different fortune befell Africa, for the reason that it was, almost to this day, a dependency of Brazil."[8] That dependency began with the complete subordination of the colony to the slave interests of Brazil. From the very beginning Angola did not serve its own independent interests, but those of the homeland, which were centralized in Brazil. Between 1575, when Paulo Dias de Novais disembarked in Angola, until 1591, 52,053 slaves were exported to Brazil, according to the contemporary chronicler Abreu e Brito.[9] By 1681 that number had reached approximately one million.[10]

Angola existed to furnish Brazil with slaves. Without slaves, no Pernambuco; and without Angola, no slaves, as Antonio Vieira was to

---

[8] Oliveira Martins, *O Brasil e as Colônias Portuguêsas,* Lisbon, 1880, p. 7; and Jaime Cortesão, "A expansão dos portuguêses em África (1557–1640)," in *História de Portugal,* Barcelos, 1933, V, 449.

[9] "Um inquérito à vida administrativa e econômica de Angola e do Brasil," (written in 1592), Coimbra, 1931, 30–31.

[10] Visconde de Paiva Manso, *História do Congo* (Documentos), Lisbon, 1877, 287.

say. The Dutch clearly understood this when they began their expansion in the Atlantic. They attacked Luanda in 1624 and in 1629 dangerously threatened it following the conquest of Bahia in 1624–25. Their conquest of Pernambuco in 1630 made the Dutch alive to the need for a source of supply for slave labor. By 1635 the shortage of slaves was critical and the management of the West Indies Company wrote to Nicholas van Ypern, governor or commandant of the Gold Coast (now Ghana) asking that Pernambuco be supplied. In 1637 Count Maurice of Nassau decided to order an attack against Mina. The expedition, which was organized in Recife and included Brazilian Indians, was commanded by Colonel Hans Coen, who tried to capture Saõ Jorge Castle, which the Count considered the "key to the Gold Coast." A thousand slaves had been sent from Guinea to Pernambuco in 1636 and 1637. With the capture of Mina, the number increased to 1,580. In a letter to Ypern, Coen proposed attacking the castle. He asked Ypern to obtain Negroes for the enterprise and suggested that the English be taken into consideration in order to avoid their opposition. So the coast of Africa was simply a hunting ground for slaves, a no-man's-land where power belonged to the strongest, not to the firstcomers or those whom the Pope had declared to be the proprietors.

In 1640, when Portugal was shaken by the disorders of the Restoration and could not give Brazil military assistance, Maurice of Nassau, following several attacks that gave him control as far as Sergipe, decided to conquer São Paulo de Luanda. As Barleus wrote, he wanted access to the most plentiful source of slaves "because the importance of a supply of Negroes from the kingdom of Angola is very great, they being indispensable as labor in Brazilian mills." Moreover Mina had proved a failure as a source of supply: the Hausas from that area were difficult to enslave, as was not the case with the Bantus from Angola and the Congo. The expedition, a large one, was organized in Recife. It was commanded by Admiral Cornelis Jol and Colonel James Henderson and consisted of three thousand men, among whom were two hundred and forty Indians, and twenty-one ships. The fleet left Recife on May 30, 1641, and on August 23 anchored off Luanda, occupying it in three days. Then the Dutch took possession of Benguela, and in October they captured the islands of São Tomé and Ano Bom. Only the fort at São Sebastião offered resistance. The offensive was completed in February of

1642 by the capture of the last Portuguese fortress on the Guinea coast, Axim.

A heavy blow was thus delivered to Portuguese Brazil. It was only from Angola, says Barleus, "that slaves are customarily transported to Brazil. . . . Moreover, only Brazil, because of its proximity, could defend and aid Angola." Now the supply of slaves from Angola, and the Congo, was cut off.

The Dutch at first thought to subordinate Dutch Angola to the government of Dutch Brazil, as under the Portuguese, though in theory the governments were separated, to all practical purposes Angola had been subordinate to Portuguese Brazil. In Brazil the Dutch attacks had been organized and based. But it was also to be Brazil that was to make Angola turn to Portugal and remain bound to Portuguese culture. Before the restoration of Angola to Portugal came to pass, however, difficulties arose between the king of the Congo and Count do Sonho, and both appealed to Maurice of Nassau in Pernambuco. Count do Sonho's emissaries, a group consisting of Dom Miguel de Castro, Dom Sebastião Manduba de Sonho, and Dom Antônio Fernandes, commanded by Colonel André Son of Angola, arrived at Recife on the ship *Het Wapen van Dordrecht* in December, 1643. They presented Maurice of Nassau with two hundred Negroes, a necklace, and a gold basin. They stated that they feared attack from the king of the Congo, despite the fact that they were allied with him against the Portuguese, and they requested that no aid be given the king. The Grand Council, which with Nassau composed the government, replied that it would seek measures to remove the discord and restore good relations between the two "nations." The Council dispatched letters to the king of the Congo and to Count do Sonho exhorting them to peace. Various gifts, described by Nieuhof, a contemporary chronicler, were sent. He observes that "the ambassadors were received with all the honors due their important mission" and showed themselves "very skilled at broadsword play, in which they exhibited the most terrible expressions and postures," and that "they understood Latin perfectly (!) and made several learned orations in that language."

Barleus adds, without giving dates, that during the same period the king of the Congo and the Duke (!) of Bamba went to see Nassau, who sent them to Holland. "They were robust and healthy, with black faces and very agile limbs that they oiled for facility of movement." They appeared in original dances, in jumps, and in sword flourishes.[11]

Colonial rivalry between the Dutch and the Portuguese increased during the years 1641 to 1661 and spread throughout the world. In the Atlantic, in the area Brazil–West Africa, it found one of its chief foci of intolerance, animosity, and competition. Between 1641 and 1648 the struggle for control of Brazil and Angola took place on land and at sea, and joined together Portugal's two largest colonial establishments in a common cause. Africa supported Brazil with human beings; Brazil returned food, money, and various products, such as sugar and tobacco. Military operations were organized from Pernambuco in 1637 and 1640; ambassadors from Negroes rebellious against the Portuguese in the Congo solicited aid from the Dutch in Brazil. In 1645 an expedition left Rio de Janeiro to attend to the requests from Massangano made by Francisco Soutomaior, successor to Pedro César de Menezes. In both Brazil and Africa, Negroes and mulattoes carried on the war against the Dutch and even confronted them with Indians.[12]

Portugal's Atlantic Empire was at this time split into two administrations, one São Jorge de Mina and the other São Paulo de Luanda, the latter including the island of São Tomé and the whole African coastline to the Cape of Good Hope, over which the Dutch finally gained control in 1652 with the arrival of Jan van Riebeeck.

The colonists at Angola communicated their misfortunes and wretched state to Bahia, the governor of which, Antônio Teles da Silva, informed the King of Portugal. His Majesty ordered Governor Pedro César de Menezes to put an end to the war against the Dutch and to

---

[11] This entire passage is based on Gaspar Barleu, *História dos feitos recentemente practicados durante oito anos no Brasil,* 1st Latin ed. 1647, Brazilian translation Rio de Janeiro, 1940, 55, 211, 215, and 254–255; Johan Nieuhof, *Memorável Viagem Marítima e Terrestre ao Brasil,* 1st Dutch ed. 1682, Brazilian translation São Paulo, 1942, 93–94; Manuel Calado, *O Valeroso Lucideno e Triunfo da Liberdade,* 1st ed. Lisbon, 1648, 3rd ed. Recife, 1942, 252.

[12] C. R. Boxer, *Portuguese and Dutch Colonial Rivalry, 1641–1661,* reprint from *Studia,* Lisbon, 1958. "É ela a raiva dos Holandeses com a guerra do Brasil ser de negros e mulatos, e mulatos e negros os que a governavam," *Correspondência Diplomática de Francisco de Souza Coutinho,* Coimbra, 1920–1955, III, 357.

make peace, while he himself would sue for the restitution of Angola and the Island of São Tomé.[13] Thus the uprisings of the Portuguese colonists and their Negro allies found no support in the homeland, which feared the strength of the Low Countries and placed faith, perhaps through weakness, in truces and subsequent negotiation for return of the colony.

In Massangano, Pedro César began to trade with the Dutch in Luanda until the cruel deportation of a hundred and sixty Portuguese colonists who were considered rebels. These people were placed in an open vessel with scant provisions and dispatched to Bahia de Todos os Santos. They finally landed at Pernambuco, eight of them having starved to death during the crossing.

For the normalcy, even the salvation, of Brazil, Angola, the "Black Mother," had to be recovered. But Portugal, already hard pressed by the struggles of the Restoration, saw even Bahia threatened in 1647 by the arrival of Sigismund von Schkoppe on the island of Itaparica. Before learning of the attack on Bahia, the King had named Salvador Correia de Sá Captain-General and Governor of Angola. Now the liberation of Bahia assumed priority. Resources were insufficient for both operations, and the ships and supplies required for Angola went instead to Antônio Teles da Silva, Governor of Brazil and Captain-General of the Royal Armada of the Atlantic.

Salvador Correia de Sá left Tejo on November 7, 1647, and on January 23, 1648, arrived at Rio de Janeiro to gather forces to liberate Angola. Despite fears of Dutch attack on Rio de Janeiro and criticism for leaving it exposed to Dutch depredations, he left for Angola on May 12, 1648, with fifteen ships and 1,400 men. Except for the five galleons furnished by the Crown, his expedition was recruited and equipped in Rio, with monies raised in Brazil.[14] Salvador de Sá sighted the African coast on July 12. When he arrived at Luanda a month later, on August 12, the Portuguese in Massangano were near total annihilation. He rapidly won victory. The surrender terms were signed on August 24, seven years after Jol had conquered Luanda. The Portuguese colony became again, as Boxer stresses, what it had been in 1641: the principal

---

[13] Manuel Calado, *op. cit.*, 253.
[14] C. R. Boxer, *Salvador de Sá and the Struggle for Brazil and Angola, 1602–1608*, London, 1952, 256.

source of slave labor for Brazil. All the *sobas* (or *sovas*, tribal chiefs) except Garcia Afonso II, king of the Congo from 1641 to 1663, immediately gave allegiance to Salvador de Sá. The peace imposed was harsh but was later mitigated by the Portuguese Overseas Council (Conselho Ultramarino). Garcia Afonso did not leave Angola for Brazil until 1652, but never again disturbed Portuguese order while Salvador de Sá governed (until 1651). The traffic in slaves was immediately reëstablished, Buenos Aires, Brazil's source of silver, now taking part in it. Angola was to be jealously guarded, Salvador de Sá said in 1651, for it was vital to Brazil and consequently also to Portugal.[15]

The recovery of Angola, accomplished by Brazil, saved the portuguese Empire from ruin. Henceforth Angola was more dependent upon Brazil. Its next governors and most important administrators came from Brazil rather than from Portugal and gave Brazil's interests priority. João Fernandes Vieira and André Vidal de Negreiros left their Brazilian struggles against the Dutch to become Angolan governors. The former was appointed to the governorship on July 8, 1654, but left Recife only at the beginning of 1658, arriving at Luanda on April 18.[16] Fearing the Dutch, he armed his ships and took along two hundred soldiers from Pernambuco, three thousand muskets and arquebusses, as well as pieces of artillery and munitions, and civil and personal servants. In Angola he was feted and visited by missions from the African chiefs, among them those of the king of the Congo, who earlier had given Salvador Correia de Sá trouble. Fernandes Vieira continued to seek obedience from Garcia Afonso and the subjugation of other rebellious chiefs. This engaged him in military campaigns and the "just war," that is, in war against infidels who refused to expel the Moors. Always concerned with the colony's defense, he devoted his activities more to military than economic problems, repairing and building forts. He had misunderstandings with his military men, complaints from the inhabitants of Massangano, and serious difficulties with Jesuits more devoted to temporal than spiritual goods. His greatest achievement was the assistance he gave Jose da Rosa's attempt to link Mozambique with Angola

---

[15] *Ibid.*, 282.
[16] The following passage is based on José Antônio Gonçalves de Mello, *João Fernandes Vieira*, Recife, 1956, 2 vols., especially II, 152–200.

by crossing the continent overland. Fernandes Vieira's administration seems to have been as irregular as others, and accusations that he had profited from the war of restoration rose after an inquiry ordered by the King. The excesses he committed were afterward reversed. What little information José Gonçalves de Melo was able to gather concerning the government of Fernandes Vieira shows him to have been like other governors, weak in initiative and services, thinking more of his own than of royal or colonial interests.

André Vidal de Negreiros, governor of Angola from 1661 to 1666, lived in the house that had been used by João Fernandes and also committed acts of violence, among others, that of deporting Angolans to Pernambuco.

Portugal had rewarded the heroes of the Pernambucan Restoration richly, granting them the government of Angola. But Portugal needed in Angola energetic men accustomed to military campaigns who could cope with Dutch attacks and African resistance. The entire west coast of Africa was now subordinate to Brazilian interests. Even the military command of the coastal fortresses was subject, like Angola itself, to the Governor-General in Bahia. When the viceroyalty was established in Rio de Janeiro in 1763, all of Portuguese Africa was closely associated with it.[17] Thus Jaime Cortesão reaffirms that "in the seventeenth and eighteenth centuries Angola was a Portuguese province of Brazil." [18]

THE COAST OF MINA AND BRAZIL

As early as the eighteenth century, sugar-growing interests no longer dominated the Brazilian economy. In 1706 Governor Dom Rodrigo da Costa wrote the Overseas Council concerning Brazil's ruinous situation, and on September 1 the Council agreed that "the suffering Brazil is experiencing, which as experience is proving may increase as time goes on, rises from the lack of Negroes and the insufficient number of them imported for work in the mills, in tobacco cultivation, and in the mines. The chief interest of individuals there is to divert to the mines those Negroes that were intended for the mills and the tobacco fields." [19]

---

[17] The Arquivo Nacional preserves the correspondence of the governors of Angola in its Viceroyalty collection.

[18] "Angola e a formação do bandeirismo," *A Manhã*, August 15, 1948.

[19] "Consulta do Conselho Ultramarino sôbre os prejuízos que causava ao Brasil a falta de negros e o remédio para os evitar," *Anais da Biblioteca Nacional*, XXXIX (1921), Document 2 913–14.

More than 150,000 slaves were used in Minas alone. Need and easy wealth made prices rise and the slave trade did not keep pace with the new economic situation because, perhaps, of a lack of ships. Negroes from Angola and the Coast of Mina were traded for bundles of tobacco and kegs of brandy, and frequently for the contraband gold that was demanded by the Dutch, who controlled most of the Coast of Mina.[20] The colonists of Bahia and Pernambuco, who possessed tobacco, brandy, and sugar, easily eliminated homeland competition and gained control of the traffic in slaves.[21]

When the trading companies of Grão-Pará and Maranhão and of Pernambuco and Paraíba were organized in 1755 and 1759, respectively it was recognized that the preservation of Portuguese America depended on commerce with the Coast of Mina "in order to supply slaves needed in the extensive gold mines, on the tobacco and sugar plantations, and in the sugar mills."

In 1757 the traders of Bahia petitioned Dom José to approve the organization of a new company that would trade with the Coast of Mina;[22] the official letter of the Viceroy, Count de Arcos, to Sebastião José de Carvalho, Marquis of Pombal, stated that undoubtedly slaves were the most important merchandise in America. "Without them, the colonists would receive irreparable damage to a commerce that is already in a state of decay."[23] Owners of sugar plantations and planters of tobacco would have the privilege of purchasing slaves—but only those from the Coast of Mina—at a fixed price. The traders' petition defended trade with the Coast of Mina, although they preferred Angolan slaves, for if those from Mina were "stronger and more robust," those from Angola were "more docile and of greater value." The Company was to be constituted with Brazilian capital and would take advantage of the provision of March 30, 1756, that permitted "free navigation to the Coast of Mina to all who wish to travel thence and to order trade in ships that carry no more than three thousand *rolos.*" The purpose of the provision being the supply "of an abundance of slaves at

---

[20] José Honório Rodrigues, "Agricultura e economia açucareira no século XVIII," *Brasil Açucareiro* (June, 1945), 78–79.
[21] "Instrução para o Marquês de Valença, Governador da Bahia, de 10/IX/1799," *Anais da Biblioteca Nacional*, XXXII (1914), Document 10 319.
[22] "Representação dos Comerciantes da Praça da Bahia, 1757," *ibid.*, XXXI (1913), Document 2 806. Also see Document 2 805.
[23] *Ibid.*, Document 2 804.

reasonable prices to the Recôncavo and backlands and mines. . . ." The English, French, Dutch, and Danes organized companies for this trade, removing almost ten thousand slaves to supply America. But the goods these companies traded were of small use to the Africans, except for English brandy. Only Brazilians had tobacco and the brandy held in esteem in Africa, and encouraged by this advantage, the traders of Bahia made their plans, already, in their statutes, establishing the prices of the slaves: the best, first quality, or choice, 140,000 *réis;* second quality, 130,000 *réis;* third, 110,000 *réis;* first choice young bucks, 120,000 *réis;* second, 100,000 *réis;* third, 90,000 *réis;* first quality adolescent boys, 85,000 *réis;* ordinary, 70,000; good boys, 70,000 *réis;* and ordinary, 60,000; good adolescent boys, 60,000 *réis;* ordinary, 50,000; choice young females, 90,000 *réis;* second-quality, 75,000 *réis;* third, 65,000 *réis;* ordinary adolescent women and good grade girls, 60,000 *réis;* pretty little girls, 50,000 *réis;* ordinary little girls, 40,000 *réis.*[24]

The Company was never created. Nevertheless the traders of Bahia carried on a considerable slave trade with the Coast of Mina, twelve to fifteen ships sailing thence annually with sixty thousand bundles of tobacco, returning with six to seven thousand slaves, including boys and girls. Pernambuco also received slaves from Mina. Not, however, Rio de Janeiro, "for it lacks the necessary commodity, tobacco, that leaf produced in the vicinity of Rio being greatly inferior in quality to that from the fields of Cachoeira, district of Bahia." Rio de Janeiro "for this reason traded with Angola and Benguela, sending goods from Europe and Asia, money in half *dobras,* brandies, and other goods, the same ships returning laden with Negroes, male and female, young and old, who are sold to labor on the land in the Recôncavo and Minas, on plantations and also in mills. Therefore few Negroes from Mina are found in Rio de Janeiro and its districts." [25]

---

[24] "Estatutos da nova Companhia, que alguns dos principais comerciantes da praça da Bahia pretendem fundar para exploração do comércio da Costa da Mina, Bahia, 3 de maio de 1757," Inventário, *ibid.,* Document 2 807.

[25] "Descrição do Estado do Brasil, suas Capitanias, Produções e Comércio," MS 13 918, British Museum; the part referring to Pernambuco is reproduced by José Honório Rodrigues in *Revista de História de Economia Brasileira,* (June 1953), 82–99. Quotations referring to Bahia and Rio de Janeiro are transcribed from the photostatic copy.

AFRICAN TRADE CONTROLLED BY BRAZIL

With the commercial decline of Portugal, the Portuguese colonists in Brazil moved to enlarge a commerce that to them was indispensable and that they alone finally would control, a commerce with an area much larger than the Coast of Mina and one that would be exercised with far more freedom than had been granted the traders who worked that coast. They went indeed directly to India, eliminating Lisbon entirely. In 1770 Martinho de Melo Castro, Portuguese Secretary of State, wrote that one could not "without great sorrow see how our Brazilian colonies have absorbed commerce and shipping on the African coast, *to the total exclusion of Portugal;* and what the Brazilians do not control, foreign nations do." He proposed the destruction of the system that had gradually been established: ships from India landed in Brazil to sell Oriental goods and buy goods for the "black trade" which then went to Angola in returning slave ships.[26] In 1779 Melo Castro wrote that the colonists of Bahia and Pernambuco had developed two kinds of commerce with the coast of Africa, one, the taking of Negroes, being licit, legal, and useful; the other, illegal, pernicious, and prohibited, consisted of the introduction into Brazil of foreign goods that were traded with the Dutch on the coast for tobacco.[27] Two years later José da Silva Lisboa, later Viscount of Cairu, observed that

African trade is of great importance here (Bahia) and is directed to the supply of slaves, yet nevertheless the profit that should accrue from it is seldom realized. Its staples are tobacco, either waste or second-grade leaf, and strong spirits. More than fifty cargoes a year depart from Bahia in corvettes and smacks; eight or ten corvettes go to Angola with European goods, while the others go to the coast of Guinea to buy slaves. The investment risked in entering this business is small. A good smack of ten thousand cruzados and a smack of twenty may be loaded upon capital borrowed at 18 per cent, and the investment is returned thirty days later when the ship reaches its destination. A cargo may consist of sixty slaves, confined to the hold for fear their desperation may induce them to rebel or leap overboard. If few die during the passage, the voyage is lucrative; if many die, the merchant is wiped out because of the exorbitant interest he must pay for

---

[26] Cf. Gastão Souza Dias, *Os Portuguêses em Angola*, Agência-Geral das Colônias, Lisbon, 1959, 235.
[27] See Note 21, "Instrução . . . ."

his capital. The trade brings not only an abundance of slaves but also much gold dust, each vessel carrying several *arrobas* purchased furtively from the Negroes without the knowledge of the Dutch, who control this aspect of the commerce strictly. If the Dutch were to learn of the trade in gold dust, they would demand satisfaction from the petty African princes who head the little dynasties that barter the gold. And as these princes are constrained in all their trade by the Dutch, because of their fear of the Dutch fortresses on the coast and the superiority of the Dutch navy, they have much difficulty in exchanging their gold.

The Dutch, Silva Lisboa continues, committed every kind of violence, compelling the Luso-Bahianos to pay a quarter of the cargo of tobacco of each ship as tribute to the Fortress of Mina; if one attempted to evade that violence, the Dutch would seize his goods.

From the Coast of Mina Brazilian ships brought home large quantities of goods purchased from the English and French. The merchants held that they were compelled to engage in this commerce—a claim Silva Lisboa does not grant—which damaged the commerce in Portuguese manufactures, because the latter, subject to high import duties, could not be handled competitively.

"More than 25,000 slaves have arrived for use in agriculture this year, 15,000 entering at Bahia alone and 10,000 at Rio de Janeiro." [28] But in truth, the slaves imported through the ports of Bahia and Pernambuco did not go to the plantations; most of them were resold to mine operators, who needed them badly and paid high prices.[29]

So Brazil was the center of a three-way commerce and was linked with Asia and Africa by trade in which Portugal took no part. This Brazilian–Afro–Asian triangle was established in the eighteenth century. It dissolved following our independence. Imported into Brazil, in addition to carpets, pepper, and Oriental textiles of cotton, silk, and damask, were slaves from Angola, Mina, Bissau, and Cacheu, and wax from Angola. Exported from Brazil were brandy, tobacco, flour, manioc, and dried meat from Ceará. José da Silva Lisboa in a letter written in 1781 observed that "half of the best leaf" in the tobacco harvest went to Portugal; "the rest, divided into rolls of three *arrobas,* goes to Africa

---

[28] "Carta de José da Silva Lisboa a Domingos Vandelli, Bahia, 18 de outubro de 1781," *Inventário, Anais da Biblioteca Nacional,* XXXII (1914), 494–506.
[29] "Ofício do Govêrno interino para Francisco Xavier de Mendonça," *ibid.,* Document 6 966.

to be exchanged for slaves, and, a large part, to Asia, reduced to powder and as contraband, to the damage of the royal contract; what remains is consumed in the internal trade of the country." [30]

Brazilians, affirms Gastão Souza Dias, were the real masters and arbiters of Angolan trade and Angola was indeed no more than a Brazilian colony. It was to end this dependency and the three-way trade that nurtured it that a decree was issued on November 17, 1761, prohibiting Indian ships from stopping in Brazil except in emergencies. But the decree was not obeyed, and vessels bound to Luanda deposited Asian goods there that were easily transported to Brazil in slave ships. New legislation (Charter of June 19, 1772) attempted to eliminate this practice, and required that Oriental goods destined for Angola must first be shipped to Portugal; thus Lisbon merchants would control the commerce, and Portuguese products would be received in Angola only when shipped with Asian products.[31]

As it was recognized that the African trade could not be stopped, and that Brazilian-African economic interests were strong, on the 20th of September, 1782, a decree was promulgated that was designed to secure and control the trade. It required the traders to disengage themselves from agriculture by October 1, 1798, and to cut back consumption of rum in Brazilian ports and increase its export to Africa.[32]

RELATIONS WITH DAHOMEY

Despite Portugal's commercial decline and loss of all territories on the west coast of Africa except Angola and Guinea and a string of isolated small fortresses that were always menaced by the English, French, and Dutch, not only the coast of Malagueta (Liberia) and the Ivory and Gold Coasts but also Nigeria were of importance in the slave trade. Since 1661, however, by the Treaty of Peace with the Low Countries (concerning Dutch possessions in Brazil), Portugal had been supposed to pay to the Dutch 10 per cent of all transactions made in the region between Rio Volta (the frontier between Togo and the Gold Coast, now Ghana), and Gabon. Now Dahomey became important in addition to Angola and Cacheu and Bissau in Guinea, which were

---

[30] See Note 28, "Carta . . . ."
[31] Gastão Souza Dias, *op. cit.,* 239.
[32] *Publicações do Arquivo Nacional,* Rio de Janeiro, 1902, III, 105.

maintained only by great effort. It was a new source of supply, thanks to the presence of Fort São João Batista in Ajuda. This outpost was manned by a small military force supported by Portugal and commanded by a Director who maintained relations with the king of Dahomey. Dahomey at first exported slaves to the islands of São Tomé and Principe, and then later to Brazil, when the expense of maintaining the fort was met by the ten *tostões* (small coins) tax collected on each head imported into Bahia.[33]

At the beginning of the eighteenth century, Brazilian trade with Dahomey increased, extending to a variety of goods carried by a large number of vessels. Dahomey became and remained one of the most important areas commercially and one of the most abundant sources of slaves. As early as 1750, the petty king in Dahomey sent a mission to Portugal, by way of Salvador, the purpose of which was to increase trade with Portugal, one of the earliest countries to hold commerce with the Coast of Mina.[34] The emissary was received with all honor in Bahia, ". . . a city which economically is in large part dependent upon Dahomey." He did not continue on to Portugal but contented himself by conversing with Count de Atouguia, the sixth viceroy. The Dahomian king may have wished to deny accusations that had been made in 1746, by Count das Galveias, the previous viceroy, concerning his part in usurping the role of the Director of the Fort, who was very dependent upon the interests of the king and the viceroy and the combinations effected between them as they exchanged presents and courtesies in the manner of one power to another.[35]

When Bahia traders made their plans to found a company to exploit the commerce with the Coast of Mina, they pointed out that the Fortress of São João offered insufficient security and control, was inconveniently

---

[33] See the excellent summary, unfortunately with no indication of sources, by J. F. de Almeida Prado, "A Bahia e as suas Relações com o Daomé," in *O Brasil e o Colonialismo Europeu,* Companhia Editôra Nacional, 1956, 114–226.

[34] Almeida Prado refers to a pamphlet on the mission without supplying bibliographical data. It is curious that the documents registered in "Inventário dos Documentos Relativos ao Brasil existentes no Arquivo do Maranhão e Ultramar" (today Histórico Ultramino) do not treat of the matter. See vol. I, "Bahia, 1613–1762," *Anais da Biblioteca Nacional,* XXXI (1913).

[35] *Inventário, Anais da Biblioteca Nacional,* XXXII, Cf. Documents 354, 426–427, 794–799, and 1 298. The directors were frequently changed.

located, and was subject to attack and violence by the petty king and men of power in Dahomey; they petitioned that its administration be given to their Company, which would rebuild the fort on a better site and man it with forces adequate for defense and even for offensive action.[36] This was not done; indeed, the Company was never organized, for its establishment would have involved the granting to Bahia and its traders of a privilege that the homeland did not care to relinquish, despite the fact that those traders already controlled the commerce in question.

Ten years after the visit of the emissary of the petty king, continuing complications resulted in the rulers of Dahomey imposing their conditions upon the Portuguese Director of the Fort.[37]

The great advantage of trade with Dahomey was that it provided a market for tobacco, especially that grown in Alagoas and Cachoeira, which was most esteemed by the Africans. Certain privateers who went to Dahomey became slave traders, doing business with Bahia.

A new emissary en route to Portugal arrived in Bahia, sent by King Adarunza, on May 26, 1795. He also was received with a great show of esteem and welcomed with festivities.[38] The King desired that the port of Ajuda, Gregue, deep in the Gulf of Benin, should become the exclusive market on the Coast of Mina for the supply of slaves for the Brazilian Portuguese. This privative arrangement was considered inconvenient by Dom Fernando José de Portugal Castro, Governor-General of Bahia from 1788 to 1800, because a monopoly would raise the price of the slaves and limit the choice among them, and because if delivery should be delayed, the tobacco to be exchanged for them would deteriorate. It was unwise, Dom Fernando added, from a security standpoint, to bring together in one place a large number of

---

[36] *Ibid.*, Document 2 807.

[37] See "Ofício do Vice-Rei Conde dos Arcos, de Agôsto de 1760," *ibid.*, Document 5 189; "Carta do Chanceler Tomás Roby de Barros Barreto, de novembro de 1760," ibid., Document 5 131; and an Ofício of the last mentioned, dated September 1761, Inventário, *ibid.*, Document 5 567.

[38] The communication from the Governor, Dom Fernando, was delivered by Luís de Souza Coutinho, Minister of State, on October 21, 1795. See *Inventário, Anais da Biblioteca Nacional,* XXXVII (1918), Document 27 102. The reply is in Document 27103, in the same vol., and an account of the expenses for the mission is in Document 27104.

slaves from the same tribes, speaking the same language. He complained of the insults and excesses practiced by the kings of Dahomey
against the Fort, stating that the forces there had been "too few to
restrain them," and that such acts, although committed by "despotic
Princes ignorant of the civilities and rights of nations," nevertheless
were quite offensive.[39]

This time the King's ambassador proceeded on to Portugal, which
returned the honor in 1796 by dispatching two priests as emissaries to
Dahomey, Vicente Ferreira Pires, a native of Bahia and an apostolic
envoy, and Cipriano Pires Sardinha. Both had accompanied Dom João
Carlos de Bragança, son of King Adarunza and known as "the
Ethiopian prince," from Bahia to Lisbon and then back to Bahia and
home to Dahomey. Father Pires in his *Viagem de Africa em o Reino de
Daomé*[40] records the prices of tobacco on the coast, mentions the other
nations (England, France, and Denmark) that traded in the region,
describes the fortress constructed in Mina by the Portuguese and in his
time in the possession of the Dutch, and tells of a visit to the king in the
interior, of the royal customs including the sacrifice of royal wives and
guards upon the death of a king, and of the ruler's unlimited power,
hereditary and defined by no constitution. In addition he describes the
Moslem customs of the people and the exploitation of prostitution by
the king and a small population of *Males*, Moorish Negroes who,
though they were from a bordering country, lived in Dahomey.

Neither the priests' visit nor the courtesies of Viceroy Count de
Atouguia and Dom Fernando Jose, who later was Viceroy of Rio de
Janeiro, calmed the impetuosity of King Adanruza. He continued to
address himself to Prince Regent Dom João in 1800, after the Director of
Fort São João had been expelled, and offered him various presents.[41] His
relations with the government of Bahia were maintained unstrained,
revealing the importance his area was acquiring, along with Angola and
Mozambique, although it was not a Portuguese colony. The King
dispatched a new mission to Bahia in 1805, to request financial support
for Fort São João, and Governor Francisco da Cunha Menezes

[39] See "Ofício de 12 de novembro de 1800," *Inventário, ibid.*, XXXVI (1916).
Transcribed in the *Revista do Inst. Hist. Geogr. Bras.*, LIX, pt. 1, 413–416.
[40] Companhia Editôra Nacional, São Paulo, 1957 (written in 1800).
[41] "Cartas (4) de Adanruzan, Bahia. 29 de outubro de 1810." *Inventário, Anais da
Biblioteca Nacional*, XXXVI (1916).

(1802–1805) decided that it should be lent at the expense of the Royal Treasury. The two ambassadors were given hospitality at the Convent of São Francisco. The governor could not understand the king's letter, and made use of interpreters. Adanruza's demands were the same as in 1795: the port of Ajuda to have a monopoly in the slave trade, gold mines in that territory to be exploited, and, finally, abolition of the Directorship of the Fort. Dom Francisco, considering the previous reflections of Dom Fernando on the matter to be sound, forwarded the latter's official report concerning it to Lisbon and sent the ambassadors on to Portugal accompanied by one of his assistants.[42]

Following this mission, Adanruza decided to send no more emissaries to the Portuguese court, but to have them remain in Bahia and communicate with the court by letter.[43] As the king's violence against the Fort at Ajuda continued, it was proposed to abandon trade in that region and establish it not in Gregué but in Porto Novo.[44] At this stage, the Portuguese government was no longer pleased by such proposals, for England was pressing for the abolition of slave trading entirely.

LUSO–BRAZILIAN–AFRICAN COMMERCE

In 1796 Angola ranked third in the importation of products from Rio de Janeiro, after Pôrto and Lisbon; and Benguela the sixth, following these three and Bahia and Pernambuco. Fourteen ships annually went to Angola and ten to Benguela, carrying sugar (402 and 200 *arróbas* [1 *arróba* = 15 kilos]), brandy (2,253 casks to Angola and 588 to Benguela), rice (2,308 and 340 *arróbas*), wheat flour (1,422 and 536 *arróbas*), dry meat (1,210 and 400 *arróbas*), tobacco (1,754 and 180 *arróbas*), bacon (84 and 160 *arróbas*), flour [manioc] (1,820 and 6,820 *alqueires* [13.8 liters]), and beans (600 *alqueires* to Benguela).[45]

[42] "Ofício de Governador Francisco da Cunha Menezes para o Visconde de Anadia, Bahia, 15 de março de 1805," "Carta do Rei do Daomé, de Abaime, 14/XI/1804," and "Anexo e Relação dos Portuguêses que se acham presos no território do Daomé," *Inventário, Anais da Biblioteca Nacional,* XXXVII (1918), Documents 27 099, 27 101, and 27 474.
[43] "Ofício do Governador Francisco da Cunha Menezes para o Visconde de Anadia, Bahia, 16 de outubro de 1805." *ibid.,* Document 27 486.
[44] "Carta de Inocêncio Marques de Santana para o Visconde de Anadia, Bahia, 17 de outubro de 1805," *ibid.,* Document 27 486.
[45] See "Mapa dos efeitos que se transportarão desta cidade do Rio de Janeiro para os portos abaixo declarados no ano de 1796," *Revista do Inst. Hist. e Geogr. Bras.,* XLVI, pt. 1 (1883), 197–204.

Bahia alone in 1804 exported products valued at 2,859,373.635 *réis* to Portugal, 268,259.000 *réis* to the Coast of Mina, 73,600.500 *réis* to Angola and Benguela, and 11,660.000 *réis* to Goa, a total of 3,481,693.595 *réis,* the chief products being sugar, brandy, cotton, rice, fish oil, coffee, hides, sweets, lumber, gold, leather, and tobacco.[46] It imported from Portugal products valued at 511,847.935 *réis,* 466,595.720 *réis* from Asia, 492,883.800 *réis* from the Coast of Mina, 209,440.000 *réis* from Angola and Benguela.

Thus, on the eve of the arrival of the royal family, and at the time when the great political and economic transformations of Brazil were just beginning, trade with Africa continued and was considerable, trade that consisted not only of the importation of slaves but also of the importation and export of products. José Antônio Soares de Souza has proved that Portuguese exports to Brazil declined from 1800 on, as the Brazilian *Capitanias* began to consume competing merchandise, especially English, that was imported directly rather than as prescribed by the colonial treaty. After 1805 especially commerce in Rio de Janeiro escaped Portuguese tutelage. When Portugal had been the intermediary in Brazilian commerce, that is, when Lisbon and Porto had taken responsibility for placing Brazilian products abroad and had received Brazilian gold, the great wealth of the Portuguese properties and mines in Brazil had been much more important than profits to be gained from the export of Brazilian manufactures and products. Now trade with and shipment of gold to Portugal were diminishing, and as a result, trade with America and Africa, indeed all commerce that was not under Portuguese control, increased. Coffee plantations were already being established, especially in the Paraiba Valley (Rio de Janeiro), when the new century began. These required slaves, and every year the number of slaves increased.[47]

According to Magalhães Godinho:

Le système du pacte colonial est fini, la liberté—la concurrence anglaise—brise le monopole portugais. La chute du trafic entre Lisbonne, Porto et

[46] "Mapa da exportação dos produtos da Capitania da Bahia, 15/III/1805," *Inventário, Anais da Biblioteca Nacional,* XXXVII (1918), Document 27 093.

[47] "O Brasil e as Manufaturas Portuguêsas, 1796–1809," and "O Brasil e o Comércio de Portugal, 1796–1809," *Jornal do Brasil,* Rio de Janeiro (June 29 and July 20, 1958).

Viana, d'un côté, et Rio de Janeiro, Bahia, Pernambuco et Maranhão, de l'autre, amène l'écroulement de tout le commerce international portugais, dont les affaires brésiliennes représentaient les 3/4.[48]

Brazil's dependence upon the traffic in slaves, which was increasing in order to satisfy the demands of the coffee industry, led to expansion of commerce with Africa, gave business to traders, and, because of the constant importation of slaves, increased the Africanization of the country.

[48] Vitorino Magalhães Godinho, *Prix et Monnaies au Portugal,* Paris, 1955, 294.

CHAPTER THREE

The African Contribution

No aspect of Brazilian-African relations deserved more attention than the African in Brazil. The chroniclers described the types of Negroes here, their qualities, virtues, and defects, fully and often with descriptive and interpretative elaboration. They did so with no greater rigor than when they described our indigenous element, our Indians. If from the beginning the latter benefitted from protective legislation and defenders of their liberty, the Negroes endured captivity with, for a long time, no voice to speak in their favor, except Father Antônio Vieira, who in his *Sermões* exhorted them to resignation, and Father Manuel Ribeiro da Rocha, who condemned the slave traffic and proposed freedom.[1] Bishop Azeredo Coutinho, on the other hand, identifying with the interests of the *latifundios,* defended slavery as "a lawful business" and a "form of commerce" the legitimacy of which had never been doubted by nations since antiquity,[2] and attacked the "French reformers."[3] The works written by Ribeiro da Rocha and Azeredo Coutinho are unique and in their defenses of liberty and slavery, respectively, present a singular contrast.

Nineteenth-century campaigns for abolition of the traffic in slaves and slavery itself occupied public opinion in Brazil and attracted minorities from the intellectual and governing classes, beginning with José Bonifa-

---

[1] *Ethíope Resgatado,* Lisbon, 1758.
[2] *Análise sôbre a justiça do comércio do resgate dos escravos da Costa da África,* Ist French ed., 1798, 2nd Portuguese ed., 1808.
[3] *Concordância das Leis de Portugal e das Bulas Pontifícias, das quais umas permitem a escravidão dos Prêtos da África e outras proíbem a escravidão dos Índios do Brasil,* Lisbon, 1808.

cio, the Patriarch,[4] and became an authentic aspiration of the Brazilian people. The Negro was now studied only from the viewpoint of advocates of abolition. This focalization may be seen in the *Catálogo da Exposição de História do Brasil,* the greatest monument of Brazilian bibliographical erudition, which contains only one section on the Negro—entirely limited to the problem of slavery and its abolition—with no listing of studies on the influence of the Negro upon, or his contribution to, Brazil. If it is true that this scholarly bias did not eliminate descriptive and other studies, among which the work by Perdigão Malheiros (*A Escravidão no Brasil*[5]) was outstanding, yet it is also true that social studies and investigations of the Negro's role in Brazil did not begin to be written until the end of the last century. Like the corresponding studies of our Indians, they grew out of the polemic on the question whether the growing differences, which had been observed and discussed for some time, between Brazilians and Portuguese were the result of the Negro element in our population or the Indian element and climactic influences, Silvio Romero[6] and Capistrano de Abreu[7] representing the respective extreme positions.

The appeals of the Indianists and the mature work of Capistrano de Abreu (including his reconstruction, with his *Rã-txa-hu-ni-ku-i,* of the language spoken by the Caxinauas, the tongue of the *gente fina;* an effort that as Karl von den Steinen noted in 1914 was altruistic and idealistic), the creation in 1910 of the Service for Protection of the Indians, which was to promote more profound examination of indigenous contributions to Brazilian culture, and, finally, the work of the National Museum, Roquete Pinto in the lead studying with his teams the cultures of various groups and the mechanisms of assimilation; all these developments brought progress in Indian studies, which today rival in bibliography and achievement those on the Negro.

Ground was first broken in Negro research by Silvio Romero, and the brightest figure in the field is Nina Rodrigues with her pioneering work *Os Africanos no Brasil* (1908).[8] Later investigations by Brazilian and

[4] *Representação à Assembléia-Geral Constituinte e Legislativa do Império do Brasil sôbre a Escravatura,* Paris, 1825.

[5] Rio de Janeiro, 1866–1867, 3 vols. Only vol. III deals with the Africans.

[6] *A literatura brasileira e a crítica moderna,* Rio de Janeiro, 1880.

[7] Three articles in the *Gazeta de Notícias,* March 9, 10, and 13, 1880.

[8] Ist ed., 1905; 2nd ed., more complete, Rio de Janeiro, 1935.

foreign authors promoted broad knowledge of slavery's cultural and social problems, of race relations, prejudice, and Negro cultures and Negro influence upon Brazil's folklore, customs, history, and language.[9]

The shift in focus of scholarship may be observed in the bibliography of this century. Tendencies in theory, changes in intellectual approach and concentration of interest, and the conclusions reached and the contributions made by scholars all reveal the growth of a whole discipline on the Negro in Brazil, although the bibliography of Brazilian studies compiled in 1949 still restricted ethnology to the indigenous groups, works on the Negro having no separate chapter but being listed in the folklore section.[10]

Well before the proliferation of these investigations, Joaquim Nabuco in the course of his campaign for abolition had pointed out that the chief effect of slavery had been "to Africanize [Brazil's propulation], to saturate it with Negro blood, as the chief effect of a great wave of immigration from China would be to Mongolize it, saturate it with yellow blood." [11] Dominated by the prejudices of his day, Nabuco considered the Africanization he saw to be a "blemish that Portugal placed on her own face, on her language, and on her only truly

---

[9] Most of these studies are listed in the *Manual Bibliográfico de Estudos Brasileiros,* Rio de Janeiro, 1949, especially in Chapter "Folclore," 299–317. Not included, however, are the following important works: Donald Pierson, *Negroes in Brazil,* Chicago, 1942, Brazilian translation, *Brancos e Prêtos na Bahia,* São Paulo, 1945; E. Franklin Frazier, "The Negro Family in Bahia, Brazil," *American Sociological Review,* VII, 1942; M. J. Herskovits, "The Negro in Bahia, Brazil: A problem in method," with "Reply" by E. F. Frazier, *American Sociological Review,* VIII, 1943; Frank Tannenbaum, *Slave and Citizen, The Negro in the Americas,* New York, 1947; Otávio da Costa Eduardo, *The Negro in Northern Brazil,* New York, 1948; Charles Wagley, *Race and Class in Rural Brazil,* UNESCO, 1952; René Ribeiro, *Cultos Afro-Brasileiros do Recife,* Recife, 1952; Thales de Azevedo, *Les élites de couleur dans une ville bresilienne,* UNESCO, 1953, Brazilian ed., *As Elites de Côr,* São Paulo, 1955; L. A. da Costa Pinto, *O Negro no Rio de Janeiro,* São Paulo, 1953; Roger Bastide and Florestan Fernandes, *Relações raciais entre negros e brancos em São Paulo,* São Paulo, 1955; Manuel Diegues Júnior, *Etnias e culturas no Brasil,* Rio de Janeiro, 1956; René Ribeiro, *Religião e relações raciais,* Rio de Janeiro, 1956; Raymond S. Sayers, *The Negro in Brazilian Literature,* New York, 1956; Édison Carneiro, *O Quilombo dos Palmares,* São Paulo, 1958; A. da Silva Mello, *Estudos sôbre o Negro,* Rio de Janeiro, 1958.

[10] See *Manual Bibliográfico de Estudos Brasileiros,* Rio de Janeiro, 1949.

[11] *O Abolicionismo,* London, 1883, 137.

successful and lasting national effort." [12] It was too high a price to pay for the incomplete, fragmentary, artificial, and exhausting development Brazil had experienced; but he added with clarity and penetration that the vitiating element in the population was not the Negro, but the Negro reduced to slavery. There was no proof, moreover, that the "white race, especially the Mediterranean peoples whose blood is so crossed with Moorish and Negro blood, cannot exist and develop in the tropics." [13] Thus he replied to that science, European, which had created a myth in order to justify the white domination of the world. Still hesitating between the teachings of European science and the contradicting lesson of human experience in Brazil, still considering Brazil to be a European people, nevertheless Nabuco foresaw the vigorous mestizo development that would soon lead to their outnumbering the white immigrants. He saw that the important influence had been the institution of slavery, not the race of the slaves, for the very air here was servile, and he concluded that the effect of slavery had been "to create an atmosphere that seizes and dulls us all, and this in the richest and most admirable of the world's dominions." [14]

Nabuco's view that the evil was slavery rather than the Negro, and the thesis presented by Gilberto Amado, in 1922, that intensification of the slave traffic had resulted in agricultural progress, a more secure government, and the creation of mestizo groups adapted to the climate and capable of living naturally in Brazil, [15] were both developed, analyzed, and interpreted in 1934 with great originality and all the rigor of modern social science by Gilberto Freyre, whose *Casa Grande & Senzala* [16] constitutes a critical inquiry without precedent. Especially important is his chapter on the Negro slave in the sexual and family life of the Brazilian. From the very beginning, writes Freyre, there existed "a distinction between the influence of the Negro as Negro (which is almost impossible for us to isolate) and the influence of the Negro as slave. The Negro in Brazil in his relations with evolving culture and

---

[12] *Ibid.*, 140.
[13] *Ibid.*, 142.
[14] *Ibid.*, 146.
[15] "Exaltação do Brasil" (1922), in *Grão de Areia e Estudos Brasileiros,* Rio de Janeiro, 1948, 157–159.
[16] 1st ed., Rio de Janeiro, 1934, 9th ed., 1958. Various translations. See especially the passages transcribed from the following pages: 348, 358, and 303.

developing society must be considered in the light of social and economic history and cultural anthropology. Hence the impossibility —let us insist on the point—of separating the Negro from that degrading condition of servitude which dulled many of his best creative and manual potentialities and accentuated other qualities, some artificial rather than natural to him, some even morbid." Establishing his criteria, Freyre goes on to examine not only rigorously but also sympathetically African influences and contributions in Brazil. "Every Brazilian," he writes, "even the fairest blond, bears in his soul, if not in both his soul and body—for there are many in Brazil whose whiteness hides a tint of black dye—the shadow, or at least the imprint, of the Negro." Long before, Antônio Vieira had written that "Brazil has its body in America and its soul in Africa." [17]

What is certain is that almost 11 per cent (10.9%) of our population is pure Negro and more than 26 per cent (26.54%) mixed Negro, Indian, and white, while only 0.2 per cent is pure Indian. If it is true that the Brazilian of the rural regions preserved pronounced Tupi facial characteristics, as Darcy Ribeiro has pointed out,[18] it is also true that the Negro strain is to be found in all regions and at all levels of society. Of the many problems engendered by the introduction of Africans to Brazil, including labor problems, problems in language, customs, and folklore, and the problem of political revolutions, the most important is presented by the mass of Negroes to be found in the population, and the degree to which miscegenation, the parent of the Brazilian people, is practiced.

The best estimates calculate the number of Indians in Brazil at the time of discovery at about one and a half millions. Some three and a half million Negro slaves were imported. The statistical difference between the two groups was established at more than two to one, therefore, and this numerical edge explains the Negro's great influence, the wealth of his cultural contributions, and his decisive role in the ethnic formation of the country. Statistical data, not very precise, indicate that over the whole course of Brazilian history more Negroes have lived here than

[17] "Sôbre o Padre João de Almeida," as quoted by João Lúcio de Azevedo, *História de Antônio Vieira,* Lisbon, 1931, 404.
[18] *Línguas e Culturas Indígenas no Brasil,* Rio de Janeiro, 1957.

whites or Indians, but that this predominance dwindled through miscegenation.

Our first Negroes came from the west coast of Africa, from so-called Guinea, a geographical term very vague and broad that seems to have included almost the whole coast between Senegal and Orange.[19] The principal slave-exporting regions around the beginning of the sixteenth century were the territories then known as the Congo and Angola. These terms were also vaguely defined. The old Kingdom of Congo may be considered to have been the region limited on the north by the Zaire (or Congo) river, on the south by the Dande, on the west by the Atlantic, and on the east by the Kvango. Angola, which seems to have been the area between the Dande and the Longa, had a vast hinterland. Imprecise geographical definitions prevent cultural classification of the African ethnic groups that populated Brazil. Modern classifications are based upon only modern data; the lack of decisive documents leaves the limits of the regions uncertain and prevents knowledge of the history of the cultural groups that here had intercourse with one another and with whites and Indians. But the two most important groups to enter Brazil during the sixteenth and seventeenth centuries were the Bantus and the Sudanese,[20] and they were distributed through the ports of Bahia, Pernambuco, and Rio de Janeiro. The Bantus came from the Congo and Angola and were rudimentary in their civilization. They were made slaves as a result of war, by tribute, or by exchange, and they accepted it relatively passively.[21] In times of peace they were procured by slave agents, called "peddlers," who were dispatched into the interior for the purpose and returned after an absence of one or two years with hundreds of Negroes whom they conducted to Luanda to be transported to Brazil. These agents were mulattoes, or even Negroes.

From the seventeenth century on, a number of products of Brazil

---

[19] See Luís Viana Filho, *O Negro na Bahia*, Rio de Janeiro, 1946, 25–26.

[20] On Bantus and Sudanese in Bahia, see Carlos Ott, "O Negro Baiano," in *Les Afro Américains*, Ifan-Dakar, 1953.

[21] The forms of recruitment were also very varied and have been sufficiently studied in Brazilian historiography, and recently such foreigners as James Duffy, *Portuguese Africa*, Harvard University Press, 1960, Charles Boxer, *Salvador de Sá and the Struggle for Brazil and Angola, 1602–1686*, London, 1952, and Fréderic Mauro, *Le Portugal et L'Atlantique au XVII⁰ siècle, 1570–1670*, Paris, 1960.

itself were used in the barter for slaves: sugar, brandy, tobacco, and cotton, and even arms and powder. A royal decree of February 16, 1720, prohibited the exchange of the last for slaves, "because these people are pagan." War provided some slaves, the so-called "Just War" in which the Portuguese were assisted by hordes of loyal, warlike Jaga cannibals.[22] Before being embarked, the Negroes were baptized and classified according to age. Prices paid for them varied according to the demand in Brazil and elsewhere.

Later, after the discovery of minerals and the beginning of mining in Brazil, the area supplying slaves was expanded to the Coast of Mina (now the Gulf of Guinea). Then began the importation of Iorubas from Nigeria, Ewes and Mandingas from the Gold Coast (Ghana), Dahomey, and Togo, Ashantis from Ghana, and Hausas and Maningas from the Sudan; finally, some Bantus came not from the west coast but from Mozambique. Thus, according to Nina Rodrigues, Brazil received Negroes not only from Angola and the Congo but also from the opposite side of the African continent.[23] The first slaves belonged to the Bantu group and came from the Congo and Angola especially, the term "Guinea" found in the sixteenth century documents being broader than at the end of the seventeenth and the beginning of the eighteenth centuries. From the Coast of Mina came equatorial groups. According to Artur Ramos,[24] the Sudanese slaves were from several Sudanese culturegroups, of which the most significant was the Ioruba, and from Guinean-Sudanese cultures (represented by the Males) in northern Nigeria and the Sudan. Negroes from the Ioruba group were usually classified Nago, which was the African language most in use and the one that, with the Bantu tongues, most influenced the Portuguese vocabulary of Brazil. Lagos was the African port of most importance in the export of Ioruba Negroes.

So Brazil's Negroes came to her from distinct cultural areas. And within Brazil there were other regional nuances. The policy was not to permit the assemblage in any captaincy of many slaves from the same tribe, nor to allow any one tribe to become numerically dominant in

---

[22] See Antônio de Oliveira Cadorneca, *História Geral das guerras angolanas* (completed in 1681). Agência-Geral das Colônias, Lisbon, 1940–1942, 3 vols.

[23] *Os Africanos no Brasil*, São Paulo, 2nd ed., 1935.

[24] *As culturas negras no Nôvo Mundo*, São Paulo, 1946, 279–280.

Brazil as a whole, in order to avoid uprisings. Bantus and Sudanese, for example, were most numerous in Pernambuco, Bahia, and Rio de Janeiro. Luis Viana Filho in 1940 studied the evolution of the slave traffic and divided it into three cycles: during the first, slaves were drawn from Guinea, and this cycle corresponded to the period of the *donatários*. During the second, which began at the end of the sixteenth century and lasted through two-thirds of the seventeenth, Angola was the major source. Last was the mixed cycle, which began at the end of the seventeenth century and corresponds to the mining period in Brazil.[25]

It is important to point out that slaves were drawn from all classes of African society, including the highest levels, a circumstance that contributed to the importance of their contributions to Brazilian culture and its laboring mass. Tollenare, for example, noted that in Sibiró there was a Negress called Teresa the Queen; she had in fact been a queen in Cabinda, but caught in adultery, was condemned to slavery and fell from her throne to the slave quarters of a Brazilian master. When she arrived she wore bands of gold-plated copper on her arms and legs and her companions showed her much respect. She was imperious and refused to work. Europeans are prompt to suppose that great reversals of fortune must awaken sympathy and consideration, but Teresa the Queen was merely whipped vigorously, whereupon she submitted to her fate and from the bad queen that she had been, became an excellent slave.[26]

It has already been observed that Congo society was stratified, with a hierarchy of classes in the free population. The greatest difference in social status existed, of course, between the freeman and the slave. As slaves could be acquired not only through purchase but also by capture in war or ambush, many freemen of the upper hierarchy came to Brazil as slaves.[27] Freyre noted that Brazil benefited from a better element of Africans than was to be found in other American countries; this may

---

[25] Luís Vianna Filho, "O trabalho do engenho e a reação do Índio. Estabelecimento de escravatura africana," *Congresso do Mundo Português*, vol. X, Lisbon, 1940, 16–17.

[26] L. F. Tollenare, "Notas Dominicais," *Revista do Instituto Arqueológico e Geográfico Pernambucano*, 1904, 425–426.

[27] M. A. de Morais Martins, *Contacto de Culturas no Congo Português*, Lisbon, 1958, 43 and 107.

have been the result of the tribal diversity, which led to larger stocks of part-Hamite Negroes, the Fula-Fulos and Hausas.[28] Morais Martins points out that the majority of our slaves came from the Congo and Angola and that among those from these areas were freemen enslaved in war or ambush.[29] In the Portuguese Congo today, he states, "descendants of slaves constitute a very important number, even the majority in some regions."[30]

Payment for slaves took many forms[31] and played a decisive role in the growth of African barter economies. Negroes were sold for sugar, rum (brandy), bulk goods, Oriental or Portuguese trinkets, tobacco, and manioc flour. Slave ships were not used solely for the transport of Negroes, but on their outward voyages carried the merchandise used in barter. The voyage back from Angola to Pernambuco required thirty-five days, forty days from Angola to Bahia, fifty to Rio de Janeiro.

As Professor Mauro has written,[32] slavery spread from the Mediterranean basin, throughout which it had been practiced continuously during the Middle Ages, to the Atlantic following the discovery of the Gulf of Guinea, and the Negro slave then replaced the Moorish slave. Brazil existed, or rather, coexisted joined to the Black Africa that lay south of the Sahara, and remote from White Africa, and saw its population and civilization become Africanized.

Despite the variety of tribes represented in Brazil, the Bantus were always preferred because they were less independent, more submissive, more reserved in behavior and loquacious in speech, and more adaptable. They accepted the religion, Christianity, and the social forms imposed upon them. The most characteristic Bantu type was the

---

[28] *Casa Grande & Senzala, op. cit.,* ed. cit., 333.

[29] Morais Martins, *op. cit.,* 107.

[30] *Op. cit.,* 55.

[31] In 1757 Negro slaves coming from the Coast of Mina cost from 5 to 20 bundles of tobacco, when formerly they were acquired for 7 to 10 bundles; the brandy used for barter was equivalent to the English type called "Roma." See "Representação dos comerciantes," *Anais da Biblioteca Nacional,* XXXII, 1914, Document 2 806.

[32] *Op. cit.,* 148. For a good description of the arrival of the slave ships and their loading, the sale of the Negroes in Recife, their origins, ethnic groups and socio-economic conditions, and the profits in the trade, see L. F. de Tollenare, "Notas Dominicais," *Revista do Instituto Arqueológico e Geográfico Pernambucano,* XI (1904), 452–458.

Angolan. Taller than other Negroes, less robust, they were communicative, talkative, and cordial. Less conformable were the Dahomeyan tribes (Jejes), the most important of which was the Nago, and the Mohammedans, who came mostly from northern Nigeria and were called Males. The least submissive Negroes in Brazil were the Hausas; they headed all uprisings in Bahia and in Brazil, being especially prominent in those of 1720, 1806, 1809, 1813, 1814, 1822, 1826, 1835, and 1838.[33] Despite uprisings, the Negro in Brazil was, as Gilberto Freyre writes, generally "the important and flexible collaborator of the white man in the work of agrarian colonization," and even played a civilizing role among the Indians: "Roquete Pinto . . . found evidence of the Europeanizing action of runaway Negroes among the populations of central Brazil."[34] I do not know to what degree that action was more Europeanizing than Africanizing. Both whites and Indians underwent a definite Africanization—in food, dress, language, music, religion, and folklore. "Brazil did not limit itself to collecting from Africa the black silt that made its fields of sugar cane and coffee fertile, its arid lands irrigated. From Africa came also 'mistresses' for the homes of colonists who had no white women, skilled labor for the mines, workers in iron, breeders of cattle and sheep, cloth and soap merchants, and master and journeymen craftsmen of Mohammedan faith."

From Africa also came certain plants, among them sago, *santo* grass, and agapanthus. The Brazilian diet came to include Indian pepper, palm oil, guava, and to be spiced by a variety of chicken dishes and such dishes as mush, *caruru,* bean cakes cooked in palm oil, *efó* (shrimps, greens, pepper, and palm oil are its ingredients), *vatapá,* which is prepared of manioc flour cooked with chicken or fish and highly seasoned, *xinxim,* and pumpkin and watermelon. The Negroes also introduced the Angolan chicken and the cola nut.[35] That beans and rice dish so common on the tables of our middle and proletarian classes dates

---

[33] Donald Pierson, *Brancos e Prêtos,* 93–103; Artur Ramos, *op. cit.,* 316; José Honório Rodrigues, *Teoria da História do Brasil,* 2nd ed., S. Paulo, 1957, 1st vol., 215; Ernesto Ennes, *As Guerras nos Palmares,* Companhia Editôra Nacional, 1938; Édison Carneiro, *O Quilombo dos Palmares,* Companhia Editôra Nacional, Rio de Janeiro, 1958.

[34] *Op. cit.,* 310.

[35] Ibid., 501–509. See also João Dornas Filho, *A influência social do negro brasileiro,* Curitiba, 1943, 15; and Donald Pierson, *op. cit.,* 311–312.

from the middle of the eighteenth century, when the cultivation and use of rice were developed.[36]

The de-Africanization of the well-to-do classes began with the re-Westernization that was prompted by the coming of Dom João early in the last century. Between 1808 and 1822 Rio de Janeiro imported no fewer than seventeen French cooks and ten French bakers.[37] In 1850, notes Freyre, Dr. Luciano Pereira Júnior observed with great satisfaction that the upper classes of Bahia and Pernambuco were modifying their cuisine toward de-Africanization, with fewer bean and pork dishes, fewer stews, and less pepper.[38]

In Bahian dress, among the lower classes the African note is apparent in the stole worn on the side, the silver ornaments, the tunics, long gowns, and skirts.

Modern linguistic studies do not admit that African tongues influenced Brazilian Portuguese. The use of Portuguese was made more secure by the fact that the slaves brought with them an African version of that language.[39] But though the structure of Brazilian Portuguese was unaffected by the Negro tongues, not so the vocabulary. Our Creole dialects are the European language as crudely learned by persons of inferior culture and social position,[40] and show verb forms simplified, inflections reduced, a morphological change. This verb simplification effected social differentiation.[41] The enrichment of our vocabulary has been the subject of several specialized studies; Quibund and Ioruba contributed to it especially. No Brazilian senses anything exotic about such words as *banguê, banzé, banzeiro, batucar, batuque, bengala, bunda, cabaço, cachaça, cachimbo, cafundó, cafuné, cambada, camundongo, candomblé, canjica, carcunda, careca, carimbo, dengue, dengoso, fubá, guri, iaiá, inhame, ioiô, mandinga, mocambo, mocotó, moleque, muamba, mucama, mugunzá, murundu, quilombo, quindim, quitanda,*

[36] Dauril Alden, "Manuel Luís Vieira. An entrepreneur in Rio de Janeiro during Brazil's eighteenth century agricultural renaissance," *Hispanic American Historical Review*, XXXIX, (Nov. 1959), 521–537.

[37] *Registro de Estrangeiros, 1808–1822,* Arquivo Nacional, Rio de Janeiro, 1960.

[38] *Op. cit.,* 509–511.

[39] See Serafim Silva Neto, *Introdução ao estudo da língua portuguêsa no Brasil,* Rio de Janeiro, 1950, 109 and 129.

[40] *Ibid.,* 130.

[41] Gladstone Chaves de Mello, *A língua do Brasil,* Rio de Janeiro, 1946, 63 and 71.

quitute, samba, senzala, tanga, xingar, and many others collected in various studies.[42]

As for pronunciation, the Portuguese language became softened in Brazil, losing that harshness that makes recordings and movies from Portugal hard for us to understand, and that we so ridicule.[43]

In music and folklore Negro influence was decisive. It is enough to recall the *reisados* [popular dramatic dances celebrating the Epiphany] and *congadas* [dances that originally celebrated the coronation of a Congo king], not to mention the *samba.* Melville J. Herskovits in a comparative study of the music of the west coast of Africa and that to be found in Africanized areas of America has pointed out the processes in the transformation of the African patterns and demonstrated the historical relations between the various traditions. In the United States, the West Indies, Central America, and parts of South America, including Brazil, Negro music shows basic African fundamentals upon which local characteristics are superimposed with other characteristics resulting from contact with European peoples. Each area therefore has its own rhythms and style. Brazil's *macumbas, jongos,* and *batuques* may be thus linked to their origins in West Africa and the Congo.[44]

African survivals, religious and folkloric, have been fully studied, particularly by Mário de Andrade, Artur Ramos, and Édison Carneiro.[45] Ramos made an exhaustive study of mytho-religious survivals in music and dance, concluding that the Negro concealed his beliefs, expressing them only through his *macumbas* and *candomblés* [annual festivities and ceremonies of Afro-Brazilian fetichistic cults] while exploiting music, dance, popular festivals, and Carnival time as opportunities to

---

[42] A. J. de Macedo Soares, *Dicionário Brasileiro da Língua Portuguêsa,* 1st ed., 1888, 2nd ed., 1954; Jaques Raimundo, *O elemento afro-negro na língua portuguêsa,* Rio de Janeiro, 1933; Renato de Mendonça, *A influência africana no português do Brasil,* 1st ed., Rio de Janeiro, 1933; 2nd ed., Pôrto, 1948.

[43] See João Ribeiro, *A Língua Nacional,* São Paulo, 2nd ed., 1933, and Gilberto Freyre, *op. cit.,* 376.

[44] *Patterns of Negro Music,* n.p., n.d.

[45] See Mário de Andrade, "Folclore," in *Manual Bibliográfico de Estudos Brasileiros,* Rio de Janeiro, 1949, 284–298, accompanied by bibliography prepared by Oneida Alvarenga, 299–317; Édison Carneiro, *O Folclore Nacional,* Rio de Janeiro, 1954 for the bibliography of these studies, and his *A Sabedoria Popular,* Rio de Janeiro, 1957; Artur Ramos, *O Folclore Negro no Brasil,* Rio de Janeiro, 1935.

pour out his unconscious. Carneiro in his book *Sabedoria Popular* criticizes studies on the Negro as tending to confuse the problem rather than to clarify it, because they are not based on rigorously scientific investigation and field work. For him, "the great folkloric contribution of the Negro lies in the entertainments that he has bequeathed us—and not in the tales nor the oral literature generally that he brought with him." Examining critically the two principal Negro cultures, Bantu (Angolans, Congolese, and Mozambiques) and Sudanese (Nagos and Jejes, Minas, Mandingas, and Hausas), he adds that "we owe much more to the Angolan than to the other Bantu Negroes, Congolese and Mozambiques. It is to him that we owe the two most important diversions of African origin: the *samba* and *capoeira* [feigned knife fights that are considered athletic contests]. . . . The influence of the Congolese Negro was less than that of the Angolan. Its presence may be seen in the *congadas* and *maracatus* [a Carnival dance], both of which look back, in different ways, to the cortege of the King of the Congo." One ought also to take account of the Mozambiques, who are quite skilled in *congadas*. The religious heritage of the Negro must also be stressed; though it belongs to him alone, and is the part of his "life in which he most resists Americanization," yet it is widespread among non-colored people too. The Afro-Brazilian cults have merited the closest attention of scholars; they are usually Nago or Jejes in origin, as Édison Carneiro attempted to demonstrate.[46]

The preservation of the fetichistic religion in forms syncretized with Catholic beliefs and rituals was, as Octavio da Costa writes, the most important element of African culture in its resistance, under all the disadvantages of slavery, to the pressures of the dominant culture.[47] Roger Bastide showed that this syncretism took place thanks to a convergence of religious and magical concepts.[48] The Afro-Brazilian cults are not practiced by Negroes only: Iemanjá, the Water Mother, confounded with Our Lady of Compassion and Our Lady of the

[46] Édison Carneiro, "O Folclore do Negro," chapter in *A Sabedoria Popular,* 65–87; and *Candomblés na Bahia,* Salvador, 1948. See also Donald Pierson, *O Candomblé da Bahia,* Curitiba, 1942.

[47] *The Negro in Northern Brazil. A Study in Acculturation,* New York, 1948, 124–128.

[48] "Contribuição ao Estudo do Sincretismo Católico-Fetichista e Macumba Paulista," *Estudos Afro-Brasileiros,* 1st series, São Paulo, 1946.

Rosary, is worshipped on the beaches of Rio with growing frequency. René Ribeiro, in research conducted in Recife, concludes that "the function of the Afro-Brazilian cults and of participation in and familiarity with the system of rituals and beliefs to be found in Brazil's Northeast is to offer the individual, especially the individual who belongs to certain socio-economic categories there, alternatives of behavior and attitude vis-à-vis the supernatural which have been incorporated into our regional subculture from the beginnings of colonization, and most benefit persons on the lowest levels of our social hierarchy." [49]

From a social point of view, though it may be true that sexual needs and the requirements of child raising may have brought master and slave into a closer relationship that was softened by the concubine, the Negro wet nurse, and house servants, nevertheless the Negro suffered greatly in his condition of servitude, as is evidenced by the punishments meted out to him, his preoccupation with suicide, the murders of masters he committed, his uprisings and his escapes. Already in 1711 Antonil was teaching that masters should treat their slaves less harshly and intransigently in order to prevent them from becoming depressed and disconsolate, from attempting to flee into the forest, and, the women, from attempting abortion "to keep their unborn children from suffering what they suffer." [50] The average life-span was low, about fifteen years; a slave was productive at the longest for only eighteen to thirty-six years, and most of them died of pulmonary tuberculosis and dozens of intestinal diseases.[51] Not until 1755 was it decreed, in a provision by the Overseas Council dated March 12, that Negroes and mulattoes found with arms should receive a hundred lashes instead of ten years on the galleys. This measure was welcomed by masters also, for they would no longer be deprived of their slaves.[52]

The corporal punishments, some of them not only painful but

---

[49] *Cultos Afro-Brasileiros do Recife; Um Estudo de Ajustamento Social,* Instituto Joaquim Nabuco, Recife, 1952, 140.

[50] *Cultura e Opulência do Brasil por suas Drogas e Minas,* 1st ed., Lisbon, 1711; 3rd ed., São Paulo, 1923, 91–97.

[51] See Stanley Stein, *Vassouras. A Brazilian Coffee County, 1850–1900.* Harvard University Press, 1957, 183 and 46; and Ubaldo Soares, *A Escravatura na Misericórdia,* Rio de Janeiro, 1958, 138.

[52] See *Anais da Biblioteca Nacional,* LXXI, 1951, Documents 19 355, 19 337, 19 405, and 19 406.

designed also and perhaps especially to degrade, provoked individual and collective resistance, for example the famous *Quilombo,* a secret haven in Palmares to which runaways fled,[53] as well as morbidity, nostalgia, and longing for Africa. Manuel Querino [54] and João Dornas Filho [55] have recorded these punishments, which soon began to be less frequent as the passage of time and the needs of life improved relations. The two races eventually ceased to be enemies, Freyre observes, as they have been and remain in some parts of the United States and throughout the Union of South Africa. Nor was Brazil ever the Negro hell described by Francisco Manuel de Melo, who would have thought otherwise if he had compared it with the Dutch or English colonies; rather it was the limbo beyond which lay the future ascension of the Negro through miscegenation and education.

Finally, as Capistrano de Abreu sums it up, "the Negro brought a note of gaiety to the taciturn Portuguese and the sullen Indian. His lascivious dances, at first only tolerated, became a social institution; his witchcraft and credos spread beyond the slave quarters. Mulatto women found their easy-going ways appreciated and lived as queens." [56] Frank Tannenbaum stresses that a characteristic of Latin American slavery distinguishing it from that practiced in the English colonies and the United States was the method of emancipation used.[57] In 1798 there were approximately 406,000 free Negroes in Brazil; following the war with Paraguay, some twenty thousand slaves who had fought in the war were freed; and in 1888, at the time of abolition, there were three times more free Negroes than slaves.

In conclusion it may be said that the Negro's major contribution to Brazil is contained in the nation's demographic composition, which is what distinguishes our populace from those of most "Latin American" countries, the number of aborigines being lower here than in some countries, the number of Negroes higher than in others, and Negrowhite miscegenation representing a very high percentage of the total. Compared with Peru, Guatemala, Ecuador, and Nicaragua, the popula-

---

[53] Édison Carneiro, *O Quilombo dos Palmares.*
[54] *O Colono prêto como fator da civilização brasileira,* Bahia, 1918.
[55] *A influência social do negro brasileiro,* Curitiba, 1943, 45 ff.
[56] *Capítulos de História Colonial,* Rio de Janeiro, 4th ed., 1954, 66.
[57] *Slave and citizen; the negro in the Americas,* New York, 1947.

tions of which are about 40 per cent Indian, Brazil is demographically another world. Moreover, as was revealed recently in the final Report of the Sixteenth American Assembly, sponsored by Columbia University, the Indian portion of the population of these countries is increasing more rapidly than the urban portion and comprises the majority in Guatemala, Peru, Ecuador, and Bolivia, although official statistics show the contrary.[58] The indigenous culture that is proliferating is non-European not only in language but in thousands of other ways.

Brazil is also to be distinguished by the relative proportion of its people who are pure Negro from other nations such as Costa Rica, Argentina, and Uruguay where the Negro has no demographic or economic importance; and from nations like Haiti and the British Federation of the Carribean (Jamaica, Barbados, Tobago) where the Negro element is dominant (more than 60%);[59] on the other hand Brazil is to be likened to Cuba, where the Negro played an important economic role and influenced cultural development and miscegenation was decisive in the ethnic makeup of the country. In short, Brazil is neither so aboriginized as some countries nor so Africanized as others; its population is more balanced and homogeneous.

It may be seen therefore that the large proportion of our population that is of African origin through miscegenation (which will be examined in the next chapter) and its importance in our economy and culture make it impossible to deny the Negro and mestizo contribution to Brazil.

---

[58] *The United States and Latin America,* Oct. 15–18, 1959, Columbia University Press, 1959.
[59] Professor Roger Bastide found it strange that in our Introduction we should omit Haiti when speaking of Cuba and Brazil as Africanized countries of America. There, however, the Negro element is predominant, which is not the case in Brazil and Cuba. See "A propos d'un livre brésilien sur l'Afrique," in *Présence Africaine,* (2nd trimester, 1962), 124.

Miscegenation and Relations
Between Brazil's Whites and Africans

MISCEGENATION AND SLAVERY IN BRAZIL

Examination of the problem of miscegenation will make clearer the multiracial composition of Brazil's population and reveal to what extent the ideal of racial democracy has been realized. We should observe at the outset that miscegenation was and is a more Brazilian and American than a Portuguese process. It occurred on a considerable scale only in Brazil, not in Africa, and during the colonial period when the country was governed by Portugal as well as after Independence. The failure of miscegenation in Portugal's African colonies and its small success in her territories in Asia—a record similar to that of other colonizing peoples—indicates that the Portuguese colonist per se was not the decisive factor in the process. Statistics compiled after five centuries of control in parts of Africa and Asia confirm neither miscegenation nor a Portuguese predilection for dark-skinned women. In Angola the number of mulattoes was thirty thousand, as compared with more than four million Negroes; in Mozambique, the figures were twenty-five thousand and more than six million. When these figures are compared with those for Brazil, it is clear that the process of miscegenation was unique here and that it must have been facilitated by local conditions. The data on the acceleration of the process in Brazil demonstrates that here miscegenation went much further in less time than in Africa.

Colonial statistics are lacking and the estimates of historians vary somewhat, but Rio Branco estimates that on the eve of Independence

1817–1818) Brazil had about 3,800,000 inhabitants, of whom 1,043,900 were white, 1,930,000 Negro, and 526,500 mulatto.[1] Thus at that time the process of miscegenation had already reached an importance far beyond what it attained in Portuguese Africa. Figures for individual captaincies, not only the strongly Africanized ones like Bahia, Minas, and Rio de Janeiro, but also the less Africanized and those, like São Paulo, where Tupi influence was important, show that the story is dramatically the same. In the city of Bahia, for example, according to the census of 1775, the population totalled 35,253; 12,720 were whites, 4,207 free mestizos, 3,630 free Negroes, and 14,696 slaves, either Negro or mestizo. Thus 36 per cent of the population was white and 64 per cent was Negro or various forms of mestizo: mulatto, mameluke, *caboclo* [white and Indian], *cafuzo* [Negro and Indian] and others.[2] In 1781 José da Silva Lisboa numbered the population at about 50,000 and stated that "only the fourth part are whites."[3] In 1807 the total was more than 51,000, 28 per cent white, 20 per cent mixed, and 52 per cent Negro.[4] In 1817 the population had grown to 150,000, and Spix and Martius noted that "a face with purely European features is relatively rarer here than in Rio de Janeiro."[5]

In Minas Gerais in 1821 the total free and slave population numbered, according to Eschwege, 696,000, of whom 131,047 were white, 211,559 Negro, and 171,572 mulatto.[6] One can see that even then it was "an admirable synthesis of [Brazilian] miscegenation."[7]

In Rio de Janeiro, according to Martius, the population before the visit of the Court was 50,000, with the number of Negro and colored inhabitants exceeding that of the whites. Thus he confirmed the observations of Sir George Stanton, who visited Rio in 1792.[8] By 1817 the total was 110,000; and between 1808 and 1822 there was an influx of

---

[1] "Esquisse de l'Histoire du Brésil," in *Le Brésil*, Paris, 1889, 151–152.
[2] Thales de Azevedo, *Civilização e Mestiçagem*, Liv. Progresso, Salvador, 1951, 54.
[3] "Carta de José da Silva Lisboa a Domingos Vandelli, Bahia, 18 de outubro de 1781," *Inventário, Anais da Bibliotecas Nacional*, XXXII, 505.
[4] Thales de Azevedo, *op. cit.*, 57.
[5] *Viagem pelo Brasil*, Rio de Janeiro, 1938, 2nd vol., 290.
[6] Guilherme, Barão de Eschwege, "Notícias e Reflexões Estatísticas da Província de Minas Gerais," *Revista do Arquivo Público Mineiro*, 1899, Vol. IV, 744.
[7] Alceu Amoroso Lima, *Voz de Minas*, 2nd ed., Agir, 1946, 97.
[8] See A. d'E. Taunay, *Rio de Janeiro de Antanho*, Brasiliana, 1942, 109.

some 24,000 Portuguese and more than 4,000 other non-Africans.[9] It was the presence of these European newcomers that made it possible for Spix and Martius to note relatively fewer Europeans in Bahia than in Rio.

Even in São Paulo, where Tupi influence was so strong that until the middle of the eighteenth century Tupi was spoken more than Portuguese, and the proportion of Negroes in the population had been small, in 1797 of a total of 158,450, 89,323 inhabitants were white, 38,640 Negro, and 30,487 mixed. Between 1811 and 1815 the population grew by 6,611, 731 of whom were mestizo.[10]

Thus throughout Brazil the proportion of mestizos in the population steadily increased. If the process continued after independence, and if in Portuguese Africa miscegenation failed, then its success in Brazil cannot be attributed solely to Portuguese psycho-social predispositions.

Gilberto Freyre was the first to stress that "in Brazil, relations between whites and the colored races were from the first half of the sixteenth century conditioned on the one hand by the system of economic production—latifundiary monoculture; and on the other, by the scarcity of white women among the conquerors." [11] But soon after "a distinction must be made between the influence of the Negro as Negro (which is almost impossible for us to isolate) and the influence of the Negro as slave. . . . Whenever we consider the influence of the Negro on the intimate life of the Brazilian, it is the slave we encounter, not the Negro per se. . . . What seems at times to be the influence of the race is purely and simply the influence of the slave, of the social system of slavery." [12] Slavery was the decisive element in easing relations between the races, relations that as Freyre points out were those of "superiors" and "inferiors"; scholars since Freyre have not failed to agree on the decisive role of slavery in this process. It was perhaps the absence of the institution in the colonization of Portuguese Africa,

[9] See Spix and Martius, op. cit., I, 95, and *Registro de Estrangeiros,* 1808–1822, Arquivo Nacional, Rio, 1960.
[10] See Florestan Fernandes, *Relações Raciais entre Negros e Brancos em São Paulo,* Anhembi, 1955, 25 and 32.
[11] *Casa Grande & Senzala,* 5th ed., 1946, I, 19.
[12] *Ibid.,* II, 525 and 526.

which despite the early dates of first occupation did not occur in the sense of settlement and economic development until the end of the nineteenth century, while abolition throughout the Portuguese colonies had taken place in 1858, that explains the failure of Luso-African miscegenation. The fact is that once the Portuguese lost Brazil, miscegenation accelerated, with a gradual softening of the prejudices and discriminations resulting from Portuguese racial policy, prejudices and discriminations which today, if they have not yet been totally destroyed, continue to be opposed and suppressed.

Miscegenation was at first a delicate flowering, a new and strange phenomenon that prompted refinements of observation, quickened the senses, and was measured and weighed with a precision unknown to us today, accustomed as we are to all hues of skin and all mixtures of blood. Tollenare observed that "the crossing of all combinations of mixed blood is so widespread, moreover, that the passage from one race to the other is by a scale which to the jaundiced eye contains all graduations." [13] And although the three ethnic groups, with their origins on different continents, seemed incapable in the beginning of being reduced and fused, yet the slavocratic system through its promotion of miscegenation gradually destroyed the dispersive factors and led to psycho-social integration.

Gilberto Freyre has written that prolonged contact with the Saracens led to the idealization among the Portuguese of the type of the "enchanting Mooress," a seductive ideal with dark eyes, enveloped in sexual mysticism. The colonists in Brazil encountered what seemed very like that figure in the nude Indian girls with long unbound hair. Freyre suggests that dark-skinned women were preferred by the Portuguese for love, or at least for physical love. [14]

It seems more logical to seek simpler explanations. In the beginning, sexual needs and needs related to child-nurture could not be satisfied by a choice between white and brown women, or Indian girls and Negresses, for only the last were, in practice, usually available. Later, the Negress who wet-nursed and cared for the new generation decided its sexual inclination. L. G. de la Barbinais, who visited Bahia in 1718,

---

[13] "Notas Dominicais," *Revista do Instituto Arqueológico e Geográfico Pernambucano,* XI, (1904), 458.
[14] *Casa Grande & Senzala,* Rio de Janeiro, 1958, 9th ed., 12–13.

observed that Brazilian Portuguese would take a Negro or mulatto girl
in preference to the loveliest white girl. "Frequently I asked them how
they had come by a taste so bizarre, that induced them to ignore their
own kind. I believe that as they are cared for and nurtured by slaves,
they receive these inclinations with the milk from the breast." [15] Sexual
desire was focussed upon the wet-nurse during the first years of infancy,
therefore, as the child nestled against the black breast. This sexual
orientation, part and parcel of the institution of slavery, opened the road
to miscegenation.

At the end of the eighteenth century, Santos Vilhena described, for all
his Portuguese prejudices, the natural development of the process:

> Negro and mulatto girls, for whom honor is only a chimerical word that
> signifies nothing, when they arrive at adolescence are ordinarily the first
> to corrupt their adolescent masters, giving them their first lessons in that
> sexuality which has enveloped the girls since infancy; and from these first
> instructions derive in the future a troop of little half-breeds who must be
> taken into their fathers' families and reared as part of the family despite the
> perniciousness they work. Many times it happens that a master who is
> affectionately called The Old Man, to distinguish him from his sons, is one
> who with his own slave girls has given his family the worst example.[16]

Before we examine miscegenation, it is well not to forget that Dom
João, Prince Regent, upon the occasion of the organization of the militia
and troops of the line of the Captaincy of Rio Grande do Sul, legally
fixed the definition of Negro. In paragraph four of the second article in
his communication authorizing these military organizations, he established that "all soldiers shall be drawn from the class of whites, which
shall consist of those whose great-grandparents were not black, and
whose parents were born free." [17] Basically this was the same rigorous
standard that even today is applied in certain states of North America:

[15] *Nouveau Voyage Autour du Monde,* Amsterdam, 1728, III, 147.

[16] Luiz dos Santos Vilhena, *Cartas Soteropolitanas e Brasílicas,* Bahia, Imprensa
Oficial, 1922, I, 138.

[17] Rui Vieira da Cunha, "Um conceito legal de branquidade," *Jornal de Comércio,*
January 17, 1954. For Dom João's Carta Régia and Instrução, see *Coleção das Leis
do Brasil,* Rio de Janeiro, Imprensa Nacional, 1891, 96–123, especially 113. See also
the Carta Régia of February 21, 1811, in *Coleção das Leis do Brasil, ibid.,* 1890,
24.

an eighth-part Negro blood means one is Negro. At the same time it defined "Negro" it also seemed to exclude descendants of whites and Indians, though their parents were born free. The object, however, was to restrain the Negro, whose frequent passage into the ranks of whites was repugnant to the white and discriminatory Portuguese legislature. We should not therefore be surprised that in the revolutionary uprisings of 1817 and 1824 there was to be found strong anti-white sentiment.

RACIAL DISCRIMINATION IN BRAZIL

Brazil's various ethnic groups were forced to adjust to one another quickly, for the divergencies in the beginning were profound and isolated everyone, native Portuguese and Creoles, whites and Indians, whites and Negroes, masters and slaves. There were many distinct groups: those born in Portugal and those born in Brazil (*reinóis* and *mazombos*), Africans born in Africa and Africans born here (Angolans and Congolese, and Creoles or *moleques*); Indians who had been converted and those who were still savages (*caboclos* originally referred to those who had been catechized). It was basically a society of two castes, the masters, the slaves, the latter constituting a herd. Yet between these castes were the landless but free *reinóis* and *mazombos,* who were cowboys, land-stewards, plantation foremen, and skilled craftsmen, and also the Negroes and mulattoes who had been enfranchised.

It was the task of the Brazilian people to overcome these differences: the European minority imposed juridical distinctions, wished to avoid racial mixture, and despised the Indian and especially the Negro. The Crown really had no racial policy, though it condemned mixed marriage. The policy of separation that it favored was not based on a racial principle but rather sought to assure the political control of the masters. Social contempt for Indians, much less than for Negroes, did not perhaps stem from racial prejudice but from the fact that whites comprised the highest social category.

Purity of blood, originating in anti-Jewish religious sentiments, became in Brazil a means to assure the privileges of the European dominant class. The caste system favored concubinage and miscegenation, which had assumed great proportions even in the sixteenth century—as may be seen in the Denunciations and Confessions of the

Inquisition—despite the fact that a liaison with a Negress was considered degrading. Even after the *Alvará* (a royal decree) of April 4, 1775[18] removed all infamy from marriages between whites and Indians, the Viceroy of Brazil, the second Marquis of Lavradio, Don Luís de Almeida (1769–1779), ordered an Indian dismissed from his post as Captain-Major because "he had shown himself to be of such base sentiments that he wed a Negress, staining his blood by this alliance and thus becoming unworthy to exercise the aforementioned post" (Decree of August 6, 1771).

It is unnecessary to recall that the slave, according to Roman tradition, was not a person before the law. The union of slaves of different sexes was not consecrated by marriage. Jorge Binci, the Jesuit author of the *Economia Cristã dos Senhores no Govêrno dos Escravos*,[19] advocated in 1705 that masters permit slaves to marry and denounced concubinage of the master with his slave and his exploitation of her in prostitution. And in 1710 Antonil declared that masters opposed marriages between slaves but were unconcerned about their own liaisons.[20] Thus legal unions that would have been inoffensive to racial prejudice and would not have shaken the foundations of the seignorial system were opposed, while liaisons that tended to dissolve the whole caste system and to bring white masters and black slaves to the same level were not discouraged.

Portuguese law in the Philippine Ordinances was limited to making clear that slaves had no public or private rights and to establishing certain prohibitions and restrictions moderating the excesses of masters. Extravagant laws twice determined that governors should punish the excesses of masters, but they were soon revoked because they resulted in disturbances between masters and slaves and shook the seignorial system.[21] Negroes, mulattoes, or Indians, although free, were prohibited in 1621 (Decree of October 20) from learning and practicing the trade of goldsmith. Although all servile work and mechanical arts fell to the

---

[18] Gomes Freire Andrade observed that "up until now no one has joined himself in marriage with one of these persons." João Lúcio de Azevedo, *Novas Epanáforas,* Lisbon, 1932, 53.

[19] Rome, 1705; 2nd ed., Pôrto, 1954.

[20] *Cultura e Opulência do Brasil por suas Drogas e Minas,* 1st ed., Lisbon, 1711; 3rd ed., São Paulo, 1923.

[21] Cartas Régias of March 20 and 23, 1688 and February 23, 1689.

Negroes, there were, according to Luís dos Santos Vilhena, few mulattoes and fewer white men who wished to be so employed. Thus, the restrictive legislation aimed only at securing the caste system, favoring Portuguese domination, and dividing the population in order to maintain the power of white masters.

Racial prejudice was not confined to the decrees prohibiting interracial marriage, which the Viceroy so severely criticized in 1771. There were colored-only brotherhoods in the Church, and colored-only regiments in the army. Vieira, in his *Sermões*,[22] proclaimed that though the Gospel of Christ announces the equality of all, "what we see in our republic, practiced not by some but by all, is completely contrary. This great republic consists of three sorts, or colors, of people: the white, the black, and the brown. . . . As all attend more to the difference in color than to the unity of profession, however, not only do we not see them united in one brotherhood or divided among two, but totally separated into three." The Negroes had their confraternity, the Rosary of Saint Benedict, and the mulattoes, who could certainly "have joined the Negroes on the maternal side," the Rosary of Guadalupe. The two confraternities, or the three, helped maintain not only the status of the white man as a "person" and that of the Negro a non-person, but also, and consequently, the seignorial system. The colored brotherhoods —black and brown—that began in the colonial period have survived into the present. These organizations did not limit themselves solely to religious objectives but also worked toward freedom by levying dues to purchase freedom for certain slaves. Their festivals, *reisados* and *congos,* which represented the syncretic aspect, always ended in visits to the churches of the Rosario of St. Benedict.[23]

---

[22] See the Sermão Vigésimo, in the series, Maria, Rosa Mística, 1688. Also see José Honório Rodrigues, "Antônio Vieira, doutrinador do imperialismo português," *Verbum,* XV (September, 1958), 313-333.

[23] See Artur Ramos, *O Negro Brasileiro,* São Paulo, 1940, and *A Aculturação Negra,* São Paulo, 1942; Joaquim José da Costa, *Breve Notícia da Irmandade de N. S. do Rosário e São Benedito dos Homens Prêtos do Rio—Capital do Império do Brasil,* Rio de Janeiro, 1886 and *Compromisso da Irmandade de N. S. do Rosário e São Benedito dos Homens Pretos, erecta na sua mesma Igreja nesta Côrte do Rio de Janeiro,* n.p., n.d. There are references to the colored brotherhoods in books on the churches and archdioceses of the various Brazilian states. See also Manoel S. Cardozo, "The Lay Brotherhood of Colonial Bahia," *The Catholic Historical Review,* XXXIII (April, 1947), 12-30.

In the army the mulattoes' Regiment (and Battalion) of Men of Color and the Negroes' *Regimento dos Henriques,* which honored Henrique Dias, reflected the conflicting interests of the slavocratic seignorial system and were an attempt to conciliate the repugnance of the whites to being placed on the same level with Negroes and colored.[24] Everything was so segregated and divided during the colonial period. Ecclesiastical law excluded Negroes and mulattoes from the priesthood,[25] and during this period it was even customary to classify by color men who distinguished themselves by their virtue or their courage.

It would be endless to enumerate the restrictions the racial policy of the Crown imposed on free mulattoes and Negroes. In 1730, in Bahia, the office of Crown Prosecutor was denied a licenced lawyer "because he is brown"; [26] earlier, in 1696, at the same place, a mulatto had been denied the right to petition and plead in the Court of Appeal (*Decree of June 28, 1696*). The law dissimulated its prejudice, now granting, now denying, now forbidding, under threat of grave penalties, Negroes and mulattoes to dress as whites (*Act of May 24, 1745*), and soon afterward revoking the prohibition (*Act of September 19, 1749*).

The Portuguese did not have the Spanish predilection for precise standards, Sergio Buarque de Holanda has observed,[27] their delight in the complicated casuistry of meticulous regulations that purported, like, for example, the *Recopilación de Leys de Índias,* to foresee and forestall everything; on the contrary their activities were conducted with unconcerned ease, being diffuse, contradictory, and sometimes rather relaxed in character. Hence the apparent contradictions that aimed through compromise to save essentials. From 1693 (*Decree of December 20*) Negroes and mulattoes were allowed to serve as mayors and law officers, and after 1773 (*Alvará of January 16*), free Negroes were eligible for all public honors and posts.

The prejudices of native Portuguese against Creoles, of whites against Negroes and Indians, and especially those of masters against slaves

[24] Oliveira Viana, *Evolução do Povo Brasileiro,* São Paulo, 1933, 3rd ed., 181–182.
[25] See Pandiá Calógeras, *A Formação Histórica do Brasil,* Brasiliana, São Paulo, 1938, 36.
[26] Quoted by Thales de Azevedo, *Ensaios de Antropologia Social,* Salvador, 1959, 100.
[27] "Le Brésil dans la Vie Américaine," in *Le Nouveau Monde et l'Europe,* Neuchatel, 1955, 66–67.

tended, as time passed, to become concentrated in a relatively few basic restrictions, especially in prohibitions on marriage, as Florestan Fernandes observes, and did not extend to extramarital unions nor impede miscegenation. The obvious explanation, says the same anthropologist, is to be found

in the meaning of family relationship in the social system; membership in the family represented the fundamental principle in attributions of social status. The incorporation of the element of color in the legal nucleus of a great family would bring with it the formal recognition of social equality between the *white man* and the *Negro* or *mulatto*. In order to avoid this, petitions were drawn up opposing intermarriage and subordinating marital relations to endogamic standards. In this sense the two racial groups had been integrated, from the beginning, in a caste system, and the prohibitions on interracial marriage secured the foundation upon which the integrity of the dominant racial group rested. . . . The prohibitions did not affect sexual relations but only marital relations. Not only were the slave sex partners not elevated to the social position of the masters, but children born of these unions remained in the same condition as their mothers.

Actually, the position of the Crown with regard to concubinage, widely practiced by masters and even by priests, was strongly influenced by the Church. Proscribed by the *Ordenações* and penalized with fines and exile to Africa,[28] and prohibited by the Brazilian Church itself,[29] concubinage nevertheless did not cease. Later legislation prohibited and punished it, but this moralistic policy did not prevent its practice and its action as an instrument of interracial contact, perhaps partially because condemnation of the practice in general did not include its practice, in particular, with Negro slaves. Gilberto Freyre, in *Casa Grande & Senzala,* writes pages of great value demonstrating the prevalence of such relations between masters and slave women. Priests living in concubinage, "incontinent or occasional fornicators," to use the expressions of the *Constituições do Arcebispado da Bahia,* although warned and admonished, did not reform and, according to the reports of gossipy travelers, allowances were generally made for them.

There was, therefore, as Florestan Fernandes says, a specific relationship between racial prejudice and the preservation of the seignorial

---

[28] See *Ordenações Filipinas,* Book 5, titles XXIII to XXX.
[29] *Constituições do Arcebispado da Bahia,* 1st ed., 1719; 3rd ed., 1853; Book 5, titles XXI to XXIV, Nos. 994–1001.

system, the former serving to perpetuate the latter by acting as a factor in social segregation.[30] If it is true, as Fernandes holds, that miscegenation cannot be said to imply an absence of prejudice (for it developed on a plane merely physical and sexual and only rarely was associated with effects that involved the acceptance of white-Negro mestizos as whites),[31] it is also true that it operated vigorously to reduce prejudice through its action in attenuating Negro physical characteristics, thus promoting the dissolution of the castes and ethnic equalization. Yet H. W. Hutchinson observed just recently in Bahia that racial nuances—the darker or lighter color, the hair and facial features—still decide the social fate of the individual.[32]

It is very difficult to establish and study the reciprocal effects of prejudice and miscegenation, for miscegenation was a hidden relationship, an extra-marital one, and historical records are lacking. Prejudice itself tended to hide and mask these relationships, preventing the facts concerning them from becoming known today in a society in which miscegenation remains an important factor. But as Gilberto Freyre observes,[33] it was miscegenation that reduced the distance between the castes by the creation of gradations of physical characteristics and educational and family opportunity.

The fact is that if we examine the Portuguese record in Africa we shall see that a declared lack of prejudice there did not lead to miscegenation.[34] When real colonization began at the end of the last century there was no slavery, with or without prejudices, to permit the use and abuse of slave women on a purely physical and sexual plane. But in Brazil, the continuation of slavery until 1888 permitted and facilitated miscegenation, which in turn made for a better interracial

---

[30] "Do Escravo ao Cidadão," in *Relações Raciais entre Negros e Brancos em São Paulo,* Anhembi, 1955, 73–74.

[31] *Ibid.,* 101.

[32] *Village and Plantation Life in Northeastern Brazil,* Seattle, 1957, 99.

[33] *Casa Grande & Senzala,* 1st ed., xv.

[34] In a recent study Charles Boxer demonstrated that miscegenation in India, stimulated by Afonso de Albuquerque, had sporadic results. It was limited to unions with women of the upper Brahmin caste from which very few *descendentes* remain today, 1,000 in a population of 500,000. See *The Colour Question in the Portuguese Empire, 1415–1825.* Reprint from the *Proceedings of the British Academy,* 1961, 127–128; and Orlando Ribeiro, "Originalidade de Goa," in *Atas do III Colóquio Internacional de Estudos Luso-Brasileiros,* Lisbon, 1959, I, 170–179.

socio-political amalgam. The process of miscegenation, which had always been based upon the Negro, was no longer regulated by European whites but by mestizos who after Independence attained high and intermediate posts. The large mestizo population, placed between the two castes of masters and slaves, had allowed the interracial mixture to expand without threatening the seignorial system. If we refer to the statistical data after Independence, we shall see the expansion still in action in the same provinces previously taken as examples because of their Africanization. The first national census took place in 1872, and of a total population of 9,930,478 inhabitants there were already more mulattoes and mestizos of various degrees than whites: 4,188,733 to 3,787,289. In Bahia only 34 per cent were white; in Minas Gerais the percentage of mestizos and mulattoes was 34.5 per cent and that of Negroes 23.14 per cent.

Miscegenation progressed freely, despite prejudice, through the influence of the economic system of master and slave. It did not, however, represent only a biological or ethnic fusing, but also a cultural miscegenation accompanied by social transformations. And this is what really interests the historian or social scientist, for it reveals the socio-cultural consequences of interracial mixture.

There are several factors that place the mestizo in a special social position: the sensitivity of one or the other parental group to physical and cultural differences, and the factors affecting the political and economic dominancy of one or the other group, as Magnus Mörner stresses.[35] And as the position of the mestizo is defined by the resistance to or his rejection by one or both parental groups, he feels rootless and insecure. Hence the tumultuous, excited, frequently insolent, and bold character of which mulattoes have often been accused in Brazilian chronicles, historiography, and social studies. Do they perchance reveal the typical personality of R. Park's marginal man attributed to them by Magnus Mörner? The fact is that since Independence new blood has entered the ruling classes, simplifying the social distinctions of the lower strata, as Charles Griffin observed.[36]

Even before abolition the socio-economic rise of mulattoes had

[35] *El Mestizage en la Historia de Ibero-América*, Estocolmo, 1960, 35–36.
[36] "Economic and Social Aspects of the Era of Spanish American Independence," *Hispanic American Historical Review*, XXIX (1949), 170–187.

become a growing process that did not meet great resistance, as Gilberto Freyre [37] and Donald Pierson [38] proved. In the colonial period Francisco Manuel de Melo noted that "Brazil is the Inferno of Negroes, the Purgatory of White Men, and the Paradise of Mulattoes of both sexes." Antonil, who took Francisco Manuel's words to be a proverb, wrote that "both sexes of the same color (mulattoes) ordinarily have the best fortune in Brazil; the white blood in their veins, perhaps from their own masters, so bewitches the latter that some of them permit and forgive them anything; and it seems that their masters do not dare to reprimand them, but are completely indulgent with them."

Capistrano de Abreu, summarizing Brazil's last days as a colony, wrote that "the mulattoes, indocile and quarrelsome people, could be restrained at intervals by acts of authority, but soon reassumed their original rebelliousness. . . . Growing in number, they were ignorant of and finally abolished distinctions of race, and were strong enough to break with the forms of existing conventions and live according to their restless nature. The levelling process was especially assisted by the feminine element, with their coyness and lascivious movements." He then recalls the following verses heard by Spix and Martius in Bahia:

> A pretty mulatto girl
> Need not practice devotion;
> She offers her dainty self
> Toward her soul's salvation.[39]

In Mato Grosso one hears also:

> A dark girl is hot spice.
> A white girl is cold soup.
> A dark one forever
> And a white one never.[40]

During the riots of February, 1823, in Pernambuco when that state was being integrated into the independent Empire, effervescent popular passions intoned discriminatory songs against whites, Portuguese

---

[37] *Sobrados e Mucambos,* São Paulo, Brasiliana, 1936.

[38] *Brancos e Prêtos na Bahia,* São Paulo, Brasiliana, 1945.

[39] *Capítulos de História Colonial,* 4th ed., Sociedade Capistrano de Abreu, 1954, 328; and *Viagem ao Brasil,* Brazilian translation, 2nd vol. 357.

[40] V. D'Almeida, "Danças, Canções e Lendas Matogrossenses," in *Terra e Gente, Mato Grosso Illustrado,* January, 1956, 50–51.

whites, former masters, wealthy merchants. The colored people translated their aspirations into quatrains such as this:

> Sailors and chalked faces
> Must all come to an end
> For only browns and blacks
> Are to live in this land.[41]

As we know, the sailors referred to were the Portuguese, and in his
Dicionário Morais says that chalking the face was a cosmetic measure
taken in order to "pass" as white. It may thus be seen that in
emergencies such as this one was, we run the danger of outbursts of
violent racial discrimination against whites, similar to those encountered today in some African nations.

It was not only the common people who sang discriminatory quatrains. José da Natividade Saldanha (1796–1831), mulatto, son of a vicar
named João José de Natividade Saldanha and a mulatto girl, Pernambucan poet, revolutionary in 1824, secretary of the Confederation of
Equador,[42] preached the destruction of the whites and declared war
against monarchy and the white population.[43] In these same years, the
German Eduardo Teodoro Bosche, who belonged to the German troop
in the service of Dom Pedro I, noted that "the hatred of the mulatto for
the white is irreconcilable."[44]

The great lesson of Brazilian history is that although we suffered the
greatest affronts externally, were menaced by ruin and disintegration,
and ran the risks of racial strife, finally an extraordinary capacity for
adjustment reconciled our extremes and without further violence found
the progressive path of liberty, equality, and democracy. It is unnecessary to refer to the wars against the Indians, to runaway slaves and

---

[41] Collected by F. P. do Amaral, *Escavações,* quoted by Alfredo de Carvalho,
Estudos Pernambucanos, Recife, 1907, 299.

[42] His biography is in F. A. Pereira da Costa, *Dicionário Pernambucano,* Recife,
1882, 591–598, and in several volumes of the *Revista do Instituto Arqueológico e
Geográfico Pernambucano.* See José Honório Rodrigues, *Indice Anotado,* Recife,
1961.

[43] See Alberto Rangel, *Textos e Pretextos,* Tours, France, 1926, 36–58.

[44] His work was first published in Hamburg, 1835; it was translated into Portuguese in the *Revista do Instituto Histórico e Geográfico Brasileiro,* LXXXIII
(1919), 226, and published as a book: *Quadros Alternados: Impressões do Brasil
de D. Pedro I,* São Paulo, 1929.

Palmares, to social struggles, the movements of Negroes and mulattoes, in order to agree that miscegenation, accompanied by socio-cultural transformations, was an elevating factor, a way to a rapprochement, to tolerance, to social integration.

But the dangers of discrimination have repeatedly assaulted us. Thus it is that in 1821 a Negro revolt broke out in Minas Gerais in support of the Constitution. A contemporary newspaper report tells us that "this revolt cost Negroes and Whites much blood: the former seized control of Vila Rica, the capital of the Province, in a most furious combat; the employees of the Diamond Junta, many Friars, and even the Bishop of Mariana put up resistance which was dissipated by the blood of a thousand Negroes." The diamond country then had more than six thousand Negro workers, there being only thirty thousand in the entire province.

Once the Constitution had been adopted in Rio de Janeiro and in other provinces (the aforementioned news story does not explain if the constitution in question was that one which would be drafted by the *Cortes* and which Dom João had promised to uphold February 24, 1821, or the Spanish one adopted in Rio by Dom João on April 21, 1821, and in effect for only 24 hours), news of it spread into the Province of Minas, the Negroes becoming persuaded that they were now all equal to the whites. At that point they had the Constitution proclaimed throughout Minas Gerais and overcame all resistance. As this province had a larger number of Negroes than the others because of its many gold and diamond washings (in Araguaia on the Rio Grande, in Jaragana, Cangeca, in Capon, where topazes were washed, in Carapata [gold], and in Mandanga [diamonds]) where proprietors and workers alike were Negroes, the Negroes gathered and organized their forces according to local customs, with the slogan, "Liberty and the Constitution."

The leader of these Negroes was Agoinos, supervisor of all the washings in Carolina and Jigonhanha, who addresses this short proclamation to his comrades:

The Constitution has been proclaimed in Portugal, which makes us equal to the Whites; this same Constitution has been adopted here in Brazil. Let us decree death or the Constitution to Negroes and whites, death to those who have oppressed us. Wretched Negroes! behold your slavery! Now you are free. Shed your last drop of blood on the field of honor for the Constitution; we want no more of slavery, nor prisons, nor oppression; we want to be equal in rights to the white Man. Our hymns are for the Constitution, and it is a joy to hear them as we wash gold and diamonds.

On June 30, this valuable commentary concludes, "the whole Province of Minas Gerais was Constitutional, the Revolution being the work of the Negroes, whose glory will last as long as this most enlightened Province." [45]

This revolution in defense of liberty and the Constitution, accomplished and directed by Negroes from Minas in localities having African names, symbolizes in Brazil the movements for independence in present-day Africa. It links us closer to their present movements for revindication and shows how, despite all dangers, we were always able to choose the path to integration, fusion, and unity.

One senses no discrimination in the Minas movement, for both whites and Negroes were to be ruled by the Constitution that was to proclaim the equality of all. But it has not always been so. Detours have always been seductive and in 1843, when progress was being made in the direction of adjustment, an illustrious man like Antônio Pereira Rebouças would plead in the Chamber of Deputies that the mulatto population be represented in the Councils of the Crown. Rebouças held that the Council of State, because of its organization and administration, did not serve as a moderating force, was not a faithful conserver of political history and the traditions of the country above all motives of partiality, but on the contrary served as a buffer behind which the ministers of State might act with impunity; and the fact that its members were deputies and senators contributed to this. Because of the vices that had been introduced into our institutions, which had been compromised and sacrificed, the monarch did not have a single source that would report truthfully and in depth the sentiments of those who were sincerely loyal. Missing in the Cabinet of January 20 (the third after the Majority) were the *maioristas,* that is, liberals who promoted the majority of Dom Pedro II; and he added, "another part of the nation that has no one to represent it in the Councils of the Crown, although the top administration is completely nationalized, is the mulatto population."

---

[45] "Notícia de uma revolução entre os prêtos no ano de 1821, em Minas Gerais," *Revista do Arquivo Público Mineiro,* year V, fasc. 1, 1900, 158–160.

Justifying representation of the mulatto population, Rebouças continued:

As they are identified with all branches of public service, it is very important that this identification have its complement in the Councils of the Crown. It is probably not so convenient, gentlemen, for the opinions of all Brazilians to be made known there openly, and the national unity to be justly represented in all the diverse groups of which it is really composed. Yes, this nation is composed of a majority of white persons native to the country, a lesser number of whites native to Portugal, and many free Negroes and mulattoes. In the composition of the ministry and councils one always tries quite rightly to make the native Portuguese proportionate to the Brazilians. Why may not other groups be considered also in proportion to their degree of civilization and intelligence? This would be no more than just compliance with the Constitution of the Empire, no more than the continuation of what was practiced in Brazil from colonial times.

He then declared that the *Cortes* distinguished between natives of Portugal and Brazilians but viewed the latter without racial discrimination, seeking to combat and abolish in behalf of colored men all the prejudice that arose and was fashionable in the colonies against the accident of their birth. And he emphatically affirmed that "in the sacred cause of Brazilian independence we all take part, always united, and have all shared the dangers of the fatherland, coöperating together for its salvation with the same loyalty and patriotic interest on all occasions, without exception."

Rebouças denounced the prejudices against color, recalling that "in every interval of general peace in Brazil, from the first period of political independence, some turbulent and inventive spirits have engaged in intrigues over the various colors. After the disorders in northern Brazil in 1824 this kind of intrigue began to be fashionable. It was discontinued somewhat during the war over Montevideo. Peace came and the same intrigue reappeared with the falsest and most calumnious imputation, which contributed to the events immediately preceding the fatal [abdication]," and it "reappeared for other reasons in 1831, was killed off by the projects of restoration parties [favoring Dom Pedro I], and was revived in 1835."

Having exposed the intrigues against the colored, Rebouças gave warning of the need for caution, restating it to be necessary "for all Brazilians to have representation at Court, [representation] which with a full knowledge of the whole population of Brazil may assure the monarch of the loyalty and love of his subjects." [46]

As one can see, Rebouças was affirming the existence of prejudices that had arisen in various periods, among them those of 1835 to which we have already referred. But perhaps because he felt them himself as a mulatto, he was guilty of discrimination when he proposed representation according to color or ethnic group, the worst path that Brazil could have taken, so broad was the racial range of its people still. He was forgetting the indigenous and mestizo population of Tupi origin. And he was forgetting also that distinctions based upon race had been ignored neither by the Portuguese *Cortes* nor by the people themselves, who were increasingly more mixed. It was not an objective nor a postulate of Portugal's colonial policy to favor interracial marriages. It merely tolerated them.

The Chamber, surprised by such an unpolitic proposal, heard with much applause and approbation the reply of Ângelo Muniz da Silva Ferraz, later Baron of Uruguaiana, like Rebouças a representative from the Africanized province of Bahia and like him, too, neither pro government nor pro opposition:

The noble deputy has said that the present Government is not national. Gentlemen, if dictionaries do not lie, if they remain what they were, if our language has not entirely changed, I believe that the word national has a meaning very different from that the noble deputy wished to give it. . . . In a political sense the present ministry is a national ministry composed of Brazilian citizens according to the Constitution, elected by the monarch, and having at heart the interest of the country. The ministry may err, may have a bad purpose, may conduct the affairs of the country badly, may be weak, ignorant, incapable, everything imaginable, and may cease to have my support, but it cannot be said that it is not national.

And to Rebouças' argument that the government was not national because "in it are not represented those who are not very light in color, or as I said, mulattoes," Ferraz replied that he did not consider that "the elector of the ministers is obliged, in the formation of the ministry, to select individuals because of their physical colors or the different political shades among which the population may be divided." And

---

[46] *Anais do Parlamento Brasileiro*, 1st Session of 1843, Rio de Janeiro, 1882, II, 820–824.

amidst much applause he declared that it was not "necessary for the ministry to have representatives from this or that circle, this or that class."

After this clear affirmation of class, but not racial, distinctions, Ferraz continued: "I believe that what the ministry must give the elector of the ministers in such an operation is a judgment whether these men are capable of conducting the affairs of state, not whether or not they belong to this Chamber, to this party or any other, to this or that class, are black or white, barrister, doctor, farmer, or merchant." And to be explicit, he declared further that "the formation of a ministry of all colors and banners" had never been attempted.

Returning to the question of the representation of mulattoes, Ferraz indicated the sure and proper way that Brazil has always taken:

What complaint can this segment of its population have in Brazil? It is placed where its ability and education carry it. Does it not occupy all the posts to which its ability and education entitle it? Does it not occupy places of great importance in the monarch's household? Does it not have a seat in the national parliament, are there not doctors and magistrates in it? . . . Do not distinguished men of this class direct our youth, teach our children? Are they not admitted to the important ministry of the Church? Do they not have a seat in all places, in all fields? In the courts and judiciary, in the military, in the national parliament, in the administration, in the Church, they serve everywhere and often they excel. And because there is no individual belonging to this class in the ministry at present, does it follow that the ministry is not national? This is too much. When this class produces educated men capable of directing public affairs, and because of their principles deserving of the monarch's confidence, I am persuaded and firmly believe that they will not be despised—they will be called.

My transcription is long, not only because it reveals the rise of the colored elites that had already become well delineated at the beginning of the second Reign, but because it shows that, if their rise did not yet reflect their percentage in the population, or if they had not yet attained the highest posts, this was not because of discrimination and intrigue but, rather, a lack of educational opportunities.

In an aside Rebouças revealed the personal frustration that tormented him: "But here am I, who judge myself as good as those in office, and no one has invited me." This could be explained, replied Ferraz, by the lack of political opportunity, in addition to the fact that Rebouças had never displayed any administrative talent.

Also involved in these debates was a mestizo who years later would be not merely a minister but President of the Cabinet, one of the greatest examples of political genius to be given Brazil by Bahia. This was João Maurício Wanderley, future Baron of Cotegipe.

This parliamentary episode shows Brazilians carrying forward the work of interracial harmony, of adjustment without regard to color, always valuing moral and intellectual attributes and qualities above variants of color, and repeatedly avoiding "pigmentocracy."

The French minister in Brazil, Alexis Guignard, Count de Saint Priest (1833–1835), wrote on June 17, 1834, that "in the division of parties found in Brazil today it would be very difficult to limit the place of persons of color, for Regent Lima [Francisco de Lima e Silva] and General Morais [José Manoel de], chief of Dom Pedro's party, belong to this group by birth. . . . It would be enough merely to see Sr. da Rocha [Justiniano José?], for Your Excellency to be convinced that no situation is inaccessible to men of color." [47]

MISCEGENATION AFTER ABOLITION

It is clear that the forms of interethnic relations changed once abolition was accomplished. Prejudice and tensions now assumed more subtle forms, which as Magnus Mörner writes,[48] makes their study more difficult, even from an historical point of view. Despite continuous racial mixing and progress in the process of acculturation, an ethnic consciousness did and does survive.

The "colorocracy" defended by Antônio Pereira Rebouças could not prevail, but a more homogeneous although culturally and ethnically mestizo society could, and without, moreover, the dangers of legalized discrimination. As stated very accurately by Professor Richard Konetzke of the University of Cologne, in one of the best and most authoritative essays on miscegenation in the Spanish Empire, slavery

---

[47] Transcription in Alberto Rangel, *No Rolar do Tempo,* Rio de Janeiro, José Olímpio, 1937, 48.
[48] *Op. cit.,* 38.

offered "a stronger obstacle to the unification of a community of races than racial differences." [49]

Now, with abolition, as Florestan Fernandes observes, the social process tended to disintegrate and destroy the seignorial-slavocratic social order. For this reason, he writes, abolition represents a landmark in the history of the Negro. It served not only to emancipate the slaves, but also to destroy the barriers to "progress" erected by the seignorial-slavocratic order.[50] Florestan Fernandes concludes that three fundamental and obvious facts may be deduced from the manner by which abolition transformed the slave into a citizen in 1888. First, "the slow transition to a system of free labor constituted a factor in interracial adjustment. . . . Second, the slow transition assured conditions for the organic transformation of the freed men and their descendents into salaried workers and to a lesser degree into capitalistic entrepreneurs. . . . Third, the slow transition permitted the formation of new social manifestations of the Negro as a worker or entrepreneur, in the midst of the white population as well as in the Negro population." [51]

Thus, because of abolition, the former slave's new role in the economy as a free worker and in politics as a citizen, the process of miscegenation continued as a new force, which is confirmed by statistics. The second census, taken in 1890, reported 6,302,198 whites, 5,934,291 mestizos, and 2,097,426 Negroes. The increased number of whites was due to increased immigration. From 1884 the wave of immigration, composed especially of Italians, had grown and been directed to São Paulo. From 1884 to 1893, 883,668 immigrants entered, 510,533 of them Italians, 170,621 Portuguese, 103,116 Spanish, and 22,778 Germans. But despite the fact that the majority went to São Paulo, the census of 1890 revealed the same strong trend toward miscegenation in the two principal and ancient "laboratories." In Bahia the distribution of ethnic types was 25.59 per cent whites, 20.39 per cent Negroes, 46.19 per cent mulattoes and 7.83 per cent *caboclos*.[52] In Minas Gerais the proportion of Negroes

---

[49] "El mestizage y su importancia en el desarrollo de la populación hispano-americana durante la época colonial," *Revista de Índias*, Nos. 23–24, Madrid (1946), 7–44, 215–237.

[50] *Relações Raciais entre Negros e Brancos em São Paulo, op. cit.*, 102 and 104.

[51] *Ibid.*, 60.

[52] See Thales de Azevedo, *Civilização e Miscigenação*, 59.

went down to 18.31 per cent and that of mulattoes was established at 34.93 per cent.[53]

The flow of Africans entering Brazil had been checked, and the gates were being opened to white European immigration. From 1884 to 1940 4,177,286 immigrants entered Brazil, predominantly Italians, Portuguese and Spanish; more than three million Negroes had been admitted up to 1850. In view of this disproportion it is natural that of a total population of 41,236,315 inhabitants, the census of 1940 should show 26,171,778 whites, 6,035,869 Negroes and 8,744,365 mestizos.[54] It is important to show the composition from 1872 to 1940 in percentages:

	1872	*1890*	*1940*
WHITES	38.14	43.97	63.47
NEGROES	19.68	14.63	14.64
MESTIZOS	42.18	41.40	21.20

As one can see, the percentage of whites increased, and that of mestizos diminished, by somewhat less than a half. The Negroes diminished very slightly between 1872 and 1890 and insignificantly between 1890 and 1940, a sign that miscegenation was no longer progressing at the rate slavery had induced.

This general population trend resulted from the influx of whites in the South and especially in São Paulo, where of a population of 7,189,493 persons in 1940, 6,104,968 were whites, only 525,423 Negroes, and 291,665 mestizos, almost as many as the 215,389 Orientals. By way of compensation the most Africanized or aboriginized states continued to show heavy percentages of mulattoes and *caboclos*. The distribution of the colored population among the various states in 1940 is given in Table I.

According to percentage, then, the states having greatest miscegenation were Bahia and Amazonas (about 70 per cent colored population), followed by Rio Grande do Norte, Pará, Sergipe, Piauí, and Maranhão (all with more than 50 per cent colored population).

The division into three groups—whites, Negroes, and mestizos—

---

[53] See Nélson de Sena, *Corografia do Estado de Minas Gerais,* as cited by Alceu Amoroso Lima, *Voz de Minas,* 2nd ed., 99.

[54] Plus 242,320 Orientals and 41,893 who did not state color.

TABLE I

Distribution of Colored Population Among the States of Brazil, and Composition of the Colored Population Within Each State, in 1940

State	Mestizos (No. & % of total population)	Negroes (No. & % of total population)	Negroes plus mestizos (% of total population)	Total population
Acre	24,774 (31.05%)	11,296 (14.15%)	45.20%	79,768
Amazonas	267,549 (61.08%)	31,408 (7.16%)	68.24%	438,008
Para	430,653 (45%)	89,942 (9.52%)	55.10%	944,644
Maranhao	314,919 (25.49%)	340,370 (27.55%)	53.04%	1,235,169
Piaui	185,155 (22.64%)	261,137 (32.06%)	54.70%	817,601
Ceara	498,449 (23.83%)	487,407 (23.30%)	47.13%	2,091,032
R. G. Norte	330,370 (43%)	102,790 (13.37%)	56.37%	768,018
Paraiba	461,340 (31.98%)	194,501 (13.41%)	45.39%	1,442,282
Pernambuco	806,649 (30.23%)	417,047 (15.63%)	45.86%	2,668,240
Alagoas	278,831 (29.29%)	131,530 (13.82%)	43.11%	951,300
Sergipe	186,351 (35.54%)	101,493 (19.35%)	54.89%	524,326
Bahia	2,000,938 (51.06%)	788,900 (20.13%)	71.19%	3,918,112
Minas Gerais	1,304,116 (19.37%)	1,297,981 (19.26%)	38.63%	6,736,416
Espirito Santo	159,769 (21.29%)	128,416 (15.78%)	37.07%	750,107
Rio de Janeiro	343,835 (18.60%)	394,076 (21.35%)	39.95%	1,847,857
D. Federal	305,433 (17.31%)	119,523 (11.30%)	28.61%	1,764,141
Sao Paulo	337,814 (4.70%)	524,441 (7.30%)	12%	7,180,316
Parana	91,414 (7.37%)	60,396 (4.88%)	12.25%	1,236,276
Santa Catarina	3,956 (0.33%)	61,382 (5.20%)	5.53%	1,178,340
R. G. Sul	153,376 (4.91%)	220,659 (6.62%)	11.53%	3,320,689
Goias	89,311 (10.80%)	140,040 (16.94%)	27.74%	826,414
Mato Grosso	172,628 (39.93%)	36,567 (8.45%)	48.38%	432,265

adopted by our censuses is extremely imprecise. Oliveira Viana had already criticized it in *Raça e Assimilação,* observing that it merely makes official the popular classification of our ethnic types. As it does not involve legal or scientific standards, it permits classification by sight, according to features, hair, and color of skin. Many light mulattoes, refined, educated, and of good appearance, must appear to be white. Mestizos appearing to be white are included as white, contrary to practice in the United States, where one-eighth of Negro blood classifies one as Negro. As Donald Pierson observes, the American criterion is based on racial descent and the Brazilian on physical appearance. As there are in Brazil many Negro grandparents who have white grandchildren, and Pierson also recognized this fact, miscegenation is a step toward the realization of the ideals of racial harmony. If the criterion were different and miscegenation less common, Brazil would have a greater number of Negroes.[55]

In the white group, then, one finds not only true whites but also white phenotypes, that is, Afro-white and Indian-white mestizos reverting to white type. In the Negro group there are Negroes and Negro phenotypes, mulattoes and *cafuzos* [Indian-Negro] reverting to Negro type. Finally, the mestizo classification shows the greatest lack of precision, for mulattoes, mixtures of Negro and white, are not distinguished from *caboclos,* mixtures of Indian and white.

For these reasons the composition by percentages presented in the tables does not reflect the type of miscegenation. If Bahia shows 71.19 per cent mestizos, with 20.13 per cent Negroes and only 28.74 per cent whites, indicating predominantly Afro-white mixture, the Negro populations reported in Amazonas and Pará are among the smallest in Brazil, these areas having been, like Mato Grosso and São Paulo, strongly under indigenous influence. Rio Grande do Sul, Paraná, and Santa Catarina are areas predominantly of white immigrant influence. In 1940 Piauí was the state having proportionately the largest Negro population, followed by Maranhão and Ceará. In the case of Piauí and Ceará this is curious, because formerly in their history they had small Negro populations, in contrast to Bahia and Sergipe with very large ones. The whitest states are precisely those that received the greatest

[55] See *Brancos e Prêtos na Bahia,* Companhia Editôra Nacional, São Paulo, 1945, 186, 188, 189.

influx of foreign settlers. The gross and proportional figures show, above all, that Brazil is essentially a nation of half-breeds.

In the 1950 census, when our population attained 51,944,387 inhabitants, 32,027,661 were white, 5,692,657 Negro and 13,786,742 mulatto, plus 329,082 Orientals.

The distribution of the colored population in that year is shown in Table 2.

By percentages, then, the states having greatest miscegenation were Piauí, Pará, Bahia, and Maranhão (all approximately 70 per cent colored population), followed by Amazonas, Alagoas, Ceará, Rio Grande do Norte, and Sergipe (all with more than 50 per cent colored population).

The proportion of whites attained its regional maximum, 87.4 per cent, in the South and its regional minimum, 31.3 per cent in the North. The total proportion of Negroes and mulattoes attained regional maximum, 68.4 per cent, in the North, and minimum, 10.5 per cent, in the South.[56]

It can be seen that the observations made with regard to the 1940 census may be repeated here. The states having greatest miscegenation are not those with the greatest percentages of Negroes; thus is revealed the presence of various non-Negroid mestizos, especially Indian-white. The states with the greatest percentages of Negroes in 1950 were Bahia, Maranhão, Piauí, and Ceará, and we know that the last three did not receive appreciable numbers of Africans during the period of the slave trade, especially the last two, which were engaged more in raising livestock than in agriculture and were dominated by Indians and Indian-white mestizos. In absolute numbers, the states with the largest numbers of Negroes were Minas Gerais, Bahia, and São Paulo; after which came Rio de Janeiro, Pernambuco, the former Federal District, now the State of Guanabara, Ceará, Maranhão, and Paraíba.

Zones of great miscegenation, like Pará and Amazonas, with minimum percentages of Negroes equal or nearly equal to those of the least Negroid states in Brazil, like São Paulo, Rio Grande do Sul, Paraná, and Santa Catarina, continue their Indian-white miscegenation while

---

[56] Alceu V. Wighman de Carvalho, "A população brasileira: crescimento, composição e tendências," Laboratório de Estatística do I.B.G.E. (Mimeographed).

TABLE 2

Distribution of Colored Population Among the States of Brazil, and Composition of the Colored Population Within Each State, in 1940.

States	Mestizos (No. and % of total)	Negroes (No. and % of total)	Negroes and mestizos (% of total)	Total population
Guaporé	22.263 (60.11%)	2.977 (8.02%)	68.13%	37,035
Acre	74,161 (64.62%)	5,980 (5.20%)	69.82%	114,755
Amazonas	305,520 (59.23%)	17,510 (3.45%)	62.68%	514,099
Rio Branco	9,648 (53.25%)	898 (4.95%)	58.20%	18,116
Para	734,574 (66.30%)	59,744 (5.31%)	71.61%	1,123,273
Amapa	24,186 (64.53%)	3,052 (8.14%)	72.67%	37,477
Maranhoa	795,707 (53.41%)	249,762 (15.96%)	69.37%	1,583,248
Piaui	616,782 (58.97%)	134,977 (12.90%)	71.87%	1,045,696
Ceara	1,233,518 (45.76%)	279,045 (10.35%)	56.11%	2,695,450
R. G. Norte	402,471 (41.61%)	91,581 (9.46%)	51.07%	967,921
Paraiba	338,120 (19.77%)	222,113 (13.54%)	33.31%	1,713,259
Pernambuco	1,386,225 (40.82%)	316,122 (9.31%)	50.13%	3,395,185
Alagoas	566,718 (51.84%)	81,260 (7.43%)	59.17%	1,093,137
Fernando de Noronha	158 (27.19%)	39 (6.71%)	33.90%	581
Sergipe	232,095 (36.01%)	91,317 (14.17%)	50.18%	644,361
Bahia	2,467,108 (51.03%)	926,075 (19.15%)	70.18%	4,834,575
Minas Gerais	2,069,037 (26.67%)	1,122,940 (14.54%)	41.21%	7,717,792
Serra dos Aimorés [57]	61,175 (38.21%)	16,986 (10.65%)	48.82%	78,161

[57] Territory in litigation between the States of Minas Gerais and Espírito Santo.

TABLE 2 (*Continued*)

Distribution of Colored Population Among the States of Brazil, and Composition of the Colored Population Within Each State, in 1940.

States	Mestizos (No. and % of total)	Negroes (No. and % of total)	Negroes and mestizos (% of total)	Total population
Espiritu Santo	253,423 (29.41%)	102,445 (11.89%)	41.30%	861,562
Rio de Janeiro	508,521 (23%)	407,136 (17.74%)	40.74%	2,297,194
D. Federal	415,935 (17.49%)	292,524 (12.30%)	29.79%	2,377,451
S. Paulo [58]	292.669 (3.23%)	727,789 (7.96%)	11.19%	9,134,423
Parana	154,346 (7.29%)	91,730 (4.33%)	11.62%	2,115,547
Santa Catarina	23,767 (1.52%)	56,948 (3.64%)	5.16%	1,560,502
R. G. Sul	226,174 (5.46%)	217,520 (5.22%)	10.68%	4,164,821
Mato Grosso	187,665 (34.68%)	51,089 (9.77%)	44.45%	522,044
Goias	384,046 (31.61%)	123,298 (10.14%)	41.75%	1,214,921

the latter reinforce their white groups with European settlers.[59] The highest percentages of Negroes now are found in Bahia, Rio de Janeiro, Maranhão, Minas Gerais, and Sergipe. Bahia has almost maintained its rank by percentage, Piauí and Maranhão having decreased respectively from 32.06 to 12.90 per cent and from 27.55 to 15.96 per cent.

The comparative table in percentages of the composition of the colored population in the two censuses of 1940 and 1950 is the following:

---

[58] There are 276,851 Orientals in São Paulo.
[59] After this study was written, the research of Fernando Henrique Cardoso and Otávio Ianni, *Côr e Mobilidade social em Florianópolis* (Companhia Editôra Nacional, 1960) was published. Their conclusions are worth reading, although they deal with a region where slave labor was less important and the percentage of Negroes and mestizos was small.

	1940	*1950*
WHITES	63.47	61.66
NEGROES	14.64	10.96
MESTIZOS	21.20	26.54
ORIENTALS	0.59	0.63

These figures show the decrease of Negroes and whites in favor of mestizos, who increased 5 per cent during the decade. The conclusion would be a strong trend toward miscegenation. But the 1890 census had pointed to an increase in the percentage of whites (43.97) in relation to the figure of 1872 (38.14) long before the 1940 results, which showed a still greater rise in the white percentage (to 63.47). And there were those who interpreted this evidence of miscegenation as an "Aryanizing" trend in our population.

THE ARYANIZATION OF BRAZIL

It was Oliveira Viana, a master of Brazilian studies and himself a mestizo, who in 1922 argued that our ethnic evolution was moving toward "Aryanization," [60] although he recognized that "the Brazilian of the future, however great the degree of Aryanization of our population, will not fail to be dark-skinned, as always," and that mestizo elements formed the bulk of the population. But despite the "darkness" of the Brazilian—and this expression [*moreno*] includes infinite varieties of finely featured mestizos—and his recognition of the mestizo as the bulk of the population, in 1933 in his *Evolução do Povo Brasileiro* he reaffirmed his thesis of the progressive Aryanization of Brazil.[61] Greatly influenced by theories of white superiority and the importance of racial factors, as presented by G. Vacher de Lapouge and H. S. Chamberlain, Viana's ideas about racial selection, the predominance of the dolicho-blond, and Teutonic superiority were destined to provoke, as indeed they did provoke, the most heated reaction in a mestizo nation, especially as their author was himself mestizo. Now we know that Vacher de Lapouge, today so discredited, showed himself a boaster to

---

[60] "O tipo Brasileiro; seus elementos formadores," *Dicionário Histórico, Geográfico e Etnográfico Brasileiro,* Rio de Janeiro, 1922, 277–290.
[61] 2nd ed., Companhia Editôra Nacional, São Paulo, 1933.

Count de Gobineau, who for thirteen months, from April, 1869, to May, 1870, was the French minister to Brazil and who previously (1853–55) had published his *Essai sur l'inegalité des races humaines* [62] in which he argued the insignificance of the "inferior" peoples and condemned them to somnolent obscurity. De Lapouge himself wrote that the Iberian adventurers who came to America showed an essentially melanistic character and their white elements were unimportant. It was the venom of miscegenation that had degraded humanity.

Gobineau condemned ethnic equalization and affirmed the superiority of the white man, and within this group that of the Aryan family. With such ideas he underwent some unbearable times in Brazil. "Il ne faut pas t'imaginer que le Bresil me soit extrêmement desagréable," [63] he wrote in a letter. He did not believe "that the ancient world offered anything similar by way of savagery"; "if the Emperor was a pure Aryan, or almost, Brazilians, on the contrary, are not only mulattoes but mulattoes of the lowest category. A completely mulatto population, vitiated in blood and spirit. No Brazilian is pure-blooded, but the combinations of marriages between whites, Indians, and Negroes are so multiplied that the shades of flesh are innumerable, and all this has produced the saddest kind of degeneration, in both lower and upper classes." There was no Brazilian family that did not have Negro and Indian blood in its veins, "resulting in rachitic natures which if not always repugnant are at least always disagreeable to see." Even the best families were crossbred with Negroes and Indians. The latter produced particularly repulsive creatures, copper-red in color. The Empress, he said, had three ladies-in-waiting: "one brown, another light chocolate, and the third violet-colored." But "je ne connais que la seconde, Son Excellence Dona Josephina [da Fonseca Costa]," and he spoke of the others, as Readers observes, in bold generalization.

Gobineau believed, in his massive prejudice, that miscegenation here or even in the United States would lead to racial extinction or degradation, for emigrants represented the detritus of Europe and were all mestizos, including the Germans, Irish, and French, and especially the Italians, who had all the defects of the Latin race. This sub-product

---

[62] 1st ed., Didot; 2nd ed., Didot, 1884.
[63] See Georges Readers, *Le Comte Gobineau au Brésil,* Paris, 1934, 11. All quotations from letters are from this book. See 32, 51, and 52.

of the European thought that later was stained by Hitlerist crime felt himself "authorized to establish the inequality of intelligence among the different races" and inspired, directly or indirectly through Lapouge, the work of Oliveira Viana, a mestizo who wrote for a Republic of Mestizos. Viana accepted this and other racial myths and the ill effects of the tropical climate, incompatible with the dolicho-blond, and gave full credence to the strength of biological determinants and the inexorable force of the race factor rather than to the forces in a diversity of cultures and collaboration among them.

In the second edition of his *Evolução do Povo Brasileiro,* Oliveira Viana declared that "given the progressive dislocation of the great foci of emigration from west to east and south in Europe, regions of Celtic, Slavic, and Mediterranean peoples," the question of the dolicho-blond lost interest. It is true that emigration between 1890 and 1901 was predominantly composed of what men like Gobineau, Lapouge, and Bryce considered the overflow of Europe: Italians, Portuguese, Spanish, Slavs. Gobineau had even written in his *Essai* that should Germans, Irish, Italians, French, and English become amalgamated with the Indian, Negro, Spanish, and Portuguese blood found in South America, "there is no way of imagining that such a horrible confusion can result in anything but an incoherent juxtaposition of the most degraded beings." [64] Bryce, also dominated by racist ideas, insisted on affirming that South America had nothing in common with Teutonic North America and was more bound to Southern (inferior in his eyes) than to Western Europe.[65]

Clearly influenced by these ideas, Oliveira Viana declared that "the representatives of Lapouge's *Homo Europeus* must be rare and may be found only mixed among currents Germanic (German, Austrian, Dutch, and English) in origin and tend naturally to settle in the southern regions, from Paraná down." [66] In effect he was himself casting doubt on Aryanization in view of the kind of immigrant required by Brazil; even further, he admitted that the theory of the racial superiority of Germanic peoples was as tendentious as the

---

[64] *Essais,* 4th ed. Paris, II, 536.
[65] James Bryce, *South America. Observations and Impressions,* New York, 1916, 520.
[66] *Evolução do Povo Brasileiro,* 2nd ed., Companhia Editôra Nacional, São Paulo, 1933, 175.

equalitarian theories that had arisen in Latin and Slavic centers.[67] He argued that a nation could not be indifferent either to the quality or quantity of its racial elements,[68] the thinking that later led to restrictions on immigration. He was alarmed by indiscriminate waves of immigration entering the country: four million Europeans in one century and a hundred thousand Japanese in less than twenty years.[69]

Oliveira Viana did not abandon his mystique of racial purity nor his belief in Nordic superiority. And many people believed this talk of the Aryanization of Brazil, despite their contempt for Lapouge, Gobineau, and other ideologists of white "Aryan" superiority. Batista Pereira, for example, in a lecture delivered in 1928, also upheld the progressive Aryanization of Brazil "as a fatal and inevitable phenomenon." [70]

The statistical revelations of the decrease of Negroes and increase of mestizos were basically true, despite their imprecisions, to which we have referred, and despite the white, South European mass, dark-complexioned and depreciated by the racists, that created the belief that our population was becoming whiter. From 1850 to 1950 the number of immigrants to Brazil reached 4,800,000, of whom 1,540,000 were Italian, 1,480,000 Portuguese, 600,000 Spanish, 230,000 German, and 190,000 Japanese. About three-quarters of these immigrants, or 3,400,000, remained in Brazil, counterbalancing the Africanization by the more than three million Negroes who had entered before 1850. The tendency for the population to become whiter as the Marxist author Caio Prado Júnior observed in 1942—and confirmed by the additional 5 per cent mestizos in the 1950 census—satisfied an ideal that exercised an important function in the ethnic evolution of Brazil, the ideal of whiteness and racial purity which found expression in the parallelism of the chromatic and social scales. This ideal plays a great role in the orientation of interbreeding, reinforcing the white man's preponderant position and prestige as procreator. Thus, sexual selection leads in the direction of greater whiteness, so that in the upper classes the whitening becomes almost complete.[71]

---

[67] *Raça e Assimilação*, Companhia Editôra Nacional, São Paulo, 1932, 21.
[68] *Ibid.*, 49.
[69] *Ibid.*, 167.
[70] "O Brasil e a Raça." Lecture at the São Paulo Law School, June 28, 1928, in *Pelo Brasil Maior*, Companhia Editôra Nacional, 1934.
[71] *Formação do Brasil Contemporâneo*, Livraria Martins, São Paulo, 1942, 105–106.

Hence, the fact that in 1835 the popular classes had attacked the "white-faces." If a Marxist historian sees a popular ideal in the "white-washing," a sociologist like Donald Pierson, who conducted one of the best and most serious investigations on whites and Negroes in Bahia, speaks of the "common pride of all classes in Brazil" in the "progressive whitening of the population." Pierson observes "that in Bahia the mestizos are increasing, but the increase seems to be at the expense of the African, who is gradually disappearing, and not at the expense of the European." The mestizos seem to be gradually absorbing the Negroes while in turn being continually incorporated into the predominantly European population. He stresses further that miscegenation leading to whiteness means racial purification and improvement "in obvious subjection to the ideas of the dominant group." "The general tendency is for the predominantly European portion to absorb the lighter mestizos while the mulattoes absorb the Negroes. This means that the Brazilian population is constantly acquiring a more European and less Negroid appearance." And finally, he records the whitist aspiration in these words: "The tendency of the mestizos is to consider themselves transitional points in an inevitable process of whitening. It is common for them to take pride in their present stage and to anticipate the final results. From mulattoes as well as whites one frequently hears this statement: 'We Brazilians are rapidly becoming a single people. Some day, in the not so distant future, there will be only one race in our country.' " [72]

Gilberto Freyre, as opposed as Caio Prado to the racist and Aryan doctrines of Oliveira Viana, also affirms the whitening of our people: "The Negroes are now rapidly disappearing from Brazil, becoming fused with the whites. In some regions the trend, so it seems, is toward the stabilization of mestizos in a new ethnic type similar to that of Polynesia." [73]

Thus, there is what Florestan Fernandes called the "mystique of whiteness, used in literature by different Brazilian authors," that translates "the attitude of those who take pride in pure ancestral blood" and "expresses the common tendency, chiefly in the lighter mulattoes, to

---

[72] Donald Pierson, *Brancos et Prêtos na Bahia,* Brasiliana, Companhia Editôra Nacional, 1945 (translated from the American ed. of 1942), 281, 392, 181, 184, 186.
[73] *Brazil, An Interpretation,* New York, 1945, 96. Brazilian ed., *Interpretação do Brasil,* José Olímpio, 1947, 187.

ignore miscegenation and the distinctions associated with gradations of
skin color (which frequently exposes them to the mockery of the darker
mulattoes and Negroes, as well as to the malicious gossip of whites).
Basically, these attitudes are responsible for the validation of sexual or
marital relations with whites (or only with lighter persons), something
to which colored individuals today refer with the expression 'improving
the race.' " [74]

For a sociologist like Guerreiro Ramos, Aryanization, more than
merely a whitening process, is an obvious rationalization for the color
prejudice in our country. The trend is reassuring, for it resolves the
racial question democratically while veiling prejudice that indeed ought
not to be liquidated by "inverting the ideological terms, proclaiming for
example that blackening of the national population would be desirable.
This position would be a kind of racism against racism." [75]

Indeed, only a misguided racism could think in ideological terms of
Brazil's becoming Negro—the prospect mentioned by Guerreiro
Ramos, himself a colored man and leftist in tendency—when this is not
in fact shown by statistics nor expressed by popular sentiment. The
feeling in favor of whitening through miscegenation of the light with
the lighter did not escape the American historian William Lyttle
Schurz when he wrote:

The trend toward the eventual absorption of all ethnic elements in a single
race was too strong to be withstood short of the old white aristocracy, and
even some of its members could not boast an unbroken lineage out of Portugal. Brazilians, reluctant to admit the tensions of a "race problem" in their
country, generally accepted the inevitable, and even made efforts to rational-
ize a situation which they could not prevent if they would. On the theory
that unrestricted miscegenation would ultimately obliterate the characteristic
physical marks of the three component races, they tended to consider the
progressive *branqueamento,* or whitening, of the population as a national
ideal.[76]

Whether or not it is a matter of aspiration or of rationalization, and
although the process of becoming white is probably in progress, a

[74] Florestan Fernandes, "Côr e Estrutura Social em Mudança," in *Relações Sociais entre Negros e Brancos em São Paulo,* São Paulo, Anhembi, 1951, 99.
[75] "Oliveira Viana Arianizante," *O Jornal,* Rio de Janeiro, December 13, 1953.
[76] *This New World The Civilization of Latin America,* New York, 1954, 172.

homogeneous Brazilian "race" is still a thing of the future. Today, says Charles Wagley, class lines generally divide the most Caucasian Brazilians from those who can be called colored people.[77]

Finally, in an investigation on the role of religion in race relations sponsored by UNESCO, René Ribeiro states that "there is a unanimity of views in Brazil in considering intermarriage extensive in the direction of the choice by the man of a woman lighter than he, a progressive whitening of our population being the result." [78]

Rationalization can lead not only to the ideal of whiteness to be observed in this century, but also to the Indianist reversion that seized our literature of the last century and whose chief exponent was Gonçalves Dias. But Indianism did not succeed in formulating an ideal or inspiring an ethnic policy such as the promotion of whiteness through control of immigration.

Indigenism persisted as an ethno-political policy in such Hispano-American countries having high percentages of Indians or Indian mestizos as Guatemala (55 per cent Indians and 44 per cent mestizos), Bolivia (55 per cent Indians and 44 per cent mestizos), Paraguay (97 per cent mestizos), Honduras (90 per cent mestizos), and Nicaragua (86 per cent mestizos).[79] In Brazil the probable million and a half Indians at the time of discovery are reduced today to a minimum of 68,100 and a maximum of 99,700, even with the most optimistic guess less than 0.2 per cent of the national population, according to the calculations of Darcy Ribeiro.[80] They were destroyed, assimilated, or integrated, providing the great coefficients of the so-called mestizo population, as we saw in the demographic tables. It is in the mestizo that one finds the Indian contribution to the formation of our people. The Indian himself was acculturated and assimilated.

Instead of recognizing that we have constituted a racial melting pot full of heterogeneous elements, a grafting of men, "a field for the

---

[77] *Race and Class in Rural Brazil,* UNESCO, 1952, 145.
[78] *Religião e Relações Raciais,* Ministério da Educação e Cultura, Rio de Janeiro, 1956, 105.
[79] Gonzalo Aguirre Beltran, "Indigenismo y Mestizage. Una Polaridad Bio Cultural," *Cahiers d'Histoire Mondiale,* VI–1, 1960, 158–171.
[80] *Linguas e Culturas indígenas do Brasil.* Centro Brasileiro de Pesquisas Educacionais, Rio de Janeiro, n.d., 47.

convergence of all the races of the world; whites from Europe, Mongols from Asia, Negroes from Africa, Malayans and Polynesians from Oceania," as Oliveira Viana himself writes—the emigration of Negroes and Japanese began to be combatted and selective immigration defended. Roquete Pinto in 1930 censured Afonso d'E. Taunay for having dedicated a chapter in the first volume of his *História das Bandeiras* to what Pinto called "the progressive Aryanization of the state of São Paulo because of the anthropological teaching that Aryan blood is Utopian." [81] Gilberto Amado criticized the "Aryan nonsense according to which only white people were to settle in Brazil in order to improve the race." [82]

IMMIGRATION POLICY

Our history of restrictions on immigration is long and reveals, like racial discriminations, the fluctuations of our ethnic policy. In the beginning there was much opposition to the entry of Chinese workers to replace Negro slaves. One of those favoring their entry was José Pedro Xavier Pinheiro, who in 1869 argued the need for these workers, especially for the cultivation of sugar cane, and explained the reasons for the failure of attempts at their importation made in 1854-55 and 1866. In the face of sustained opposition, the idea was abandoned; there was fear of "the superstition of the Chinese, their repulsive ugliness, the crossing of their race with others in the country, their extravagant habits, their language and even their dress." [83] Thus, our view of the Chinese was dominated by fear of defiling the purity of our blood! What might they have thought of us?

Having excluded the Chinese, the defenders of the whiteness, the European-ness of our people began to oppose the entry of other Orientals and Negroes. It was the Republic that began discrimination. Decree No. 528, dated June 28, 1890, made the entry of natives of Asia and Africa subject to special authorization by Congress, so that they did not have the same liberty of immigration as others. [84]

---

[81] Reception of Sr. Afonso Taunay, May 6, 1930, in *Dirçursos Acadêmicos,* Academia Brasileira de Letras, Rio de Janeiro, 1937, 231.

[82] *Sabor do Brasil,* Rio de Janeiro, 1953, 53.

[83] José Pedro Xavier Pinheiro, *Importação de Trabalhadores Chins,* Rio de Janeiro, 1869.

[84] Artur Hehl Neiva, "Getúlio Vargas e o Problema da Imigração e da Colonização," *Revista de Imigração e Colonização,* Year III, No. 1, (April, 1942), 27.

On July 28, 1921, Andrade Bezerra and Cincinato Braga offered Congress a proposal the first article of which stated: "The immigration of individuals of the black races is prohibited in Brazil." Two years later, on October 22, the deputy from Minas, Fidélis Reis, offered another proposal relative to the entry of immigrants, the fifth article of which was as follows: "The entry of colonists of the black race into Brazil is prohibited, and as regards the yellow, entry will be permitted annually in numbers corresponding to 5 per cent of the individuals present in the country." This proposal was criticized in the press by Evaristo de Morais, Tito Castro, Clóvis Beviláqua, and Teixeira Mendes. Like Oliveira Viana, Fidélis Reis belonged to the group supporting Brazil's Aryanization, and with Gobineau, Lapouge, and their like, accepted "the decisive and incomparable influence of the blond dolichocephalic type on the progress of all civilization." The fifth article prohibited the entry of Negroes and Japanese, while the first stated: "The government is authorized to promote and assist the introduction of European farm families wishing to move to Brazil as colonists." [85] In the expression "European" Fidélis Reis concealed his admiration for Aryans and the dolicho-blond type. What he wanted, he said, was to direct large numbers of Italian immigrants to Minas Gerais; and in opposition to Councilor Antônio Prado's action to save the coffee harvests, he advised against the entry of Japanese. And he added: "In no way must we be short-sighted and sacrifice the ethnic type now emerging by the introduction of elements incapable either of being assimilated or of being assimilated advantageously." Inclined toward accepting white superiority, he warned: "Let the error of introducing the Negro suffice. Let us not fall into the same error with the Oriental. What do temporary economic interests matter? Let us learn from the example of the United States (in prohibiting the entry of Japanese), although as regards the Negro we may because of special circumstances be resolving our problem more successfully, despite ethnic prejudices in the generations involved in his absorbtion." He praised the earlier proposal of Andrade Bezerra and Cincinato Braga but declared that his was "less irritating" and revealed a broader outlook.

But clearly the objective of Reis proposal was to confront what was

---

[85] *Anais da Câmara dos Deputados,* Session of October 31, 1923. Rio de Janeiro, 1928, X, 140–149.

considered a threat: immigration to Brazil of the American Negro, inspired by the United States government, which desired to free itself of that blot upon its Teutonic yearnings. This, said Fidélis Reis, would be the equivalent of a disaster; it was an imminent danger that should cause serious apprehensions, for even admitting that as a slave the African Negro had helped Brazil, it would have been preferable had he not come to us, for he prejudiced the "Aryan" goal of our racial evolution; furthermore, "biologically, the mestizo is a degenerate."

In keeping with the false image that racists have of themselves, Fidélis Reis said: "In addition to the reasons of an ethnic, moral, political, social and perhaps even economic order that bring us to reject *in limine* the entry of the Negro and the Oriental into the ethnic forging that is in process in our land, . . . there is perhaps another reason to be considered, the esthetic one. Our Hellenic conception of beauty could never be in harmony with the types resulting from such a fusion of races." Beauty for Sr. Fidélis Reis and his colleagues was Hellenic, but it was not for the majority of the Brazilian people, not even for the people of Minas whom he represented and of whom between 1890 and 1940 almost 50 per cent were Negroes or mulattoes.

Some applauded Reis' pseudo-scientific nonsense and gave him further support, as for example when Carvalho Neto declared: "In the fusion of the two races the superior one is triumphing: within seventy years the Negro will disappear in Brazil." Fidélis Reis replied that it was as a result of miscegenation with the Negro that "a large portion of the ennervated, backward, and wretched population of our interior was formed." Balanced, clear, logical minds were exhibited by Leopoldino de Oliveira and Vicente Piragibe. The former in addition to denying the inferiority of the Negro demanded attention to health problems; Piragibe said: "Much of what we are we owe to the Negro and mulatto."

When consulted, Oliveira Viana, who directly or indirectly had inspired Reis' proposal, said that he was "radically opposed to the immigration of American and any other kind of Negroes to Brazil. I am also opposed to the immigration of all other races that are not white European races. . . . We owe much to the Negro, but no doubt it would have been infinitely better if he had not constituted one of the great factors in the formation of our nationality." He was against "the inferior interbreeding that retards our progress so" and favorable "to races rich in eugenism" (!).

Also consulted was Afrânio Peixoto, who offered a contradictory, superficial, and literary opinion, full of the customary questions and reticences and somewhat suspect in its white racism, which concluded with this patriotic tirade: "Well, then! Even with weapons in his hand, no, never! God help us, if He is Brazilian" (!).[86]

Prejudice against the Negro and miscegenation, whether disguised or open, still continued, led by a Europeanized majority that on the basis of its racial doctrines could not believe in the growth of Brazil, for we had an inferior population and our first task should be to improve it eugenically by the mass immigration of selected groups of Europeans, preferably dolicho-blonds. "Make mestizo, dark-skinned Brazil fair" was the motto of these pseudo-scientists.

In 1933 when the Constitution was being drawn up, racial discrimination disguised as eugenic selection disclosed other Aryanists, such as Artur Neiva, Miguel Couto, and Xavier de Oliveira, who offered the following emendations; Artur Neiva (No. 1,053): "Only the immigration of elements of the white race will be permitted, concentration in mass in any part of the country being prohibited"; Miguel Couto (No. 21E): "The immigration of Africans or persons African in origin is prohibited and that of Asians permitted only at the annual rate of 5 per cent of the total immigrants of this origin resident in the national territory"; Xavier de Oliveira (No. 1,164): "The entry into the country for purposes of residence of elements of the Negro and Oriental races, of whatever origin, is prohibited." [87]

Fortunately, once the Constitution was drawn up, it revealed the usual Brazilian good sense and did not include specific discriminations of this nature. Article 121, paragraph 62, established the system of quotas (2 per cent of the total number of the respective nationalities) in order to "guarantee ethnic integrity," which would be interpreted as discriminatory in favor of the white man. The radicals saw an error in this solution, "a victory of Japan over Europe and over the most sacred

---

[86] See criticism and résumé of these debates in Tito Carlos, *A Imigração Negra,* Rio de Janeiro, 1924.

[87] See Artur Hehl Neiva, "O Problema Imigratório Brasileiro," *Revista de Imigração e Colonização,* Year V, No. 3 (September, 1944), especially 515–517.

interests of Brazil," for of the 79,544 European immigrants that we
could accept we received only 9,358, and during the same time we
admitted 3,305 Japanese.[88]

But the truth is that, far removed from these cogitations regarding
preservation of the ethnic balance, which always meant the defense of
whiteness and the extreme racist theses of certain deputies, the people
glorified the Brazilian mulatto woman in the streets, singing a song that
animated the Brazilian Carnival for many years:

> Don't deny your hair, *mulata,*
> For in color you are *mulata,*
> But color is not contagious, *mulata,*
> So I want your love, *mulata.*[89]

In 1937 the New State, which was inspired by Nazi-Fascist models
and directed by Getúlio Vargas, who never hid his admiration for the
thinking of Oliveira Viana, established the doctrine of restricted immigration, which was not anti-Negro only because there was no threat of
Negro immigration, but was directed against Asians in general and
against the Japanese in particular. Article 151 of the Constitution
adopted in 1937 established the same principles as the Constitution of
1934 because of the continued dominance of the notion that the
Brazilian people should be whitened and all entry of non-European
groups averted. Little was it imagined that in a quarter of a century
Europe and its dolicho-blonds would lose their world supremacy, and as
the German historian Ludwig Dehio writes, see "the Second World
War accelerate the fall of the West from its precarious position of
domination over the colored races, with unforeseeable consequences." [90]

Indeed, the "Nordic" or "Teutonic" peoples who were to purify us
ethnically were so far from fulfilling the aspirations of the Aryanists
that from 1884 to 1940 Brazilian immigration was composed of 78.57 per
cent Latins. In a way to know that we were becoming "Latinized" was
encouraging, although our real ethnic route lay in miscegenation. But

---

[88] Antônio Xavier de Oliveira, "Nova Contribuição ao Estudo do Problema Imigratório no Brasil," *Revista de Imigração e Colonização,* (December 1944), 645.
[89] The song was composed by Lamartine Babo in 1932.
[90] *Germany and World Politics in the Twentieth Century,* London, 1959, 36.

no one then had the courage of Gilberto Amado to declare that he preferred we acknowledge ourselves a "Half-Breed Republic" and that *caboclos,* Indians, mestizos, *curibocas* [Indian-white], *cafuzos,* and Negroes cannot be Latins.

The Constitution of 1934, with its North American system of quotas and selection, represented one of the greatest examples of alienation by a minority by imposing on a mestizo population immigrants chosen to improve it ethnically. It was an incredible outrage that Decree No. 406, of May 4, 1938, prescribed the preservation of the "ethnic and social composition of the Brazilian people," and that this was reaffirmed in Decree No. 7,967, of September 18, 1945, establishing in Article 2 that "in the admission of immigrants attention will be given to the need for preserving and developing in the ethnic composition of the population those characteristics most suited to its European origin as well as to the safeguarding of the national labor force."

Through its leaders and through Congress itself, Brazil thus had its share of laws of racial discrimination that excluded certain ethnic groups and offended the liberal, democratic, and anti-discriminatory principles of its people.

By stating that "laws governing the selection, entry, distribution, and settling of immigrants will remain subject to the exigencies and conditions determined by the national interest," the Constitution of 1946 freed itself of any blot of racial discrimination and respected the human rights established by the United Nations Charter to which Brazil had subscribed.

In the same year the restrictions directed against the Japanese, not against Negroes, received serious censure from the anthropologist of German origin, Emílio Willems. I do not know to what degree his arguments opposing the pseudo-science prevailing before 1946 may have influenced the legislators, but in combating the concept that immigration of Japanese was "a factor for degeneration," Willems gave scientific support to the anti-discriminatory spirit of 1946.[91] Japanese immigration, begun in 1908, had attained its maximum percentage of the total

---

[91] "O Problema da Imigração Japonêsa," *Estado de São Paulo,* São Paulo, May 18, 1946; and especially Hiroshi Saito, *O Japonés no Brasil,* Editôra Sociologia e Política, São Paulo, 1961.

immigration between 1934 and 1943, i.e. 23 per cent, falling between 1944–1953 to 0.7 per cent and reaching 9 per cent between 1954–1958. In reality, setting aside the political problem presented by Japanese settlers during the Second World War, which was similar to that of our German "Aryans," the policy against Japanese immigration disclosed a feeling of ethnic discrimination incompatible with our democratic objectives and our proven capacity for assimilation and integration.

What was demonstrated was the formulation of policy that was still timid, subject to temporary variations caused by a group of leaders more or less bold in their preference for white European domination but always opposed by the mestizo majority and by the attitude of whites and Negroes disposed to contact, absorption, and assimilation. Since 1933, Roquete Pinto has written that "policy in the populating of Brazil was from the beginning based upon detrimental expedients: (a) decimation of the Indians; (b) the importation of Negro slaves—which indeed was a necessity—and the deliberate avoidance of steps to civilize them, educate them, and prepare them for freedom; (c) the procurement, at their weight in gold, of white settlers, who were not selected nor examined for physical fitness but were provided at once with capital, land, dwelling, implements, and all assistance; (d) the abandonment of our best national elements to the bitter fate of poverty." [92]

For this reason Donald Pierson believes that

although Brazil seems never to have had a formal racial directing force, the traditional behavior, which originally arose and was formed under the influence of immediate and spontaneous responses to the circumstances and conditions of colonial life, produced an informal racial directing force . . . which may be summarized in the best possible way by the following commonly heard expression: "We Brazilians are becoming a single people!" The great Brazilian homogeneity and predominant miscegenation suggest and inspire this belief and aspiration, which in turn results in a plastic ethnic policy of compromise and adjustment. The ethnic policy of the people is miscegenation, and there is a racial problem only when a group resists absorption and assimilation, as was the case of nuclei of Germans and Japanese, or when it sees itself threatened or is persecuted, and then the great majority comes to its defense.

---

[92] *Ensaios de Antropologia Brasiliana,* Companhia Editôra Nacional, São Paulo, 1933, 125.

No attempt at racial persecution has ever been made in Brazil, except in the colonial period when the Inquisition persecuted the Jews. When Brazilian Fascists set up a program of anti-Semitic discrimination they were considered contemptible and criminal by the great majority of the Brazilian people. The racist myths of this or past centuries have never seriously undermined our ethnic democracy. Those privileges originally denied colored people were, as we have seen, gradually won in the course of time and especially in the zones of great Negro and mestizo concentration, as Gilberto Freyre stresses. "It is curious to observe that Minas Gerais seems always to have taken the lead in movements of social democratization opposing prejudices of whiteness and legitimacy." [93]

POLICY OF RACIAL BROTHERHOOD

It was precisely the areas of most intense miscegenation that proved to be most fertile in great men, further states Gilberto Freyre,[94] especially great politicians. Among the most Africanized zones, Bahia and Minas Gerais have always been distinguished in Brazilian political life, especially the latter, which from the time of Independence to the present, and regardless of its economic importance, has never entirely lost decisive or influential political control. The reason for this—and we do not know to what extent there may be African influence here—is that the politician from Minas is capable of hiding his maneuvers and aims while operating with innocent casualness to weave a complicated web through which he triumphs without even seeming to have won a victory. The man from Minas is seldom a radical; he prefers to compromise, to be congenial, to appease and adjust rather than impose or seem intransigent. Hence his infinite victories, his political control of the country independent of his economic power, which was overwhelming only during a certain colonial phase when politics in Brazil were not in the hands of the Brazilians.

From this control by zones of great racial confrontation and adjustment comes the Brazilian policy of brotherhood that is the essence of

---

[93] *Casa Grande & Senzala, op. cit.,* 5th ed., 2nd vol., 743, note 7.
[94] *Sobrados e Mucambos,* Companhia Editôra Nacional, São Paulo, 1936, 376.

our ethnic policy. Hence Donald Pierson's statement that although more Negroes were imported into Brazil than into any other part of the world, they never constituted a racial unity but were and continue to be absorbed, dissolved into mulattoes and culturally integrated into one Brazilian people.[95] And this took place under slavery, for as Florestan Fernandes observes, "the abolitionist campaign contributed only partially to modifying the attitudes and expected behavior of white men toward Negroes and toward their own mestizo descendants whom they treated as 'Negroes.' It was not accompanied by a feeling of horror as in the United States, and it served to reëducate Brazilian abolitionists to the point of appreciating the moral greatness of certain Negro and mestizo personalities." [96]

Abolition, then, contributed to the proletarization of the mass of Negroes but did not interrupt the process of social ascension of mestizos that had begun in the previous century, as Gilberto Freyre demonstrates in his *Sobrados e Mocambos*. On the contrary, according to Florestan Fernandes, "the slow transition to the free labor system was a factor in interracial social adjustment, and through social localization of resentments, permitted the formation of new social concepts of the Negro as a worker or entrepreneur, in the midst of the white as well as the Negro population." [97]

Prejudice in Brazil is more social than racial, more of classes than of race, and is found referring to whites as well as to the ascending Negro or mestizo. For this very reason the rise of the colored elites develops normally and progressively, as Thales de Azevedo recently showed.[98] They are represented at all occupational levels, in the Church, the army, the judiciary, the press, in higher education, public administration, and the three branches of the government. We have already had a mulatto as President of the Republic; and this elevated "status" is recognized by the entire community, by all the people, with rare exceptions among the discriminatory elements that exist everywhere, even in Brazil.

---

[95] *Brancos e Prêtos na Bahia, op. cit.,* 417.

[96] "Côr e Estrutura Social em Mudança," in *Relações Raciais entre Negros e Brancos em São Paulo, op. cit.,* 105.

[97] "Do Escravo ao Cidadão," in *Relações Raciais entre Negros e Brancos em São Paulo, op. cit.,* 60.

[98] *As elites de côr, Um estudo de Ascensão Social,* São Paulo, Companhia Editôra Nacional, 1955.

Research conducted in São Paulo, which today has quantitatively the third largest Negro population in Brazil, proves for example that "social class appears as a factor for integration stronger than the segregating influence of racial differences." [99] It is curious that the inquiry sponsored by the magazine *Anhembi* in São Paulo, like Thales de Azevedo's observations in Bahia, shows color prejudice to exist in the Portuguese colony, which explains the low rate of miscegenation in Portuguese Africa today and distinguishes our behavior from that of the Portuguese. [100]

In the social ascent there is no racial minority or caste, as Donald Pierson stresses, but "a system of free competition." Not so free, we add, for lack of opportunity, poor education, and various other conditions make competition difficult. Statistical data on literacy according to color always reveal the inferiority of Negro and mulatto groups, who are on lower socio-economic levels. [101]

But persons from those groups who overcome these barriers may have and already have had possibilities of attaining the highest positions. The rise of persons of color in the present framework of Bahian society revealed by Thales de Azevedo shows that "high society and the prestige professions were much less mixed fifty or eighty years ago, although the participation of mestizo individuals in such groups is an old Brazilian tradition." He further reveals that in 1872 the slaves were totally illiterate and "today more than 50 per cent of the Negroes and more than 60 per cent of the mestizos over 5 years of age are literate, and their number in secondary and higher education is growing annually, opening the way to the liberal professions, in which they are already found in varying proportions." He concludes that "facilities for the social rise of colored persons are increasing in Bahia," and further,

---

[99] E. Williams, "Races, Attitudes in Brasil," *The American Journal of Sociology,* IV, No. 5, 1949, 402–408. Excellent reports by Sílvia Donato show the prejudices which in dissembled and polite forms are to be found in other countries as well as in various parts of Brazil, such as São Paulo, Santa Catarina, Bahia, Nordeste, and Triângulo Mineiro, where the Negroes live always on the lowest social level. See *Jornal do Brasil,* February 1, 5, 12, 14, and 19, 1963.

[100] Roger Bastide, "Manifestação do Preconceito de Côr," in *Relações Raciais entre Negros e Brancos, op. cit,* 129, and Thales de Azevedo, *As Elites de Côr, op. cit.,* 97.

[101] I.B.G.E., *Contribuição para o Estudo da Demografia do Brasil,* 1961, 399.

TABLE 3

Literacy of the Population of Brazil in Certain Age Groups,
According to Color

	Maximum number of literates per 100 individuals of the age-groups specified			
	Men		Women	
Color	*1940*	*1950*	*1940*	*1950*
Whites	63.58	67.81	51.48	60.04
	(yrs. 30–39)	(yrs. 20–29)	(yrs. 10–19)	(yrs. 20–29)
Browns*	39.34	40.28	28.52	32.33
	(yrs. 30–39)	(yrs. 20–29)	(yrs. 10–19)	(yrs. 20–29)
Blacks	29.29	35.94	21.97	29.35
	(yrs. 30–39)	(yrs. 20–29)	(yrs. 10–19)	(yrs. 10–19)
Yellows	80.40	93.95	71.45	90.88
	(yrs. 20–29)	(yrs. 20–29)	(yrs. 10–19)	(yrs. 10–19)

* Including those inhabitants who would not state their color.

TABLE 4

Numerical Index of Literacy among Blacks, Browns, and Yellows,
according to Sex and Age, as Compared with Whites

Age	Whites		Browns **		Blacks		Yellows	
	Men	*Women*	*Men*	*Women*	*Men*	*Women*	*Men*	*Women*
5–9	100.0	100.00	32.8	33.9	33.1	34.6	189.0	180.4
10–19	100.0	100.00	47.2	49.3	49.5	52.7	156.2	152.7
20–29	100.0	100.00	53.0	46.7	59.4	53.8	138.5	142.9
30–39	100.0	100.00	51.1	37.6	59.0	47.1	135.0	128.7
40–49	100.0	100.00	45.9	31.5	56.5	42.7	129.0	117.0
50–59	100.0	100.00	42.0	27.1	55.0	39.3	119.9	117.4
60–69	100.0	100.00	37.0	23.9	53.9	38.0	109.3	99.4
70–79	100.0	100.00	29.3	17.7	49.4	33.0	99.9	83.3
80 and older	100.0	100.00	21.5	12.7	42.3	25.6	116.6	88.4
5 and older *	100.0	100.00	47.2	41.8	52.7	48.4	138.7	138.2

* Exclusive of inhabitants who would not declare their age.
** Inclusive of inhabitants who would not declare their color.

that "the principal channel of social ascension by which a great number
of Negroes and mestizos have acquired high *status* is education in the
twofold sense of good manners and high-level instruction, in addition to
adherence to the *mores* and concepts of the dominant culture, which in

the final analysis is a problem of acculturation or more complete integration of colored masses into society." [102]

Leadership in Brazil always included mulattoes and Negroes: some of the greatest writers, like Machado de Assis, Gonçalves Dias, Natividade Saldanha, Olavo Bilac, Caldas Barbosa, Tobias Barreto, Lima Barreto, Teodoro Sampaio, Cruz e Souza, José do Patrocínio, José Maurício, Luís Gama, Evaristo Ferreira da Veiga, José Ferreira de Menezes, both Rebouças, Antônio and André, Bishop Dom Silvério Gomes Pimenta, and Don Luís Raimundo da Silva Brito; statesmen like José Maurício Wanderley, Baron de Cotegipe, Francisco Gê Acaiaba de Montezuma, Viscount de Jequitinhonha, and Sales Tôrres Homem, Viscount de Inhomirim, Francisco Glicério, Bernardino de Campos; diplomat Domício da Gama; psychiatrist Juliano Moreira; not to forget one of our greatest colonial artists, the sculptor Antônio Francisco Lisboa, "Aleijadinho." [103] Many of these men were of the same scientific and cultural level as the best European minds, and above that of white Aryans considered superior in Europe, the United States, or South Africa. Many white men on those continents who reveal their idiosyncrasy regarding skin color would not have the moral and intellectual qualities to rise to the level of these men, despite all the prejudices in their favor facilitating their ascension. For this reason they indeed are as inferior as many whites in Brazil or anywhere, and as many Negroes in Brazil or anywhere, independent of color.

Thus, through the processes of acculturation and integration, colored men in Brazil have been participating in Brazilian life, like the Indians and like white and Oriental immigrants as they gradually adjust to the patterns of our culture—as they become "Brazilianized"—participating

---

[102] *As Elites de Côr, op. cit.*, 196, 197, 198.

[103] See Manuel Querino, "Os homens de côr preta na História," *Revista do Instituto Geográfico e Histórico da Bahia*, 1923, 353–363, and by the same author, *O colono prêto como fator da civilização brasileira, Bahia*, 1918. We have already referred to the great Negro personalities of Africa today, politicians and writers, who have triumphed despite the prejudices of Europeans, men like Leopoldo Sédar Senghor, Sékou Touré, Ousmane Socé Diop, Bernard Dadié, Camara Laye, Aké Loba, Sembène Ousmane, and other figures of the *Présence Africaine*. See Mercer Cook, "The Aspirations of Négritude," and Ezekel Uphahlele, "The Importance of Being Black," both in *The New Leader*, October 24, 1960, 8–9, and 10–11, respectively.

in the elaboration of a new, original civilization in a mestizo synthesis. For this reason Brazil is much more homogeneous in terms of culture, language, and historical stages than other regions of comparable size. We are one and indivisible, without racial or cultural minorities, and our imbalances or divergencies are regional, which is common to all continental countries and may exist even in small countries like Italy.

There is a general opinion among both Brazilian and foreign scholars that our color prejudice is based more on class than on race, as may be seen from the testimony of the great majority of travelers in the last century [104] and from present socio-anthropological studies.

Despite all our faults in the matter of racial prejudices, we constitute the most perfect racial democracy. Racial democracy is our creation, as political democracy is an Anglo-American creation. Charles Wagley writes that we must attempt to preserve our "characteristically Brazilian traditions, from which the rest of the world will have much to learn, especially concerning relations between races." [105]

The mestizo populace has by its own example been eliminating racial discrimination. Our elites are not based upon lineage but derive from all ethnic groups, although leadership is not yet vested only in persons of exceptional ability, intelligence, or technical and human qualities, capable of providing the nation with the efficiency that Toynbee says Brazil needs to become a world power. The people show themselves superior to the ruling minorities and to the new personalities, especially those in social circles, who seek to base status upon lineage. The people believe in the collaboration of cultures, the accumulation of human experiences from all ethnic groups, and they continuously oppose the impositions of those who stand in the way of progress, pretending always to conform to those impositions but overcoming them through ridicule and passive resistance. For this reason the history of our race relations shows continuous progress—mild, without bitterness, fear of strife, or extreme impositions. And in this way the most serious problems of our psycho-social integration have been resolved. But because some minorities, more social than ruling, resist the mestizo

---

[104] See a good synthesis of these opinions in Donald Pierson, *Brancos e Prêtos,* 139–167, and Manuel Cardoso, "Slavery in Brazil as described by Americans," in *The Americas* (January 1961), 241–260.
[105] Preface to Thales de Azevedo, *As Elites de Côr,* 11.

popular will, it has been necessary to resolve some problems of racial equality by law. Our legislative action against racial discrimination is slight compared to that of countries like the United States, where there is a Negro minority of 10.50 per cent (according to the 1960 census), or of European countries where there is discrimination against small racial minorities. The Afonso Arinos Law (No. 1,390, July 3, 1951) transfers to the field of penal infractions, with rapid trial, actions arising from racial prejudice. In 1961 the author of the law, as Secretary of State, recommended to the director of the Rio Branco Institute where Brazilian diplomats are trained "the most rigorous and strict application of the law, so that by obeying the principles of President Jânio Quadros all racial prejudice, open or disguised, may be abolished within the service of the State Department." [106]

In 1960 Aurélio Viana in the Chamber of Deputies denounced the Brown Root Engineering and Naval Construction Company, which lays pipes for Petrobrás, for refusing to hire colored Brazilian workers.[107] President Quadros has also taken measures to restrain the publication of classified advertisements containing racial discrimination.[108] But if all this reveals our imperfections, its beneficial aspect cannot be denied, as Abdias do Nascimento, director of the Negro Experimental Theater, emphasized.[109]

Because we are the most advanced ethnic democracy and the most extreme contrast to the Union of South Africa, as Kenneth Little stresses,[110] we have not only the greatest responsibilities toward South African segregation but the greatest triumphs to gain in winning the friendship of the new African nations.[111]

BRAZIL, A MESTIZO REPUBLIC

Only in this way, as President Kennedy said in his *Strategy of Peace,* will we be able to help the colored peoples to rid themselves of the stain of inferiority imposed on them by the white European peoples, and

---

[106] See *O Jornal,* Rio de Janeiro, March 21, 1961.

[107] *Diário do Congresso Nacional,* November 22, 1960, 8,551.

[108] Story in *O Jornal,* Rio de Janeiro, March 18, 1961.

[109] *Ibid.*

[110] *Race and Society,* UNESCO, 1952, 24.

[111] See the chapter on "União Sul-Africana e Brasil," *ibid.,* II (*África do Sudoeste*).

ourselves prove that miscegenation does not produce degenerates but world champions, as Brazilians have been in football, basketball, tennis, boxing, and other athletic sports. Furthermore we have exceptional social advantages, not only in ethnic composition but in the respect with which we have permitted the preservation of African cultural complexes. Based on his research, Pierson affirms that "with the exception of Brazil and certain areas of the Caribbean, there is no country outside of Africa where a people of African origin has attempted to preserve African culture."[112] Even in 1835 Bahia was the seat of the *iman,* that is, the leader in Brazil of all the African disciples of Mohammed. Apart from the many Africanisms that have enriched our mestizo culture, discussed in the chapter on the African contributions to Brazil, "African survivals still persist, somewhat separating a part (relatively small) of the Negro population from that of European descent."[113]

The preservation of African traditions, the adoption of those of European origin and the degree of amalgamation in the process of acculturation reveal the freedom of racial and cultural contacts. The preservation in Brazil of the Negro religions—especially in the *candomblés*—differing in ritual or music according to the African "nations," and survival of the cult of Iemanjá, which is practiced today even in Rio de Janeiro, show that we have always followed the path of tolerance and coexistence and that our culture, as Gilberto Freyre writes, is a complex that soon freed us "from a strictly colonial and sub-European status." We do not have the racial resentments, however slight, that Charles Boxer has shown were manifested toward all Afro-Asians by the Portuguese.[114]

We can and must discriminate against Europeans with superiority complexes, or who are resentful and bitter because of their colonial experiences. In this sense I believe, like Gilberto Freyre when he pointed out the dangers of Dutch immigration from Indonesia, that the announced influx of Belgians from the Congo will not serve us well.[115] Basically we are tired, as Ronald Ngala, President of the Democratic

---

[112] Pierson, *op. cit.,* 48.

[113] *Ibid.,* 421, note 19.

[114] C. R. Boxer, "S. R. Welch and his History of the Portuguese in Africa," *Journal of African History,* I, 1 (1960), 63, and notably, by the same author, *The Colour Question in the Portuguese Empire, 1415–1825,* reprint of *Proceedings of the British Academy,* XLVII, London, 1961; see especially 137.

[115] News stories of March 18, 1961.

African Union of Kenya, has said, of the supremacy of Europeans and of exploitation by them. We are tired of all supremacies and superiorities.

In an excellent study on *Brasil e o Colonialismo Europeu,* J. F. de Almeida Prado summarizes the thought of all free Brazilians when he says that Europeans "in general are becoming perfectly odious, together with compatriots of the same [colonialist] mentality. Formed by centuries of rapine, their psyche does not yet permit them to comprehend those who are different." [116] This is the image that we have of them today—except for those who have divested themselves of colonialist intentions, racial myths, and the myth of their intellectual superiority—, an image of which we boast but one that is held here, as throughout Asia, Africa, and America, by only a small minority.

It is certain, as Giorgio Mortara observes, that the process of whitening is accelerating and that it has come to group with those of European ancestry all those of mixed blood who are sufficiently light-skinned. One hundred and twenty-five years ago these "whites" did not constitute a third of the population; today they constitute almost two-thirds. The remaining third is composed mostly of colored, that is, of the brown-skinned, products of miscegenation who are not quite light enough to pass as white, and of a much smaller group of blacks and a few Orientals (Japanese). The relative increase in whites is the result in part of their lower death rate, as well as of infusions of European immigrants during the past eighty years. [117] The high Negro mortality rate is a consequence of the low socio-economic situation of the Negroes. Despite the fact that two-thirds of the population is now classified white, Aryanization may not be inferred—that would be an absurdity, for the standard for whiteness is one that would not be used in Europe, North America, or South Africa, including as it does large numbers of light-skinned mestizos. Ethnically and culturally we are a Republic of Mestizos; [118] we are not ashamed of this but rather are honored to serve the world as an example of peaceful racial coexistence.

---

[116] Companhia Editôra Nacional, São Paulo, 1956.

[117] "A População do Brasil e seu Desenvolvimento nos últimos anos," *Boletim Geográfico,* (March–April, 1961), No. 161, 273.

[118] The Minister of France in Brazil, Count Alexis de Saint Priest (1833–35) wrote in a dispatch dated August 8, 1835, that Brazil was a mulatto monarchy that had nothing "pure" except the royal blood. See Alberto Lamego, *No Rolar do Tempo,* 50.

The Brazilian Contribution to Africa

In spite of all the studies on Africans in Brazil, Africa itself continued to be forgotten and in Brazil the Negro was the Brazilian Negro. In 1888 Sílvio Romero wrote that it was "a shame for science in Brazil not to have devoted any of its efforts to the study of African languages and religions."[1] If Brazilian scholars wished to focus on Africa by analyzing, comparing, and relating the origins of groups acculturated in Brazil, that desire was never realized. From 1850 to the present, despite Afro-Brazilian studies, no research has been concerned with the African continent, nor has there been any definition of the interest that Brazil had and has still in Africans past and present.

Limiting themselves to Brazil, our scholars failed to prepare public opinion and alert diplomacy to the importance of Africa. Because of the objective nature of their studies and because of European and United States influence on our foreign policy, which has concerned itself with the La Plata River, Latin America, and the United States, we set aside the African aspect of three centuries (1550–1850) which if they Europeanized us, also Africanized us. Consequently we have not attended the changes undergone by Africa as we should have in the interest of maintaining good economic, political, cultural, and military relations with that continent.

On the other hand, our relations with Africa have not been limited to what we received from areas at first broad and later more reduced: Guinea, Nigeria, Dahomey, Gold Coast (Ghana), Ivory Coast, Central

[1] *Estudo sôbre a poesia popular do Brasil,* Rio de Janeiro, 1888.

Sudan (Sudanese Republic), Senegambia (Mali Federation), Sierra Leone, Liberia, Congo (ex-French and ex-Belgian), Cabinda (northern Angola), Angola, and Mozambique. Influences and contributions, rather, were reciprocal precisely because of the profound similarities of soil and climate, vegetation and biological environment.[2] "Geographically, Brazil is more closely related to Africa than to Europe."[3]

The similarities are so numerous that it is possible to make unexpected comparisons. Pierre Gourou shows, for example, and we shall summarize here, the analogies of the physical environment of the Amazon and the Congo.[4] The same equatorial climate with nearly the same average temperatures and minimum and maximum humidity and total annual rainfall in São Gabriel do Rio Grande and Iangambi. Similar natural vegetation, the humid, evergreen forest, the most beautiful example of which is the Amazon forest (3,000,000 sq. kms.). The two regions have the mightiest rivers in the world, with vast basins (6,900,000 sq. kms.); in area drained, equatorial fullness, and evenness of flow these majestic rivers are similar—even to their blackness. Climate, topography, and even identical vegetation make the two regions parallel. What distinguishes them are the rapids that cut the Congo River and make it inaccessible between Matadi and Leopold-ville. When they discovered the mouth of the Congo, the Portuguese did not explore it and therefore did not learn that its estuary is the outlet of an enormous river basin.

To Africa went Brazilian tobacco as a medium of exchange for slaves, and the Africans took to it from the beginning; to Africa went manioc, which even today is in the hottest regions of the world what the potato is in Europe. If the banana was known in Asia and Africa, what the first chroniclers here called the *pacoba,* i.e. the "golden" banana, was not. The pineapple, whose flavor made chroniclers of all nationalities enthusiastic, came from Brazil and invaded Europe and Africa and introduced the word *ananasi* (*nanasi, nananzi,* and *nanasa*) into Kicongo. The "Irish" potato came from here and has fed Europeans and

[2] See Pierre Monbeig, *Quelques traits géographiques de l'Amérique Latine,* Paris, 1954.
[3] Gilberto Freyre, *Interpretação do Brasil,* Rio de Janeiro, 1947, 180.
[4] "Étude comparée de l'Amazonie et du Congo Central," *Atas,* III Colóquio Internacional de Estudos Luso-Brasileiros, Lisbon, 1959, 147–153.

Africans ever since; wild rice covered expanses of swampy soil near rivers both in central Africa and in Brazil, although it had been known elsewhere from the earliest times; Bahian coconut palms were taken to Cape Verde, as Gabriel Soares de Souza testifies, "where they covered the earth and there would be infinite numbers if they did not dry up after eight or ten years"; and our cashew has sweetened African palates.

But no item introduced exceeded the importance of manioc and corn, which came to constitute the bases of African diet. As a tropical cereal, corn "replaced or was combined with inferior traditional cereals, various species of millet and sorghum." And not only corn but also "manioc served as a dietary staple for societies on the African continent," while the cashew was both beverage and food.

For this reason the geographer Orlando Ribeiro writes that "between Brazil and Africa relations are in a way even complementary. If it is true that Africa helped to make Brazil, or rather, helped to make America from the southern United States to the Rio de la Plata, by means of the Negro slaves that it furnished, it is also true that products introduced from America, especially corn and manioc, aided in mitigating the traditional hunger of the African continent."[5]

Pierre Gourou affirms that Africa was not dying of hunger, for its farmers had at their disposal good tubers, such as yams and taros, banana trees, cereals such as sorghum and wild rice, sesame, and fruits and vegetables.[6] Pernambuco and Rio de Janeiro imported squash from Guinea, as José de Anchieta noted. There was the horsebean, very frequently cultivated here but originating in southern Africa and Guinea;[7] ginger came from São Tomé and was declared contraband to maintain the value of that brought by the Portuguese from India; the banana came from São Tomé, and "the Negroes from Guinea are fonder of these bananas than of *pacobas* and grow them on their farms," wrote Gabriel Soares de Souza; and date trees were

---

[5] Orlando Ribeiro, *Aspectos e problemas da expansão portuguêsa,* Fundação da Casa de Bragança, Lisbon, 1955, 31.

[6] Pierre Gourou, "Les Plantes Alimentaires Américaines en Afrique Tropicale. Remarques Géographiques," *Atas,* III Colóquio Internacional de Estudos Luso-Brasileiros, Lisbon, 1959, I, 51–59.

[7] Our information is taken from F. C. Hoehne, *Botânica e Agricultura no Brasil,* Companhia Editôra Nacional, São Paulo, 1937, 107, 186.

introduced in the sixteenth century and "even in 1929 an official was sent to Africa in search of them";[8] the first cows to arrive in Bahia and Pernambuco came from Guinea.[9] If Africans could give us so much, then obviously they were not dying of hunger; but, as Gourou writes, they were glad to receive America's contributions.

Gourou believes that as regards tubers the reasons for the African adoption of Brazilian plants are clear enough. The Iorubas of Nigeria remained loyal to the yam, although it was economically inferior to the potato and manioc: part of the harvest of yams must be used to plant the next crop, which is not the case with manioc; yams are difficult to keep and require special care, while manioc requires nothing similar. The method by which the yam is produced is archaic and the only reason for preferring it is taste. The yam continues to provide 48 per cent of the Ioruban diet. The Iorubas are not interested in the potato, which was successful in other areas of Africa. The Brazilian tubers offered obvious economic advantages, so much so that manioc came to provide 23 per cent of Ioruba food production, but neither the potato nor the other tubers could replace the yam.

Despite the Sudanese soybean and millet, Brazilian corn was also utilized in Guinea, Dahomey, Nigeria, and Angola. To counterbalance this, Guinea sent us millet which was introduced in Bahia, as Gabriel Soares de Souza testifies, "but it is not considered a food there, and I still say that manioc is more healthful and beneficial than good wheat because it is more digestible." Millet was used only for the "feeding of horses, chickens, goats, sheep and pigs; and it is given as fruit to the Negroes from Guinea, who do not want it as a food although it is the best their land offers."[10] Hence the success of our corn and especially of manioc. Even the Brazilian method of preparation was imported, and in Kicongo one says *madioko*. The inhabitants of Gabon, Gourou adds, prepare a product that is very similar to the Brazilian and is known as *farinha* [manioc flour].

Manioc spread eastward in Africa, occupying 75 per cent of the land devoted to carbohydrates in the western territories of the Belgian

---

[8] *Ibid.*, 179.

[9] *Ibid.*, 179.

[10] Gabriel Soares de Souza, *Tratado Descritivo do Brasil em 1587*, Companhia Editôra Nacional, São Paulo, 1938, 199–200.

Congo, this percentage falling to below 50 per cent in the east and to 15 per cent in the territories where, although physical conditions are not hostile to it, food habits remain attached to cereals and bananas. Gourou further reminds us that manioc has its dangers, and Kwashiorkor is a disease caused by insufficient protein, which was avoided in Brazil by the consumption of beans. So the commodities on which the African native diet is based, like corn, sweet potato, and manioc, are Brazilian in origin; if we add *massango* and *massambala* to the bean, a dish so familiar to our cuisine, the African popular diet is complete.

So long as these foodstuffs imported from Brazil were not cultivated in Africa, our ships annually carried food supplements to the Portuguese zones. About 1629 the first steps were taken for the cultivation of food vegetables on small plantations situated around Luanda. Plants of American and Brazilian origin also went to the Congo.[11] Corn, manioc, sweet potato, pineapple, mammee, coconut, guava, and peanut, cultivated along a broad strip of Africa and already abundant in the seventeenth century, were transplanted from Brazil. And later, from Bahia, where the city alone consumed more than a million *alqueires,* "infinite flour" was sent to Angola and the Coast of Mina "for the sustenance of slaves bought there and of the crews of the slave ships." [12]

The Cape Verde islands, according to Professor A. Jorge Dias, seem not to have been inhabited prior to the Portuguese occupation, "but some of them were suitable for settlement and cultivation. However, only after the introduction of Brazilian corn (second quarter of the sixteenth century), the germination needs of which were magnificently adapted to the local climate, was it possible to produce in abundance a cereal that might serve as a basis for the diet of the inhabitants." [13]

Rubber also was taken to Angola at the beginning of this century, and the Brazilian crisis caused by Malayan rubber production was shared by many Angolan towns, like Camaxilo.

---

[11] See Morais Martins, *Contato de culturas no Congo Português,* Lisbon, 1958.
[12] Letter from José da Silva Lisboa to Domingos Vandelli, *Anais da Biblioteca Nacional,* XXXII, 503.
[13] "Contatos de Cultura," in *Colóquios de política ultramarina internacionalmente relevante,* Lisbon, 1958, 65. See also Fernando Ortiz, "La Cocina Afrocubana," in *Estudos e Ensaios em Homenagem a Renato de Almeida,* Rio de Janeiro, 1960, 143–152.

And our contact with Angola was even broader. It was from Brazil that the first stallions and mares went to Angola. A *carta régia* dated February 6, 1706, ordered that four stallions should be transported to Luanda, but some petty official substituted mares, the arrival of which Raimundo José da Cunha Matos reports with a certain sense of calamity: "I am most dubious of the wisdom of the government in sending these mares to Angola, and fear that this day may prove as fatal as was the day the horse was introduced among the Indians of Chile and Brazil, who today gallop upon those animals in raids and war. If the Negroes of the Congo ever come to have calvary, the supremacy of the Portuguese soldier here, which is based upon the horseman, will have ended." [14]

There was interchange on the human level also. Important persons moved from one side of the Atlantic to the other to fill successive posts in the colonial empire. Antônio de Albuquerque Coelho, for example, was governor of Rio de Janeiro, Maranhão, São Paulo and Minas, Macau, and Angola. Caldeira Brant, later Marquis of Barbacena, served in the army of the governor of Angola, Dom Miguel Antônio de Melo, as his adjutant-general. On the 7th of April, 1797, *Desembargador* (High Justice) João Joaquim Borges da Silva sailed for the islands of São Tomé and Principe to investigate the actions of their governors, João Resende Tavares Leite and Ouvidor Antônio Pereira Bastos Lima Varela Barca. Nor should we forget that General José de Oliveira Barbosa, afterward Baron of Passeio Público, governed Angola from 1780 to 1816. But the human interchange was not limited to high officials. Many Brazilians went to Angola as soldiers, sailors, convicts, civil servants, peddlers, businessmen, prostitutes, and exiles.[15]

African passenger travel by means of the wooden or Congo horse and primitive palanquins was replaced by slings similar to Brazilian hammocks. Social changes took place as a result of the need for slaves in Brazil. Society in the Congo, for example, was highly stratified with a hierarchy of classes among the free population. The greatest difference in social status was between the free man and the slave; but as soon as

---

[14] *Compêndio Histórico das Possessões de Portugal na África,* Rio de Janeiro, Arquivo Nacional, 1963, with Preliminary Note by José Honório Rodrigues, 602, 310.
[15] Cunha Matos, "Compêndio," 665.

Brazilian plantations began to demand labor in abundance the structure changed, because in addition to the great chiefs others could not resist the temptation to possess slaves and captured free Negroes in ambush.

The slave traffic between the coasts of Brazil and Africa generated a process of intercommunication and transculturation between the various African and Luso-Brazilian ethnic groups.

Portuguese Africa owes much to the great cultural and scientific services of two Brazilians: to the Cariocan Elias Alexandre da Silva Correia (1740–?), who in 1790 came to Rio de Janeiro to take the post of Captain in the Grenadiers,[16] the authorship of one of the best-known sources of Angolan history, written in the seventeenth century and recently published in Lisbon;[17] and to the Paulist Francisco José de Lacerda Almeida (1753–1789), named Governor of Rios de Sena (Mozambique), the first attempt to cross Africa, linking Mozambique and Angola. The diaries of his travels in Africa were published in this century by the Agência-Geral das Colônias[18] and by the Instituto Nacional do Livro.[19]

Because of Portugal's insatiable demands for gold some Brazilians suffered bitter exile in Africa. In the sentence dated April 18, 1792, condemning Tiradentes to death and determining that he should be drawn and quartered, each quarter to be nailed to posts on the roads of Minas "where he engaged in his infamous practices," the following were also condemned to exile for life in the military installations of Angola: Tomás Antônio Gonzaga, Vicente Vieira da Mota, José Aires Gomes, João da Costa Rodrigues, and Antônio de Oliveira Lopes.

Convict Gonzaga to go to Pedras, convict Vicente Vieira to Angocha, convict José Aires to Embaqua, convict João da Costa Rodrigues to Novo Redondo, convict Antônio de Oliveira Lopes to Caconda, and if they return to Brazil they will be sentenced to life imprisonment and half of their property will be confiscated by the Treasury and the Royal Chamber. Convict João Dias da Mota is condemned to ten years of exile in Benguela, and if he returns to

---

[16] See *Publicações do Arquivo Nacional*, Rio de Janeiro, 1902, III, 71.

[17] *História de Angola*, Lisbon, 1937, 2 vols.

[18] *Travessia da África*, Lisbon, 1936.

[19] *Diário de Moçambique para os Rios de Sena, 1797–1798*, and *Diário da Vila de Tete para o interior da África, 1798*, Rio de Janeiro, 1944. He also wrote diaries of his travels in Brasil.

this state of Brazil and is apprehended, he shall be sentenced to life imprisonment and a third of his property confiscated by the Treasury and Royal Chamber. Convict Vitoriano Gonçalves Veloso is condemned to public whipping in the streets, three turns around the prison, and exile for life in the City of Angola, and if he returns to this State of Brazil and is apprehended, he shall be sentenced to life imprisonment and half of his property confiscated by the Treasury and Royal Chamber. . . . Convicts Fernando José Ribeiro and José Martins Borges are sentenced, respectively, to exile for life in Benguela and to a fine of 200,000 to cover the cost of the Tribunal.[20]

These were later joined by all those who had received the death sentence, that is, Francisco de Paula Freire de Andrade, José Alves Maciel, Inácio José de Alvarenga, Domingos de Abreu Vieira, Francisco Antônio de Oliveira Lopes, Luís Vaz de Toledo Piza, Salvador Carvalho do Amaral Gurgel, José de Rezende Costa Pai, José de Rezende Costa Filho, and Domingos Vidal Barbosa,[21] whose sentences were commuted through the "mercy" of the Queen on October 15, 1790, to exile for life in the military installations of Angola and Benguela, with the death penalty if they should return to America. The difference is that for the latter group the punishment was not only exile and but also imprisonment in Africa, while for the former it was exile in the African dominions, meaning Mozambique and Rios de Sena, for as many years as might seem convenient.[22] In view of the royal colonialist clemency—no longer colonialist according to one historical view that is really pseudo-historical and pseudo-popular, because Brazil was now called a State—the Tribunal ordered on April 20, 1792, that convict Francisco de Paula Freire de Andrade should go to Pedra de Ancochi, José Alvarenga Manuel to Mosango, Inácio José de Alvarenga to Dande, Luís Vaz de Toledo to Cambambe, Francisco Antônio de Oliveira Lopes to Bié, Domingos de Abreu Vieira to Machimba prison, Salvador Carvalho do Amaral Gurgel to Calata, José de Rezende Costa Pai to Bissau, José de Rezende Costa Filho to Cape Verde, Domingos Vidal Barbosa to the island of São Tiago.[23] This new decision led those

---

[20] "Acórdão da Relação . . . in *Autos da Inconfidência Mineira.* Rio de Janeiro, 1938, VII, 195–197.
[21] *Ibid.,* 194–195.
[22] *Ibid.,* 226.
[23] *Ibid.,* 233.

who had earlier been sentenced to exile to appeal their sentences and finally succeed in having them reduced. Thus, on May 2, 1792, Tomás Antônio Gonzaga had his exile commuted to ten years in Mozambique, Vicente Vieira da Mota to ten years in Rio de Sena, José Aires Gomes to eight years in Inhambana, João da Costa Rodrigues to ten years in Mosoril, Antônio de Oliveira Lopes to ten years in Macau, Vitoriano Gonçalves Veloso to ten years in Cabeceira Grande [?], Fernando José Ribeiro to ten years in Benguela, and João Dias da Mota to ten years in Cacheu.[24]

This is hardly a Brazilian contribution to Portuguese Africa, but in the history of our relations we cannot forget that men who aspired to liberty went to live there, as today many Angolans and Mozambicans with similar aspirations seek not exile in Brazil but the inspiration to fight for national freedom and to escape sinister eyes and denunciations.

> What frightful times are in store,
> after a trial so sore?
> Who in the future will know
> what is approved or no
> Oh you new humanity,
> what will your spirit be? [25]

So great was the contempt of Portugal for the African colonies that they were a place of exile either for rebels, our heroes of the Inconfidência, or for idlers and delinquents, as may be seen from the order from the Court to the Viceroy in Rio de Janeiro, ordering that vagrants, delinquents, and volunteers be sent annually to Angola and Benguela.[26]

When in 1843 the problem of naturalization was discussed and objections were raised against certain privileges granted to Portuguese, the great conservative Bernardo Pereira de Vasconcelos said in the Senate that it was necessary to avoid the barbarous tendencies that would result from the abolition of the slave trade. Indignant, the liberal Costa Ferreira retorted: "Africa has been a civilizing force"; and the

---

[24] *Ibid.,* 274.
[25] Cecília Meireles, *Romanceiro da Inconfidência,* Rio de Janeiro, 1953, 206.
[26] See "Correspondência da Côrte de Portugal com os Vice-Reis do Brasil," *Publicações do Arquivo Nacional,* III, 1901, 121.

other replied: "That is correct. Africa is civilizing America! . . . I see other countries that have tried to become Africanized in part." [27] It is true that the conservative politician was defending the interests of the great estates and slaveowners, but it should not be forgotten that, as he himself used to say, there is no moral civilization without material civilization, and the latter in Brazil depended on the importation of Africans without whom the country would fall into decay—especially if we consider that the average life-span of a slave was ten years. They were the instruments of our wealth and production, as Lopes da Gama said, but he could not "agree that they brought moral and intellectual civilization with them."

Many years later in 1867 when the abolitionist campaign reached its height, Perdigão Malheiros added to these considerations when he wrote that there were people who said that Brazil owed its progress and civilization to Africa,

But what civilization did Africa and those Negroes who were imported have? On the contrary, slavery and the traffic merely served to prevent the immigration of free, civilized people such as Europeans from developing and to hinder the greater development and progress of the country. Not even materially or economically, that is, with regard to production alone, has any such development been shown to have accrued from slavery; it has been demonstrated that free labor produces in much greater quantity and value because of the human faculties and powers, it makes use of intelligence and will.

Indeed, during our three centuries of isolation from Europe, of intercourse with Europe limited to the Iberian area, we underwent a marked African and Oriental influence.[28] The social changes brought about by Dom João by the opening of our ports meant Europeanization that the abolition of the slave trade and the entry of immigrants reinforced.

Bernardo Pereira de Vasconcelos' attitude was realistic and free of the fundamental dependence adopted by the Brazilian elite with respect to

---

[27] Senate Speech, April 25, 1843, transcribed in the *Jornal do Comércio* April 30, 1843, No. 115, and cited by Otávio Tarquínio de Souza, *História dos Fundadores do Império*, V: *Bernardo Pereira de Vasconcelos*, Rio de Janeiro, José Olímpio Editôra, 1957, 247.

[28] See Gilberto Freyre, *Sobrados e Mucambos*, Companhia Editôra Nacional, 1936.

Europe. The Negro was of essential assistance in the Brazilian historical process and it cannot be judged whether the process would have been better with free labor. Internal development and change were accomplished by Africanization as much as by Europeanization and Orientalization until the process of Westernization became dominant not only because historical conditions made such dominance possible but also because the leading minorities approved of changes that would bring us closer to the Western nations.

Finally, could not one classify as a Brazilian contribution to Africa the emigration of three hundred Portuguese from Recife to Angola in 1848 at the time of the Praeira Revolution, which was radical and nationalistic in tendency with a program that included the nationalization of retail trade—which was in the hands of the Portuguese? But the fact was that Portugal, deprived of Brazil and forced to look more attentively to Africa, did not have human resources and did not feel that it could divert emigration from Brazil to Angola, because this would represent sacrificing the Brazilian gold sent to Portugal from Portuguese emigrants' savings, that covered the Portuguese financial deficit.

The colonization of Mossâmedes, accomplished with Portuguese from Pernambuco, was an exceptional case, not only of mass repatriation to a colonial zone that did not compete with Brazil in its attraction for Portuguese immigrants, but also because Huíla, which was where they went, is considered a triumph of Portuguese colonization in the tropics. "On the Huíla plateau in Angola the capacity of the Portuguese to triumph peacefully over the Nordic in the conquest of tropical areas was proved experimentally," writes Gilberto Freyre.[29] But this region, which is the only triumph of white Portuguese colonization in the two African provinces up to the twentieth century, does not, as James Duffy critically points out, constitute a tropical area, for climatically it resembles the great areas of the Union of South Africa colonized by Nordic peoples. Huíla today, he adds, is the most Portuguese region in Angola and its plantations are replicas of those existing in Portugal and Madeira.[30]

Tropical or not, Huíla was colonized victoriously by Portuguese acclimated to tropical Pernambuco and their descendants consider

---

[29] *Aventura e Rotina*, Rio de Janeiro, 1953, 399.
[30] *Portuguese Africa*, Harvard University Press, 1959, 100, and 354, note.

themselves more Angolan than Portuguese, as many Portuguese considered themselves Brazilian on the eve of our Independence.

Thus, it is not the common experience of former Portuguese occupation that justifies the relations we must maintain with Africa today, but
the historical process of mutual acceptance and reaction, of cultural
donations and contributions that make Afro-Brazilian friendship and
coöperation as important as our European, Pan-American, or Latin-
American alliances.

Modern Relations: 1800–1960

England aspires to dominate all of Asia, as through the settlements and wars that it is undertaking in Africa one must suppose it aspires to complete dominion over that great region. The countries of both regions have the same commodities and products as Brazil, and as the British must prefer outlets for their own, they will seek by all means to set up obstacles for us, and to achieve this there is no better way than to deprive Brazil of additional labor: this is the true British policy.

CUNHA MATOS,
from his Speech in the Chamber of Deputies, July 3, 1827.

TREATIES BETWEEN GREAT BRITAIN AND PORTUGAL.
1810–1817

At the beginning of the nineteenth century, even before the Portuguese Court was established in Brazil, the commerce of Rio de Janeiro had escaped Portuguese control and trade had increased with Africa and America. The act that opened our ports on January 28, 1808, merely legalized a *de facto* situation. Afro-Brazilian commerce and the slave trade had grown, especially between Angola and Brazil.

As the seat of the monarchy Brazil ruled the Empire, even before it became a kingdom itself in 1815. As Martinho de Melo e Castro had predicted in 1770, the volume of trade and navigation that was making Rio de Janeiro the center of an intercontinental commerce between Asia and Africa passed definitively into the hands of Brazil where the Throne was now established and, consequently, the whole diplomatic life of Atlantic South America was to be found.

Azeredo Coutinho in his *Ensaio Econômico sôbre o Comércio de*

Portugal e suas Colônias[1] argued for a close relationship between colonies and mother country such that, the richer a colony should be, the more it should owe, and the closer it should be bound to, the mother country. Nevertheless economic and political divergence occurred. The change in Portuguese colonial policy was made to serve the interests of the oligarchy that controlled both mother country and colonies and who, as Azeredo Coutinho pointed out, "only fear when they have something to lose; and the more they have to lose, the more they fear, and the more they fear, the more obedient they are. Therefore the interests of Portugal and the colonies must be bound together, nor should the latter be treated as rivals."[2] So later it happened in Brazil that having nothing to lose, we were not afraid, and fearing nothing, we refused to be obedient but, rather, achieved our independence.

Here also was the ideal center for English commercial expansion aimed to conquer the immense regions of America, for the English had been excluded generally from Europe because of the Napoleonic War, and from commerce with the United States because of the Non–Importation Act (1809).

Since that time two irreconcilable currents have clashed in the course of our history. The first took us to Africa in search of slaves to satisfy the increasing needs of our agricultural development, both in sugar, which moreover was the economic basis of our independence, and in coffee, which was cultivated in the province of Rio de Janeiro, especially in the Paraíba valley. The second current moved us away from Africa because of the English insistence on abolition of first the slave trade and afterward slavery for the economic and humanitarian interests found together in Protestant Christianity. This clash between national needs and English demands was the essence of our history in the first fifty years of the nineteenth century.

Thus Africa was the fundamental basis of our being or not being. We needed slave labor but Dom João and consistent Portuguese policy, which governed us according to Portuguese interests and not ours, depended on the protection of the British, and this required abolition.

---

[1] 1st ed., Lisbon, 1794. Various later editions and translations. Concerning them, see Sérgio Buarque de Holanda, "Introdução" in *Memória sôbre o Preço do Açúcar,* reedição do Instituto do Açúcar e do Álcool, Rio de Janeiro, 1946.

[2] See *Ensaio,* 1st ed., Capítulos I, II, and III. Quotation, 110.

Contradictorily, then, while our slave interests were growing and the importation of slaves was increasing, British pressure for abolition became greater.

For two years Lord Strangford, the British Minister to Brazil (1808–1815), struggled so that once the European war was over the English might be in an advantageous position to compete here with other nations. On February 19, 1810, Prince Regent Dom João signed two treaties with Great Britain, one of Alliance and Friendship, with secret articles, and one of Commerce and Navigation. Article X of the first treaty stipulated the obligation to abolish the slave trade gradually, limiting that commerce to the African dominions of the Portuguese Crown. It also recognized that Portugal had not abdicated its rights to the territories of Cabinda and Molembo, disputed by France, nor was there any limitation or restriction of commerce with Ajudá and other African ports situated on the so-called coast of Mina belonging to or claimed by the Portuguese Crown.[3] The rights of Portuguese or Luso-Brazilian subjects to trade in Africa were not, however, limited to the dominions but were recognized in a broader area covering the coast of Mina, Dahomey, Cabinda, and Molembo to the northern Congo. And the traders would know how to take advantage of this recognition, establishing a powerful network of communications on both coasts, agents and posts for trade which were acknowledged in Brazil or in other cases kept secret.

So although the treaty of Alliance and Friendship established the principle of gradual abolition of the slave trade, at the same time it recognized its existence and permitted its continuance. In this sense it was a victory for Brazilian slave interests. In return, Portugal ceded Bissau and Cacheu, where the traffic in slaves was to be restricted and entirely abolished, for a period of fifty years.

By the treaty of Commerce and Navigation Portugal armed Great Britain with the great weapon to dominate Brazil, the preferential tariff of 15 per cent for English products. By securing these preferential rights Great Britain became mistress of our economy and established its

---

[3] See "Treaties" in Antônio Pereira Pinto, *Apontamentos para o Direito Internacional*, Rio de Janeiro, 1864, I, 33–84.

preëminence until 1844 when the treaty of 1827 renewing those privileges expired. Among several other astonishing privileges having no time limit, His Britannic Majesty had succeeded in having the port of Santa Catarina declared a free port (Art. XXII), in obtaining for his subjects in Brazil the protection of their rights and privileges by an English judge, and for his consuls, jurisdiction over their inheritance and succession, along with permission granted in perpetuity for the English to trade with Portuguese possessions situated on the east coast of the African continent (Art. XXIV).

These treaties generated an enormous wave of protest and deep sentiment against British imperialism. By 1814 Lord Strangford was writing to Viscount Castlereagh, the British Foreign Minister, that the inhabitants of Bahia and those places where the slave trade constituted the main commerce were desperate in the face of the measures taken by the British fleet for the suppression of the trade, measures that had brought about the ruin of many of the principal firms engaged in it. The traders in Rio de Janeiro also had suffered severely from the opening of free commerce with the countries of Europe, for they had lost the monopoly on imports and exports that they had enjoyed previously; they blamed England for this, which together with their irritation at the seizure of many of their ships created an irreconcilable animosity against the British name and nation.[4]

But the desperation of Bahians and Cariocans did not, as the English representative thought, mean acceptance of the English actions opposing their interests and those of the nation. On the contrary, after 1810 the slave traffic increased, its organization was perfected, and it became the most important business in the country, with a network of ships that mocked the British cruisers, of well-managed establishments on the African coast, and of Luso-Brazilian agents and capitalists in Brazil. It is sufficient to recall that from Angola and Benguela alone between 1812 and 1815, the date of the new agreement with Portugal on the traffic, the number of slaves that arrived annually in Rio de Janeiro from these colonies was, respectively, 6,891 and 5,015, 6,121 and 4,404, 7,730 and

---

[4] See Charles Webster, *Britain and the Independence of Latin America, 1812–1830,* Oxford University Press, 1938, I, 171, document 58.

3,576;[5] in addition, Bahia alone received more than 40,000 slaves from the coast of Mina between 1813 and 1817.[6] The number of slaves brought to Pernambuco also showed the same increase, despite the efforts of British cruisers.[7]

Thus, there was no gradual abolition of the traffic, nor was it limited as prescribed by the treaty of 1810 to the Portuguese possessions. Great Britain could not meet the competition of the low-cost labor of slave-holding nations and consequently insisted on the abolition of the trade, which would mean the abolition of slavery. For this reason Castlereagh's foreign policy (1815–1822) proceeded unceasingly in efforts to assure universal abolition of the slave trade. After several negotiations Palmela, the Portuguese representative to the Congress of Vienna, agreed to abolish the traffic north of the Equator, Portugal receiving 300,000 pounds as compensation for unsettled claims, being freed from the payment of a loan, and accepting parts of the treaty of 1810 against which it had always protested. Finally, a general declaration was made condemning the traffic in African slaves as repugnant to the principles of humanity and universal morality.[8]

During his whole ministry Castlereagh devoted a great part of his time and energy to the movement for abolition, responding to tremendous pressure from abolitionist societies and by his action affecting relations with several nations. The special declaration of the Congress of Vienna, which was followed by abolition in several countries, had not been adopted by Portugal and Spain, and at the end of hostilities England lost its wartime right of search and seizure. The English knew that the treaty of 1810 had had no effect and believed that Dona Carlota Joaquina and members of the Court had interests in the trade.[9]

Palmela's agreement in Vienna was ratified by the Prince Regent in

[5] Edmundo Correia Lopes, *A Escravatura, Subsídios para a sua História*, Lisbon, 1944, 147.
[6] *Ibid.*, 144–145.
[7] Pernambuco received slaves only from Angola, from 1810 to 1815, 1,254; 2,489; 3,265; 3,911. *Op. cit.*, 139–141.
[8] Charles Webster, *The Foreign Policy of Castlereagh*, 1812–1825, London, 1931, 1st vol. 419 ff.
[9] *Ibid.*, 2nd vol., 454–459.

Rio de Janeiro on June 8, 1815.[10] It declared that "desirous of terminating amicably all doubts relative to the places on the coast of Africa where Portuguese subjects might, in conformity with the laws of Portugal and existing treaties with His Britannic Majesty, continue the commerce in slaves," and that in view of the fact that ships had been seized and condemned because of the illegal traffic, a commission was being appointed to idemnify those Portuguese prejudiced by such seizures. For this purpose Article 1 provided for a sum of three hundred thousand pounds to be paid in London, to a person designated by the Regent, for the establishment of a fund to attend to claims, and Article 2 considered the aforementioned sum a total payment of all Portuguese claims arising from seizures made prior to June 1, 1814.

The agreement was followed by the treaty, also signed in Vienna on January 22, 1815, and ratified on June 8 in Rio de Janeiro. After stating that in Article X of the treaty of 1810 the Prince Regent had declared his resolution to coöperate with His Britannic Majesty in the cause of gradual abolition of the slave trade, the trade was prohibited in Article I of the new treaty "on any part of the coast of Africa north of the Equator under any pretext or in any way whatever," except for those ships that had sailed from Brazilian ports prior to publication of the ratification, up to a maximum of six months after publication. In Article II His Britannic Majesty bound himself not to cause "any molestation to Portuguese vessels en route to engage in the slave trade south of the line, or in the present dominions of the Portuguese crown," or in the territories over which the said Crown had reserved rights in the aforementioned treaty of Alliance (1810).

As may be seen, the slave trade was now permitted only south of the Equator, and the area of acquisition was thus restricted by the elimination of the markets of Dahomey, Ajudá, and the other Portuguese possessions in the north, except for Cabinda and Molembo north of the Congo River. Furthermore, the treaty of 1810 was considered nullified

---

[10] See the *Convenção* between the Prince Regent, Dom João, and George III, King of Great Britain, to terminate issues and indemnify the losses of Portuguese subjects in the African slave trade, signed in Vienna January 21, 1815, and ratified by Portugal June 8 and by Great Britain February 14, in A. Pereira Pinto, *op. cit.,* I, 124–127.

and the two parties bound themselves to fix in a separate treaty the time by which the slave trade was to cease completely. Finally, the traffic south of the line could not be conducted under the Portuguese flag "for any purpose other than that of supplying slaves to the transatlantic possessions of the Portuguese crown." [11]

All these Portuguese concessions, prejudicial to our agricultural interests at the time and made in Rio de Janeiro by a ministry composed exclusively of Portuguese, were not to be valid. In its dealings with Great Britain Portuguese diplomacy always maneuvered with cunning shrewdness, or in other words, because of its weakness developed the faculty of temporizing, the skill of compromising in order to gain time, a conciliatory and opportunistic artifice, which under threatening circumstances pretended to sacrifice its interests but had no intention of complying with the imposed obligations, and by delay gained the most of what history already considered lost. But "English tenacity," as Pereira Pinto wrote, "does not tire, and if it appears sometimes to give in before energetic opposition, it surges forward again, always demanding, always arrogant." Pereira Pinto also wrote that "when such an element [slavery] has long been implanted in a country, when agricultural interests cannot fail to be shaken by the absence of slave labor, great prudence in execution is required and must be accompanied by adequate means to lessen the difficulties in transforming the extremely important establishments of the nation that are its only source of wealth." [12]

The slave traffic continued stronger than ever, organizing more efficiently to escape the British cruisers and to meet the demands of agriculture. In 1815, 1816, and 1817 Rio de Janeiro received from Angola alone 7,730, 6,115, and 4,645 slaves; Pernambuco received 3,911, 5,499, and 5,932; [13] and Bahia received on the average 4,200 annually from below and above the Equator, more than 2,000 Sudanese and less than

---

[11] *Ibid.*, I, 128–132. In Article V Great Britain renounced payment of the loan of 600,000 pounds sterling contracted by Portugal in 1809. Great Britain also obliged itself in secret Article III to satisfy His Royal Highness' just claims in case of the capture by British cruisers of Portuguese ships after June 1, 1814, until the end of the period during which total abolition of the slave trade north of the Equator was to be accomplished.

[12] *Ibid.*, 150–151.

[13] See data in Edmundo Correia Lopes, *op. cit.,* 147, 139, and 141.

2,000 Bantus.[14] Studies made by Nina Rodrigues and others made later by Luís Viana Filho and Carlos Ott show that, despite the agreement to abolish the trade north of the Equator, we received more Sudanese Negroes than Bantus, that is more northern than southern Negroes, at least in Bahia. If by the treaty of 1810 the slave trade with other than the Portuguese dominions had become illegal, in 1815 its legal exercise was recognized by Great Britain only below the Equator, whether originating in Portuguese dominions or markets to the north. Convinced of total Portuguese indifference to the treaty and of the northern traffic, Great Britain was to insist two years later on an addition to the treaty of January 22, 1815, for the purpose of preventing any illegal trade.

The agreement of 1817 was a "sad inheritance bequeathed us by the Metropolis" and would oblige us at the time of Independence to accept the treaty of 1826, the source not only of difficulties for our agriculture but also of great insults to our sovereignty and dignity perpetrated by the British fleet in our very ports. By the additional agreement both governments bound themselves—and actually only Great Britain had any economic interest in this—to "mutual supervision that their respective subjects not engage in illegal slave trade, now clearly defined by the first two articles." [15] In the first the traffic was prohibited in British or Portuguese ships, or under British or Portuguese flags, or for the account of subjects of another power, and in all ports or stopping places on the coast of Africa, both north of the Equator and outside the dominion of Portugal. In order to restrict still further any possibility of liberal interpretation facilitated by the treaty of 1815, the second article declared in which African territories the slave trade would continue to be legal: "on the east coast of Africa, the territory between Cabo Delgado and the Bay of São Lourenço; on the west coast, the whole territory and Bay of São Lourenço; on the west coast, the whole territory between the eighth and eighteenth degrees of latitude south," which meant limiting the trade to Angola, except for the territories of Molembo and Cabinda from the fifth and twelfth minutes to the eighth latitude south. Both powers further obligated themselves in Article III to promulgate a law determining the penalties to be incurred by their

---

[14] See Nina Rodrigues, *Os Africanos no Brasil,* São Paulo, 1935, 2nd ed., 45.
[15] See Pinto, *op. cit.,* I, 155–174.

subjects engaging in the illegal trade, and at the same time to renew the already existing prohibition on the importation of slaves into Brazil under any but the Portuguese flag; Portuguese ships engaging in the traffic were to be provided with a passport, as per the form attached to the treaty (Art. IV). In Article V the British Navy was granted the right of visit and seizure for judgment by special tribunals. This greatest concession gave rise to the gravest difficulties between the two nations, and later, transferred to the treaty of 1826, legalized the offense inflicted on our merchant ships until 1856, and afterward independently and without our consent in the name of the Aberdeen Bill of 1845. For judgment and appeal in causes of seizure two mixed commissions were established (Art. VIII), composed of an equal number of nationals from both powers, one having its seat in Brazil and the other in Sierra Leone. No indemnization, it was immediately stipulated, would be granted to Portuguese ships captured with slaves taken north of Cabo de Palmas, or, after six months from the exchange of ratifications of the treaty of 1815, with slaves taken at stops north of the Equator. Compensation in cash for unjust seizures and payment of the three hundred thousand pounds promised in 1815 were to complete the bargain.[16] In case no other adjustment should be stipulated, the new agreement was to remain in effect for fifteen years from the date of total abolition of the slave trade by the Portuguese government.[17]

Of this entire British diplomatic offensive to have the illegality of the slave trade recognized by other nations, especially by Spain and Portugal, in whose American dominions slave labor was considered indispensable, the most positive result was concession of the right of visit, search, and seizure of any ship suspected of illicit cargo. Through this right Great Britain could verify if the agreement was being obeyed and thus prevent any nation from enjoying the advantage of imported slave labor and, consequently, low production costs. Great Britain, which had abolished its slave trade by the law of 1807, in effect from January 1, 1808, and slavery in its colonies by the law of August 29, 1834, now by means of Castlereagh's policy forced universal abolition of the slave trade except south of the Equator.

---

[16] See "Regulamento para as Comissões Mistas," in Pinto, *op. cit.,* I, 174–186.
[17] Separate Article of the Agreement, September 11, 1817, in Pinto, *op. cit.,* I, 187–188.

Whatever the importance of these treaties, the abolition of the traffic depended on more than restrictions on paper, as Sir Charles Webster wrote.[18] The really effective agent was the British fleet, whose cruisers became expert, states Webster, in detecting the slavers and pursuing them to their bases of operation on the coast of Guinea. The mixed Commission functioning in Sierra Leone, whose decisions were final, sought to give legal approval to the English seizures. But all the concessions of little nations like Portugal, won by intimidation and corruption, would be of small use if the British could not count on the support of the United States and France. In the latter, realists and the commercial classes believed that abolition was merely an instrument to maintain British supremacy,[19] and in the United States, non-Portuguese and Brazilians found the ships and flag with which to confront the British cruisers successfully.

Neither France nor the United States recognized the right of visit. John Quincy Adams, Minister of the United States to Great Britain (1815), Secretary of State at the time of Monroe (1817–1825) and sixth President of the United States (1825–1829), declared that the American Constitution prohibited the judgment of its citizens by a foreign tribunal such as the one established in Sierra Leone, and stated that England's persistence in the right of visit aimed only at a hypocritical advantage for itself. The most that the English obtained was a suggestion that British and American fleets might coöperate in their efforts to liquidate the traffic. Castlereagh did not, then, obtain the practical measures that he desired.[20] Nor did the English succeed in overcoming the organization and astuteness of the Luso-Brazilians engaged in smuggling slaves, whose trade increased in spite of all treaties and agreements obtained at the cost of Portuguese weakness.

Henceforth the official records no longer show the origin of slaves imported from above the Equator, although as Nina Rodrigues shows, the importation continued "after 1817 as vigorously or perhaps more so than before." [21] However, Luís Viana Filho writes "that if Sudanese Negroes still came to Bahia as contraband, they were far fewer in

---

[18] *The Foreign Policy of Castlereagh, 1815–1822*, II, 460.
[19] Charles Webster, *op. cit.*, 461.
[20] *Ibid.*, 465.
[21] *Os Africanos no Brasil*, 2nd ed., 46.

number than the Bantus, for it is improbable that with the Angolan markets open, which were closer to Bahia, Bahian traders should continue to risk the dangers of tenacious English vigilance north of the Equator. Officially, from this time until 1830 all African emigration is recorded as coming from Angola, and if this is not the whole truth, it is correct to assume that actually the greater part of the trade did seek out ports below the Equator, which were as abundant as the others and where difficulties with British cruisers did not exist." [22] Correct or not, as Luís Viana Filho may prefer, it is certain that Carlos Ott's research proved that between 1800 and 1828 more Sudanese than Bantus entered Bahia and that between 1838 and 1860 the difference in favor of the Sudanese was greater, demonstrating therefore that the trade north of the Equator was successful in overcoming British insolence. [23] Contributing to that end were the great and ever-growing search for slaves, now forbidden merchandise, the ever-increasing prices, the large capital invested in the business, and the activity of the traders who were organized with extreme efficiency.

The close internal relationship between Brazil and Africa continued, and the intercourse maintained by the trade had become the business of large interests. The story of this Luso-Brazilian traffic shows how the coast of Africa continued to be dependent on Brazil. This dependence was accentuated with the arrival of the Court in Rio de Janeiro, which became the seat of the whole Empire. Political dependence was now added to economic dependence, and continued to the time of Brazilian independence. [24]

The immediate transition from the regime of colonial monopoly to that of open ports and free entry of general trade (then however limited to the English) exercised great pressure on Luso-Brazilian commerce, but it was especially prejudicial to the outfitters and proprietors of heavy ships comprising the fleets transporting our produce to Portugal. Removed from European maritime trade by English competition, both before and after the war, many ships were turned to trade with the

---

[22] *O Negro na Bahia,* Rio de Janeiro, 1946, 80.
[23] "O Negro Baiano," in *Les Afro-Americains,* Ifan-Dakar, 1953, 144–145.
[24] All the books of Royal Orders directed to the Azores, Madeira, Cape Verde, São Tomé, Goa, and Mozambique between 1809 and 1821 are to be found in the Arquivo Nacional. Missing are the Orders relative to Angola.

dominions of the Empire, especially with Africa, thus increasing the possible tonnage of slave cargo, and others became useless hulls in our ports. But the successive Portuguese concessions in the treaties of 1810, 1815, and 1817 definitively removed these ships from the slave trade; the traders had to acquire new ships, especially American ones, with which to confront the British cruisers. The steps taken in this regard, as well as in the construction in 1819 of warehouses to accommodate slaves, reveal the care with which the traders organized themselves or proposed measures to the government which could facilitate growth of the traffic.[25]

Commerce with Angola increased annually; in 1819 we received 17,500 slaves, plus 2,732 quintals [hundredweight] of wax and 266 quintals of ivory; in 1820, 18,957 slaves, 2,144 quintals of wax and 320 of ivory;[26] in 1821, 20,000 slaves entered Rio and 15,000 in the first six months of 1822 alone.[27] In this same year Rio received 57 ships from Europe and 54 from Africa.[28] Colossal fortunes were made in this Angolan-Brazilian commerce, for example, that of the merchant João Barbosa Rodrigues who when he died left an estate of 3,000,000 cruzeiros; this was sent to Rio de Janeiro by the Governor of Angola on the war frigate *Dom Pedro,* where it was necessary to bribe high royal officials so that one of Rodrigues' heirs might receive it.[29] Or that of Manuel José de Souza Lopes, whose commercial house had an annual volume of over a million cruzeiros.[30] Rio de Janeiro and Bahia were the

---

[25] In 1819 400 *réis* were levied per Negro in order to construct the warehouses. See *Correio Brasiliense,* 1819, XXIII, 304.

[26] Official Letters from the Governor of Angola, Manuel Vieira de Albuquerque Tovar, giving information on the economic situation in Angola, signed in Luanda, January 23, 1821, and directed to Tomás Antônio de Vilanova Portugal. Arquivo Nacional, Box 642, Package 2, 1821.

[27] Alan K. Manchester, *British Preëminence in Brazil,* 1933, 182. For a documented example of commercial movements when Rio de Janeiro was the seat of the Portuguese Empire, see Olga Pantaleão, *Aspectos do Comércio dos Domínios Portuguêses no Período de 1808 a 1821.* Reprint from *Revista de História,* No. 41, São Paulo, 1960.

[28] See *Correio Brasiliense,* London, 1820, No. 25 267–280, and Luís Gonçalves dos Santos, *Memórias para servir à História do Reino do Brasil,* Lisbon, 1825, 2nd ed., Rio de Janeiro, 1943, II, 737.

[29] *Correio Brasiliense,* 1819, XXIII, 447.

[30] Document dated November 26, 1821, in Arquivo Nacional, Box 645, Angola, 1821, packages 2, 6.

centers for all legal or illegal business, in slaves or other commodities, conducted between South America and Africa, especially with Angola and Dahomey. One arrived from and departed for Africa at Rio de Janeiro.[31] But the most important business was the illegal slave trade conducted in forbidden zones by Portuguese and Brazilians, which from 1817 to 1850 attained an extraordinary volume.[32]

BRAZIL DOMINATES PORTUGUESE AFRICA. 1818–1826

With the slave traffic growing and with the expansion of commerce between Angola, Dahomey, and Brazil, there was an increase in the degree of dependence of the coast of Africa on our interests. It was not only because of the competition of cheaply or relatively cheaply produced Brazilian and Cuban products, sugar production being especially cheap in comparison with production of the British West Indies, that Great Britain insisted on abolition of the traffic[33] but also because the British desired, in order to have a free hand in future action, to break the solid bonds that the west coast of Africa was weaving with Brazil, particularly with Bahia and Rio de Janeiro. In that final act of insolence known as the Aberdeen Bill of 1845, the aim was to undo Afro-Brazilian relations with a view to the subjection of Africa that was to be promoted by the colonial powers, led by Great Britain with France following, from the middle of the century and especially after 1870.

The repatriation of Africans from Brazil was not uncommon, as Nina Rodrigues showed with respect to Hausas and other groups from Bahia to Dahomey, nor was it rare for Africans of the upper castes to come to Brazil to be educated, especially in Bahia. This was the case of "Xaxá" Souza's second wife, the daughter of the king of Dahomey.

---

[31] See *Registro de Estrangeiros*, 1808–1822, Publicações do Arquivo Nacional, 1960.

[32] The history of the traffic and its traders has not yet been written. It was Nina Rodrigues who called attention to this question by outlining the activities of Félix de Souza in Ajudá. J. F. de Almeida Prado collected much information, unfortunately without giving his sources. See his chapter, "A Bahia e suas Relações com o Daomé," in *O Brasil e o Colonialismo Europeu*, São Paulo, 1956, 115–226.

[33] F. Buxton in the House of Commons defended the policy of impeding the entry of Brazilian and Cuban sugar in order to favor that from the Antilles. Transcribed in *Jornal do Comércio*, July 31, 1850.

More than once when slave ships were captured, it was said that the Negroes were going to Brazil to be educated.[34]

We have already seen from the statistical data collected by the Governor of Angola, Manuel Vieira Albuquerque Tovar, how Angolan trade was concentrated upon Brazil, as well as the number of ships coming here. Brazil paid Empire expenses incurred in Portuguese Africa, and the entire Empire was seated at Rio de Janeiro; it is true that the Empire was governed by European ministers with Portuguese more than Brazilian interests at heart, but even so they felt the importance of working to the advantage of Brazil, which they still believed was also to the advantage of Portugal. It was in Rio de Janeiro on September 17, 1819, that the document was signed that made a city of the town of Mozambique.[35]

While Brazilian commerce with Africa was growing unceasingly, that of Portugal with Africa was decreasing annually. As Hipólito José Pereira da Costa Furtado de Mendonça wrote in the *Correio Brasiliense* in 1820, Portugal's smallness, the decadence of its agriculture and industry, and its total lack of resources were obvious; "however badly administered Brazilian resources are, they are superior to those that Portugal can manage in its present state. The population there is greater than Portugal's; the products of the soil are greater in quantity; finances are better, the food supply is more abundant, materials for the construction of ships are more available." [36]

Before Independence was realized, the lack of unity between the two kingdoms was evident, it no longer being possible to subordinate our interests and far greater resources to those of Portugal. The history of the Constitutional *Cortes* clearly shows that the new Portuguese political generation did not understand, nor could it, that Brazil was now more powerful than Portugal, not merely because the monarchy was established here but also in economic reality; it was in fact already the head of a community not yet ripe for establishment. As Francisco de Sierra y Mariscal wrote of the Brazilian Revolution, "before His Most Faithful Majesty went to Brazil there already existed a great conspiracy

---

[34] This was the case of Negroes imprisoned on the ship *Legítimo Africano*. See J. F. de Almeida Prado, *O Brasil e o Colonialismo*, 166.
[35] Transcribed in *Correio Brasiliense*, 1819, No. 22, 457.
[36] *Ibid.*, 1820, No. 24, 631.

against His royal authority." [37] And the conspiracy only continued to grow as Congress demonstrated its narrowness and expressed that hostility to Brazil which resulted from a feeling of inferiority, as may be seen in the fluency with which Deputy Trigoso stated what was needed to reduce Brazil again to the position of a Portuguese vassal state: "First, return the Royal Prince; second, remove the troops now there; third, send troops to subdue those now there; fourth, abolish some tribunals."

Against this background of over-simplification Chief Magistrate José Albano Fragoso wrote in 1820 that many Portuguese "were succumbing to the venom of jealousy"; the whole nation was fearful of becoming subjected to Brazil, for the stocks of colonial products to be sold only in Portugal were depleted, the provisioning of the colonies exclusively through the mother country had ended, and unlimited free commerce was bringing directly to Brazil trade that formerly went through Portugal.[38] All this was ending any possibility whatever of union, and the disunited kingdoms would follow their own destinies.

But before this, elections were held for the representatives from the Afro-Asian territories of the United Kingdoms of Portugal, Algarves, and Brazil to the *Cortes* Gerais [General Assembly] in Lisbon. Elected deputy from Angola was Counselor Euzébio de Queiroz Coutinho, father of our Euzébio de Queiroz Coutinho Matoso Câmara, both Angolans. The Counselor, a former colonial judge in Benguela, general magistrate in Angola, and then chief magistrate in Bahia practicing in the district of Sêrro Frio, had been chosen to be one of the founders of the new tribunal in Pernambuco. Euzébio de Queiroz preferred to serve in that tribunal as prosecutor for the Crown, appointed by José Bonifácio, rather than in the *Cortes,* as he was a partisan of African independence and union with Brazil; he remained here in his capacity as magistrate, and in 1828 became a member of the Supreme Tribunal created in that year.[39] His son, the fifth born but oldest of those

---

[37] "Idéias Gerais sôbre a Revolução do Brasil e as suas Conseqüências," *Anais da Biblioteca Nacional,* XLIII–IV, Rio de Janeiro, 1931, 59.
[38] Advisement dated in Rio de Janeiro, May 18, 1820, in Ângelo Pereira, *D. João IV Príncipe e Rei. A Independência do Brasil,* Lisbon, 1956, 310–315.
[39] Clemente José dos Santos, Barão de São Clemente. *Documentos para a História das Côrtes Gerais. . . . ,* 1883, I, 128.

surviving birth, was born in São Paulo de Luanda December 27, 1812, and came to Brazil at the age of three.[40] He was a judge here, chief of police, chief magistrate, deputy, minister, one of the most highly considered leaders of the conservative party, and in his opposition to the smugglers, author of the law bearing his name and abolishing the slave trade. A senator in 1854, Euzébio de Queiroz died on May 7, 1868. From these biographies of father and son it can be seen that Angola chose as its representative a judge who had served there, but who was living in Brazil at the time; born in Angola, his son as a politician in Brazil put an end to the Afro-Brazilian traffic in slaves.

The other deputies, Fernando Martins do Amaral Gurgel e Silva and Manuel Patrício Correia de Castro, came to Rio de Janeiro to discuss the advantages and disadvantages of going on to the *Cortes.* The *Cortes,* according to the words of Borges Carneiro on June 27, 1822, attributed the delay of its Angolan deputies to the hostility of Dom Pedro, which was keeping the Afro-Asian representatives from continuing their voyage from Rio.[41] It was even thought that they had been detained.[42] Euzébio had decided immediately in favor of Angolan independence and union with Brazil; the other two, coming from Angola, hesitated when they learned of the political course being followed by Brazil. Their dispute over what should be done may be seen in the proclamations that both sent to their Angolan compatriots, published in the *Correio do Rio de Janeiro* of June 20, 1822.[43]

Manuel Patrício did not think that Angola should go along with Brazil's complaints against the *Cortes,* although he recognized that commercial, political, and geographic relationships associated it with Brazil. He says that he was the first to hasten to Rio, "the place designated where all three deputies were to meet to go to Lisbon; the

---

[40] S. A. Sisson, *Galeria dos Brasileiros Illustres,* São Paulo, 1948, 2nd ed., 19–22. On the father, see Laurênio Lago, *Supremo Tribunal de Justiça e Supremo Tribunal Federal. Dados biográficos.* Imprensa Militar, 1940, 34–35.

[41] Passage from "Diários das Côrtes," transcribed in D. José de Almeida Correia de Sá, *D. João VI e a Independência do Brasil,* Lisbon, 1957, 39.

[42] In the research that I conducted from newspapers and documents of the National Archive I saw no confirmation of these rumors.

[43] The proclamation of Manuel Patrício Correia de Castro, "Compatriotas Angolenses," was signed on June 7; that of Fernando Martins do Amaral Gurgel e Silva, "Dulcis Amor Patriae," is dated June 21.

first of your representatives, elected unanimously by you, was already here" [Euzébio de Queiroz]. He thought that it would be a contravention of Angolan wishes if he deviated in any way from Euzébio de Queiroz' enlightened wisdom. He had gone to speak with him and the latter had advised him to delay his going, which would be "the surest act of prudence and the safest policy." He was not convinced, though he sensed that his other colleague, Amaral Gurgel e Silva, was of the same opinion as Euzébio de Queiroz, who had decided not to leave in view of the complaints of the Brazilian provinces against the Courts; he declared, "as you [the Angolans] are not part of the Kingdom of Brazil you must not enter into a duel for which you cannot even be called as witnesses or seconds." But he recognized that "your commercial relations must indeed lead you to embrace the cause of Brazil; you wish to have resources here, not so far from you, thus avoiding a long journey to the capital of the monarchy." For this very reason, however, he maintained that the deputies should present themselves at the Congress as quickly as possible, for only there could such a petition be made. He also recognized that the claims of the Angolan deputies "will receive no better attention than did those of Brazil." In this hesitation between Angola and Brazil and Angola and Portugal Deputy Patrício took leave of his colleagues and went on to Lisbon. If one must be on bad terms with anyone, writes the commentator of the *Correio do Rio de Janeiro,* better with Brazil than with Portugal.

More sensitive to Euzébio de Queiroz' arguments and to Brazilian political opinion, Amaral Gurgel e Silva preferred, as he writes in his proclamation, to await word from Angola and to see in the light of new circumstances, the possible separation of Brazil from Portugal, what ought to be the leaning of Angola, more bound to Brazil than to Portugal:

Circumstances unforeseen by you and by me at the time of the elections have caused me if not to turn back at least to halt my voyage, and I was seized by a certain remorse upon being compelled to delay my arrival at the Congress. But what else should I do, illustrious Angolans? At this Court I found spirits aggrieved by legislation of the sovereign Congress that seemed little in keeping with the category and dignity of kingdom to which Brazil has been elevated; the result was an urgent request from the Senate and people to install the Cortes in this capital, which was granted by the decree of His Royal Highness dated June 3 of this year; and knowing that our commercial relations and geographic position have much in common with Brazil, should I be so imprudent as not to halt my voyage to give pause for reflection? What benefit could accrue to my fatherland by a precipitous arrival in Portugal on my part? No, beloved compatriots, I am sensitive to the misfortunes of despised Angola; I have seen and wept for the evils that have long afflicted her. This is the occasion on which I hoped she would be saved from the last decline to which she was exposed by some of the pashas who have governed her. I hoped that a wise and foreward-looking Congress would make her rise to the equal of the rich provinces of the Lusitanian monarchy; but it is on this occasion that Brazil, resentful of the preparations and hostile measures revealed by the English newspapers as brought against it by the government in Lisbon, is taking broad steps toward its emancipation. What! would you not consider my conduct criminal if in such thorny circumstances I should not consult your will as to how to maintain union with both kingdoms?

What does Amaral Gurgel e Silva seek to obtain through this manifesto favoring union of the two kingdoms of Brazil and Angola? He desires the same mandate that will be given to the representatives of the Brazilian provinces to the Constituent and Legislative General Assembly of Brazil. As is known, in the second session of the Council of State, June 3, 1822,[44] the attorneys-general of the province had petitioned Dom Pedro to summon a general assembly. Amaral Gurgel wishes to represent Angola in this assembly and not in the *Cortes* of Lisbon, sensitive as he is to the misfortunes of Angola, the grievances of Brazil, and the hostilities of Portugal. "Send me your instructions, then, in a clear and decisive manner. Consider what means may effectively benefit our country."

The unity of Brazil and Angola in their patently common destiny seemed so clear that of three representatives two chose this path, leaving Deputy Patrício to follow the direction of metropolitan colonialism alone.

In Portugal the loss of Brazil was felt to be a threat, even if the African possessions were preserved. "Consider . . . with what skill Mr. J. B." (João Bernardo da Rocha Loureiro), wrote the *Gazeta Univer-*

---

[44] "Atas das Sessões do Conselho de Estado em 1822 e 1823," "Publicações do Arquivo Nacional, Rio de Janeiro, XVIII, 1918, 9. The Council of State was created by the decree of February 16, 1822, and the first session was held on June 2 of the same year.

sal,[45] "is conducting our interests among the select population of Angola, Pedra Encoje, Rio de Sena, Mozambique, and Cape Verde, in place of the degenerate Brazilians! Who can doubt that although the African colonies have not previously been advanced by the Portuguese, despite our having ruled them for almost four hundred years, they have now begun to make rapid growth in production and wealth after our sad farewell to Brazil?" But the situation was worse, for there were reports in Angola of the events in Lisbon and of the Brazilian move toward independence, which made the retention of Angola problematical because of its greater attachment to Portuguese America than to Portugal.

In Angola there was insecurity over the political situation, and the governor, Manuel Vieira de Albuquerque Tovar (1819–1821), communicated his apprehensions to Tomás Antônio Vilanova Portugal on March 31, 1821, when Dom João still resided in Rio de Janeiro. One of the leaders in the disorders of 1821, Joaquim Aurélio de Oliveira, had fled to Rio de Janeiro without permission and without passport.[46] Rio was the center for liberals and Masons aspiring to civil liberties. "Your Excellency knows," Angolan conservatives had written the Governor,[47]

that Elias Vieira de Andrade came here as a prisoner from Benguela, and they say that his chief crime was having been found with a catechism of the *Pedreiros livres* [48] on his person; the magistrate ordered him freed and he went to live at the home of Captain-Major Joaquim Aurélio, and later he was put in prison. On the day that the captain-major fled, he first went to see Vieira de Andrade at prison; the captain-major's flight was known to and arranged by his associates and companions, of whom the first was the Bishop and the second the magistrate; the Bishop already belonged to this group in Rio de Janeiro and the magistrate to one in Viana, and for this reason they immediately contacted one another; they and Felix Figueiredo, the surgeon-general, Campos, Souza Lopes, and others of the same crowd provided money and letters and all assisted his flight, the chief abettor being

---

[45] Transcribed from *Correio do Rio de Janeiro,* No. 46, June 4, 1822.

[46] "Ofício do Governador M. V. de Albuquerque Tovar a Thomás Antônio de Vilanova Portugal," 31/III/1821, in "Ofícios do Governador da Angola," Arquivo Nacional, Box 642, Package 2.

[47] Communication to the Governor, unsigned, of March 26, 1821, in "Ofícios," Aquivo Nacional, Box 542, Package 2.

[48] Who were uniformly liberal.

Meireles, the owner of the ship on which it is thought he fled, in whose house the Bishop is to be found almost every day. This gang is of long standing in Angola, dating from the time when their leader, Regimental Colonel da Linha Cabreira, was alive. Your Excellency knows well all the discussions that have taken place since the news from Portugal; they and others say that we must follow Portugal and change the government; they want to send Your Excellency to Rio de Janeiro.

Joaquim Aurélio, the leader of the disorders, was a captain-major who had gone to Angola from Minas Gerais, of which he was a native, and who had fled to Rio de Janeiro carrying papers signed by the rebels that the Bishop had given him. Manuel Vieira had been able to overcome this first rebellion, and as a good subject had in July sent Cavalry Captain Paulo Antônio to Rio whence he was to go to Lisbon to kiss His Majesty's hand,[49] after first paying his respects to the Regent of Brazil, Dom Pedro. Constantly menaced by the Angolan liberals, Vieira did not govern long, and on August 23 he communicated to Count de Arcos that he was in Pernambuco on his way to Lisbon and excused himself for not presenting himself to Dom Pedro.[50] His replacement, Joaquim Inácio de Lima, governed no longer than a few months, for on February 6, 1822, the Provisory Junta was installed, composed of seven members presided over by Bishop Friar Dom João Damasceno Póvoas.[51] It was to these people, accused of belonging to the Rio faction, that Deputy Amaral Gurgel e Silva addressed himself. As in Brazil, strong liberal currents were striving for a more autonomous regime and many dreamed of an association with Brazil, as we shall see below.

In Mozambique, with a small population in 1821 of 552 settlers and

---

[49] "Ofício de Manuel Vieira de Albuquerque Tovar ao Conde dos Arcos," July 2, 1821. Arquivo Nacional, Box and Package cited. In the Ofício of July 3rd he reports that he had just discovered that Dom João had left for Lisbon.
[50] "Ofício de Manuel Vieira de Albuquerque Tovar ao Conde dos Arcos, de Pernambuco," July 23, 1821. Arquivo Nacional, Box and Package cited.
[51] Friar Dom Damasceno da Silva Póvoas was a minor reformed religious Franciscan from the Province of the Conception in Rio de Janeiro, and was appointed by Dom João on December 17, 1812. See Arquivo Nacional, "Roma e Nunciatura, 1809–1817," Codicil 271, Book 1, 63. In the Archive there are several documents by him, the most interesting being the one in which he justifies the lack of pomp and commemorative celebrations at the restoration of Angola on August 15, 1648. His greatest concern was the education and ordination of the Indian clergy in Brazil.

4,400 slaves,[52] Governor João da Costa Brito Sanches was deposed as
soon as the liberal movement was discovered on June 25 of that year and
replaced by a junta composed of the Bishop of São Tomé, Brigadier João
Vicente de Cardina, Joaquim Antônio Ribeiro, Francisco de Paula, and
Baltazar Manuel de Souza e Brito. The new governor, sent from Rio de
Janeiro and still appointed by Dom João, left Brazil on March 23, but
the Provisory Government in Mozambique prohibited his landing, later
granted in his capacity as private citizen, for they would recognize only
the authority of the *Cortes*. But the troops took his side: he was a
lieutenant-general, and so was elected president of the junta, with the
Bishop as vice-president.[53]

Mozambique, which had not elected deputies to the *Cortes* because of
its small population, saw itself involved in the question of the deputies
from Goa, who had arrived there on the transport ship *Leucônia* on
October 1, 1822, on their way to Lisbon, but were afraid of stopping at
Rio de Janeiro, for the news of Brazil's liberty made them fear reprisal or
detention—besides which they did not trust Commander Desidério
Manuel da Costa who was close to the government of Rio de Janeiro.[54]
Antônio José de Lima Leitão, Bernardo Peres da Silva, and Constâncio
Roque da Costa, the deputies from Goa, alleged that the Provisory Junta
of the Government of India had paid the commander of their ship a fee,
partly in currency and partly in saltpeter, to deliver it to the Junta of the
Public Treasury in Rio de Janeiro, plus 300,000 réis as payment for
passage and rations for them and two servants; they further said that

---

[52] This is the population given by Bordalo (see the following note), but the ofício
of João Manuel da Silva to José Bonifácio, October 1, 1822 (Arquivo Nacional,
Box 728, Package 1), calculates it at more than 3,000 settlers.

[53] Francisco Maria Bordalo, *Ensaios Sôbre Estatística das Possessões Portuguêsas,* continuation of the work of J. J. Lopes Lima, Lisbon, 1962, IV (Mozambique), 127. The movement is described in a very rare pamphlet by Joaquim
Antônio Ribeiro, printed in Rio de Janeiro, *Memória Descritiva, da forma por
que foi estabelecido o sistema do Ex-Governador e Capitão-General J. da Costa
Brito Sanches e do seu sucessor Tenente-General João Manuel da Silva,* Rio de
Janeiro, Oficina de Silva Pôrto, 1822.

[54] "Ofícios de João Manuel da Silva a José Bonifácio de Andrada sôbre os sucessos
em Moçambique de três deputados eleitos às Côrtes pela Província de Goa."
Mozambique, October 1, 1822. With enclosures. Arquivo Nacional, Box 748,
Package 1.

the commander ridiculed and spoke out against the political regenera-
tion of the monarchy and insisted in continuing to Rio de Janeiro and
not directly to Lisbon, when from the papers and public rumors it was
known that "the Royal Prince and the dominant party in Rio de Janeiro
have taken a hostile attitude against the Portuguese in Europe, the
Cortes and the King, even preventing the voyage of the deputies from
Minas and Angola to Lisbon, which greatly disturbs the petitioners who
sincerely love and defend the integrity of the present Portuguese
monarchy with its absolute equality of rights and possible equality of
opportunity." The commander "publicly stated that he was responsible
only to the Prince Regent of Brazil, even after this ill-advised Prince had
refused due obedience to the *Cortes* and King." For this reason they
demanded an inquiry into the conduct of Desidério Manuel da Costa,
the commander, and his imprisonment and removal to Lisbon, "in
order to be investigated there in accord with the decision that created
the Commission on Infractions," and they further wished that the
money paid by the Junta of the Treasury of Goa to that of Rio de
Janeiro for their rations be turned over to them. Without entering into
political questions, the commander of the transport declared himself
disposed to deliver the money to the Governor "with the precautions
necessary for my exoneration in Rio de Janeiro"; that "the 300,000 réis
for rations were spent during the ninety-day voyage, which was exactly
the time required for the voyage to Rio de Janeiro," and that if "this
sum seemed large to the petitioners," it was "the least amount paid from
India to Rio de Janeiro," for "the usual cost is 400,000 réis for no better
rations."

João Manuel da Silva denied the requests of the Goan deputies, barely
granting them food and lodging while they were there, and immediately took precautions against, especially, Lima Leitão and Peres who
were going about agitating Mozambicans, publishing proclamations,
and demanding elections and reforms of the government. Alleging that
no election had been held because of the small number of inhabitants
but promising to take measures inasmuch as "other peoples of less
political importance have sent their deputies," João Manuel da Silva
imposed order and declared that the decree of February 27, 1822, had
ordered the preservation of the governments on the coast of Africa with

their former powers. He affirmed in an edict that "the authority of the government will permit of no change, and those who oppose it will be considered guilty of treason."

In his communication to José Bonifácio, João Manuel da Silva hoped that with the departure of the Goan deputies Mozambique would become peaceful. As they wished to continue directly to Lisbon, "without touching the ports of Brazil, which are hostile to Portugal," they were going on to the Cape of Good Hope. They would leave "because of the war they have declared here between Brazil and Portugal." The Goan deputies requested their passports for Table Bay on September 3, although they had formerly arranged for passage on the galley *Flor de Cintra* sailing to Pernambuco. "The news now is that there is almost complete anarchy in Pernambuco, the government has no authority and the insubordinate colored rabble is insulting and killing Europeans and even the most respectable people of the country."

The two deputies, so prejudiced, so anti-Brazilian, so badly informed on the supposed detention of the Angolan deputies, two of whom in point of fact favored the union of Angola and Brazil, insisted in view of the situation at the ports of Rio de Janeiro and Pernambuco that their transport—"a ship of war belonging to the nation and having no function in Rio de Janeiro, unless it be that of being sent on some expedition against the mother country or some other part of the Monarchy that may be attached to it (*sic*) (perhaps Angola?)"—should have no other commission than that of "taking the Indian deputies and their government's important official papers to the *Cortes*."[55]

The fact was that despite all their protests and demands and the decision of December 21, 1822,[56] giving approval for the organization of Brazilian privateers to attack "the commerce, ships, and properties of the Portuguese of the Kingdom of Portugal, in view of the many varied

---

[55] The transport came to Rio whence it continued to Vigo. The Portuguese authorities there requested that it be turned over to them and the Spanish ordered it to leave port. See Clemente A. de O. Mendes e Almeida, "Memorando," in *Publicações do Arquivo Nacional,* Rio de Janeiro, 1903, IV, 146.

[56] Session of the Council of State, No. 23, December 21, 1822, in "Atas das Sessões do Conselho de Estado em 1822 e 1823," *Publicações do Arquivo Nacional,* Rio de Janeiro, 1918, XVIII, 42.

attacks of their government against the Empire of Brazil and the person of its Emperor," the deputies arrived separately in Rio: Bernardo Peres on the galley *Flor de Cintra* and Lima Leitão on the ship *Príncipe Regente,* on January 16 and 20, 1823. Dom Pedro was informed that the aforementioned deputies, "in addition to being generally considered enemies of the cause of Brazil, are equally known as anarchists and revolutionaries, which has been verified by official communications sent from that city [Angola] where by their scandalous and detestable procedures against the government and public tranquility their perversity became most notable," and ordered the chief magistrate of Paço, the General Superintendent of Police, "to have them forthwith placed in custody in one of the fortresses of this port; however, Constantino Roque da Costa, who is detained on board the aforementioned galley, shall be set free and in full liberty." [57] So the presumptuous gentlemen whose activities in Mozambique against Brazil were reported by João Manuel to José Bonifácio ended up in the fortress of Santa Cruz, where they remained from January 23 to February 17, when Dom Pedro decided that they should be transported on a Danish ship en route to Lisbon.[58]

While Rio de Janeiro, with or without the King Dom João, was the political center of the problems of popular representation of Angola, Mozambique, and Goa, in Cape Verde, Cacheu, and Bissau the *Inconfidente* José de Rezende Costa, who as we have seen had been exiled there, was elected deputy to replace two deputies, Manuel Antônio Martins and Dom Antônio Coutinho de Lancastre, the latter a native of Pôrto, ex-governor of the islands of Cape Verde, and then residing in Rio de Janeiro, as was Euzébio de Queiroz. The irritating boldness of sending an *Inconfidente* like José de Rezende Costa as a replacement to represent Cape Verde was an obvious threat to the integrity of the colonies that were influenced by Brazilian ideas and by the politics of Rio de Janeiro. The elections of Dom Antônio Coutinho

----

[57] See "Registro do Gabinete de José Bonifácio de Andrade e Silva," in *Publicações do Arquivo Nacional,* Rio de Janeiro, 1918, XVIII, 110. The order is No. 109, dated January 23, 1823.

[58] *Ibid.,* Dispatch No. 115, p. 112, and Notice No. 114, both dated February 17, 112 and 60.

de Lancastre and his replacement, José de Rezende Costa, were set aside and another election approved by the *Cortes* was held.[59]

This whole series of events throughout Portuguese Africa and Asia shows the web of relationships, the coördinated influence exercised by Brazil upon the Portuguese Afro-Asian world, not to mention the effect of the traders and freed slaves returned to Africa taking Brazilian customs, traditions, and language to Dahomey and the whole Gulf of Guinea.

The visit of the representative of the King of Benim and Onim (Nigeria) was another curious event that revealed the close bonds existing between Brazil and Africa even after our independence. He arrived in Rio on the schooner *Mariana* on July 6, 1824, when the difficult negotiations about the recognition of Brazilian independence were under way. He was given an audience by Dom Pedro, attended the solemn christening of the prince, but was granted not even a second interview. The representative of Benim referred to his friendship with Dom João and stated that his "Emperor and King" was first in recognizing Brazil's independence. Dom Pedro, however, looked to Africa for a steady supply of slaves, not for official relations with tribal chiefs.[60]

Large parts of the African coast felt Brazilian influence, and not only Portugal but also Great Britain, which was beginning its second imperialist expansion, preferred to see these increasingly close ties broken. For this reason, when Brazilian independence was achieved there was obvious fear of an Afro-Brazilian union, already suggested to the Angolans by Euzébio de Queiroz and Amaral Gurgel in Rio de Janeiro. What should Dom João, Portugal's king, do? Remain inactive, merely trying to defend the colonies on the coast of Africa, or attempt to occupy some part of Brazil? That was one of the urgent questions confronting the Council of State he convoked in January of 1824,[61] when British pressure to separate Portugal from Brazil and Brazil from Africa, and thus to impose itself freely, became greater.

---

[59] Barão de São Clemente (Clemente José Dos Santos), *Documentos para a História das Côrtes Gerais da Nação Portuguêsa*, Lisbon, 1833–1889, I, 128.
[60] Arquivo Histórico do Itamarati. Ambassador Manoel Alves of Lima, 1824–1826, 273, I, 13.
[61] See Ângelo Pereira, *D. João VI Príncipe e Rei, A Independência do Brasil*, Lisbon, 1956, 364–371.

It was recognized then that Portugal did not have the means in men or money to subjugate Brazil and that Great Britain was interested in Brazil's freedom, while Monroe's declaration had to be kept in mind. For all these reasons there was fear not only of hostilities from Brazil, harassment of commerce and of Portuguese loyal to Portugal, and seizure of Portuguese ships in Brazilian waters, but even of the intention attributed to the Brazilian government, by the Goan deputies, "to place a small fleet under the command of this officer [John Taylor] for the purpose of seizing several Portuguese possessions on the coast of Africa." [62] This last report reached Lisbon in 1824, after a movement for independence and approval of Brazilian freedom had already begun in Benguela. Events in Brazil caused a profound impression in Angola, especially in Benguela where union with the new American state was considered.[63]

Euzébio de Queiroz the elder was not far from the truth, then, when he attempted to induce his two fellow-deputies to take Brazil's side, to support Angola's independence and union with the new Empire. His effort failed, but it showed the strength of economic relations between Angola and Brazil and the strength of liberal ideas.

It has been proved by statistical data that after complete separation from Brazil, Portugal supplied a little over one-fifth of Luanda's imports, the remaining four-fifths coming from Brazil. Lopes Lima writes: "I see from an official map that in 1823 imports from Brazil amounted to CR$686,000 and those from Portugal CR$131,000, to which countries Luanda sent more than four-fifths of its exports with Portugal receiving less than one-fifth." [64] As the two deputies from Angola stated in their proclamations in Rio in 1822, Brazil's commercial superiority over Portugal was clear. For this very reason, in the peace negotiations between Brazil and Portugal when an attempt was still being made to find bases for union, and in the subsequent treaty, it was expressly declared that "the possessions of the Crown in Asia, Africa, and islands

---

[62] Clemente A. de O. Mendes E. Almeida, "Memorando em que se consigna uma notícia fidedigna e na máxima parte documentada," in *Publicações do Arquivo Nacional,* Rio de Janeiro, 1903, 144.

[63] *História de Portugal,* ed. by Damião Peres, Barcelos, 1935, VII, 565. See also J. J. Lopes Lima, *Ensaios sôbre Estatística das Possessões Portuguêsas na África Ocidental . . . ,* Liston, 1844–1862, Book 3, 125; and Francisco Castelbranco, *História de Angola,* Luanda, 1932, 183–194.

[64] J. J. Lopes Lima, *op. cit.,* Book III, Part I, XXXVII.

adjacent to the continent shall forever continue to be considered dependencies of the Crown of Portugal." [65]

This occurred in 1824 when Dom Miguel, Count of Vila Real, was returning to Portugal from his mission in London. He feared as did Dom João and the constitutionalists that the Portuguese possessions would follow Brazil's example and then join the Brazilian Empire. In 1823 in Rio de Janeiro, however, Dom Pedro had informed Henry Chamberlain, the British Minister, that "With regard to Colonies on the coast of Africa, we want none; nor anywhere else; Brazil is quite large enough and productive enough for us, and we are content with what Providence has given us." [66] The Portuguese fear was unwarranted, therefore; Dom Pedro's ambitions were limited to Brazil, as were those of the ruling minority in Brazil, who merely felt injured by English demands for abolition of the slave trade. We were born free of colonialist aspirations, although we were an Empire.

In 1822 George Canning wrote to the Duke of Wellington that the Allies could be certain that no new state in the New World would be recognized by Great Britain unless it had openly and completely abolished the slave trade.[67] And in 1823 he affirmed that recognition was a question of time, but made clear that

The Brazilian Government cannot be unaware how deeply the faith and honour of this country are engaged in the compleat and final abolition of the Slave Trade. The Crown of Portugal is the only European Crown which has with-holden its consent from the principle of that measure, and it has done this expressly on the plea of providing for the cultivation of Brazil. The altered relations of Brazil and Portugal altogether invalidate that plea, for it is preposterous to suppose that Portugal can at once declare Brazil in rebellion and pretend to a right to keep up a trade, admitted to be otherwise indefensible, for the benefit of Brazil. But if Brazil should take that abominable trade into its own hands, and if Great Britain should, at the moment when that new trade begins, hasten to recognize the Power which undertakes it, I leave M. de Andradà [José Bonifácio] to judge what

---

[65] "Bases para o auto de reconciliação entre Portugal e o Brasil, enviadas pelo Gabinete de Lisboa para Londres," 1824. In Clemente A. de O. Mendes E. Almeida, "Memorando," *Publicações do Arquivo Nacional,* Rio de Janeiro, 1903, IV, 205, Base No. 13.

[66] Henry Chamberlain to George Canning (secret), from Rio de Janeiro, April 2, 1823, in C. K. Webster, *Britain and the Independence of Latin America,* Oxford University Press, 1938, I, 222.

[67] September 27, 1822, *ibid.,* II, 74.

would be the sentiment excited in Europe, what in Portugal herself, upon whom we have never ceased to urge the expediency and duty of abolition. The Recognition of Brazil would in that case be not only the Recognition of a new Power, but of a Power distinguished from all other States in the vast extent of the New World by its solitary adherence to the Slave Trade.[68]

George Canning's entire correspondence always insists on this same point: recognition depends on the abolition of slavery, "the great question hanging over this country," "the only great market for the slave trade." But mercantile interests in the United Kingdom required the continuation of commercial relations and could not understand that taking part in the quarrel between Portugal and Brazil placed Britain on the side of the Mother Country which, contrary to the treaty of 1810, had raised the duty on English goods to 30 per cent while Brazil had contented itself with the 15 per cent stipulated in the treaty.[69]

In this weighing by Great Britain of its commercial interests in Brazil and in the abolition of slavery, and of Brazil's interests in not abolishing the importation of slaves, the great idea of British diplomacy—along with the imposition of abolition, obviously, to which Brazil would subscribe without wishing to comply—consisted of forcing the separation of Angola from Brazil, thus also satisfying the Portuguese objective of retaining its best possession. And for this reason the Treaty of Peace and Alliance between Dom Pedro, Emperor of Brazil, and Dom João VI, King of Portugal, that recognized the independence of Brazil stated in Article III: "His Imperial Majesty promises not to accept the proposals of any Portuguese colonies to join the Empire of Brazil." [70] Now the close commercial relations already noted, which would continue to be important for a decade, the movements in Angola and Benguela, and Dom Pedro's insistence on recognition as Emperor, while Dom João was only King, made the former's intentions suspect and increased fears of a movement on the part of the African colonies to join the new State. And this would be inadmissible not only to Portugal but also to Great Britain, the intermediary in the negotiations whose recognition was considered indispensable.

The interpretation of the third clause of the treaty leaves no doubt

---

[68] George Canning to Henry Chamberlain, February 15, 1823, *ibid.,* I, 220–221.

[69] Memorandum from Canning to the Cabinet, November 15, 1822, *ibid.,* II, 395.

[70] For the Treaty, see in A. Pereira Pinto, *Apontamentos para o Direito Internacional,* Rio de Janeiro, 1864, I, 323.

that it was an English imposition, despite Dom Pedro's affirmations to the contrary. Hildebrando Accioly has written that "this clause was no doubt very important to Great Britain, interested as it was in abolishing the slave trade, because as the slaves imported into Brazil came from the Portuguese colonies in Africa, it is easy to understand that the union of those colonies to the Empire of Brazil would make the suppression of the traffic more difficult, while if they continued under the dominion of Portugal England could induce the Portuguese government to prohibit such commerce." [71] If Dom Pedro acceded to this yet not to suppression of his title of Emperor, which also made the negotiations quite difficult, it was because the English raised their heaviest objections here. He had been amply warned, both by the French representative, Count Gestas, and by the Austrian, Baron Wenzel de Mareschal. The former, writing to the Viscount of Paranaguá, Minister of Foreign Affairs, inquired concerning the negotiations of Sir Charles Stuart: "Was it a matter of Emperor of Brazil only, or of Emperor of Brazil, the Indian Colonies, and Africa?" [72] And Mareschal had advised Dom Pedro not to renounce the inheritance of the Portuguese Crown and the possibility of joining it to that of Brazil, so that one day he might reign over more than four million subjects, as well as acquire vast dominions in Asia and Africa. [73]

The treaty of 1825 was the first in a series of steps taken to cut the bonds uniting Brazil and Angola. The second was to be the agreement of 1826, which satisfied the English demand for abolition that had been a preliminary to the Agreement of 1825. In it the Emperor of Brazil and His Majesty the King of the United Kingdom of Great Britain recognized that because of the separation of Brazil from Portugal they should renew, confirm, and fully enforce the stipulations of the treaties for the regulation and abolition of the slave trade on the coast of Africa. It was not a question of making the previous stipulations binding on Brazil; Article I agreed that three years after the exchange of ratifications (exchanged in London on March 13, 1827) it would be illegal for Brazilian subjects to engage in the slave trade on the coast of Africa

[71] *O Reconhecimento da Independência do Brasil,* Rio de Janeiro, 1927, 214.
[72] "Do Conde de Gestas a Paranaguá," Rio, October 26, 1825, in *Arquivo Diplomático da Independência,* Rio de Janeiro, 1922, III, 290.
[73] Tobias Monteiro, *História do Império, O Primeiro Reinado,* Rio de Janeiro, 1939, I, 417.

under any pretext or in any manner whatever. Henceforth its continuation would be considered and treated as piracy.[74]

The price of recognition was therefore not only special favors, concessions, and privileges, but especially the agreement to abolish slavery, a step that promised to ruin Brazil's agriculture. On April 23, 1823, José Bonifácio told Henry Chamberlain that abolition had been discussed the previous day by the Council of State, which had become convinced of the impropriety of the slave trade and the advisability and propriety of putting an end to it. José Bonifácio further told Chamberlain that he knew that the British government was very anxious about this point, and that the Brazilian government was ready to fix the period in which the trade should cease completely with regard to Brazil. But he was obliged to state frankly that abolition could not be immediate for two reasons, one economic and the other political. The first was based on the absolute need to assure an increase in the white population prior to abolition so that agriculture might continue, for with the supply of slaves cut off, it would regress and suffer great damage. So far no step had been taken in that direction, but thought was being given to measures to attract European emigrants, thus diminishing the need for Africans. The Brazilian government sincerely desired to see that moment arrive. The second consideration was based on political advisability and referred to the popularity and perhaps even the stability of the government. The government could risk facing the claims and petitions of merchants and others involved in slave commerce, but could not without great danger—which no sensible man would think of incurring—attempt at that time to suggest a measure that would indispose the whole population of the interior. Almost all agricultural labor was done by Negroes and slaves. The whites unfortunately worked very little, and if landowners should see their supply of workers suddenly curtailed, the consequences for the government and even for the country would be unpredictable. All classes would consider their prosperity cut off at the roots.[75]

---

[74] For the Agreement, see in A. Pereira Pinto *Apontamentos para o Direito Internacional,* I, 389–393.

[75] Dispatch from Henry Chamberlain to George Canning (secret), Rio de Janeiro, April 26, 1823, in C. K. Webster, *Britain,* I, 223–224. This same opinion was expressed by José Bonifácio in his instructions of February 24, 1823, to Marshal Felisberto Caldeira Brant Ponte, Brazilian agent in London. See A. Pereira Pinto, *Apontamentos,* I, 312, No. 11.

GREAT BRITAIN EXPELS BRAZIL. AGREEMENT OF
1826 AND PARLIAMENTARY DEBATES

Despite this clear explanation of the consequences of immediate abolition, the Agreement of 1826, ratified by the Emperor in 1827, extended
the legality of the traffic for only three years. The result was to be the
lasting conflict that until 1850 complicated our relations with Great
Britain, which attempted to enforce exact compliance with the agreement while the traders organized the greatest contraband in our
history.

In an official letter addressed to the Chamber, the Minister of Foreign
Affairs, Marquis de Queluz, explained the government's difficulty in
concluding the arrangement with the British Plenipotentiary in view of
the legislative proposal to abolish slavery within six years. The Brazilian
government had stressed that it preferred to wait in order to proceed
"with all circumspection in an affair of such vital importance to the
nation," but the representative of Great Britain had replied that he did
not believe His Majesty's sentiments had changed and that he had been
sent not to prolong but to shorten the length of time granted for the
liquidation of the slave trade; that, furthermore, as the traffic was
already prohibited north of the Equator, His Britannic Majesty had
wished to show his consideration for the interests of the Empire by
ceasing to require the Portuguese government to comply with its
existing treaties with England according to which the traffic was
prohibited. "Otherwise, within six months Brazil would have no port at
all at which to conduct the traffic except as contraband; for resistance on
the part of the Brazilian government would be completely useless"; the
British would either make Portugal close its African ports to the Brazilian slave trade or would use the British fleet to deny access of Brazilian
ships to them. The government, concluded the Marquis de Queluz, João
Severiano Maciel da Costa, had acted for the "good of the nation by
conceding willingly what would have been taken from it by force." [76]

---

[76] "Ofício from Marquis de Queluz to the Secretary of the Chamber of Deputies,
José Antônio da Silva Maia," May 22, 1822, in *Anais do Parlamento Brasileiro,*
Session of 1827, Rio de Janeiro, 1875, I, 154. The Ofício is reproduced in III, Session of July 2, 1827. The Marquês de Queluz was substituted in November 20,
1827, after the debate was over, by the Marquês de Aracati, João Carlos Augusto
de Oyenhausen, a Portuguese by birth, who after the abdication of Dom Pedro
I accompanied him, and was Governor of Mozambique in 1837.

On June 16 of the same year the Diplomatic Commission discussed this official letter and in its opinion approved the agreement by a three to two vote, then sending it to the Legislative Commission for proposals for laws "concerning piracy and the control of its necessary circumstances and requisites." The opinion stated that "this agreement deprives Brazil of great revenues and of labor for its agriculture." [77]

The two dissenting votes were those of Brigadier Raimundo da Cunha Matos (1776–1839) and Luís Augusto May. The former had come to Brazil in 1816, after having served in Africa for nineteen years, had embraced the cause of independence and became identified with the agricultural interests, being one of the founders of the Sociedade Auxiliadora da Indústria Nacional.[78] His vote and his speeches in the plenary session are decisive and enlightening. For him the agreement was "derogatory to honor, interest, dignity, independence, and Brazilian sovereignty" for several reasons: (1) because it attacked the fundamental law of the Empire, for by it the government attributed to itself the right to legislate, a right that could be exercised only by the Assembly; it submitted Brazilian subjects to English tribunals and justice, which were totally incompetent, and deprived them of the liberty to trade and traffic in slaves in African ports free and independent of the Crown of Portugal; (2) "because it is enormously prejudicial to the national commerce, which is excluded from the best markets by British and French competition favored in the concessions of the treaties of 1810 and 1826"; (3) "because it ruins agriculture, the vital foundation of the nation's existence, which depends on slaves"; (4) "because it destroys our shipping," the most substantial part of which was engaged directly or indirectly in the slave trade, not to mention the removal of the means

---

[77] *Anais do Parlamento Brasileiro*, Session of July 16, Rio de Janeiro, 1875, II, 79–80.
[78] For bibliography, see in Inocêncio José da Silva, *Dicionário Biobibliográfico Brasileiro*, VII, 52–53; Sacramento Blake, *Dicionário Biobibliográfico Brasileiro*, VII, 112–115, and the various biographies in *Revista do Instituto Histórico e Geográfico Brasileiro*, especially that by Manuel de Araújo Pôrto Alegre, XI, 1st ed., 219–234. His work, "Compêndio Histórico das Possessões de Portugal na África," may be found in the Instituto Histórico e Geográfico Brasileiro, and was published in 1963 by the Arquivo Nacional, with a preliminary note by José Honório Rodrigues (7–21). His unpublished "Estado Presente das Colônias Portuguêsas no Costa da África," may be found in the Gabinete Português de Leitura.

of subsistence for a very large number of persons who had an interest "in the African and Asian markets, where despite repeated acts of British intervention there is still great consumption of our brandies and tobaccos (the only commodities in which they cannot compete with us); thus [we are] *losing our ancient* and valuable commerce in gold, ivory, palm oil, wax, textiles, resin, and many other goods in which we formerly traded"; (5) "because it is a cruel blow to the revenues of the State," for the public treasury collected an import duty of more than 20 per cent on each slave and on other items imported in quantity and passing through customs; (6) "because it is premature," as "we do not now have in the Empire a large enough population to permit us to reject the heavy recruitment of Negro people who through the course of time and mixture with other races will eventually give us active citizens and intrepid defenders of our fatherland"; [79] (7) "finally, because it is inopportune," "having been arranged at a time when the Chamber of Deputies had already presented a proposal to reduce the importation of slaves into Brazil gradually and when the islands of the Azores, from which we could receive a great number of laborious settlers to populate the shores and hinterlands of our Empire, no longer belong to us."

After stating these fundamental points, Cunha Matos expressed the belief that our negotiators had been filled with panic terror before the English threats and that the example of other nations was of no use to us, especially as the English and North Americans had not been coerced into declaring the trade piracy; they had acted spontaneously of their own free will. "Each governs its affairs as it sees fit." It was not the Legislative Assembly that made the law: "It was the English who dictated it, the English who are imposing it upon us and the English who are to execute it against the unfortunate Brazilians so harshly threatened by them." He showed that the situation of the English and North American population was entirely different from ours and concluded his dissenting vote in the Diplomatic Commission with this

[79] Cunha Matos was one of the first to examine the problem of immigration. See "Memória Histórica sôbre a População, Emigração, e Colonização que convém ao Império do Brasil," 1837, in *O Auxiliador da Indústria Nacional*, 1873, 344–364. He was also one of the first to collect statistics on our population. See Relatório presented to the Comissão de Estatística da Câmara dos Deputados, Session of October 8, 1827, in *Anais do Parlamento Brasileiro*, Rio de Janeiro, 1875, V, 108–III.

vigorous declaration: "I disapprove therefore of the agreement made with the British government on the enforced abolition of the slave trade (enforced by threats of hostilities in the case of opposition on our part). I disapprove of the unconstitutional decree [that the trade constitutes] the crime of piracy and of all the barbarous consequences that will follow, and I declare that the government and Brazilian nation were coerced, obliged, oppressed, subjected, and compelled by the English government to an onerous and degrading agreement that concerns internal, domestic, and purely national affairs in the exclusive competence of the free and sovereign legislative power and the august head of the Brazilian nation." [80]

The other dissenting vote was that of Luís Augusto May (1782–1850), deputy from Minas Gerais, founder and director of *A Malagueta*.[81] This agreement and any other treaties concerning "the interest and security of the State presented to this Chamber after ratification, without having been communicated to the legislative body between their conclusion and ratification, cannot be the object of deliberation . . . , for such deliberation would be completely academic in the eyes of all parties." Its tardy submission to the Chamber was a fiction to which the government had had recourse in order to place responsibility on some one, when it should be seeking "to improve the plight to which Brazil is reduced by the rapid conclusion of the British treaty . . . and the consequent future problems of the paper currency and of the total cessation of commerce." [82]

The debates against the agreement in the sessions of July 2, 3, and 4 were tempestuous, beginning with a long and very able speech by

---

[80] The vote is transcribed in *Anais do Parlamento Brasileiro*, Session of June 16, 1827, Rio de Janeiro, 1875, II, 80–81 and in *Anais*, Session of July 2, 1827, III, 11–12. In this last session it is accompanied by his speech in the Plenary Session, 12–18.

[81] Political newspaper of Rio de Janeiro, published from December 18, 1821, to June 5, 1822, followed by *Malagueta Extraordinária*, published from July 31, 1822, to August 10, 1824. See on L. A. May and the *Malagueta*, Hélio Viana, *Contribução à História da Imprensa Brasileira* (1822–1869), Rio de Janeiro, 1945, 503–534, and facsimile reprint of *A Malagueta*, Rio, Zélio Valverde, 1945, with introduction by Hélio Viana.

[82] The declaration was transcribed in *Anais do Parlamento Brasileiro*, Session, June 16, 1827, Rio de Janeiro, 1875, II, 81, and III, 10–11.

Cunha Matos.[83] He did not propose to defend the justice and perpetual suitability of the slave trade for the Brazilian Empire, said Cunha Matos, but maintained that "the moment has not arrived for us to abandon the importation of slaves, for although it is an evil, it is a lesser evil than not importing them"; the commerce "should terminate only when, and by the means, judged most convenient by the Brazilian nation, admitting no influence from Britain, whose views were diametrically opposed to development of the great Brazilian resources that may one day be prejudicial to Great Britain's ambitious designs." In this three thoughts may be seen already clearly delineated: (1) the disadvantage of abolition for the national interests: (2) opposition to British interventionist policy; and (3) the future expansionist action of Britain in Africa in opposition to Brazil. Indeed, it was easier to defeat Portugal in its claims to broad dominion on the African coast than to prevent close ties between Brazil and Africa later.

Cunha Matos maintained that the treaty was invalid, first, because it had been extorted from our government by force, violence, and threats; second, because of the great harm resulting from it to Brazilian agriculture, commerce, and national revenue; and third, because it contravened the fundamental law of the Empire by subjecting Brazilian citizens to judgment before foreign tribunals, a situation that Adams had rejected as unacceptable to the United States. He then analyzed the reduction in national commerce, which had been dominated by the English and French since the opening of the ports; he showed that our merchants had been obliged to limit themselves to trade with the African coast and Asia, trade that was now totally disrupted by the agreement, and he declared that "the English wish to become the lords of Africa." "Formerly it was we who derived sole benefit from these great riches. Today it is the English." Always very clear, very independent, and very nationalistic, Cunha Matos stated that with Dom João's departure almost thirty thousand persons had abandoned Brazil, the German settlers "worth their weight in gold" had not been employed in agriculture and were few in number, while the British Colonies were flooded with about two hundred and fifty Negroes to nineteen whites per league. The treaty of 1810 had already reduced our navy to nothing,

---

[83] *Anais,* II, 12–18.

ruined our shipyards, forced the surrender of our commerce, channeled the flow of Brazil's precious metals to London, and even the small factories in Minas manufacturing cotton textiles and blankets had been destroyed. The English had begun this destruction and the French had completed it. "I do not reproach the English, they are doing what for them is right; I merely reproach our insensitivity!" And he returned to his basic thesis, which he was one of the first to hold that the English fight for abolition was moved by the desire to separate us from Africa in order to possess it for England. This was the English objective. "If the English today still import some commodities from Brazil, in addition to precious metals, it is only because they have not yet concluded their great project for the colonization of Africa. And what was the reason for the continued visits to the African interior by the Englishmen Ledyard, Brown, Lucas, Houghton, Park, Salt, Valence, and others? What was the reason for the expeditions to celebrated Timbuctu and Hausà? What was the reason for the voyage to the Zaire? The purpose is quite clear: to make it possible for them to do without Brazil, to weaken Brazil, and to take from Brazil only precious metals."

And so firm was his idea, and so skillful his prognostication, that on July 3 in the following session, when replying to his colleagues who had not accepted his arguments, Cunha Matos repeated it: "Here, gentlemen, are the motives behind the renowned British philanthropy with regard to the slave trade: Brazilian agriculture and the agriculture of other countries in South America that do not belong to the English must end because the British wish to make themselves masters of the coast of Africa, to close its ports fast to all foreigners, and to destroy the sources of the wealth that inconveniences them." [84]

Cunha Matos showed himself to be without racial prejudice, and prior to Bernardo Pereira de Vasconcelos believed that without its Negroes Brazil would not have been civilized. "I have declared many times that I do not defend the slave trade for an indefinite period, but ask what would Brazil be today if the ancient Portuguese laws based on jealousy and distrust had been followed and no Negroes admitted to this continent? Would it not still be populated by Indians living under barbarous conditions?" This idea that our Negroes saved us from

_____

[84] *Ibid.,* II, 33.

barbarity was new at the time; Bernardo Pereira de Vasconcelos was to repeat it in the Chamber in 1843 with the expression "Africa civilizes Brazil," a remark that surprised some of his colleagues and puzzles his biographer, Otávio Tarquínio de Souza, who hesitates to state whether it represented Pereira de Vasconcelos' taste for contradiction or his association with the slave interests.

A speech delivered also in the July 3 session by the Bishop of Bahia, Dom Romualdo Antônio de Seixas,[85] one of the members of the diplomatic commission who had approved the opinion on the agreement, opposed a "liberal system of settlement" and the civilizing of the Indians to the possible lack of slave labor, for "in forests of my province alone there are more than twenty thousand Indians who are suited to all kinds of work and industry, but their labor has unfortunately been lost to the state because of absence of a good system of instruction, civilization, and colonization, and perhaps because of the false ideas commonly held concerning their indolence and lack of intellectual capacity." He believed in the ability of the Indians, especially mentioning the Mundurucús,[86] and was persuaded that they could be transformed into "farmers, artisans, and sailors, infinitely more useful than those wretched Negroes on whose existence the prosperity of Brazilian commerce, industry, and shipping is made to depend." Thus, despite "the complaints and pretexts put forward by greed and self-interest," "innovations and reforms, which are moreover healthful and necessary" would lessen only "the profits and advantages of a few individuals." If the period within which slavery must be abolished were not three years—during which half of Africa could be transplanted to Brazil—but twenty years, when that time should end "the same complaints would arise and it again would be argued that Brazil needed to prolong this execrable importation."[87]

---

[85] D. Romualdo (1787–1869) was the deputy from Pará and an orator of the old classical school. His sermons and pastoral orations are listed in the Catálogo da Exposição de História do Brasil (1881); his *Discursos Parlamentares* was published in Bahia, 1836. His work seems to be criticized in all literary histories; see Sílvio Romero, *História da Literatura Brasileira,* Rio de Janeiro, 1949, 4th ed., 205–208.
[86] Today the total with whom we have permanent contact is about 1,000 to 1,500. See Darcy Ribeiro, *Línguas e Culturas Indígenas do Brasil,* Rio de Janeiro, 1957, 56.
[87] *Anais do Parlamento Brasileiro,* Session of July 3, 1827, 22.

"Ah! the Bishop's Indians!" replied Cunha Matos. "We have been Christianizing the Indians for three hundred years, and except for those few gathered in villages by the Jesuits, they have been of little profit and less utility to the state. I know what the expenses were in the province of Goiás for the resettlement and conversion of the Indians: it was all in vain, because the poor savages found exploiters in the villages who were more barbarous than their former chiefs." [88]

Replying to the Bishop and supporting Cunha Matos, José Clemente Pereira said in the same session: "I have heard people talk about the Indians, and they say that we have two hundred thousand who can immediately settle Brazil. This is easy to say, but let us observe what has been demonstrated by so many years of experience; what progress has the attempt to civilize the Indian made, despite more or less efficient efforts on the part of the government? Little or none, Mr. President, either because we have not found the true way to win over the Indians, or because of their nature and habits: what I am sure of is that the Indians continue to inhabit their forests and to wage war on those who wish to invade them, and that if we advance in the conquest of territory, there is no advance the winning of the population. But let us concede that the Indian can be civilized. When will his labor be profitable to Brazil? No doubt that will come late and very slowly, while the shortage of Africans is immediate and sudden." [89]

Without the Negro work was not possible because of the scarcity of whites and their prejudices against manual labor. And work was necessary to civilize Brazil, was Cunha Matos' thesis. According to Bishop Dom Romualdo, however, a liberal system of colonization and especially the stability of our political institutions would attract "honest families and hard-working men" from Europe. His view was seconded by José Lino Coutinho, the deputy from Bahia, and the only one in all these debates to manifest racial prejudices, when he stated that "white men enjoy a greater share of intellect." Cunha Matos replied that, of the small European immigration to Brazil that cost its weight in gold, a large number of immigrants had not been employed in agriculture and others had soon returned to their native lands. The immigrants were the

[88] *Ibid.,* 32.
[89] *Ibid.,* Session of July 4, 1827, 42.

refuse from the population of Hamburg, Lubeck, Bremen, and Freiburg, plus a few soldiers and officers, a total of seven thousand from 1821 to 1827. José Clemente Pereira was of the same mind in the July 4 session: "We have also attempted to raise hopes with the arrival of European labor . . . European labor! Mr. President! Ah! what a vain hope! I see no more than the illusions of dreams in this idea. Are we not well acquainted with the falseness of this theory from sad experience? Where are those settlers who have been purchased for Brazil at such great expense?" He analyzed this hopeless possibility and said that if immigrants came, Brazilian agriculture could not count on them because "they would much prefer to have their own businesses than to hire themselves out." [90]

The sessions of July 3 and 4, 1827, presented divergencies on aspects of the question, but in their conviction that immediate abolition of the trade would bring evil upon agriculture, Nicolau Pereira de Campos Vergueiro and Miguel Calmon du Pin e Almeida, two of the greatest experts on the problems of Brazilian agriculture,[91] aligned themselves with Cunha Matos. Both recognized the treaty as concluded and ratified, but both recognized its evils. "As this commerce so directly and indirectly influences all the sources of national wealth, is it fitting that it shall cease at the time stipulated without plans to replenish the great void that it will necessarily leave?" asked Vergueiro. "Clearly not. It behooves us to prepare for the shortage of labor that we shall necessarily

---

[90] *Loc. cit.* Eduardo Teodoro Bösche, first Sergeant in the troops in the service of Dom Pedro I, speaks of Wallenstein's bandits and states that their "officers are from the riffraff of Europe and with the few exceptions of certain dissolute barons are nothing but vagabonds and gamblers." See "Quadros Alternados" (1836) *Revista do Instituto Histórico e Geográfico Brasileiro,* 1919, LXXXIII, 155–156.

[91] Nicolau Pereira de Campos Vergueiro (1778–1859), later Regent, Senator, and Minister of State, initiated large-scale importation of European workers for agriculture in São Paulo. He founded Fazenda de Ibiacapa e a Vergueiro & Co. See Djalma Forjaz, *O Senador Vergueiro, sua Vida e sur Época,* São Paulo, 1924. Miguel Calmon du Pin e Almeida (1796–1865) was Minister of State, Senator, and President of the Sociedade Auxiliadora da Indústria Nacional. The owner of a sugar plantation, he wrote the significant work on the reformation of the sugar industry at the beginning of the nineteenth century, *Ensaio sôbre o Fabrico do Açúcar,* Bahia, 1834, studying the economic problem of the decrease in slavery and the lack of foreign settlers; he also wrote the *Memória sôbre a Cultura do Tabaco,* Bahia, 1835.

experience, by promoting the emigration of European colonists." [92]
Calmon also approved of the agreement as just in its objective, but he
censured the negotiation preceding it. "It is quite painful for me to say
it, Mr. President, but the negotiation that preceded this treaty, or
agreement, is worthy of censure by the representatives of Brazil;
because it has colored with force an act that should have been
spontaneous, because it has made almost foreign and an inglorious
sacrifice the resolution to abolish the iniquitous traffic in Africans;
sacrifice, I say, because whatever may be said to the contrary abolition
will bring a great reduction in our revenues and a great decline in our
so-called colonial culture; and I say *inglorious* because such a sacrifice,
in view of the negotiation, must be attributed rather to the force that
extorted it from us than to the justice that should have dictated it to
us." [93]

What was clearly demonstrated was that the agreement did not serve
our national interests, that it represented intervention in our internal
affairs, and that it had been torn from us under pressure and the threat
of force. The British Minister to Brazil, Charles Gordon, must have
been surprised by the extreme nationalist current led by Brigadier
Cunha Matos. Accompanied by general applause, the latter declared
that the agreement was "the most direct attack that can be made upon
our Constitution, dignity, and national honor, and upon the individual
rights of Brazilian citizens," [94] and he protested against the opinion that
abolition of the traffic was the result not of threats from Great Britain
nor of concessions from the Brazilian government, but of an humanitarian ideal that was of honor to Brazil.[95] It had been torn from us by
force, the definition of the trade as piracy had been imposed, and
Brazilians had been made subject to foreign courts.

The speaker with most reason in the parliamentary storm that
overtook the House on July 2, 3, and 4, 1827, was Brigadier Cunha
Matos who dared to invite the Bishop and other deputies and the
foreign diplomats, including the English, to divest themselves of their

---

[92] *Anais do Parlamento Brasileiro,* Session of July 3, 1827, II, 35.
[93] *Ibid.,* III, 45–46.
[94] *Ibid.,* 43.
[95] Document No. 10 of the Foreign Office, cited by Alan K. Manchester, *British
Preëminence in Brazil,* University of North Carolina Press, 1933, 215, No. 108.

slaves in the name of Christianity, recalling that even Mohammed—and this was one of the reasons for his great penetration in Africa—had ordered that any slave embracing the doctrine of the Koran should be liberated immediately.

Some, like Holanda Cavalcanti and Clemente Pereira, knew that Great Britain despite its threats would be incapable of abolishing the slave traffic by force, and thus foresaw in 1827 what Euzébio de Queiroz was to say in 1850: the traffic would end only when Brazil wanted it to end. Holanda Cavalcanti believed that the government had been coerced and should not have signed: "I should like to see the British fleet in action, which would certainly be more difficult than the English agent's utterance of words to the Brazilian minister." [96] Clemente Pereira recalled that at this time "England is in the midst of great internal convulsions because of a labor surplus of sixty thousand for which it can find no employment. . . . It is precisely at this time, too, that Great Britain considers itself in some danger because of the ruin of many of its bankers . . . and it is also at this time that the Holy Alliance is deliberating a great plan against England . . . and that France has just celebrated a treaty of alliance and commerce with Brazil. Under such circumstances, would it behoove the acute and most far-sighted English policy to carry out the hostile acts with which its minister plenipotentiary frightened our negotiators?" [97]

As was later borne out, Britain could not cope with the slave traders nor abolish the trade, which indeed soon reached figures never before attained. Her threats hid her real objectives, disclosed by Cunha Matos with his superior experience of nineteen years in Africa, in a clear historical prognostication: "England aspires to dominate all of Asia, as by means of the settlements and wars that it is undertaking in Africa one must suppose it also aspires to complete dominion over that great region. The countries of both regions have the same commodities and products as Brazil, and as the British must prefer their own territories, they will seek by all means to set up obstacles for us; and to achieve this there is no better way than to deprive Brazil of additional labor: this is the true British policy. I believe with all my heart that Brazil will come

---

[96] *Anais do Parlamento Brasileiro*, Session of July 3, 1827, 25.
[97] *Ibid.*, Session of July 4, 1827, 44.

to receive cotton and rice from Benguela, wax from China, and sugar from Tonkin: if this does not occur in my time, it will happen in my children's time, who will perhaps remember my prophecy." [98] Thus the future Field Marshal foresaw British expansion in west Africa, economic competition with Brazil, and the expulsion of Brazil from Africa that would force upon us an isolation that, because it would be against our interests, we would accept only twenty-three years later. The coast of Africa occupied such an important position in the plans for our security and the defense of our interests that in 1828 the Minister of the Navy declared in his report to the General Assembly that there was "an absolute need to maintain a naval division on the coast of Africa and to replace it every six months." [99]

THE SLAVE TRADE

The two major consequences of the agreement of 1826 and the Treaties of 1827 with France and Great Britain [100] were general repugnance for all treaties with European powers, and more rational and efficient organization of the slave traffic. In his speech of July 2, 1827, Cunha Matos confessed "that frequently I recall the opinion of that wise Brazilian, Sr. José Bonifácio de Andrade, when he said that Brazilian policy . . . should be one of friendship with all the powers of Europe, unbound by treaties of any nature whatever; it is with the American nations that we must have intimate diplomatic relations, both because they are our neighbors and in order to oppose the wild pretensions of old Europe. . . . All agreements and treaties that we make with European powers will be treaties between wolves or lions and lambs! Where there is extreme inequality there is not nor can there be perfect reciprocity: the greater must supplant the lesser and the weaker must pay the costs." [101]

In a budgetary discussion of August 1827, Nicolau de Campos Vergueiro also expressed aversion to treaties and the policy of subordination to Europe: "Looking at the trade agreements, I do not see what

---

[98] *Ibid.,* Session of July 3, 1827, 34.
[99] *Relatório à Assembléia Geral do Império do Brasil pelo Secretário d'Estado dos Negócios da Marinha, Diogo Jorge de Brito,* Rio de Janeiro, 1829, 23.
[100] Text in A. P. Pinto, *Apontamentos para o Direito Internacional,* I, 43–59.
[101] *Anais, do Parlamento Brasileiro,* Session of July 2, 1827, II, 16.

advantages they offer us or that we have derived from them . . . ; however, [it is clear] we do grave harm by subjecting ourselves to receiving foreign merchandise at fixed duties and binding ourselves not to alter those duties; such treaties are shackles placed on the administration." With regard to commercial relations he defended the article of the *Carta régia* of 1808 which had opened Brazil's ports to all nations and imposed duty of 24 per cent. That letter had done everything, but everything had been undone by the subsequent treaties; there was no reciprocity, for "commerce is conducted by foreigners, we concede them all advantages, and they concede us nothing at all." And he proceeded by saying: "There is another treaty that is not commercial and in which I see only our act of faith in a powerful nation; I believe that everyone knows that I am referring to the treaty for the abolition of slavery (*cheers*). It was called a treaty, but is an obligation only on our part, for it is a treaty by which we bind ourselves without the slightest concession on the part of the other nation. I cannot consider this a treaty; it could be considered so only during a state of war in which the victor imposes onerous and crushing conditions on the loser. To make in a state of peace a treaty by which we compromise a right without the least compensation from the other nation is the most extraordinary thing imaginable." [102] He recommended the isolation of Brazil with respect to Europe in view of the fact that Europe treated us as though we were in a true state of war, in order to attain the greatest advantage and our disadvantage. Europe did this everywhere to enrich itself at the expense of other nations; the United States owed its strength largely to its isolationism and to the firm, independent determination not to allow such concessions as Dom Pedro and the Marquis de Queluz had granted.

Campos Vergueiro was much more hostile to the agreement now than in July, as was Vasconcelos, who also was convinced of the evil of treaties with Europe. "What do we want with old Europe? America belongs to America; let Europe belong to Europe and all will be for the best." He stated that he was against the Holy Alliance, declared that he was still a great admirer of Great Britain, and said in relation to the treaty with France: "I confess that such a strong indignation takes hold of me and that my spirit is so greatly perturbed when I cast my eyes

---

[102] *Ibid.,* Session of August 20, 1827, IV, 165.

upon it that I find myself obliged to fling it far from me." And he continued: "Today it is generally recognized that treaties cannot fail to be, if not hostile, at least most odious acts that serve only to provoke and indispose nations. . . . I am the declared enemy of that European policy which is not based on the enlightenment of our age and tends to cause the human spirit to regress on the brilliant path that it is following and to return to the obscurity of those times when only might made right." Warmly applauded, he concluded: "We want nothing, *nothing,* to do with Europe." [103]

It was the interventionist policy of the Holy Alliance that frightened some of our politicians, but the harm done our national interests by Great Britain and France especially opened eyes to European plunder and the policy of force that grasped everything for self-profit. "Gentlemen," said Cunha Matos, "I have passed in this Chamber for an enemy of the English government; I am an enemy not of that government but of English egoism. Let us not think that England will defend us for our good looks; Great Britain will take our part only if this suits its interests and will abandon us when it finds that we are no longer useful." [104] Cunha Matos held that we are not nor should be enemies of any nation but, rather, friends with our own national interests, and that an independent policy is always the best policy. Speaking on the treaty with Prussia, Holanda Cavalcanti attacked "the mania for treaties that have been the dishonor and shame of Brazil." [105]

The first consequence of this general uneasiness, felt even by the governing minority, about the privileges granted to Europe, was the alienation of Dom Pedro from Brazil as its patriots deserted him. The price of the agreements and treaties was his abdication, as later the price of abolition was the fall of the Empire. The second consequence was the commercialization and reorganization of the slave trade. The merchant speculators concentrated on profit and methodically confronted and overcame the British fleet up to the time when the until then dominant agricultural interests should find another solution and dispense with slave labor. The economic crises and panics that frequently disrupted our rural economy did not make us accept British imposition of general paralysis or radical transformation.

---

[103] *Ibid.,* Session of July 20, 1827, IV, 169.
[104] *Ibid.,* Session of August 20, 1827, IV, 172.
[105] *Ibid.,* Session of May 12, 1828, I, 62.

Neither in the colonial phase nor during Dom João's residence had the traffic in slaves been so efficiently organized in the form of a rational capitalism that took into account the possibilities of the market—that is, the economic opportunities, in the strict sense of the expression, for large sales. Unfortunately, no study has yet been made of the traffic, the traders, their capital and their methods. It is known from statistical data that after 1826 the trade increased greatly and that the law of November 7, 1831, freeing all slaves imported from outside the Empire and imposing penalties on the importers, was not enforced. The influence of those in power, writes Tavares Bastos, weakened the enforcement of the law to the point that it became a dead letter. Later it was recognized that a forgotten and unpopular law could not be revived, and it was necessary to proclaim another.[106]

Using as a basis the statistical data of the English commission on the traffic, Tavares Bastos states that from 1788 to 1829 the lowest annual number of slaves imported into Brazil was 18,000 and the highest 65,000.[107] In 1823 José Bonifácio calculated the annual average at 40,000,[108] and for the years 1826 to 1829 Walsh gives the respective totals of 33,999, 29,787, 43,555, and 52,600.[109] As there are no systematically collected official data, the variation among the estimates is great, although all figures reveal a growing influx of slaves beginning in 1826. Reverend C. S. Steward calculates the yearly average from 1809 to 1829 at 20,000, but in this last year alone there were 60,000, and from January 1 to April 14 there were 13,000.[110] For Bahia alone in 1826 Miguel Calmon gives 7,858; in 1827, 10,186; in 1828, 8,127; in 1829, 12,808; and in 1830, 8,425.[111] With the development of coffee plantations, Rio de Janeiro was always requiring a greater number of slaves, perhaps an

---

[106] C. A. Tavares Bastos, *Cartas do Solitário,* 3rd ed., Companhia Editôra Nacional, São Paulo, 1938, 155.

[107] *Ibid.,* 175.

[108] *Representação à Assembléia-Geral Constituinte e Legislativa do Império do Brasil sôbre a Escravatura,* Paris, 1825.

[109] Rev. R. Walsh, *Notices of Brazil in 1828 and 1829,* London, 1830, 2 vols.

[110] *A Visit to the South Sea, in the United States ship Vincennes, during the years 1829 and 1830; including scenes in Brazil, Peru, Manilla, the Cape of Good Hope, and St. Helen,* London, 1832, I, 80–81. Reverend Walter Coulton gives the average of 10,000 to 15,000 in 1846. See *Deck and Port; or incidents of a cruise in the United States frigate Congress to California, with Sketches of Rio de Janeiro, Valparaiso, Lima, Honolulu, and San Francisco,* New York, 1850, 111.

[111] Transcribed in Luís Viana Filho, *O Negro na Bahia,* Liv. José Olímpio, 1946, 98.

even greater percentage of the total than is generally attributed to Bahia. In a speech delivered July 4, 1827, on the agreement of 1826, Clemente Pereira declared that 25,000 to 30,000 slaves entered regularly through the port of Rio de Janeiro although they might be distributed throughout other provinces. Furthermore, despite all affirmations of the fertility of Negroes, Clemente Pereira states that encouragement of breeding had been neglected, there being plantations with no Negresses, and only one Negress being imported from Africa for every three or four males.[112]

From 1831 on the clandestine nature of the traffic makes it difficult to know the numbers involved. The government began officially to denounce the obstinacy of plantation owners who insisted on believing that without slaves agriculture would languish,[113] as well as the greed of some merchants who joined them "in the plan to Africanize Brazil."[114] It was recognized that "industrious white people were needed," and the Ministry of Foreign Affairs tried officially to attract them, as may be seen in the Reports of 1835, 1838, and 1847.[115] But what stands out clearly from these documents is the number of slave ships and slaves seized by English ships. Both contraband and smugglers found "sympathy and protection among a large part of the inhabitants," reports a document of 1837.[116] When in 1840 statistical data reappear, they show that repression stimulated demand, or at least the interest of agriculture in taking advantage of a source of labor of which it might later be deprived. Following are the data on the importation of slaves from 1840 to 1851, totaling 371,615:

1840—30,000	1844—22,849	1848—60,000
1841—16,000	1845—19,453	1849—54,000
1842—17,435	1846—50,324	1850—23,000
1843—19,095	1847—56,172	1851— 3,287 [117]

---

[112] *Anais do Parlamento Brasileiro*, Session of July 4, 1827, 42. There was a ratio of seven men to three women for the Africans in Vassouras, between 1820 and 1829. See Stanley J. Stein, *Vassouras. A Brazilian Coffee Country, 1850–1900*, Harvard University Press, 1957, 76–78.

[113] *Relatório do Ministério dos Negócios Estrangeiros*, Rio de Janeiro, 1834, 5.

[114] *Ibid.*, 1831, 10.

[115] *Ibid.*, 12, 16, 25.

[116] *Ibid.*, 1837, 5.

[117] *Ibid.*, 1853, 8.

In 1862 Tavares Bastos presented somewhat different data for the period 1840–1847, totaling 249,800, which were based on English statistics although those of the Brazilian Ministry were already known:

1840—30,000	1843—30,500	1846—52,600
1841—16,000	1844—28,000	1847—57,800 [118]
1842—12,200	1845—22,700	

According to the Brazilian statistics the annual average was 27,134, and according to the English 28,875, while the average of immigrants was 9,241. As may be seen, the process of Brazilian Africanization, which had led first Cunha Matos and later Vasconcelos to proclaim in the Chamber that Africa was civilizing Brazil, accelerated at the peak of British persecution, despite scattered affirmations that Brazil needed white European colonists to counterbalance that process.

Around 1835 the rapidly expanding cultivation of coffee required more slaves, and the government, whether sympathetic to the trade or not, did not have the power to attempt abolition, for it was identified with the interests of the rural class. Hence the increasing influx of slaves and the inefficiency of official measures. From 1839 a new factor made contraband more difficult, and for this reason further stimulated the trade by increasing prices and compelling better organization. This was the English demand for abolition of the trade in the Portuguese colonies. From 1834 on the Brazilian Ministry of Foreign Affairs denounced the protection of contraband under the Portuguese flag.[119] In order to abolish this inhuman traffic, the Imperial Government in 1836 addressed itself to the English and Portuguese governments and to the republics of Uruguay, Buenos Aires, Chile, and Peru, proposing an agreement to obtain that end. There are stories about a clever subterfuge invented at that time by the traders of calling the Africans settlers, "because this protected them from the cruisers that they met, after which they unloaded them on our coasts, as happened in the case of the Portuguese schooner *Amizade Feliz* and the brig *Orion*, whose master had the *sang-froid* to affirm in court that the Negroes

[118] A. C. Tavares Bastos, *Cartas do Solitário*, 175. (1st ed., 1862.) On p. 161 Tavares Bastos gives a total of 221,800 Africans, with a minimum of 14,200 (1842) and a maximum of 57,800 (1847). The yearly average was 27,725.
[119] *Relatório de Ministério dos Negócios Estrangeiros*, Rio de Janeiro, 1834, 5.

carried on his ship were settlers collected in Angola to be taken to Mozambique." [120]

It was Palmerston who as Foreign Minister of Great Britain (1830–1841) demanded energetic measures of Portugal in order to end the slave trade in its colonies. Great Britain then, as always, held a dominant position in the political and economic life of Portugal.[121] Palmerston required of Portugal a treaty similar to the one obtained from Brazil permitting the right of search and capture. This, as here and in the United States, would have meant an abdication of sovereignty. As always great powers, Great Britain in the past and others in the present, demand treaties and support by force principles contrary to national interests. At times they lose patience and threaten with their fleets. Palmerston confessed that the words with which a September general (Revolution of September, 1836) attacked the "infamous policy" of the English had reached their mark. In May of 1838 he set a date for the negotiations, and when the Portuguese procrastinated, prepared a "bill" authorizing the British fleet to seize Portuguese ships and have them tried by the tribunal in Sierra Leone. To Portuguese Minister Moncorvo's protest he replied that Portugal could declare war if it pleased and thus facilitate the affair. It was a harsh measure, as when they dealt with us, and it provoked Portuguese resentment. Palmerston made all kinds of threats, including that of taking Goa; in 1839 he almost did take it.

It is curious to observe that the British commanders were free to decide what should be done with their prizes and to make contracts of deposit with charitable institutions. The eighty-five Africans taken from the Portuguese schooner *Flor de Luanda* in 1836 were entrusted to the Santa Casa, a charitable hospital in Rio. As they were well behaved, they were freed in 1846 after serving eight years with the hospital paying the British, or their agents, for the Negroes' services.[122]

The English were applying pressure because the slave trade, although abolished by the decree of December 10, 1836, continued even after

---

[120] *Ibid.*, 1836, p. 5.
[121] Sir Charles Webster, *The Foreign Policy of Palmerston, 1830–1841*, London, 1951, I, 479–494.
[122] See Ubaldo Soares, *A Escravatura na Misericórdia*, Rio de Janeiro, 1958, 107–108.

positive instructions to the governor of Angola, Admiral Noronha, who had celebrated a provisory agreement on May 20, 1839, with Captain Tucker, Commander of the English naval forces on the African seas.[123] Palmerston's Bill, which was published in Portugal August 9, 1839, subjected to seizure and judgment by the Tribunal of the British Admiralty any ship sailing under the Portuguese flag suspected of being employed in the slave trade. The measure was insolent and offensive and was based on the system of intimidation that we were to endure later with the Aberdeen Bill; like the latter, it led to violation of territorial waters, and British cruisers invaded the ports of Luanda and Mozambique.[124] Relations were broken off and the Brazilian government, after deploring the "controversy," declared itself "neutral in the contention between Great Britain and Portugal, neutral therefore with respect to the Bill, which in no way affects Brazil," and stated that it consented, under the principles and conditions of the Right of Peoples, to the entry of English cruisers with their prizes.[125]

The English action and Palmerston's Bill resulted from the conviction that the slave trade was conducted most intensively in the Portuguese colonial ports. Apprehended ships were navigating under the Portuguese flag and the slaves came especially from Angola. Aureliano Coutinho, our Secretary of Foreign Trade, had revealed this as early as 1834,[126] and in 1837 Limpo de Abreu wrote that the Imperial Government "has on several occasions sent communications to the Portuguese and British Governments informing them that the Portuguese flag was being used to protect African contraband." Dubious of the efficacy of the decree just promulgated by the Portuguese Government, Limpo de Abreu proposed that the sale to Portuguese subjects of Brazilian and foreign ships intended for navigation off the coast of Africa should be regulated so as to exclude the possibility of their use in the traffic.[127] In 1838 it was repeated "that all or almost all ships engaged in the slave traffic belong to the Portuguese nation, to whose subjects the trade is prohibited only in ports north of the Equator." [128]

---

[123] Published in *Diário do Govêrno* of October 4, 1839.
[124] C. T., *Lord Palmerston: A Opinião e os Fatos,* Lisbon, 1865.
[125] *Relatório do Ministério dos Negócios Estrangeiros,* Rio de Janeiro, 1840, 78.
[126] *Ibid.,* 1834, 5.
[127] *Ibid.,* 1837, 5–6.
[128] *Ibid.,* 1838, 15.

Although after 1826 Brazil could not carry on the traffic, now defined as piracy, Portugal, which had signed no agreement, had felt free to engage in that commerce. On July 3, 1842, however, the Anglo-Portuguese Treaty defined the slave trade as piracy, and regulated the apprehension, and constituted special commissions for the judgment of ships engaged in it, all as had been established in the Agreement of 1826 with Brazil. After 1842, therefore, the traffic was legally considered contraband by the three interested parties and its practice became more difficult. It did not, however, cease to grow, as we have seen. The most rigorous repression resulted in greater cleverness in evasion and stimulated imaginative subterfuge. British cruisers no longer limited themselves to search on the high seas; they now exercised strict vigilance along our coasts. Ernesto Ferreira França, who in the 1827 debates had shown himself to be compliant, believing that "if we should wish to make a law concerning this [the traffic], we would do well to call in the English to make it with us," [129] in 1845 as Secretary of Foreign Trade did not conceal his rebellion against the English affronts: "If such excesses by British cruisers (apprehension of ships giving no indication of slaves aboard and sailing within the territorial waters of the Empire) . . . be not restrained and restitution made, our coastal navigation, which is the area in which our national shipping holds an advantage over foreign shipping, will remain subject to the greatest inconveniences and prejudices; the agreements . . . that re-strict the right of visit and search, permitting it only on the high seas and in cases when slaves are indeed being transported, would be a dead letter; our very sovereignty and national dignity would not be duly respected." [130] The British cruisers no longer submitted ships captured on the high seas to the Mixed Commissions of Sierra Leone, but took them to the Vice-Admiralties of Demerara and the Cape of Good Hope, both incompetent tribunals.

On March 12, 1845, Ernesto Ferreira França advised the British that the period of fifteen years for abolition of the traffic agreed upon in the Agreement of 1817 incorporated in that of 1826, effective since 1830 had elapsed. But the British took no notice of this communication and continued to exercise the right of visit and search and to maintain in

---

[129] *Anais do Parlamento Brasileiro,* Session of July 4, 1827, 48.
[130] *Relatório do Ministério dos Negócios Estrangeiros,* (presented to the 1st Legislature) Rio de Janeiro, 1845, 19.

operation the Mixed Commission of Sierra Leone. Limpo de Abreu's protest of 1845 was also not taken into consideration, despite its proposal of a new adjustment. Unilaterally, on August 8, 1845, Great Britain repeated with regard to Brazil what it had done with Portugal: the Aberdeen Bill gave to the Tribunal of the Admiralty and to any Vice-Admiral the right to take cognizance of and proceed to adjudicate any ship flying the Brazilian flag engaged in the traffic of African slaves and detained and captured by any person in the service of His Britannic Majesty. Henceforth the traffic became a most complicated Brazilian diplomatic problem, for its repression by the British involved acts manifestly offensive to Brazilian sovereignty and independence.[131]

The vigor and success of the traffic increased, despite British vigilance, the detentions, and the seizures. The years 1846 to 1849 saw the greatest importation of Africans; after the Aberdeen Bill, the slave traders received the greatest support of the population, for the success of the traffic was seen as the most adequate reply to British insolence. In 1847 Baron de Cairu renewed the expressions of displeasure with treaties and of rejection of the European powers heard from nationalist leaders twenty years earlier in the Chamber:

The evil effects of treaties entered into a few years after Brazil's political emancipation, resulting from recurrent clashes between their provisions and the true interests of the nation and the difficult future bequeathed us by certain commitments still binding upon us, as well as other reasons, have produced a general opinion that treaties are not the best means of strengthening bonds between nations; that as the Empire experienced a period of continuous constraint on its social development because of treaties, it must now be cautious and concede absolutely nothing. . . . Such a doctrine, good in the abstract, may not be the most sound, in view of the need for the Empire to procure adequate markets for its products; circumstances may advise negotiations at times, especially with those nations having no colonial interests to protect.[132]

---

[131] See the two protests against the Bill, signed by José Marques Lisboa, head of the Legation in London (July 25, 1845), and by Antônio Paulino Limpo de Abreu (October 22, 1845), in *Relatório de Ministério dos Negócios Estrangeiros,* 1846, Notes 3 and 4, 6–12. See also note of July 23, 1845, by the English Minister, Hamilton Hamilton, preceding the Bill, and the Bill itself, translated in the same Relatório, Notes 27 and 28, 77–82.
[132] *Relatório do Ministério dos Negócios Estrangeiros,* Rio de Janeiro, 1847, 23.

In Luanda in 1846 Portugal, then as always very submissive to Great Britain, was already apprehending and trying Brazilian ships suspected of the traffic, although the slave trade was knowingly protected under the Portuguese flag. The most arbitrary acts were committed at this time, even against legitimate commerce, both Brazilian and not, carrying Brazilian products to the coast of Africa. Our protests against the right of visit and search exercised by Great Britain, now assisted by France and Portugal, went unheeded and our entire legitimate, non-slave trade with Africa was threatened with destruction.

Such destruction was the intention of the colonial powers: of Great Britain and France, which were later to take possession of the African coast and now wished to break not merely commercial but all Afro-Brazilian ties, and of Portugal also, officially associated with them in order to retain what it possessed and to remove Brazilian influence from its colonies. Clandestinely, under the Portuguese flag, the slave trade expanded, for it was the most important business of the Portuguese colonies and their citizens. Great Britain refused to revoke the Bill unless Brazil would submit to a treaty similar to the one with Portugal of 1842, that is, one conceding the right of visit and search recognizing the mixed commissions, the conditions that had been imposed on us in 1826, and that we had endured until 1845.

What Portugal granted in 1842 Brazil would no longer grant and did not grant until final abolition of the traffic, which it effected of its own free will. On the contrary, despite British pressure we did not renew the Treaty of 1827, and as of August 12, 1844, we established new import duties [133] ending preferential rates. The large commercial interests of Great Britain and France suffered a great blow, for half of the goods consumed by Brazil was furnished by the English,[134] while French

---

[133] Decree No. 376, August 12, 1844, ordering implementation of the Regulations and Tariffs of the Imperial Customs, signed by Manuel Alves Branco; *Coleção de Leis do Império do Brasil,* Rio de Janeiro, 1844, 171 ff.

[134] Statement of Honorio Hermeto Carneiro Leão in *Relatório do Ministério dos Negócios Estrangeiros,* presented to the 2nd Session of the Fifth Legislature, 1843, 5. One must not forget that in 1825, 1830, and 1839 Brazil was by itself already absorbing almost half of the goods exported to all of South America and Mexico combined, while Great Britain purchased little from Brazil. See A. K. Manchester, *British Preëminence in Brazil,* 207.

merchants filled Ouvidor, Ourives, and Ajuda Streets with articles of fashion.[135]

If in its struggle with Great Britain Brazil lost not only Africans but also commercial relations with Africa, as Cunha Matos had foreseen, nevertheless English and French commerce encountered greater obstacles to the importation of its products. In 1850 the budget provoked diplomatic protests by raising import duties by 80 per cent.[136]

All of the excesses of the British, all of their impositions, all of the abuses of their strength and all of their violations of our territorial waters, our ports, and our ships from 1845 to 1850 did not succeed in ending the traffic but rather revitalized it, for the greater risk increased prices and profits and required greater capital. In three years the price of an African slave rose from 630,000 *réis* to 1,350,000 *réis*,[137] and from 1846 to 1849 imports always attained numbers in excess of 50,000, which had never occurred before. English violence succeeded only in expanding the traffic; to evade and overcome British vigilance was the means of avenging Brazilians for British insolence; to confront the arrogance of the stronger power, which, abusing its strength as other powers do today, did not have the patience to wait for Brazil to find itself the solution that it desired, was a form of redress.

Was the Brazilian government also unsuccessful in ending the traffic? "And why have the English not put an end to this contraband, despite all their cruisers?" inquired the Deputy from Rio de Janeiro, Bernardo Augusto Nascente de Azambuja, interrupting the old patriot Francisco Gê de Acaiaba Montezuma. The latter had just come from the struggles for independence and was heard most attentively by the Chamber after the tempest provoked by the partisan accusations of the opposition that the government had risen to power on the ladder of African interests, and the government's reply that the opposition wished to rise on the ladder of English interests. Attempting to calm the debates, Montezuma stated that Great Britain would act the same whether Brazil's government were liberal or conservative, and he appealed to the

---

[135] See the speech by Cunha Matos, July 3, 1827, in *Anais do Parlamento Brasileiro*, 35.

[136] See *Relatório do Ministério dos Negócios Estrangeiros*, 1850, 12; documentation, 118–119.

[137] Stanley J. Stein, *op. cit.*, 228–229.

opposition for the government, which had been behaving in a prudent, noble, generous, and energetic manner, to be granted the entire confidence of the Chamber, "all the moral strength demanded by the present emergency."[138]

It was true. English forces were mobilized in the Atlantic against the traffic, but were unsuccessful in ending it. Now the Brazilian government decided over the strong opposition of the slave traders not to prolong the situation further, not only because the plans being made for new immigration promised an advantageous alternative but also because the latest English action, the attacks upon and destruction of coastal ships suspected of carrying slaves, without even taking them before the Admiralty for judgment, necessitated a decision that would end the disrespect to our sovereignty that we could not oppose with force. After the British squadron was strengthened by Admiral Parker's ships, which had been stationed in Greece, and by cruisers from the Rio de la Plata, British prowess showed itself in acts of piracy, the sacking and burning of ships, with the spoils transferred to the British fleet.[139]

The Tenth Cabinet of 1848 was determined to settle the question. Upon consultation the Council of State advised abolishing the traffic; the Viscount of Maranguape, Caetano Maria Lopes Gama, made this statement:

In view of the nature of these facts, I consider Brazil under two pressures: one is that of the slave traders and the other consists of the means used by the British government to repress the trade. Only with the cessation of the first pressure shall we be able to achieve that of the second. . . . This solution consists in taking serious measures against the traffic immediately, in establishing such conditions for navigation between Brazil and the coast of Africa as . . . to render the slave trade difficult if not impossible. . . . In order to make these measures more effective, it will be advisable to use the press for the enlightenment of those Brazilians who suppose the coast of Africa to be the source of our wealth, showing them that they are in

---

[138] *Anais do Parlamento Brasileiro,* Session of June 28, 1850, 2nd Session, Rio de Janeiro, 1879, I, 588–592. It was Deputy Joaquim Antão Fernandes Leão, Minister of the Navy in the previous Cabinet (March 8, 1848 to October 28, 1848), who made the grave accusation.

[139] See *Relatório do Ministério dos Negócios Estrangeiros,* 1851, by Paulino José Soares de Souza; and José Paranhos da Silva, *Cartas ao Amigo Ausente,* Rio de Janeiro, 1953.

error and blind to their true interests and that slavery is dangerous to our country.[140]

The matter was resolved by the Brazilian decision to end the slave trade. That solution was due to Paulino José Soares de Souza and Euzébio de Queiroz, the Minister of Justice. In a speech on July 15, 1850, the former gave the history of the problem and revealed the decision of the government to liquidate the traffic. The conclusions of the British Parliament's Commission on the Slave Trade, approved March 12, 1849, had shown:

1) that since 1845 the vigor and efficacy of the British naval forces assigned to repression of the trade had reached a point never before attained and that those forces were now assisted by those of France and the United States, in accordance with the treaties;

2) that the number of Negroes freed by British cruisers in the years 1846 and 1847 was slightly more than 4 per cent of the total exported from Africa in those years;

3) that the expenditure made in suppression of the slave trade appeared to be no less than 650,000 pounds sterling per year (approximately 6,500,000,000 *réis*);

4) that the traffic in African slaves conducted by Brazil was very profitable, and was managed and organized with such confidence that it thwarted as never before the efforts of the nations engaged in suppressing it;

5) that the extension and activity of the traffic in African slaves, although in part neutralized by foreign interference and sometimes restricted by the action of the governments of Cuba and Brazil, were controlled principally by the European market for goods produced by slave labor;

6) that the importation of slave-produced sugar for British consumption had contributed to the great increase in demand for products so produced, so that it had become more difficult than ever to suppress the trade in African slaves;

---

[140] Reproduced in José Antônio Soares de Souza, *A Vida do Visconde do Uruguai*, Companhia Editôra Nacional, São Paulo, 1944, 209–210. The diplomacy of Paulino José Soares de Souza in this question is magnificently treated in this book. Paulino remained in the post of Foreign Minister from September 29, 1848, to September 5, 1853.

7) that the sufferings and mortality of slaves in depots and transports were frightful to humanity and without precedent in the history of slavery.

The question, said Paulino, was not a party issue, for both parties faced the same difficulties. Even in the British Parliament a motion had been presented requesting the revocation of endeavors requiring the effective maintenance of a fleet on the coast of Africa. The Parliamentary Commission had shown that blockade of African ports was insufficient to abolish the traffic. The motion had not passed, but it had been demonstrated that "the cruisers off the coast of Africa were not in themselves an adequate system and that it was necessary to take other measures." This testified to the failure of the system that had been adopted by all British administrations. "It is an enterprise," added Paulino, "In which Great Britain has expended enormous sums, in which it has used every recourse of its skilled diplomacy, and which it has pursued, chiefly since the Treaty of Vienna, over the long space of thirty-five years with unfailing activity." Furthermore, the treaty between Britain and the Argentine Confederation in 1849 had enabled the former to divert warships from the Rio de la Plata to cruising against the traffic, and Admiral Parker's forces had come from Greece in 1851. Hence the renewed violence, but it had been most successfully countered by the traders, who had managed to smuggle in a larger number of slaves than in 1841–1842 despite France's consent to repression and the United States agreement to employ a squadron of no less than eighty guns. Experience from 1841 to 1850 had proved the ineffectiveness of the cruisers and the blockade. Paulino declared that "there has been some vacillation and incoherence," that at times we had moved forward and at other times backward, and it was necessary "to come out of the state in which we find ourselves" and "encounter a broad, sincere and open solution for all these problems . . . which are hindering our progress toward the development of the country's resources and prosperity." Finally, he informed the nation very objectively as to the inadvisability of continuing the traffic and the consequences of abolition for Brazilian agriculture: "When a powerful nation like Great Britain pursues the objective of ending the traffic with tireless perseverance and unfailing tenacity over a span of more than forty years; when it resolves to spend 650,000 pounds per year merely to maintain its cruisers in order to repress that traffic; when it obtains the acquiescence of all European and American maritime nations; when the traffic is reduced to Brazil and Cuba alone, shall we be able to resist the torrent? . . . I believe not. Moreover, gentlemen, if the traffic does not end by these means, nevertheless some day it must end."

He also informed the Chamber that England had made treaties with the chiefs of many African nations at many points on the coast of Africa, "where the traffic is no longer conducted." The true objectives of Great Britain, so clearly exposed by Cunha Matos, were thus confirmed in 1850. Nothing was comparable to the expansion of the Second British Empire and for it to succeed, it was indispensable to abolish the slave traffic and isolate those nations, especially Brazil, with growing influence among the various African chiefs. Once this was done, division of the African territories between Great Britain and France would soon begin. The portions progressively conquered by Great Britain were vast, for it had established a mission among the Ashanti (Gold Coast) since 1817 and warred on them several times; in 1821 it set up trading posts in territory subordinate to the government of Sierra Leone; in 1843 it annexed the Cape Colony, the Orange Colony in 1848; and in 1852 and 1854 it recognized the Transvaal's independence from the Orange Free State.

Paulino finally obtained a large vote of confidence resulting in a firm decision to abolish the trade with Law No. 581, dated September 4, 1850 (implemented by Decree No. 731, November 14, 1850).[141]

Repressive measures exercised by Brazil against the traders made importation fall from 23,000 (1850) to 3,287 (1851) and 700 (1852), but "the excesses perpetrated on our coast, in our ports and before our fortresses" nevertheless did not cease immediately. British arrogance was provoking sentiments of reprisal, if not by an impossible physical struggle at least by strengthening commercial relations with other nations and making importation of British products more difficult. In the case of the

---

[141] See *Coleção de Leis do Império do Brasil,* 1850. The law defines the crime, criminals, and accomplices, decrees the sale of ships apprehended, the reexportation of slaves to their ports of origin or their employment under Government tutelage, and establishes that passports to African coast ports would be issued to merchant ships only after an affidavit has been signed by a responsible officer and bond posted equal to the value of the ship and cargo.

Piratinim, which was transporting slaves between provinces,[142] English piracy reached the point of transferring thirty-seven crates of fine and coarse china, four garden statues, one glass chandelier, Madeira wines, sherry, preserves, and sweets to an English warship and setting the *Piratinim* on fire.

Feelings were so high that the government feared violent popular reprisals. José Maria da Silva Paranhos, editor of the *Jornal do Comércio* and future Minister of Foreign Affairs, wrote on August 3, 1851, that the people

> must warm themselves in the sacred fires of independence and national honor and prepare to resist in Milanese fashion, as soon as the patriots who will serve as their examples give the signal that the moment has arrived. Let us respect the life and property of those British subjects who are among us and are not responsible for the evil acts of their government; but if reprisal be necessary, let us deprive ourselves of all or almost all articles produced by the British; such reprisal will be worth more than powder and shot, and in this way we shall force English commerce here and in London, Liverpool, Manchester, and so on, to pay for the hospitality and profits that we give it, and to announce itself opposed to the insults and violence of which we are the victims.[143]

Previously in 1850 Deputy Nascente de Azambuja had proposed raising import duties on British merchandise [144] and Antônio Peregrino Maciel Monteiro, Deputy for Pernambuco and ex-Minister of Foreign Affairs (1837), defending the government against the accusations of opposition member Melo Franco, according to whom such a hostile step would not be adopted by the government, had stated that "the administration intends to repress the traffic by all appropriate means

---

[142] With the diminution of the traffic resulting from governmental prosecution of traders and from the English cruisers, which between 1848 and 1851 captured 90 slave ships, and from the loss of capital invested, transfer was begun of slaves from the provinces of the North to the Paraíba Valley, which needed them more and was more powerful. The data are as follows: 1852, 4,409; 1853, 2,010; 1854, 4,418; 1855, 3,532; 1856, 5,006; 1857, 4,211; 1858, 1,993; 1859, 963. See Sebastiao Ferreira Soares, *Notas Estatísticas sôbre a Produção Agrícola e Carestia dos Gêneros Alimentícios no Império do Brasil,* Rio de Janeiro, 1860, 135–136.

[143] *Cartas ao Amigo Ausente,* Rio de Janeiro, 1953, 312. Description of the piracy against the *Piratinim,* 211–213.

[144] I have not found this proposal, except in references in the speech of Deputy Manuel de Melo Franco, confirmed separately by Deputy Azambuja himself. *Anais do Parlamento Brasileiro,* Session of July 20, 1850, II, 249.

and intends also to preserve intact the . . . sovereignty of the country, reserving the right to employ all extraordinary measures whether as acts of reprisal or as economic and financial expedients." [145]

In 1854 Antônio Paulino Limpo de Abreu announced in his Report that only two cargoes of slaves had been unloaded; in the following year, however, he declared that since December 1852 there had been none. "Which is a very satisfactory result and if possibly some important case arises in some part of our vast territory, where despite the most careful precautions this crime cannot always be detected, it will be investigated and the most energetic measures taken to punish those participating, and to recover and free the Africans involved. Several indications have come to the knowledge of the Imperial Government that these nefarious speculations still continue, but the risk that they run in the Empire have caused them to take another direction." [146]

In 1855 it was also affirmed that no slaves had been disembarked, despite rumors to the contrary, but in 1856 José Maria da Silva Paranhos reported an attempt to land a cargo in Sirinhaém on September 11, 1855; this was the last attempt. Despite efforts of the government to end the traffic and to encourage colonization, such as the Land Law decreed September 18, 1850, this case provoked the British insult expressed in a note from the Legation on March 7, 1856.

The undersigned [W. Stafford] hopes, therefore, that the Imperial Government, through its appreciation of its own dignity and position in this hemisphere, will not consent to be deceived by pretexts or the lax behavior of its subordinates, for if this continues it will inevitably place the country in difficulties with a Power that considers it its strict duty, consequent upon the obligation to which it is so deeply committed, total abolition of the traffic . . . to summon the Imperial Government to compliance with that obligation in the most honorable and complete manner; and if this should not occur, to have recourse to those means which Great Britain has a perfect right to adopt.

José Maria Paranhos da Silva in reply gave the history of the Brazilian efforts, showed that only internal prosecution had effectively liquidated the traders, who had made light of the British cruisers, and rejected the

---

[145] *Ibid.,* 252.
[146] *Relatório do Ministério dos Negócios Estrangeiros,* 1853, 8; and 1854, xii and xiv.

note: "The threat addressed to the Imperial Government in such offensive terms in the name of His Britannic Majesty cannot, then, produce the effects that are said to be in view." On the contrary, because of its contempt for Brazil's national spirit, it provoked popular support for the slave trade.[147]

In 1857 it could be affirmed that no new instance of the trade had arisen, although there might still be discussions with the Legation on problems relative to claims on illegal seizures. After 1859 there was no further indication of activity by the traders, and José Maria da Silva Paranhos declared that the questions in which we were involved with Great Britain having been resolved, "relations between the two peoples are therefore entering a state of perfect understanding and friendship." The traffic had ended, but English domination, disguised by humanitarian pretenses, did not, with the result that in 1863 we broke off relations with Great Britain after the insults of W. D. Christie. But that is another story.

THE TRADERS

The history of the slave traffic is not only that of the movement of British imperialist expansion into Africa, an expansion that excluded any and all able to menace the free exercise of British power, except France with which the conquest had to be shared in order to pacify French ambitions, and, later, Belgium and Germany. It is also the history of the traders with their economic power, their penetration along the African coast, and their rapprochement with the African chiefs. Despite humanitarian affirmations and the general belief that slavery was an evil, the truth was that everyone made use of it, and as early as 1827 Cunha Matos showed that Great Britain had engaged extensively in the trade, the port of Liverpool alone using more than 1,200 ships in it; he acknowledged the evil treatment on slave ships but was not unaware that many slaves who went to America freed themselves of the sacrificial customs that hung over them. He inquired why priests and diplomats, especially the English, used slaves, not white servants, and did not free them.

Without entering into these digressions that so divided international

---

[147] *Ibid.*, 1856. Sirinhaém Case, 17. Note, Appendix B, 19–20; Reply, *ibid.*, 20–24.

and national opinion, the truth is that the assured demand for and sale of slaves for agriculture challenged the greed of traders. On May 12, 1837, in his censure of "the horrible commerce in human flesh," Martim Francisco reported to the Chamber that a ship that had sailed from African ports, pressed by contrary winds and lack of provisions, had cast two hundred and fifty Africans overboard.[148]

Nina Rodrigues recognized the correctness of the government's claim that Africans captured in the traffic preferred to remain in Brazil rather than be sent home.[149] The slave traffic between Africa and Brazil was the work not only of Brazilians but also and especially of Portuguese, and it was carried on under Brazilian, Portuguese, Spanish, and United States flags. As early as 1834 Aureliano Coutinho revealed that the Portuguese flag was protecting slave ships; in 1838 it was recognized that the owners of slave ships found in the Portuguese colonies facilities for use of the Portuguese flag through fraudulent sales.[150] As repression became stronger, the Brazilian flag ceased to be used and was increasingly replaced by the Portuguese, Spanish,[151] and finally the North American. The last instances of the trade were those of the schooner *Mary E. Smith,* apprehended in the port of São Mateus, Espírito Santo, and the *Vickery,* both in 1855.

At the beginning of 1840 President John Tyler (1841–1845) informed the Senate that there were well-founded suspicions that American ships were engaged in the trade. In 1844 the United States Minister to Brazil wrote that "it is a fact that cannot be hidden or denied that the slave trade is almost entirely conducted under our flag and in ships constructed by Americans, sold here and licensed to traders for the coast of Africa. The scandalous trade could perhaps not be so extensive if it were not for the use of our flag and facilities granted in the licensing of American ships to take cargoes and products useful in the purchase of slaves to the coast of Africa." Furthermore, added the Minister, the traders made sport of the British squadron; if they encountered it, it was sufficient for them to unfurl the American flag.

---

[148] *Anais da Câmara dos Deputados,* Session of 1837, Rio de Janeiro, 1887, I, 52.
[149] *Os Africanos no Brasil,* 2nd ed., 155.
[150] See *Relatórios do Ministério dos Negócios Estrangeiros* of 1834 and 1838.
[151] *Ibid.,* 1850, 11, and speech of Paulino José Soares de Souza, *Anais do Parlamento Brasileiro,* Session of July 15, 1850, II, 201.

Lawrence F. Hill [152] explains that this use of the United States flag resulted principally from the American practice, based on a law of 1792, of granting maritime licenses to ships sold in foreign ports by one American citizen to another. The law, aiming to encourage maritime construction, limited neither the duration nor the destination of voyages made after transfer to new proprietors. American citizens, then, bought ships from their compatriots and applied to American consuls for permission to sail for the African coast, and the latter could not refuse although they might suspect the nature of the voyage. Such ships were rented by Brazilian traders, ostensibly to transport merchandise and passengers to the coast of Africa. Part of the purchase price was paid only after one or more voyages to Africa had been made. Lawrence Hill relates the activities of three ships, the *Agnes,* the *Montevideo,* and the *Sea Eagle,* in the slave trade between 1843 and 1844; we may be sure that in practice it was the American flag that protected the transport of Africans to Brazil. In 1845 Henry Wise, American Minister to Rio de Janeiro, requested energetic measures of the President of the United States, saying:

We are a "bye word among nations"—the only people who can now fetch and carry any and every thing for the slave trade, without fear of English cruisers; and because we are the only people who can, are we to allow our proudest privilege to be perverted, and to pervert our own glorious flag into the pirate's flag—the slaver's protection—the Brazilian and Portuguese and Spanish passport to a criminal commerce against our own laws and the municipal laws of almost every civilized nation upon earth? . . . Our flag alone gives the requisite protection against the right of visit, search, and seizure; . . . In one word, the sacred principle of the inviolability of the protection of our flag, is perverted in the ports of Brazil into a perfect monopoly of the unhallowed gains of the navigation of the African slave trade.[153]

Between 1840 and 1845, sixty-four American ships were sold and bought in Rio de Janeiro alone, and no doubt used in the slave trade: in this same period fifty-six American ships left the Brazilian capital for or

---

[152] *Diplomatic Relations between the United States and Brazil,* Duke University Press, 1932, especially Chapter V, "The Abolition of the African Slave Trade to Brazil," 110–145, which is based on official documents. We summarize this study, with additions.

[153] *Ibid.,* 127–128.

entered it from Africa.[154] Many Americans served in the traffic in one way or another, and it is calculated that thousands and hundreds of thousands of Negroes were transported from Africa to Brazil with the help of Yankees. The Minister himself, David Tod, communicated to the Secretary of State on January 8, 1850, that

Citizens of the United States are constantly in this capital [Rio], whose only occupation is the buying of American vessels with which to supply the slave importers. These men obtain sea-letters, which entitle them to continue in use the United States flag, and it is this privilege which enables them to sell their vessels to slave traders, deliverable on the coast of Africa at double, and sometimes more than double, the price for which they were purchased on the preceding day. The vessels take over slave goods and slave crews, under the protection of our flag, and remain nominally American property until a favorable opportunity occurs for receiving a cargo of slaves; and it is not infrequently the case that our flag covers the slaves until the Africans are landed upon the coast of Brazil.[155]

Hill reveals that during the period of greatest American participation in the traffic, between 1839 and 1849, the ministers and consuls never ceased to inform their government and that Presidents Van Buren, Tyler, and Taylor recommended objective measures in messages to Congress. After all, although use of the American flag was permitted by law on ships sold in foreign ports by one American to another, had not American participation in the traffic been considered piracy since 1820?

None of the Secretaries of State modified the policy, however, nor did the American Congress give greater attention to the problem. And probably it did not because the government had no interest in helping to liquidate the traffic to Brazil. American capitalists, ship builders in New York, Providence, Boston, Salem, and Portland, or Philadelphia and Baltimore, profited greatly from the sale of their ships, built—and they knew it—for the trade and sold deliberately for voyages to the coast of Africa.[156] The officers and crews that took the traders to the coast of

---

[154] *Ibid.*, 129–130. Figures for the other ports are equally high, especially for Bahia, but much lower than for Rio.

[155] Dispatch of Minister Tod to the Secretary of State, January 8, 1856, in L. F. Hill, *ibid.*, 129.

[156] The description of the process and the confirmation that northern ships were those used by the traders appear in the dispatch of December 9, 1846, from Henry A. Wise, Minister to Brazil, to James Buchanan, Secretary of State, in W. R. Manning, *Diplomatic Correspondence of the United States,* Washington, 1923, VII, 370.

Africa and frequently were themselves involved in the traffic came, naturally, from the shipbuilding centers. It is interesting, observes Hill, whose chapter we are summarizing, that the region of America that fought most for the abolition of slavery was precisely the area that gave most encouragement to the slave trade; it was not rare for a man to preach abolition and yet to participate in the construction of slave ships, which was a very lucrative business. As for the United States government, it preferred to avoid helping Great Britain establish naval hegemony in the Atlantic by means of the right of search and seizure and sow the seeds of future domination of Africa by forcing out Brazilian products by establishing a monopoly of British products, and by negotiating deals with African chiefs, all done carefully under the mask of humanitarianism.

The Brazilian authorities knew of the use of American ships, and in 1856 José Maria da Silva Paranhos stated in his reply to the insolent official communication from the English minister, W. Stafford, dated March 7, 1856, that "the traders, whose negotiations are premeditated and begin in United States territory, will not fear British cruisers"; in 1857 he declared that the Imperial government had attempted to obtain information on the speculators, "especially in the United States, Portugal, and Spain and their possessions, where it appears certain that the smugglers have established their principal bases of operation." [157]

Clearly the traders here and on the African coast were rich and powerful men, capable of improvising new means to deceive English vigilance and of inventing legal recourses, such as the purchase of American ships, or illegal ones; for the traffic was one of the richest businesses in Brazil during the first fifty years of the nineteenth century.

Basing it on English documents and pamphlets, Tavares Bastos in 1862 gave a summary of the activities of certain traders at the peak of the traffic between 1840 and 1850, but it was Nina Rodrigues who first outlined the history of the Brazilian trade and especially the figure of Félix "Xaxá" de Souza and his political machinations in Dahomey, where he dethroned chiefs in order to forward his dealings. It is not known when Souza came to Africa, but in a short time he became the

---

[157] See *Relatório do Ministério dos Negócios Estrangeiros,* Rio de Janeiro, 1856, 20–24; and 1857, 20.

most opulent and famous of the traders, monopolizing the supply to
Cuba and Brazil, especially that to Bahia. Nina Rodrigues thought that
he was a Cariocan mestizo, but Almeida Prado states that he came from
Bahia and supposes that he must have gone to Ajudá as a governmental
functionary. The monies that paid African expenses, including those of
São Tomé and Principe, came from Brazil. The activities of "Xaxá"
Souza and his sons in the slave trade continued until the definitive
abolition of the traffic.

The history of the traders, collected by Nina Rodrigues [158] from
English authors, has been great expanded by J. F. de Almeida
Prado,[159] who recounts the activities of Souza, Domingos José Martins,
André Pinto da Silva, Francisco José Medeiros, Cerqueira Lima,[160] and
other Brazilian slave traders. Félix de Souza was a powerful man both
in fortune and social position and his second wife, descended from an
African chief, came at the age of eight to be educated in Bahia. He
impressed many travelers who visited his home with his splendor, his
harem, his numerous children (53–80!), the abundance of his table.
Prince de Joinville, brother-in-law of Dom Pedro II, who visited him in
1842 when he had suffered the loss of thirty-four ships captured by the
English, write that nothing stood out more than the personality of
"Xaxá" Souza himself. Long before he died—in 1840 according to Nina
Rodrigues, or in 1849 according to Almeida Prado—Félix de Souza was
a powerful man, for as early as 1822 he considered himself capable of
offering the protectorate of Dahomey to Dom Pedro I.[161] His son Isidor,
who continued his father's activities, died in 1858 when the commerce in
slaves was ending in Brazil.

Almeida Prado also summarizes the activities of Francisco José
Medeiros, equally well established in Dahomey, born in the United
States, supplier of African palm oil and slaves. Brazilian influence was
enormous in Dahomey, and the preservation of Portuguese words and
place names is owing more to Brazilians than to the Portuguese,
especially if we include numerous former slaves who returned from

---

[158] *Os Africanos no Brasil,* Companhia Editôra Nacional, São Paulo, 2nd ed., 1935,
51–55.
[159] "A Bahia e as suas Relações com o Daomé," in *O Brasil e o Colonialismo
Europeu,* Companhia Editôra Nacional, São Paulo, 1956, 115–226.
[160] On the activities of Cerqueira Lima, see Luís Viana Filho, *Os Negros na Bahia,*
87–88.
[161] All this information is based on Almeida Prado, *op. cit.*

Brazil. Domingos José Martins also became one of the principal figures on the coast, especially in Dahomey, dealing in palm oil and slaves; his business attained the volume of $200,000 a year.

But the history of the traders is not complete if one does not know it from this side of the ocean. This was the center of the activities, of the plans and of the corruption. The famous report made by Alcoforado and presented to the police in 1853 exposes in incorrect language but in detail the entire vast network of the traders active in Brazil.[162] Most prominent and numerous among them were the Portuguese, beginning with José Maria Lisboa who around 1832–1833, using old ships that were destroyed soon after the slaves were disembarked, traded in slaves he bought for twenty to thirty thousand reis and sold for from two hundred and fifty thousand to three hundred thousand reis.

Payment was usually in installments. Selection of the site for disembarcation and delivery was made in advance. Between 1833 and 1834 the most important slave trader was José Bernardino de Sá, later Baron (Portuguese) de Villa Novo do Minho, who established his agents south of the Equator, used English fabrics for his bartering and the Portuguese flag for his ships, and had no difficulties because the British cruisers did not go south of the Equator.

The scale of the traffic enlarged in 1834–1835, despite the pitiless[163] suppressive measures of João Paulo dos Santos Barreto, the Minister of the Navy. The incident of the Portuguese schooner *Angélica* revealed the strength of the slave smugglers and the extent of their influence. The ship was captured but the officer responsible for this mistake was forced to pay a large indemnity. Large hangar-like shelters for the reception of the slaves were openly constructed. Justices of the peace were liberally bribed. Various disembarcation points were established along the coast of the State of Rio de Janeiro (São Sebastião, Ilha Grande, Mangaratiba, Marambaia). It was at this time that Brazilians like José Breves, his father-in-law, and his brother began to engage in the trade using the Portuguese flag always and hiring naval officers who had left active service and were bored. The father-in-law of Aureliano de Souza e Oliveira Coutinho, Viscount de Sepetiba, was investigated

---

[162] I j⁶–525 of Arquivo National. This document is the basis of what follows.
[163] So considered in the Report. See previous note. At the height of the contraband between 1844 and 1848 Santos Barreto was also Minister of War for several months.

because of his enormous power and influence, but was acquitted of participation in the traffic. A point of disembarcation was even established in the fortress of São João by a Colonel Vasques, a Portuguese.

In 1836 and 1837 the traffic was blatantly open. Traders disembarked their cargoes practically anywhere they chose, bribed officials, and took their slaves up into the mountains and sold them for up to half a million reis. With rare exceptions—the police report mentions only Breves—the traders were Portuguese of great and little influence. The official whose duty it was to inspect all ships bound for Africa received eight hundred thousand reis for expediting a departure.[164] The chancellor of the Portuguese legation received one million reis for arranging the use of the Portuguese flag. The justice of the peace in Santa Rita, whose duty it was to take care of the ships' papers, received eight hundred thousand reis, and his clerk, half that sum. Energetic action by Francisco Gê Acaiaba de Montezuma, Minister of Foreign Affairs in 1837, and chief of the customs service resulted in the capture and detention of more than thirty ships that afterward were released by lower officials.

Now for a time the smugglers concealed and dissimulated their activities, disembarking in lonely places, then sailing to Montevideo and returning to Brazil with cargoes of meat. In 1837 and 1838 Manoel Pinto da Fonseca, assisted by his brothers,[165] entered the traffic; he soon became famous.[166] His ships sailed beyond the Cape of Good Hope as far as Mozambique and Quilimane, where slaves could be purchased cheaply.

The traders' audacity reached its climax in 1841 when they captured within the breakwater at Campos a British gig with its crew and officers. Thereafter the British cruisers became more vigilant, seizing ships within the waters of our coasts and forcing the traders to change tactics. João Manuel Pereira da Silva, later a deputy and a well-known historian, became the attorney for the smugglers in 1840 and

---

[164] The Report (preceding notes) mentions Manoel Moreira de Castro, later editor of the *Jornal do Comércio* and a Sr. Midosi. Moreira Castro was later accused by Euzébio de Queiroz.

[165] All are included in the list of traders and counterfeiters prepared in 1864, covering the period 1841 to 1861. Documents Ij–480 and 56–472 of the Arquivo Nacional.

[166] L. F. Hill, "The Abolition of the African Slave Trade to Brazil," *Hispanic American Historical Review*, XI (May, 1931), 169–197.

obtained for them, it was said, the protection of high officials. The ports of Macaé, Cabo Frio, and Paranaguá began to be used, as well as others. Generous bribes were distributed: two hundred thousand reis to a port captain, four hundred thousand to a customs agent, the same amount to a municipal judge, two hundred thousand to the judge's clerk.

About forty thousand slaves were disembarked in 1840. The slave ships sailed now not from Rio de Janeiro but from the above-mentioned ports. Alcoforado stated in his report, which is here summarized, that the traders had become so powerful that they could successfully oppose the cabinet. They boasted of their influence and claimed that they controlled the elections in three states, Minas, São Paulo, and Rio de Janeiro. In truth these men were very powerful, for they commanded vast sums and were aided by their allies the great landowners and also by the British commercial interests, from whom they obtained credit, in return granting the right to do business in the areas they controlled. With the publication of the British Bill, the traders changed tactics still again: the Portuguese flag now was no longer useful, so they turned to the American. The agent of this new arrangement was Manoel Pinto da Fonseca, in association with Manoel Maria Bregaro and with J. M. Pereira da Silva as attorney to deal with two American agents.

Alcoforado states that the ships purchased by the slave traders were loaded with cloth trade goods and sailed under the United States flag to Africa, without being molested by the British. There the American crews were exchanged for Portuguese (who were waiting in Africa or had made the voyage also, as passengers); they awaited their opportunity, embarked their cargo, and returned to Brazil the same way. From 1840 until 1848 the traffic was protected by the American flag, and during that time about sixty thousand slaves were landed in Brazil. The slaves could be seen for the looking; politicians encouraged the traffic and promised the traders their assistance. "It is clear that all political parties paid homage to the smugglers, except for a very few men who were not interesting in helping those in power who protected the smugglers from 1844 to 1848." [167]

---

[167] Of the Cabinets from February 2, 1844 to May 31, 1848, José Carlos Pereira de Almeida Tôrres, Visconde de Macaé, was three times Prime Minister, and Manoel Alves Branco, Visconde de Caravelas, was President of the Council in the Cabinet of May 22, 1847 and an outstanding figure in three others.

Indeed the traffic had become scandalous. Slaves were disembarked at Ilha Grande, at Campos, at Macaé, and even in the fortress of Santa Cruz, where the smugglers maintained a depot. The business was the monopoly of the Portuguese, who had formed a company together with the principal speculators in slaves: Maia, Saraiva, Barroso, Guimarães, Rocha, and Brandão.[168]

The steamship entered the trade for the first time toward the end of 1846. The Portuguese Tomás da Costa Ramos, slave smuggler and counterfeiter, owned the steamer *Teresa*. She was a small ship with space for only four hundred slaves, but Ramos crammed her with twelve hundred. On one occasion the use of a new device to purify drinking water resulted in the death of the entire cargo. Devices such as that, introduced in the American vessels, killed many Negroes.

Close to fifty or sixty thousand slaves arrived in Rio de Janeiro in 1847 and 1848. Following the seating of the cabinet of the Viscount de Olinda, Minister of Justice Euzébio de Queiroz, an Angolan by birth, set out to suppress the traffic. The police, who were always involved in the smuggling, were warned that serious measures including prosecution were going to be taken. The traders, however, especially Manuel Pinto da Fonseca, did not credit the firmness of Euzébio de Queiroz, and relied upon the protection they had formerly enjoyed and their access to the proceedings at secret meetings of the Chamber of Deputies. Two ships of Fonseca's were indeed released by local authorities following their detention. But in January of 1851 Euzébio de Queiroz destroyed the depots and sheds at Caju, Praia de Fora at the foot of Santa Cruz, at the Ostras river, and at Campos Sombrios, seized ships loaded with slaves, prosecuted the traders, and as they were Portuguese, deported them. Pinto da Fonseca escaped. The reëlection of Euzébio de Queiroz made it clear to the dealers in slaves that their former influence was no more. They had reached their last days.

That suppression obviously did not depend solely and exclusively on British cruisers. "Let His Majesty's Government rest assured that what disheartens and frightens the traders," wrote Paranhos da Silva, "is the prosecution at home that deprives them of all possibilities of profit. Without this internal repression, which will long remain as active and

---

[168] All of these names are recorded in the police list of 1864 already mentioned.

vigilant as it has to date, the bold and insidious traffic would make light of all the British cruisers." [169] It was Brazil's measures that reduced the activity on both sides of the Atlantic. From the two hundred Portuguese, Brazilians, Spanish, and mestizos of all origins practicing the trade in Ajudá around 1850, the number was reduced in 1865 to five Portuguese, thirteen Brazilians and four women, plus ten free Negroes from Brazil.

In 1856 Sinimbu, then Court Chief of Police, reported the strength of the traffic to the Minister of the Empire, José Tomás Nabuco de Araújo, as follows:

In the port of Ambriz on the coast of Africa there are three slave-trading posts, one belonging to Manuel Pinto da Fonseca, another to Ferraz Correia, both merchants from Bahia, and the third to Tomás Ramos, also known as "Maneta" because he has only one arm. The last post is the most powerful; Maneta is in Lisbon, but his agent, whose name is Fonseca, is on the coast. On the Congo River there are two posts, one preparing slaves for Havana and belonging to Zulueta, whose agent on the coast is José Ojea, and another that formerly belonged to the aforementioned Manuel Pinto da Fonseca. On the Quicombo River there is a post belonging to Rivarosa. On Cape Lopes there are three posts, one belonging to Havana and directed by a certain José Pernéa, another that did belong to José Bernardino de Sá, while the third is Rivarosa's, whose brother resides in Havana. They say that José Antunes de Carvalho e Côrtes was Rivarosa's manager and partner for a time, and that if he is not here he will probably be at the post. In Pôrto Novo the only proprietor preparing Africans exclusively for importation into the Empire is Domingos José Martins, who there is reason to suspect is attempting new efforts in the trade. In Onin the most notable trader is Luís Laminier, who became a naturalized Spaniard although French by birth. The points on our coast at which most shipments have been disembarked are Rio de Ostras, Macaé, Cabo Frio, Ponta dos Búzios, and Itapemirim. There is information that several ships have recently left Lisbon for the coast, that two of these unloaded in Havana while the others sailed for the Empire. [170]

In 1851 some of the traders were sought by the police, for example, Commander Joaquim José de Souza Breves who controlled the area of

---

[169] *Relatório do Ministério dos Negócios Estrangeiros,* Rio de Janeiro, 1856, 24.
[170] Joaquim Nabuco, *Um Estadista do Império, Nabuco de Araújo. Sua Vida, suas Opiniões, sua Época,* 2nd ed. São Paulo, Companhia Editôra Nacional, 1936, I, 166.

Marambaia where ships were frequently unloaded; another, the Portuguese Joaquim Pinto da Fonseca, was deported.[171] In police correspondence with the Ministry of Justice there are two lists prepared after 1864 containing the names of about three hundred and eighty-eight persons involved in the trade, none of them persons active in Ajudá, except Francisco Antônio Monteiro. Outstanding among them are Commander Joaquim José de Souza Breves, Canon Antônio Correia de Carvalho, and Antônio de Menezes Vasconcelos de Drumond; national and foreign nobility, such as Baron de Gamboa, José Manuel Fernandes Pereira, Baron do Itapemirim, Baron de Eylesh, Joaquim Pinto da Fonseca, the Cavalcanti Wanderley Lins and Barros Wanderley Lins, and the Cavalcanti de Albuquerque Maranhão; Frenchmen; Jews such as Moisés Ludwig; Italians; Spanish; and, the vast majority, Portuguese.[172]

BRAZILIAN POLITICS AND SUPPRESSION OF THE TRAFFIC

The Tenth Cabinet September 29, 1848, presided over by Viscount de Olinda and later by Viscount de Monte Alegre, was as Joaquim Nabuco writes, "one of the strongest and most homogeneous that the country ever had," for "it suppressed the traffic, put down the Pernambuco Revolution, overthrew Rosas, and at the same time laid the foundations for great reforms and improvements that later were realized." [173] If as Minister of Foreign Affairs Paulino José Soares de Souza engaged in extraordinary activity with skill, competence and assurance, as Minister of Justice Euzébio de Queiroz, another of the great leaders of the Conservative Party, on September 6, 1850, obtained Law No. 581 for repression of the traffic and on October 14, 1850, Decree No. 708, which implemented that law.

As Minister of Justice Euzébio de Queiroz strove for enforcement of the law so successfully that between 1848 and 1850 only 819 imported slaves were apprehended, while in 1850 the figure was 1,678, and in

---

[171] *Cartas ao Amigo Ausente,* 44.

[172] These two lists, Documents I j. 480 and 56–472 of the National Archive, covering traders from 1841 to 1864, have been consolidated and will soon be published as one list by the Arquivo Nacional.

[173] Joaquim Nabuco, *Um Estadista do Impéiro,* São Paulo, Companhia Editôra Nacional. 1936, I, 83–84; and J. A. Soares de Souza, *A Vida do Visconde do Uruguai,* São Paulo, Companhia Editôra Nacional, 1944, 196–197.

1852 1,006.[174] The traffic continued to decline because of difficulties imposed by the government, the action of the public ministry, the diligence of the police, and especially the untiring and determined action of the Angolan-Brazilian Euzébio de Queiroz Coutinho Matoso Câmara.

The struggle for abolition of the trade finally depended, therefore, more on the action of the Brazilian government than on British cruisers. All the efforts of the English, their whole squadron, which was strengthened several times, all their diplomatic pressure, their threats and disrespect to our national sovereignty, had found that Milanese resistance spoken of by Paranhos in his *Cartas ao Amigo Ausente:* nothing was accomplished, because no decisive action was taken by the Brazilian government. And why did the government not collaborate in liquidation of the trade? First, as has already been seen, because abolition affected rural interests, so identified with national interests, and the rural aristocracy was not persuaded of the value of the about-face in favor of colonization. "Fortunately the opinion, previously so general, that the death of our agriculture was inevitable as soon as there should be no further importation of slave labor, is disappearing," wrote Euzébio de Queiroz in 1851.[175] It was a difficult opinion to overcome, for in 1851 there were only 142,403 free persons in the capital, with 13,461 freed persons and 110,602 slaves; in the Province of Rio de Janeiro there were 262,526 free persons, 293,554 slaves and only 18,761 colonists.[176] But the government had begun to attend more to colonization and in 1858 admitted 14,650 immigrants; in 1859 there were 28,507 immigrants and 78 official, semi-official, and private colonies.[177]

This merely proves that the change in opinion was concomitant with active repression. It was now possible to show that the national were not the rural interests, or rather, the interests of the slave traffic. Formerly the big business, the big national contraband, was the traffic, and the traders with their large resources functioned as an economic pressure

---

[174] *Relatório do Ministério dos Negócios da Justiça*, Rio de Janeiro, 1851, 9; and 1852, 2.

[175] *Ibid.*, presented at the 2nd Session of the Eighth Legislature. Rio de Janeiro, 1850, 12.

[176] *Relatório do Ministério dos Negócios do Império*, Rio de Janeiro, 1851, 23 and 25.

[177] *Ibid.*, 1858, 24; and 1859, illustrative map.

group obstructing official action. This was recognized in the Chamber and some deputies even accused the government of connivance with the slave interests. In 1846 the United States Minister to Brazil, Henry A. Wise, wrote to Secretary of State James Buchanan that

There are only three ways of making a fortune in Brazil—either by the slave trade, or by shaving, or by a coffee commission business. The foreign merchants alone engage in the latter, & to be a Brazilian "man of consequence" all have to partake, more or less, directly or indirectly, in the two former. And *all who are of consequence* do partake in them both. Here you must be rich to profit by usury, & to be rich you must engage in the slave trade. The slave-traders, then, are either the men in power, or are those who lend to the men in power & hold them by the purse-strings. Thus, the Government itself is in fact a slave trading Government against its own laws & treaties.[178]

These most grave accusations came, it is true, from a very suspect man whose hatred for Brazil and Brazilians was outspoken in the various dispatches that he sent the Secretary of State. "This degraded and corrupt people who are ignorant of the first rudiments of administrative or judicial justice," [179] he writes in a passage from his correspondence accusing the Chief of Police of prevarication and of having received 2,000 *réis* to forge the will of a deceased rich man.[180] In another dispatch he accuses the Ministers, Councilors of State, Senators, and Deputies of being involved in the slave traffic.[181] Actually, according to the mutual accusations that were heard in the Parliament, although the police lists to which we have already referred do not mention them it seems that many people in high positions were indeed involved in the traffic, if not directly at least indirectly.

In his famous speech of July 15, 1850, Paulino José Soares de Souza reported the difficulties, the advances and retreats of the government, and said that "those who know how things are done among us will absolve my predecessors of any rebuke that may be made them in this

---

[178] William R. Manning, *Diplomatic Correspondence of the United States. Inter-American Affairs, 1831–1860,* Washington, 1932, II, 370.

[179] *Ibid.,* 369.

[180] The Chief of Police at that time was Magistrate Luís Fortunato de Brito Abreu Souza e Menezes.

[181] Dispatch of April 12, 1847, from Henry A. Wise to James Buchanan; Manning, *op. cit.,* 380.

respect." [182] By this he made it clear that the greater importation of slaves, 129,100 or more in the two years that the liberals were in power,[183] was not to be attributed to any kind of connivance. But the opposition pressed the issue in the session of July 20, 1850, when they declared that the Imperial government was helping supposed Brazilians "who by engaging in the traffic have been protected by the government in countries to which they have been taken as prisoners." Melo Franco was suggesting Imperial protection to foreigners employed in the trade, especially Portuguese, mentioning the case of a Portuguese firm established in Rio de Janeiro that claimed an indemnization of 60,000 *réis* for damages sustained on the coast of Africa, in Ambriz, at one of its trading posts attacked by Portuguese government forces. The suggestion was obvious and Maciel Monteiro did not miss the opportunity: "Now it is known that you were protecting the traffic." Melo Franco replied: "All the parties are more or less compromised in this illlicit commerce, but if there is a party that has raised its banner, declaring that civilization has come to us from the coast of Africa, that party is yours, for its most eminent member raised that banner in the Senate." Melo Franco was referring to Bernardo Pereira de Vasconcelos' statement that Africa had civilized Brazil.[184] After much interruption by the majority members, Melo Franco finally presented a petition requesting information as to the basis of the Imperial government's claims upon Portugal in behalf of the proprietors of the post in Ambriz, as to the number of Brazilian ships apprehended by British cruisers that year, the actions of the government, and finally, the number of free Africans distributed to private persons.

Maciel Monteiro, representing the majority, did not oppose the petition; he considered it important, but took advantage of the opportunity to reaffirm that according to the statistical data submitted to the Chamber by the Minister of Foreign Affairs, and which neither party had amassed, "it is evident that during the period of the present opposition's government, of evil memory, the importation of Africans into the Empire was extraordinary." If that government, now the

[182] *Anais do Parlamento Brasileiro,* Rio de Janeiro, 1880, II, 201.
[183] This figure appears in the same speech; *ibid.,* 200.
[184] *Ibid.,* 110 and 152.

opposition, had *not* tolerated the traffic, he asked, how could it have been possible to import such a large number of Africans? "Those who may wish to make a judgment on this question relating to protection or non-protection of the traffic, taking all ministries into account, cannot fail to recognize the grave imputation that must be made by the present administration." Maciel Monteiro believed that there had been tolerance on the part of the liberal government, and yet Melo Franco had wished "to cast doubt on the party to which I belong by repeating the indiscreet remark of an individual who belongs to our party that the coast of Africa civilized the Empire." In cases such as these he would rather be guided not by words but by facts, and the enormous importation of Africans during the past administration was a fact. "But even if one wishes to malign an entire party because of the very private and even absurd opinion of one individual, even if one wishes to establish the consensus of an entire party on the opinion of one of its members, I shall tell the noble opposition that it also is not exempt from such an opinion. Let the noble deputy recall that one of the eminences of his party, a Senator from Minas (I may name Sr. Vergueiro without being indiscreet),[185] is reputed to favor the traffic, and there is even indication (I shall not be the one to accuse him, for I do not carry my indiscretion to that extreme) that he gave special protection to the traders." And after referring to the opinion of Senator Paula Souza, a liberal, that the Empire was relieved of all obligation to repress the trade because the Agreement of 1826 no longer existed, he concluded: "It is therefore known and verified that if one wishes to judge by the facts in respect to protection or non-protection granted the traffic by the nation, to the noble opposition belongs the imputation of having protected the traffic when it was in power." [186]

So the opposition again saw itself openly denounced, as it had been in the session of June 28 when Deputy Joaquim Antão Fernandes Leão, ex-Minister of the Navy in the previous government, had declared to the cabinet ministers: "Destroy the ladders by which you have risen to

---

[185] In the report on the traders to which we have already referred (note 162) there is the name of a José Vergueiro who between 1839 and 1850 was engaged in the trade. Might there be some relationship?

[186] *Anais do Parlamento Brasileiro,* Session of 1850, Rio de Janeiro, 1880, II, 248–251.

power and you will have done the country a service." "What ladders?" asked the majority members, and Antão replied: "Can it be that the noble ministers did not require the support of friends in the slave traffic in order to come into power?" The accusation raised a storm of protest: "Outrage! Calumny! Nonsense!" "A party that would make use of traders must be a sorry one indeed," continued Antão. Joaquim Otávio Nébias, a magistrate and deputy from São Paulo then exclaimed forcefully: "The trust of the Crown is not controlled by traders" (applause, asides, whispers). But Antão insisted: "Reject this support, have enough energy and patriotism to tell your friends in the traffic . . ." He did not finish his sentence, for Deputy Joaquim José Pacheco from São Paulo interrupted to exclaim: "What is shameful is to fawn upon the foreigner! Let us all unite against the foreigner!" Both sides exacerbated their nationalism in the face of the English threats.

The disagreeable incident provoked by Deputy Antão from Minas had its reply in a speech by Deputy Pacheco. To the insinuation that Africanist ladders had raised the Conservative Party to power, he parried with the English ladders on which the Liberal Party had risen. But it was obvious that never had there been such an effort to abolish the traffic as now with the Tenth Cabinet presided over by Viscount de Olinda. Pacheco asked what efforts the Liberals had made to repress the traffic and accused them of having strengthened the traders morally "when you decorated many smugglers, thus abusing your stewardship" (great applause). It was Montezuma's task to restore calm by calling for national unity.[187]

On July 4, 1852, Paulino clearly established the non-partisan nature of the question. After denying that men in the government had connections with the traders or that it had been painful for his party to take repressive measures, he declared: "Gentlemen, let us say it, because it is the truth: during the periods when fifty to sixty thousand Africans entered the country annually, when speculation regarding Africa was at its peak, there were many people more or less directly involved in the trade. Who among us did not have relations with someone engaged in the traffic at times when it was not condemned by public opinion? . . . I believe therefore that repression of the traffic must not be a political

---

[187] *Ibid.*, 1875, Session of July 28, 1805, I, 577–592.

weapon (applause); it is in the general interest of the nation." [188]
Returning to the matter on July 16, he further clarified it:

Let us be frank; the traffic in Brazil depended on the interests, or rather, on
the presumed interests, of our farming community: and in a country where
agriculture has such great power, it was natural that public opinion should
show itself in favor of the traffic, public opinion which has such great influence not only in representative governments but even in the most absolute
monarchies. (Applause) What is so astonishing, then, in the fact that our
politicians bent to the law of necessity? What is astonishing if all of us,
friends or enemies of the traffic, bent to that necessity? Gentlemen, if this
were a crime, it would be a general crime in Brazil (applause), but I
maintain that when in a nation all political parties share power, when all
politicians have been called to exercise it, and all are agreed on a course
of action, that action must be based on very strong reasons; it is impossible
for it to be a crime (applause), and it would be foolhardy to call it an
error (applause).

He then continued:

When Brazil annually imported fifty to sixty thousand slaves a year, the
importation of slaves tending, as we know, to restrain free labor, our great
landowners, our politicians, in short the people of Brazil, who even without
knowing the statistics could not fail to note the increase in the traffic, must
necessarily have been struck by the imbalance that it was producing between
the two classes of labor, free and slave, and by fear of the very grave dangers
to which this imbalance was exposing us.

Then even those who considered cessation of the traffic a calamity for the
country's finances, because it would diminish our means of production and
therefore the national wealth, began to recognize that the dangers of its
continuance were much more serious and that between the two evils they
should unhesitatingly decide in favor of cessation of the traffic.

To this consideration were joined the interests of our farming community;
at first, believing that an increase in their profits depended on the purchase of
a greater number of slaves, our farmers, not realizing the very grave danger
threatening the country, were concerned merely with the acquisition of
new slaves, buying them on credit, with payments due in three and four
years, and paying very high interest in the interim.

Now, it is known that the majority of these slaves soon died off in the
first years because of the unfortunate state to which they are reduced by
evil conditions on the ships, changes in climate, food, and their whole way of

---

[188] *Ibid.*, 1877, I, 173.

living. The slaves died but the debts remained, and as a result, lands were mortgaged to speculators, who bought Africans from traders in order to resell them to farmers. (Applause) In this way our property passed from the farmers to the speculators and traders. (Applause) This experience awakened our farmers and made them realize that they were being ruined, whereas they had thought to become wealthy (applause), and henceforth the trade was completely condemned. Its days were numbered, and our only merit was to have recognized and profited energetically from the occasion in order to institute repression; but with the revolution that had gradually taken place in the ideas and public opinion of the country, whatever the party, whatever the ministry, the government *had* to be sincerely in favor of repressing the traffic, as we were.[189]

Having put the question in these terms, Paulino explained that the then particularly violent British actions had been designed "to contest any merit of ours in this important service lent by Brazil to the cause of humanity." Great Britain had seen all its efforts thwarted by the tenacity of the traders; the traffic had tripled since the proclamation of the Aberdeen Bill. Only the law of September 4, which had the general support of the nation, succeeded in reducing and then abolishing it.

This was perfect and complete enlightenment. The business of the traders represented enormous profits, approximately 100,000 or 200,000 *réis* on each sailing vessel arriving at its destination, as Paulino showed in his speech of July 15, 1850.[190] These profits were made especially by the Portuguese principal traders, it being confirmed that a hundred and forty of them returned to Portugal with a collective profit of 1,000,000 pounds sterling.[191] Many of them were on the police lists as traders and counterfeiters, and they were relentlessly prosecuted by the police. Accused, sentenced, and deported from the country for their slave-trading activities, many became naturalized Brazilian citizens between 1852 and 1856 "solely to be able to rely on the protection of the laws of the nation and be free of the demands and denunciations of police spies."

---

[189] *Ibid.,* Session of July 16, 1852, II, 249, Rio de Janeiro, 1877.

[190] *Ibid.,* II, 200. According to L. F. Hill, art. cit., the profits of the traffic varied in 1840 between 100 and 200 per cent.

[191] R. Coupland, *The British Anti-Slavery Movement,* London, 1933, 184. The author does not indicate the source of his information and sees the problem only from the British point of view.

As always they dared to hire the services of the press to attack the country and its authorities: "What country is this that has different laws for each nationality; humble to the point of abjection before the strong, and arbitrary to the point of insolence before those who fear it?" This is to be found in a communication [192] telling of the supposed arbitrary acts against the Portuguese trader Antônio Severino de Avelar, arrested in Rio de Janeiro and taken to Recife, accused of being connected with the unloading of slaves in Sirinhaém. The communication censures the Portuguese authorities for not protecting their subjects, as though the latter could escape Brazilian law or we were still in the time when Portugal had ceded custodianship to Great Britain, an arrangement that we received as our national heritage and that caused us much humiliation and from which we struggled to be free. Antônio Severino de Avelar, a trader known to the police,[193] made frequent trips to Africa, the United States, and Lisbon. The Portuguese were deeply involved in the slave trade and in counterfeiting; the latter caused us to protest to the Portuguese government in 1861 and 1862.

The first and most important consequence of abolition of the traffic was the release of the capital tied up in it and the freeing of the farming interests involved with the traders. That capital could now be applied to agriculture. "Abolition of the slave trade suddenly brought a great influx of capital to the country valued at more than 16,000,000 réis." [194] "Typical of this period are great commercial activity, satisfactory business negotiations, the creation of utility companies, the reduction of discount rates, which in 1851 declined to 3 and 4½ per cent, and then rose to 6 and 7 per cent, and a rate of exchange generally of 27 and 28, sometimes going as high as 30 and seldom down to 28. There is a surplus of money on the market: there is security, an abundance of capital, and business is satisfactory. This bright picture was not darkened either by the effects of the war in the Rio de la Plata or by

---

[192] *Jornal de Comércio,* January 11, 1856, 3.

[193] His name appears on the list to which we referred earlier.

[194] *Relatório da Comissão Encarregada pelo Govêrno Imperial . . . de proceder a um Inquérito sôbre as causas principais e acidentais da crise do mês de setembro de 1864.* (The Commission was composed of Councillors Angelo Muniz da Silva Ferraz and José Pedro Dias de Carvalho [replacing Bernardo de Souza Franco], Dr. Francisco de Assis Vieira Bueno [replacing José Maria da Silva Paranhos] as Government Inspectors). Rio de Janeiro, 1865, 24.

the Crimean War, which could have influenced consumer markets for our products." [195]

"Bonds rose to a level never hoped for, companies were formed to build railroads, banks were founded, new settlers entered the country, capital was abundant in Rio." [196]

Sebastião Ferreira Soares[197] expressed himself in similar fashion when he wrote that upon abolition of the slave trade, "the great sum of capital that was being employed in this anti-Catholic cycle reëntered our principal commercial centers seeking new employment"; material improvements that had thus far been neglected were now explored. In the unanimous opinion of historians, the about-face in our history in the direction of material progress dates from that time.[198]

WITHDRAWAL FROM AFRICA

Brazil's withdrawal from Africa took place between 1850 and 1858, and the tradition of three centuries' of ethnic-cultural contacts was broken. The few commercial relations that still persisted between Lagos and Bahia, the return of freed Africans from Brazil to Africa and even the founding of African cities by Afro-Brazilians, to which Nina Rodrigues and Gilberto Freyre refer, do not disguise the break nor hide the alienation henceforth felt by Brazil toward Africa. If we dominated Angolan commerce until 1835, if commercial relations with other African groups were close, if slavery was the source of our agricultural labor, after 1826 our relations were disturbed by European interests, especially British, and became an internal and international problem. Before 1850 the principle that Africa had civilized Brazil could be proclaimed, first by Cunha Matos and then by Bernardo Pereira de Vasconcelos. "Today, however," said the writer of an article in the *Jornal do Comércio* in 1850, "sentiments more Christian and principles more honest are professed. The slothful and impure civilization imported from Africa is increasingly more discredited, opinion is clearly

---

[195] *Ibid.*, 25.
[196] See note 162.
[197] *Esbôço ou Primeiros Traços da Crise Commercial do Rio de Janeiro, em 10 de setembro de 1864.* Rio de Janeiro, 1865, 33.
[198] See Capistrano de Abreu, "Fases do Segundo Império," in *Ensaios e Estudos,* 3rd series, Sociedade Capistrano de Abreu, 1938, 119 ff.

changing, and now it requires some courage for anyone to boast of the profession of slave-trader." [199]

Actually, as may be deduced from transcribed discussions and debates, in Cunha Matos' time people were able to distinguish between slaves and Africans, and the part of our African intercourse of three centuries against which there were now recriminations was the importation of slaves. The later effects of the twenty-five-year seige, however, were the repudiation and isolation of Africa and the birth of slavocratic complexes that led Brazil to think of the African only as a Brazilian slave soon to be liberated. Outwardly our policy became Latin-Americanized and turned entirely toward the Rio de la Plata, and a new attempt was made to Westernize a nation to which the Portuguese had been unable to transplant European culture intact or even almost intact. Tupi and African influences over three centuries had made basically intractable the European and Occidental institutions that the Portuguese had wanted to impose on us. The Brazilian triumph over barbarism was ethnically and culturally a syncretic product, and backwardness was the penalty for the intractability of European institutions in a foreign environment with non-European and heterogeneous peoples by whom mechanical imitation was impossible. As the dominant minorities did imitate, they were alienated and frequently found themselves threatened with losing their control over the majority.

Brazil's withdrawal from Africa was an instrument of differentiation and growth to keep the imported institutions from becoming fatuous and ephemeral, to adjust them to changes and thus permit them to be creative and original. It was practically complete. Anyone examining our foreign policy will see that even in the distribution of diplomatic posts we always concentrated on Europe. As early as 1831 Francisco Carneiro de Campos wrote that he was "intimately convinced, and moreover the vote of the Assembly-General is in agreement, that— although we have had to date, and perhaps for a long time must continue to have, the closest relations with the Old World—it is convenient to begin as of now to establish and preferably to strengthen

---

[199] "O Tráfico," signed P. R. in *Jornal do Comércio*, July 11, 1850.

the bonds that in the future must closely link the units in the political
system of the American hemisphere," [200] a policy he expected to "repel
the unjust pretensions of infatuated foreign nations." Nonetheless, more
attention continued to be given to Europe than to America, and in the
latter, most attention was given to the Republics of the Plata because
proximity created constant problems.

In the opinion of Great Britain, as later in that of the United States,
the policy that was suitable for us, the only one in which we ought to
be protagonists, was that of "Latin" America. To regionalize foreign
policy, prevent it from being active, from having extra-continental
interests, has always been the objective of the two great nations during
their periods of rise to power. Witness the example of our isolation from
Africa during the past century and note today the Atlantic organization, which is contemptuous of South American Atlantic nations.

Distribution of diplomatic posts shows that in 1833 we had ten
representatives in Europe and only four in America, and that despite
constant variation motivated by debate in the Assembly during
examinations of the budget, our diplomatic representation was always
greater on the old continent. For the first time in 1844 the Foreign
Minister's Report divides representation according to continents. In the
Afro-Asian world we had three consuls without remuneration: at the
Cape of Good Hope, in Canton, and in the English and Portuguese
dominions. Even in 1840, however, Pedro José da Costa Pacheco had
been our Consul-General in the English and Portuguese dominions of
Asia, and João Stein had represented us at the Cape of Good Hope. This
was for a long time our only representation in Africa, although we had
petitioned for a consulate in Angola since 1847. "The Imperial
Government, convinced of the most urgent necessity to establish
Brazilian consulates in certain Portuguese possessions in order that
subjects of the Empire may receive due protection there," wrote
Saturnino de Souza e Oliveira in 1847, "has given instructions to the
legation in Lisbon so that it may effectively insist on the admission of
Brazilian vice-consuls in those possessions, emphasizing the reciprocity
that must be accorded the government of Brazil, which has permitted

---

[200] *Relatório do Ministério dos Negócios Estrangeiros.* Rio de Janeiro, 1931, 6–7.

the Portuguese government to name vice-consuls in Brazilian ports." [201]
But Portugal did not want our presence in Africa, and thus we
maintained twenty-one vice-consuls in metropolitan territory and in
Madeira but none in Africa.

In 1850 Portugal continued to place obstacles to the admission of
Brazilian consular agents to the ports of their overseas possessions, ports
that had been opened to foreign commerce by the law of June 5, 1844.
The Brazilian legation in Lisbon made repeated requests stressing the
principle of reciprocity and the convenience of having Brazilian agents
attend the interests of Brazilian citizens, and alluding to the vexations
Brazilians had suffered from Portuguese authorities; but to no avail.
"The Imperial government will continue to give this matter the
attention it merits," wrote Foreign Minister Paulino José Soares de
Souza, future Viscount of Uruguay.[202]

Not until 1855 did Portugal enter into an agreement to admit
Brazilian consular agents to all ports in the overseas possessions. An
agent was named for Angola, with residence in Luanda, and instructed
both "to attend to Brazilian interests and to inform the Imperial
Government promptly of any efforts that may be made to revive the
extinct traffic in slaves." [203] The agent appointed, Frederico
Hermenegildo de Niterói, did not, however, go to Luanda; his
successor, Inacio José Nogueira da Gama, who departed in May, 1856,
was in December replaced by Saturnino de Souza e Oliveira,[204]
who remained until 1861. Souza e Oliveira was instructed by the
Foreign Ministry to make a study of Brazilian-Angolan commercial
relations to learn "why certain of our agricultural products that in
former times had a large market in this part of Africa today are sold
there on a very small scale," so that measures to reëstablish the old
supremacy of our products could be taken.[205]

---

[201] *Ibid.*, 1847, 18.
[202] *Ibid.*, 1850, 5.
[203] *Ibid.*, 1855, x.
[204] *Ibid.*, 1856, 7. Saturnino de Souza e Oliveira Coutinho was the son of the
Conselheiro of the same name, a politician in the State of Rio de Janeiro and
nephew of Aureliano, Viscount of Sepetiba.
[205] "Instruções de 10 de dezembro, 1857." Arquivo Histórico do Itamarati. Re-
partições Consulares, Angola.

The instructions give an interesting rapid summary of our African trade, dividing it into three phases:

The first phase begins in colonial times and ends in 1830 with the Treaty of 1826 which abolished slavery.

The second phase consisted of illicit trading in slaves and ended when the slave traffic was suppressed.

The third phase is that in which we find ourselves today and dates from 1850.

During the first period, commerce was on a large scale and Brazil was truly the Metropolis of the Portuguese possessions on both African coasts. In the second period, the theater of speculation was not so large, but because of the sums involved, we may say without error that the period was more important than the first. In both these periods, our exports were exchanged for slaves. In the second period, however, certain of our products began to be excluded, and those foreign products which we reexported to Africa were excluded entirely. Since 1837, our exports to Africa have dwindled steadily until they have dropped to the present level.

The end of the traffic in slaves, however, resulted in an increase in agricultural production in Angola, with exportation to Europe. One of these products, wax, is shipped to Lisbon and reëxported to Brazil. It is obvious that it would be advantageous to us to import such products directly from their source, an objective that will be achieved only when our own products have a larger market in Angola than at present.

Brazil produces products that are esteemed in all Africa. Our brandy is a drink much appreciated and has no rival among the beverages that are substituted for it; Africans will sacrifice everything for this liquor. Our sugar and our processed tobacco are consumed there in quantity.

So Your Excellency can see that there are elements upon which a prosperous trade between the Empire and the district of your consulate may be based. It would be convenient for Brazil to secure that trade. Besides immediate profits, we must keep in mind that the introduction of our products to Africa cheaply and in quantity will make difficult the cultivation there of similar products, thus preventing African competition in European and American markets.

It was further recommended that the consul oversee the estates of deceased Brazilians who had been residents of Angola—for large sums had for a long time lain stagnant in the coffers of the Angolan treasury; and finally that he maintain a careful watch upon dealers in slaves in order to frustrate their attempts to take slaves to Brazil. Before the establishment of this consulate, Brazil had agents only in Lagos,

Bombay, and Macao. On May 7 and 20, 1892, the vice-consulates of Mozambique[206] and Quilmane were established, and in 1896, that in Goa.[207]

In this manner, only at the end of the century, when spheres of influence in Africa were already established and Brazil had been practically isolated from it for forty years, was our presence again permitted in Luso-African territories. It must not be forgotten that in 1848 we still maintained "considerable commerce with those overseas provinces," according to Paulino José Soares de Souza in his Report, and that in 1895 we renewed the political relations with Portugal that had been broken in 1893 because of the asylum given the Armada rebels.

According to Article 4 of the Agreement of November 4, 1826, Brazil had obligated itself to maintain one of the two mixed commissions in Sierra Leone which, together with the other in Rio, was charged with judging cases of slave contraband. As early as 1831 the Brazilian government did not wish the continuance of the Commission because of the annual cost to the National Treasury of 5,000 *réis,* but it was maintained until 1845 when the fifteen-year period of the agreement expired. On several occasions, as in 1839 and 1840, the posts of judge and arbiter for Brazil were vacant; from 1841 to 1843 our commissioner-judge was Frederico Hermenegildo de Niterói, who in 1850 was to be our representative in Monrovia, capital of Liberia, proclaimed a republic in 1847 by Negroes emigrated from the United States.

The Empire also maintained relations with Morocco. In 1878 the Imperial Government was informed that Moroccan Jews were coming to Brazil to seek their fortune, becoming naturalized Brazilians, and returning to Morocco, frequently with children born in Brazil and therefore also Brazilians. They came to Brazil "because of the good treatment that they receive there and the advantages that commercial life in the Empire offers them." Upon their return to Morocco they refused to submit to the laws of that country. The Council of State advised that by law, or by an agreement with the government of Morocco, a presumption of renunciation of naturalization should be established when the naturalized citizen returned to his native country

---

[206] See *Relatório do Ministério das Relações Exteriores,* 1892, 31.
[207] *Ibid.,* 1899, 90–92.

and settled or remained for two years.[208] Consular protection was temporary and individual; nevertheless the Moroccans still refused to follow the laws of the country, and complaints continued until 1882 when an agreement was signed, establishing the principles of the right to protection, Great Britain, France, Spain, and other countries joining it.[209] As abuses continued, it was proposed in 1896 to remove the consulate at Tangier.[210]

Relations with Africa during the Empire were merely formal, in these cases as in that of January 7, 1882, recognizing supervision of the Transvaal's foreign policy by the Queen of England,[211] or that of August 14, 1888 accepting Leopold II's ignominy in the Belgian Congo.[212] Finally, on August 14, 1888, the Empire was "apprised that the Italian protectorate was solemnly established and declared in Zula, south of Massuá."[213]

It was a sad thing to witness the formality of these acknowledgments and how indifferently we observed the European powers carving into bloody strips the Africa with which we had had such close and solid connections. The treaty of June 11, 1891, signed between Portugal and Great Britain, recognized and protected the remnants of the Portuguese possessions in Africa. Cunha Matos' prediction was being realized: with Brazil isolated from Africa, Great Britain, France, Belgium, and Germany were pillaging to their own advantage and preparing African competition to our own tropical products.

If the Empire had been forced to turn its back on Africa and to concern itself with the African only as slave, the Republic pretended complete ignorance, not only because it did not have the power to pursue an independent policy to censure European colonialism, but also because it was controlled by theories of the superiority of Anglo-Saxon white skin or European ancestry.

In 1899, before the general alliance of the European powers and the

---

[208] *Relatório do Ministério dos Negócios Estrangeiros,* Rio de Janeiro, 1878, 16–17.
[209] *Ibid.,* 1822, 30–33, Appendix No. 114, pp. 253–267. For the Agreement, see 261–267.
[210] *Ibid.,* 1896, 67.
[211] *Ibid.,* 1882, 333–334.
[212] *Ibid.,* 1886, 52–53. Documents Nos. 22 and 23; pp. 37–40.
[213] *Ibid.,* 1889, Documents Nos. 99 and 100; pp. 172–173.

formation of their all-pervading policies, Ruy Barbosa warned the
Latin-American peoples that it was a foolish and short-sighted attitude
to believe that they had assured their independence for all time.
"Having struggled with two nations in profound decline, supported by
the sympathy and assistance of one that had by then already undertaken
to rule the seas, they were left with the illusion that they had given
Europe an unforgettable lesson, that the defeat of Spain and Portugal
would discourage the Old World from similar attempts and that, if
perchance these should arise, they would just as easily, successfully, and
immediately be repulsed." Now, continued Ruy Barbosa, the European
population was expanding, crossing immense stretches of ocean and
"disputing the scattered population of these emancipated dependencies
its virgin soil, ready wealth, and certain future." It was necessary to
prepare, to join with other peoples in view of recent examples: "We
have seen colonialist policy fascinate the most sedentary nations, and
Asia, Africa, and Oceania have disappeared under the claws of Europe.
In short, we have seen the law of nations become practically the law of
the cannon." [214]

Our minorities, so depreciated and "penalized" by the campaigns
against the traffic and for abolition of slavery, limited themselves to
strengthening relations with Europe and the United States and to fixing
their attention on South America, trying especially to resolve the
problems of establishing frontiers, the definitive work of Rio Branco, in
defense of Brazil's territorial status quo. It was not only Africa that did
not exist for us; neither did the Orient; only China was known to us,
very superficially; with China the Empire had signed a Treaty of
Friendship in 1882, and the Republic had negotiated an agreement on
emigration in 1893 and signed a new treaty in 1913; and also Japan, with
which we had also negotiated a treaty in 1893 designed to facilitate emigration. This last was finally approved in 1896.

Examination of the distribution of diplomatic and consular representation shows that in 1914 and 1915 most of our representation was
spread through Europe (there being 61 consular agencies in Great
Britain, 27 in Spain, 26 in Italy, 25 in France, 24 in Germany, 20 in

---

[214] "Desleixo Latino-Americano," in *A Imprensa,* May 4, 1899, reproduced in
Campanhas Jornalísticas, Casa de Rui Barbosa, 1957, 99–101.

Portugal) and 86 in America (26 in the United States and 11 in Argentina). In Asia we had diplomatic representation only in China, where foreign consuls still had extra-territorial rights, and in Japan; in Africa there were only consular agents.

In 1923 we recognized the independence of Egypt;[215] in 1925 we made out first agreement with an African country, Liberia, designed to solve controversies arising between the two republics (Paris, July 15). Egypt, with all the reservations imposed upon it by Great Britain; Liberia, "protected" by the United States, which already was rich in colonial possessions;[216] China, subjected to a series of capitulations; and Japan, these were the free countries of the Afro-Asian world with which we maintained more formal than positive relations. Of those countries under foreign domination we had the largest representation in Morocco, as always, because of greater economic interests. Everything was under the vasselage of Europe.

From 1919 to 1923 Brazil still dominated the world coffee market (more than 64 per cent) and Africa contributed only 2 per cent, but the magnificent prices of the decade 1920–1930 stimulated coffee-growing extraordinarily throughout the world.[217] In Africa, especially in Eritreia, Uganda, Kenya, the Belgian Congo, Nigeria, French West Africa, and Rhodesia plantations were started to compete for the world market. Africa was to reappear as our competitor, stimulated by Europe to benefit eternally malignant world power.

AFRICA RETURNS

It was around 1929–1930 that African competition to Brazilian products began to be noticed. Waldir Niemeyer wrote an essay in 1929 on Afro-Asian competition to Brazilian agricultural production,[218] showing that Great Britain and France, the two powers having the largest colonial empires, were transforming their colonies into great centers

[215] Great Britain communicated that it had ended the British protectorate. See *Relatório do Ministério das Relações Exteriores,* 1924, I, 14 and 59.
[216] *Ibid.,* 1928. In *Relatório do Ministério das Relações Exteriores,* 1928, the United States appears with those of its colonial possessions where we had consular agents.
[217] Afonso d'E. Taunay, *História do Café no Brasil,* Rio de Janeiro, 1941, Vol. XII, 269 and Vol. XV, 209.
[218] *Nossos Concorrentes. O Brasil, sua Produção Agrícola e os Concorrentes da Ásia e África,* Rio de Janeiro, 1929.

supplying raw materials and foodstuffs for their internal markets and consuming their varied manufactured articles. Although he stated that he saw nothing ominous in the perspective of colonial competition, because Brazil was already becoming an industrial nation, he indicated that concern with African production was growing. His comparisons between the production of the African colonies and that of Brazil showed, for example, that in 1927–1928 Uganda was already producing more cotton than Pernambuco, which had been the principal center of production; that in 1913 the Gold Coast (Ghana) was already the greatest producer of cacao in the world (234,900 tons), followed at a great interval by Ecuador (37,400 tons) and Brazil (31,000 tons), so that in 1927 its contribution had been 50 per cent of world production; that Nigeria was already the greatest center in the world producing palm oil, third in the production of peanuts, and competing with Bahia in cacao; that Guinea (having more or less the same territory as Piauí) was already producing more rice than all of Brazil. But not even these facts of economic importance presented in a pioneer study succeeded in awakening our attention. Africa continued to be unknown, distant, without interest.

After the 1930 Revolution, Foreign Minister Afrânio de Melo Franco attempted to initiate a new commercial policy "by means of commercial agreements capable of encouraging expansion of our production and providing new markets for our exports."[219] The agreement between Brazil and Great Britain, concluded September 11, 1931,[220] and giving reciprocal treatment to the natural products and manufactured articles of the two countries no less favorable than that granted to any other country, was extended in 1932 to the colonies, protectorates, and territories under British mandate, such as the Gold Coast, Togo, Nigeria, Northern Rhodesia, Sierra Leone, Somaliland, Tanganyika, Uganda, and Zanzibar.[221]

From this time on the interest of our authorities in Africa began to awaken, and in the Presidential Message to Congress of May 3, 1937, there was the statement that "negotiations are continuing in London for the conclusion of a new agreement with Great Britain and a careful

---

[219] *Relatório do Ministério das Relações Exteriores,* Rio de Janeiro, 1931, xvi.
[220] *Ibid.,* 63–65.
[221] *Relatório do Ministério do Exterior,* 1932, Rio de Janeiro, 1935, 39–40.

study is being made of the stipulations referring to the Dominions and possessions having self-government with which we maintain constant and considerable commercial interchange." [222] But that trade was in point of fact neither so constant nor so considerable, for between 1934 and 1938 Algeria, the first African country in commerce with Brazil, was twenty-fifth among other countries, the Union of South Africa twenty-sixth, Egypt thirty-third, and Rhodesia thirty-fifth, the first and the last being colonial countries.[223] Moreover, in 1942 Africa accounted for only 3 per cent of the total value of Brazil's foreign trade, with America representing 70.21 per cent (45.64 per cent for the United States alone), Europe 26.03 per cent (16.45 per cent for Great Britain alone) and Asia 0.22 per cent.[224] The First World War had modified the situation, for in 1938 it was stated that "Africa, North and Central America, Asia, and Oceania have given us a positive balance totaling 3,401,405 pounds; South America and Europe a negative balance totaling 3,372,646 gold pounds." [225] With the war "our commerce, which had already been having a difficult struggle to equalize its balance of trade, totally or partially lost for a period that cannot yet be calculated several consumer markets" represented by the belligerent countries and even by the neutrals, in view of restrictions imposed on commerce because of the arbitrary classification of merchandise as war contraband.[226] Coffee was then being sold at slight profits and African production jumped from 2 per cent of world production to 12.13 per cent, while ours fell to 50.13 per cent.[227]

---

[222] The part relative to the Ministry of Foreign Affairs is reproduced in the *Relatório* of the Ministry, 1936, Rio de Janeiro, 1938, Appendix A, p. 7.

[223] *Relatório do Ministério das Relações Exteriores,* 1938, Rio de Janeiro, 1943, 265–322. In the case of Algeria, there was a commercial agreement signed with the French Embassy in 1932. The commercial agreement with the Union of South Africa is dated April 18, 1939. Brazil's exports to Africa for 1937–1939 were 1.44%, 1.28%, and 1.35% of its total exports. See *Anuário Estatístico do Brasil,* 1939–1940, 395.

[224] A war year. See *Relatório do Ministério da Fazenda,* Rio de Janeiro, 1942, 98. Between 1944 and 1946 Africa accounted for 2.87%, 3.57%, and 2.82% of Brazil's total exports. See *ibid.,* 1959, 157.

[225] *Relatório do Ministério das Relaçõs Exteriores,* 1938, Rio de Janeiro, 1943, 24.

[226] *Ibid.,* 1939, Rio de Janeiro, 1939, 12.

[227] See *Anuário Estatístico do Departamento Nacional do Café,* cited by Afonso d'E. Taunay, *História do Café no Brasil,* XV, Rio de Janeiro, 1943, 209.

During the Second World War a new interest in Africa was born, an interest at first only in North Africa. Foreign Minister Osvaldo Aranha decided to send a diplomatic agent to the African theater of operations, which was important in the overall war picture, and it was Vasco Leitão da Cunha who performed this function in Equatorial Africa and in French North Africa, studying the possibility of the consulate in Algeria which was later established. Military missions also sent at that time studied military coöperation in the campaign on the side of the Allies before the arrival of the F.E.B.[228]

After the war, however, there was a new break in relations, a total estrangement, and between 1945 and 1955 we did not attend to the evolution of Africa. There were merely statements, as that in 1951 that "the decision of the Egyptian Government to put an end to the presence of British troops in its territory and the demonstrations of the Moroccan people for their independence have attracted the attention of the Brazilian Government," which was following the matter "with a most friendly interest in conciliation." [229] The great preoccupation was, as always, American politics and the bond with Western Europe, although union with all peoples in the work of international conciliation was affirmed. The formality of these tranquilizing and fatuous declarations served only to show that we accepted our limitations in the international field, which restricted us to the American continent and to the European powers, which as a result treated us as they saw fit.[230]

Commenting on the presidential message of 1955, Senator Lourival Fontes examined our foreign policy, conducted "without any organizing thought, consistency of action, or firm and sure guidance." He reminded Brazil that, together with Canada, it was the middle power that had most contributed to the Second World War, yet our diplomacy was content "with making the grand gesture," while our allies and

---

[228] *Relatório do Ministério das Relações Exteriores,* 1943, Rio de Janeiro, 1944, 10–12.

[229] *O Itamarati em 1951.* Ministério das Relações Exteriores. n.d., p. 35. In 1951 a cultural agreement was signed with Egypt. See *Coleção de Atos Internacionais,* No. 334.

[230] Message of President Café Filho, March 15, 1955 (*Diário Oficial,* March 16, 1955), makes the same statements.

associates, who so desired to see us limited to continental defense, seek outside the continent, far from the hemisphere,

the tropical products that have their habitat or origin here. They go to Malaya for rubber. They go to Indonesia for quinine. Coffee plantations are flourishing in Ethiopia. Plantations of sugar cane and copper mines are being developed in Durban and the Belgian Congo. The sources of supply of wheat, corn, bananas, rice, and potatoes are in western Africa. The jungles and forests of that lush continent are already being prepared for cattle raising and meat production on a large scale. They go to Egypt and the Sudan for cotton for their industrial needs. Even today the United States imports more than 90 per cent of its industrial and strategic raw materials which are specifically American. Its sources of supply for products native to America are located many miles from the hemisphere.

Lourival Fontes then warned that the great threat hanging over Brazil was that of African competition, for depleted Europe was taking that last opportunity to make a new future and life for itself as an industrial and military power, American capitalism also was making a tremendous effort to exploit the wealth of Africa. Our policy was leading Brazil to a position of isolation and segregation, for "we were shutting the doors on our commercial expansion toward almost a billion customers and consumers composing the population of the Soviet Union, China, and the popular democracies." [231] The perceptiveness of this view of our passive foreign policy clashed with its lack of perception in hoping for Americanization of North American policy, and with the prophecy that "if today Africa is the hope of Anglo-American capitalism, tomorrow it will inevitably pronounce Latin America's death sentence." How could we reconcile the hope of internationalizing our ports and products with the facts of American continentalization, expanding on the one hand and restricting on the other, or further, how follow an anti-colonial policy while seeing only our death sentence in the growth of the African nations? [232]

Lourival Fontes' views of African competition in 1955 as a mortal threat and of the African problem in general did not make the least

---

[231] Speech delivered April 23, 1955, in the Senate, *Diário do Congresso Nacional,* 922–924, reproduced in *Discurso aos Surdos,* Rio de Janeiro, José Olímpio, 1955.
[232] In May of 1960 the author prepared a study on "Brazil, the United States and Latin America," soon to be published, in which he develops this question.

impression on one of our great parties, for upon approving a motion concerning the goals of our foreign policy during a convention in 1957, not the slightest reference was made to the whole problem of European and American colonialist policy, much less to Africa.[233]

But the inevitable was to happen when the colonialist policy of France, Great Britain, and Belgium in Dark Africa came to an end. After the victory of the Arab revolutions in Morocco and Tunisia, and the recognition of these new governments by Brazil,[234] the upheavals in the Sudan and its recognition as a free country,[235] the interminable war in Algeria, the Afro-Asian conference at Bandung (1955), the independence of Ghana, also recognized by Brazil,[236] and our participation in the Egyptian question, there had arrived not only the Dark Continent's great moment but also the decisive occasion for us to give our attention to African independence and to define our position vis-à-vis colonialism and the projected European Common Market. It was already perceived that the latter "would constitute a threat to Brazilian products, especially coffee, produced also by the overseas territories of some of these countries. In the meeting of the contracting members of G.A.T.T. [General Agreement on Tariffs and Trade] last October [1956], Brazil expressed its reservations and showed the dangers of such an initiative, which could favor these products to the detriment of similar ones of Brazilian origin." [237]

The policy of the Juscelino Kubitschek administration concentrated on the Pan-American Operation, and on developing Latin America. No attitude in support of African aspirations could have any bearing on the essence of the objectives he proposed. It was during his government that the explosion of African independence took place; in 1956 there were eight independent countries (Egypt, Ethiopia, Union of South Africa, Libya, Morocco, Tunisia, and Sudan) and by 1960 twenty new countries had obtained their freedom. For this reason the government, although

---

[233] See Motion I, approved at the Convention of the U.D.N. (National Democratic Union), transcribed in *Diário do Congresso Nacional*, April 9, 1957, 1841–1842.

[234] See notes in *Relatório do Ministério das Relações Exteriores*, 1956, 51.

[235] *Ibid.*, p. 52.

[236] *Relatório do Ministério das Relações Exteriores*, 1957, 79.

[237] *Ibid.*, 9, 187, 209.

limited by its continentalism and by the establishment of the P.A.O., could not fail to be attentive to the problems created by the new African countries, to the possibility "that new markets may be opened to us on that continent, thus establishing a profitable exchange of commerce." [238]

In 1958 the independence of Guinea and the U.A.R. (United Arab Republic) were recognized and the delegates of independent African states who had met in Acra (Ghana) [239] in that same year were received; it was decided in 1959 to establish diplomatic missions in Tunis and Rabat, as well as to begin negotiations for the establishment of diplomatic relations with Ghana; in 1960 support was given to the "Declaration on Granting Independence to Colonial Peoples and Countries" [240] and the independence of the following nations was recognized: Cameroons (January 25, 1960), Togo (April 24, 1960), Madagascar (June 25, 1960), Belgian Congo (June 28, 1960), Somaliland (June 30, 1960), Upper Volta (August 13, 1960), Ivory Coast (August 13, 1960), Dahomey (August 13, 1960), Niger (August 13, 1960). Central African Republic (August 13, 1960), Chad (August 13, 1960), Gabon (August 16, 1960), Congo (August 17, 1960), Federation of Nigeria and British Cameroons (September 19, 1960), Free Republic of Mali (October 7, 1960), and Mauritania (November 28, 1960). Furthermore, several diplomatic missions were sent to the commemorative festivities and plans were made for the establishment of diplomatic missions in Conakry (Guinea) and Acra (Ghana) and for the reëstablishment of consulates in Lourenço Marques and São Paulo de Luanda.[241]

Clearly, our most effective action was limited to the formalities of recognition and ceremonial missions, and it was the head of the government himself who in his New Year's Message declared that "the West is undoubtedly correct to concern itself with Africa, which is awakening and seeking to be integrated into modern civilization. It even behooves Brazil to execute a dynamic policy with respect to the African nations. But to admit therefore that our interest in Africa must receive priority over that owed Latin America is a tragic error, with

---

[238] *Ibid.*, 1958, xiv.
[239] *Ibid.*, 21–23.
[240] *Ibid.*, 1959, 7 and 19.
[241] *Ibid.*, 1960, xv, 26–29.

consequences that may be extremely harmful and even fatal to the values that it is incumbent upon the West to safeguard." [242]

As if its incoherent voting in the U.N. were not enough, sometimes supporting Portugal, Belgium, and France in fundamental questions on colonialism, sometimes abstaining from the vote, Brazil's aspirations did not go beyond the continent and it was forgotten that no one could defend the West in Africa better than Brazil—if this were really the objective. Brazilian international policy in relation to Africa was a mistake made at a time when we should *not* have regionalized and Latinized our foreign policy, but rather, defined it in proper balance between our interests in Africa and in America, as a stage toward the greater internationalization of a country that is already a middle power.

Our lack of attention to Africa, whose westernmost point is a few hours in flying time from our northeastern coast, and the importance of the South Atlantic, the basis of our plans for economic coöperation and strategic defense, impose new directions on our foreign policy. Neither the lesson of the Great War, recalled recently by Cordell Hull in his *Memoirs,*[243] nor our ties with Africa taught us that a broad, intercontinental policy designed to improve our defense and security and develop our foreign trade is probably the manifest destiny that has emerged from the past, is colliding with the present, and will advance in the future.

---

[242] *O Jornal,* January 1, 1961.
[243] *Memoirs of Cordell Hull.* London, 1948, 2 vols.

Afro-Brazilian Politics

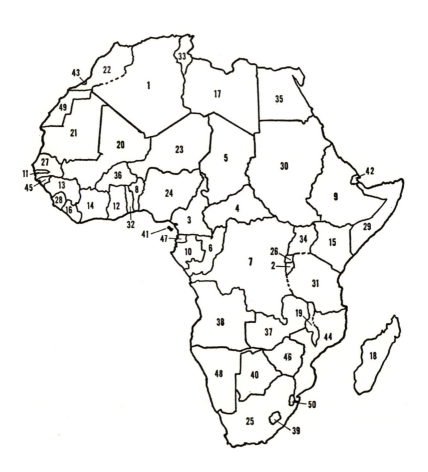

Countries of Africa (1965)
Independent Countries

Ref. No.	Country	Capital	Year of independence	Approximate population (thousands)
1	Algeria	Algiers	1962	10,784
2	Burundi	Kitega	1962	2,600
3	Cameroun	Yaoundé	1960	4,560
4	Central African Republic	Bangui	1960	1,250
5	Chad	Fort Lamy	1960	3,000
6	Congo (Brazzaville)	Brazzaville	1960	900
7	Congo (Leopoldville)	Leopoldville	1960	15,000
8	Dahomey	Porto Novo	1960	2,200
9	Ethiopia	Addis Ababa	——	22,000
10	Gabon	Libreville	1960	453
11	Gambia	Bathhurst	1965	316
12	Ghana	Accra	1957	7,340
13	Guinea	Conakry	1958	3,357
14	Ivory Coast	Abidjan	1960	3,500
15	Kenya	Nairobi	1963	8,847
16	Liberia	Monrovia	1847	2,500
17	Libya	Tripoli	1951	1,270
18	Malagasy Republic	Tananarive	1960	5,862
19	Malawi	Zomba	1964	2,950
20	Mali	Bamako	1960	4,305
21	Mauritania	Nouakchott	1960	770
22	Morocco	Rabat	1956	12,360
23	Niger	Niamey	1960	3,127
24	Nigeria	Lagos	1960	55,653
25	Republic of South Africa	Cape Town Pretoria	1961	17,075
26	Rwanda	Kigali	1962	2,665
27	Senegal	Dakar	1960	3,280
28	Sierra Leone	Freetown	1961	2,183
29	Somalia	Mogadishu	1960	4,500
30	Sudan	Khartoum	1956	12,831
31	Tanzania	Dar es Salaam	1964	10,046
32	Togo	Lomé	1960	1,559
33	Tunisia	Tunis	1956	4,290
34	Uganda	Kampala	1962	7,016
35	United Arab Republic	Cairo	——	27,303

Ref. No.	Country	Capital	Year of independence	Approximate population (thousands)
36	Upper Volta	Ouagadougou	1960	4,500
37	Zambia	Lusaka	1964	3,500

Countries without Self-government

Ref. No.	Country	Capital	Administrative Country	Approximate population (thousands)
38	Angola	Luanda	Portugal	4,936
39	Basutoland	Maseru	U. K.	727
40	Bechuanaland	Mafeking	U. K.	332
41	Fernando Pó	Santa Isabel	Spain	63
42	French Somaliland	Djibuti	France	81
43	Ifni	Sidi Ifni	Spain	49
44	Mozambique	Lourenço Marques	Portugal	6,640
45	Portuguese Guinea	Bissau	Portugal	549
46	Rhodesia	Salisbury	U. K.	4,010
47	Río Muni	Bata	Spain	250
48	South-West Africa	Windhoek	South Africa	526
49	Spanish Sahara	El-Aiun	Spain	23
50	Swaziland	Mbabane	U. K.	283

Brazil, the Atlantic, and Africa

UNDERDEVELOPMENT AS A BOND

Obscurantism has its basis in the underdevelopment of a large part of the humanity of Latin America, Africa, Asia, and parts of Europe.[1] They differ from one another, but are united by poverty and lack of technology. What links them is not insufficient political stability, legal guarantees, or maintenance of order, or the lack of a high degree of organization—for political disorder, revolutions, and dictatorships are common to the super-industrialized nations of Europe—but, rather, inadequate technology and low level of real per capita income. Excluding continental China, this sub-world contains demographically 1,600,000,000 inhabitants, increasing at the average rate of 2 per cent annually, while the developed nations have 870,000,000, growing at the rate of 1.4 per cent annually. The per capita income of the latter varies between $800–$2,600 with an average of $1,500, while that of the former is between $80–$400 with an average of $120. The disparity between the developed and the underdeveloped has been the object of studies by economists, research by institutions, and debates and resolutions by the United Nations.

It does not matter that in the underdeveloped world there are developed and underdeveloped areas, as in the case of Brazil, nor that some areas attempt to develop themselves and underdevelop others, as in the case of Portugal and its "provinces." As the economist Simon S. Kuznets has observed, the present levels of per capita income in today's

[1] Especially Spain, Portugal, Ireland, Greece, and Turkey in "Western" Europe.

underdeveloped countries are much lower than those of the industrialized countries in their pre-industrialization phase. It is also true that
even in the underdeveloped world some countries began their move
toward development when they reached an annual growth of over 5 per
cent, such as Mexico, Brazil, and India; and others began the
preparatory phase, such as Afghanistan, Ceylon, Pakistan, and Indonesia.[2] Similarly, Latin America is more westernized than Africa, and in
the latter the contrasts are less violent, as Lord Hailey has pointed
out.[3]

So great are the differences between the various territories and regions
of Africa in its present stage of development, writes S. H. Frankel, that
it is difficult to express them briefly in statistical form.[4] If in Africa the
per capita income is below $200,[5] and if industrialization is functionally
related to development, only the Federation of Rhodesia and Nyasaland, Egypt, Algeria, Morocco and probably the Belgian Congo are
between the Union of South Africa and the rest of the African
continent.[6] Dark Africa is least developed. Industrial activity in other
parts is relatively diversified, but the segments that characterize a stage
of advanced development are not yet important; it may even be said
that its dimensions are in general very small. The per capita income is
higher for non-Africans than for Africans, and among the latter it is
higher for salaried workers than for those who devote themselves to
traditional agriculture.[7] Indices of growth also vary from region to
region, and if the Gold Coast (3.1%), Ghana (3.1%), the Sudan
(3.0%), and Southern Rhodesia grow at the average rate of 3 per cent,
Tunisia (1.2%), Tanganyika (1.8%), and Kenya (1.6%) do not attain
an average of 2 per cent.[8]

In any case, development encounters formidable barriers, and eco-

---

[2] C. W. Rostow, *The Stages of Economic Growth,* Cambridge, 1961, 44.

[3] "The Differing Faces of Africa," *Foreign Affairs* (October, 1957), 144–155.

[4] "Economic Aspects of Political Independence in Africa," *International Affairs*
(October, 1960), 140–146.

[5] *Étude sur la situation économique de l'Afrique depuis 1950.* Economic and
Social Council of the United Nations, 1959, 25.

[6] *Ibid.,* 136.

[7] *Ibid.,* 168 and 184.

[8] *Economic Bulletin for Africa,* United Nations, Addis Ababa, Ethiopia, 1962,
#2, p. 9.

nomic historians like S. Kuznets and W. Rostow describe the periods of
initiation, maturity, and mass consumption that characterize the
advance of industrial nations. "It is quite possible," said Miguel Osório
de Almeida representing Brazil in the United Nations, "that the present
low levels of income are not only the result of centuries of stagnation,
but also, in many cases, of a real process of economic deterioration. This
seems to be the case in Brazil, for example, where the per capita income
seems to have deteriorated from 1830 to 1900. This regressive process in
many underdeveloped countries may have been a factor in unleashing a
series of social and political explosions that are now backfiring as
obstacles to growth."[9] The Brazilian delegate then calculated the
investment necessary to double the per capita income of the underdeveloped group during the decade of development launched by United
Nations Resolution No. 1710 (December 19, 1961), and foresaw that, if
the present rates of economic development and demographic growth
should persist for both areas, in a generation the underdeveloped
countries would go from an average of $120 per capita income to $251
and the developed from $1,500 to $3,630.

The disparity, then, would only be accentuated and the rich and
healthy would not help the backward and poor through Christian faith
or philosophical motives. There is nothing more practical and realistic
than imperialism. Why will Americans, Englishmen, and Europeans in
general pay more taxes to help victims of social injustice? Because of
Christian sentiment, adherence to a social philosophy, the awakening of
a more alert social conscience, the same old wish for political domination, or because of fear of social revolution that may surround them
with hostility and hatred and threaten their privileges?

Some modern scholars attempt to show that these problems can be
solved only with long-range plans and that even if the super-developed
West and the Soviet Union, which control the majority of the world's
capital, levied 5 per cent of their national income annually to assist
underdeveloped peoples, it would require three generations for the

---

[9] "Speech delivered in November 1962 in the Second Commission of the Seventeenth Session of the United Nations General Assembly," mimeographed and
distributed by the Ministry of Foreign Affairs, in "News Bulletin" No. 45 in
Portuguese, January 11, 1963, and in English, April 9, 1963. Transcribed in
Tempo Brasileiro (March, 1963), 254–275.

other three-quarters of humanity to be able to enjoy Western and Soviet standards.[10]

The revolution in expectations of growth is encouraging all peoples comprised in the great majority of humanity and is progressing more swiftly than the real possibilities for rapid and substantial satisfaction. This universal phenomenon is raising the hopes of the African nations, subjugated until recently, as it does those of the Latin Americans, liberated for more than a century. All believe that the end of their afflictions is in sight, but whether in Africa or in America, all are equally suspicious that help may bring economic dependence and be accompanied by sinister intentions.

The problem of development has been receiving attention in the United Nations since Resolution No. 520 (VI) A, dated January 12, 1952, which recommended the creation of organs to finance economic development on non-commercial bases. It was concluded that technical assistance, on which United Nations action was concentrating under American direction, was a palliative in view of the enormity of the problem. In order to finance economic development of underdeveloped nations the International Bank for Reconstruction and Development (1946) and the International Finance Corporation (1956) were created, which together could not attend to investment needs. They were merely of a supplementary nature and the sums involved never attained significant proportions. The proposal to create a Finance Fund met with the irreconcilable opposition of the United States and the United Kingdom; the only result finally obtained was that the American government accepted the idea of creating another unit for technical assistance, the Special Fund, whose resources were to be $100,000,000, but they barely attained $26,000,000 in the first year of operations.

In 1959 it was already realized that the policy of the underdeveloped members of the United Nations to have a substantial sum of capital employed in development did not have the expected results. Other proposals have been made but disparities in fact continue, and only a few have, by their own efforts and sacrifices, attained the initial phase or pre-phase in overcoming difficulties. In 1953 it was proposed that

---

[10] Andrew Shonfield, *The Attack on World Poverty*, London, 1961.

developed countries should take measures to insure that "income will be taxed only or principally in the country where it is produced." [11] The developed countries opposed this plan because it did not provide a favorable "climate for investment."

No more enlightened consciousness at that time existed to orient the problem. It was probably the *World Economic Survey* of 1958 that promoted this enlightenment. It studied the impact of recession in the most advanced capitalist economies and on economies exporting raw materials. The expansion of capacity to produce raw materials and the fall in prices of basic products, together with the increase in prices of manufactured products, represented a loss of two billion dollars in real income and in the importing capacity of the less developed economies in 1957–1958. The study further showed that, in contrast to the fall in imports of basic products in the industrialized countries, importation of manufactured goods by the less developed economies tended to exceed their rate of economic development. Thus there was little likelihood that commerce between developed and less developed countries could contribute external resources that would permit the less developed economies to attain the rate of growth of the developed nations. [12]

These findings and conclusions of an official publication of the United Nations soon awakened the attention of the delegates from both developed and underdeveloped countries. The former, alarmed by conclusions that could unleash a series of consequences, attempted to diminish their importance. Outstanding in this task, in the very midst of the Economic and Social Council (Twenty-eighth Session, Geneva, June–July, 1958), were the chief of the delegation from the United States and his successors, who declared that the publication had exaggerated the problem of raw materials. They also showed displeasure at the breadth of the study made by the *Survey* and the attention it had given to the speech of the Secretary-General, who had faced this problem as one essential to normalization of the world's economic situation.

The analysis made by the Economic Commission for Latin America

---

[11] Resolution No. 486 (XVI) of the Economic and Social Council, July 9, 1953.
[12] *World Economic Survey*, United Nations, 1958, 3 and 10.

(ECFLA) also confirmed that the rate of industrial expansion of this region had decreased in 1958, for the gross production of the region had increased by 3 per cent as compared to 5 per cent in 1957, and as the population had grown by 2.5 per cent, it was seen that the per capita production of the region had had an insignificant increase.[13]

Since then the deterioration of the underdeveloped economies because of the relationship of commercial exchange with the developed nations has continued and been recorded regularly in the economic studies of the United Nations. The lowering of world prices of the principal agricultural products exported from Africa has diminished the value of the exports, although total exports have continued to increase. If in 1958 the volume of export of the underdeveloped countries was not materially affected by the recession yet the value of the exports showed a substantial decline; between 1958 and 1959 the total quantitative expansion of exports from the exporting countries attained a record increase of approximately 9 per cent; and yet this growth in trade did not bring about a comparable increase in profit. Consequently, despite the much greater increase in volume of their exports, the increase in value was not more than 5 per cent.[14]

The process has continued and in 1961 the *World Economic Survey* stated that, as "in previous years, the changes in import prices are generally less than in export prices. As the latter are falling almost universally—relatively in Latin America and severely in southeast Asia—there has been a generalized deterioration in terms of commerce. It has been less in Latin America, where foreign trade has remained notably static in the period 1958–1961, and greater (about 5 per cent) in Africa and south and southeast Asia, where the incidence of change in the prices of raw materials has been noted more. On the average, countries exporting raw materials have had to export 2 per cent more in 1961 than in 1960 in order to acquire from foreign trade the sum necessary to maintain the same volume of import." [15]

Commercial relations between the underdeveloped and industrialized

---

[13] *Economic Survey for Latin America,* 1958, 1.

[14] *Economic Bulletin for Africa,* Economic Commission for Africa, United Nations, Addis-Ababa, Ethiopia, I, 1, p. 5.

[15] United Nations, 1962, 150. See this page also for changes in the terms of trade for countries exporting raw materials, by region, from 1960 to 1961.

nations and the promotion of inter-regional commercial coöperation have annually attracted greater attention in the United Nations General Assembly. It was considered paradoxical that the progressive expansion of aid from the industrial nations should not be accompanied by equal progress in the reduction of obstacles to the growth of trade. The less developed nations have manifested a preoccupation with the fact that 73 per cent of their $25.6 billion in exports went to the industrial nations in 1959.[16] The principal difficulty lies in the industrial nations' policy of protecting agriculture and in formulae mitigating the instability of raw materials by means of compensatory action. In 1962 the current value of total exports for the underdeveloped regions indicated a record for the trimester of almost 2 per cent over the previous year's figure. But in order to compensate for the lowering by almost 1 per cent of the value per unit, it was necessary to increase the volume of export by 3 per cent.[17]

Thus, the process of deterioration has continued to present the same characteristics. Production and international trade of primary materials, which in 1960 attained record high levels, continued to expand in 1961, but at lower prices. International prices, which have generally had an annual decline since 1957, continued to fall in 1961.[18]

The tendency reflected the constant excess of supply over demand in foodstuffs, a decline in the consumption of diverse raw materials and, in the case of some of these, an excess of supply or productive capacity over demand, despite increase in consumption. In contrast to the continuous decline in the prices of primary materials, the average value per unit of manufactured goods in international trade, which in 1959 had resumed the slow upward trend interrupted in 1958, continued to rise in the first half of 1961 and during the year as a whole by approximately 1 per cent over the previous year's level. Thus, the terms of exchange fell to a new low in 1961, reducing the purchasing power of a unit of raw material in international trade in terms of manufactured goods by a

---

[16] United Nations, Document E/3520, June 7, 1961, par. 83.

[17] *Current Economic Indicators,* United Nations, III, 1, 1962, 17.

[18] See Index on Volume of Production, Volume of Trade, Prices of Primary Materials, and Total Industrial Production, in *Commission on International Commodity Trade,* May, 1962, 2.

little more than 2 per cent, compared with the previous year, 17 per cent less than in 1953, and 27 per cent less than in 1950.[19]

Despite the decline in prices of primary materials, the gains in total exportation by countries exporting primary materials rose during the first three quarters of 1960 and 1961 to $500,000,000, or 2 per cent.[20] In this group of exporters of raw materials, the underdeveloped countries had gains of $300,000,000 or 1.5 per cent, reflecting an expansion of almost 4 per cent in quantity and a fall of a little more than 2 per cent in the index of unit value for such exports. The foreign trade situation of underdeveloped areas worsened in 1961. The official gross total of gold and foreign currency of these countries declined in the course of 1961 to $11,500,000,000 at the end of September, which when compared with the data at the end of the previous year is the lowest figure since 1954.[21]

In view of these data it was natural that the underdeveloped nations should seek common means to stabilize variations in prices and volumes of production in the international market. In the Fourteenth General Assembly of the United Nations in December, 1959, Brazil and Pakistan succeeded in obtaining approval for the formation of a group of experts to study the problems of raw materials and the advisability of establishing in the U.N. a mechanism capable of compensating for the effects of variations in prices on the balance of payments, giving special emphasis to the financing of compensations. In January of 1961 this group gave its report under the title of "International Compensation for Fluctuations in Commodity Trade." On December 19, 1961, the U.N. adopted Resolution No. 1707 (XVI) which recognized "international

---

[19] *Commission on International Commodity Trade,* United Nations, May 1962, 3. The passage is taken from this study. See same page for Indices of Prices in International Trade, 1950–1961.

[20] *Ibid.,* 3. The smallest deterioration revealed by Table 3 reveals that a part of the imports of underdeveloped areas consisted of raw materials whose unit of value declined. See "Index of the Unit Value of Imports and Exports and Terms of Trade of Underdeveloped Countries" (Table 3) and "International Export of Developed and Underdeveloped Areas between 1953–1961" (Table 4).

[21] Since 1956 the total exports of the less developed areas have grown only 2% per year, while those of the industrial areas have grown 6.5%. See William Butler, "Trade and the Less Developed Areas," *Foreign Affairs,* January 1963, pp. 374 and 377. The situation in Latin America is very grave, for sixteen nations depend on only one product for more than half of their export profits.

trade as a fundamental instrument for economic development."

In the Punta del Este Charter of August, 1961, it was also decided to call together a technical group of the Organization of American States, which in April, 1962 presented its report and a plan for a compensation fund. In the Second Punta del Este Conference in January, 1962, it was further resolved that it was necessary "to free the exchange of raw materials by eliminating undue restrictions and to try to avoid violent fluctuations in their prices." [22]

The international and regional solutions differed in the manner of confronting the market fluctuations, and while the first suggested two types of compensation for short- and long-term variations, the second limited itself to short-term fluctuations. Furthermore, it is evident that the regional solution may suffer the consequences of its limited remedies before the fluctuations of the immense underdeveloped world.

For that very reason the struggle was to develop on all sides. In Rome, during the Tenth Session of the Commission on Basic Products of the U.N., there was a study on the creation of a financial mechanism to compensate for losses caused by the fall in quotations, with a proposal to create a Security Fund for income from exports and thus to confront the basic problems: instability of export income, low level and insufficient increase of exports to finance development programs and, finally, a tendency to lowered capacity to import manufactures.[23]

The Cairo Conference, convoked through the initiative of the United Arab Republic and Yugoslavia, with thirty-one participants and eleven observers meeting in July, 1962, expressed in the Declaration of Countries in Development its apprehension that the regional economic grouping of industrialized countries, if conceived and executed in a restrictive or discriminatory manner, might affect the interests of developing nations. The Declaration affirmed also that "the joint action of those countries in the process of development could resolve many of their problems and would promote more rapid progress on broad

[22] *O Brasil em Punta del Este,* Ministério de Relações Exteriores, Rio de Janeiro, 1962, 19.
[23] *Commission on International Commodity Trade,* Report of the Tenth Session, May 15–23, 1962, United Nations.

international bases." [24] Although there was no specific reference to the European Common Market, it is the latter that has inspired these positions because of its policy of breaking traditional routes of world commerce. Brazil was one of the countries that contributed to formulating the Declaration. "In this document," said Miguel Osório de Almeida later, "it is recognized with apprehension that there is a growing disparity between standards of living prevailing in different parts of the world and that the economic development of underdeveloped nations is encountering growing difficulties resulting in part from international factors out of their control and from tendencies that may result in the perpetuation of old structures in international relations." [25]

The fact that international trade represents 20 per cent or more of the total economy of underdeveloped countries, against 8 per cent for the American economy, and that the total exports of underdeveloped areas reached $30 billion in 1960 while the total financial assistance from industrial nations (including private foreign investment) was only $8 billion,[26] shows the significance of foreign trade to development and the need for a critical examination to bring forth immediate solutions.

Recognition of the existence of adverse factors foreign to the underdeveloped or developing nations and the discriminatory action not only of the Common Market but of an institution like G.A.T.T., created by the industrialized countries to serve their objectives, have caused growing opposition in the United Nations and suggested the adoption of urgent and objective measures. "In the field of international trade there are disquieting tendencies acting to the detriment of the interests of underdeveloped nations; there is also on the part of the major nations and commercial blocs or their sub-groups the tendency to adopt economically unnecessary institutional measures that operate, or

---

[24] Document E/3682, July 27, 1962, United Nations. Otávio Dias Carneiro, then Minister and Brazilian delegate to the Rome and Cairo Conferences, gave the Brazilian position concerning the role of commerce in the process of development with extreme objectivity.
[25] Speech delivered to the Second Commission of the Seventeenth Session of the General Assembly of the United Nations, November 1962. Mimeographed and distributed by the Ministério de Relações Exteriores, January 11, 1963.
[26] William Butler, *op. cit.*, 372.

tend to operate, to the detriment of the international trade of the underdeveloped countries," declared Miguel Osório de Almeida. On the negative side of the scale, weighing more heavily against the interests of the underdeveloped nations, is the non-ratification of the International Trade Organization approved at the Havana Conference of 1948. In its place a temporary agreement was concluded preparing the way for the G.A.T.T., in which under American leadership the interests of the great industrial nations are predominant [27] and the underdeveloped nations and those obliged to bear the heaviest burden of trade restrictions have been isolated.[28]

Years of struggle, debate, and indecision enlightened the underdeveloped nations. It was then recognized that international trade more than assistance was an indispensable factor in growth and difficult phase of overcoming obstacles; it was considered that international agreements functioned for the benefit of the industrialized countries that dominated them; reliable official statistics showed the enormous prejudices imposed by the developed on the underdeveloped nations and that the fall in prices of primary materials benefitted the industrial countries; it was proved that the total exports of developed countries went from $37.2 billion to $85.4 billion, while the exports of the underdeveloped increased only from $19.1 billion to $27.3 billion. It did not require much to arrive at the conclusion that the underdeveloped countries were helping the developed ones to develop still further. Dissatisfaction with the organs that defended a policy favorable to industrialized nations, discontent with international relations that were characterized by the constant and progressive deterioration of conditions in underdeveloped countries and accelerated progress in industrial areas, and finally, lack of coördination between the various international organs led to the victory of the convocation of the International Conference of Trade and Development.[29]

When in December of 1961 the Assembly General adopted Resolu-

---

[27] In the "Speech" referred to, the structure of this agreement and its basic defects are studied from the point of view of the developing nations.

[28] *World Economic Survey,* United Nations, 1961, 81.

[29] *Report of the Economic and Social Council,* General Assembly, Seventeenth Session, August 5, 1961, to August 3, 1962, United Nations, 19–20.

tion No. 1707 (XVI), which recognized international trade as a fundamental condition for economic development, the Secretary-General was requested to consult with the member states of the United Nations and with specialized agencies on the advisability of promoting an international conference on problems of international trade. The opinions gathered by the Secretary-General in the discussion of the Economic and Social Council expressed great support for calling the conference, it being recalled that in the Cairo Declaration thirty-one nations had shown themselves in favor of the project and, moreover, that the foreign trade of underdeveloped countries had suffered serious set-backs with the trend to lower prices of basic commodities. They had further noted that even if there were much greater international financial assistance their position would remain precarious in view of the short-term fluctuations in basic commodities. At the end of the debate the Council adopted Resolution No. 1785 calling together an International Conference on Trade and Development [30] that should have as its objectives: 1) the elimination of preferential systems discriminating against basic commodities and of subsidies to domestic production of primary materials by countries forming "conventional" markets; 2) elimination of artificial devices restricting access to industrial or semi-manufactured products in "conventional" markets; 3) entry into the trade system of the socialist countries (COMECOM), which are growing at a higher rate than the "conventional" markets, are extraordinarily elastic in demand for our exports, and can thus constitute a growing market for our products.[31]

That is a most important point. The so-called leftist tendency in the diplomacy of the developing or underdeveloped countries means above all an awareness to real national needs. The doors to trade with the super-developed countries of western Europe are closed or open only to the trade of certain underdeveloped countries, and those that are not chosen are threatened with stagnation. Trade relations with other developed countries is all to their advantage: the loss in purchasing

---

[30] *Report of the Economic and Social Council, August 5, 1961, to August 3, 1962,* United Nations, 1962, 19–20.
[31] Synopsis of an interview with Ambassador Jaime de Azevedo Rodrigues, "Noticiario" of the Ministry of Foreign Affairs, January 23, 1963.

power of Brazilian exports to the United States between 1955 and 1961 alone came to $1,486,000,000.[32] On the contrary, the socialist countries resolutely oppose the regulations imposed by disciplinary organs such as G.A.T.T. on trade relations in the capitalist world and are at the same time becoming rapidly industrialized, whereas their agricultural production is stationary or shows slow growth. Their economic growth has been associated with a considerable expansion in foreign trade (average annual rate of 12% in one decade), representing a value equivalent to triple the rate of growth of trade for underdeveloped countries and greater by a third than that attained by the developed economies in the rest of the world.[33] The Brazilian representative to the United Nations, Miguel Osório de Almeida, has therefore rightly said that "the opening of these countries to international trade could represent a dramatic step in the field of positive international coöperation."[34]

The first difficulties having been overcome, broad, objective, and diversified trade with the socialist countries means a step toward emancipation and characterizes the diplomacy of those countries really desiring development for their people.

Trade with the socialist countries is in harmony with the decade of development projected by the United Nations in Resolution No. 1710, dated December 19, 1961, and with Resolutions Nos. 1717 and 1718 of the same date on the economic and educational development of Africa. At the last meeting of the African nations promoted by the United Nations in the Congo, there was discussion concerning the creation of bases on which to strengthen industry and agriculture, and the subjects of foreign trade and South American competition were much debated.[35] The representatives of thirty-two countries in a meeting marked by a spirit of coöperation planned a program of economic development that is to begin in 1963 with a true inventory of all mineral

---

[32] Unless the United States is disposed to removing its restrictions on trade in primary materials. The National Planning Association has calculated that removal of these restrictions on commodities from Latin America would result in an increase of export gains, for this region alone, of from approximately $850,000,000 to $1,700 billion annually. See W. Butler, *op. cit.,* 382.

[33] *World Economic Survey,* United Nations, 1961, 106.

[34] The speech cited (note 38), p. 16.

[35] On planning for development in Africa, see *Economic Bulletin for Africa,* United Nations, Addis-Ababa, June 1962, II, 2, Ch. III, 29–44.

deposits in their territories and of sources of potential energy in the various regions. The United Nations have approved the coördinated program of development, granting an initial credit of $7,500,000 for 1963.

Diplomacy directed to development is leading the underdeveloped peoples and will unite them in their march, which must not be disturbed by purely regional motives such as the one now being disputed by Africans and South Americans with respect to the European Common Market, for discriminatory concessions may be sinister and mean subjugation. "If independence is the first objective," said Kwame Nkrumah, "development comes immediately after it, and no leader in Asia or Africa can escape this pressure."[36]

THE COMMON MARKET, AFRICA AND BRAZIL

The process of European integration already has its past, its present, and its future. As W. O. Henderson has shown,[37] the past includes successive attempts to liberalize international trade, although they always tended to make it discriminatory, as have the two recent attempts of the European Economic Community (Common Market) and the European Free Trade Association (E.F.T.A.), as well as others that regionally have followed the European model. The European Common Market was created in the Rome Treaty of 1957 by France, West Germany, Italy, Belgium, the Low Countries, and Luxembourg, impelled by their changing economies to make an attempt at integration. Having overcome the obstacle of sovereignty by the joint decision, the role given to the Parliamentary Assembly, and the process of continuous consultation, the Common Market was constituted as a closed system of selective trade excluding outsiders and including so-called overseas territories.

The Rome Treaty (Art. 131 ff.) defined the association as including the latter,[38] but their independence has obliged the member states to create a new constitution on the basis of equality of sovereign states.

---

[36] "African Prospect," *Foreign Affairs* (October, 1958), 45–53.
[37] *The Genesis of the Common Market,* London, 1962.
[38] J. J. van der Lee, "The European Common Market and Africa," *The World Today* (September, 1960) 370–376.

Working against the association were the colonialist heritage and the political implications of states preferring not to be committed internationally. Several conferences took place before the period of association expired on December 31, 1962.[39] Like the first, the new arrangement established the preferential system, a development fund, non-discrimination among the Six and their associates and, finally, the Council of Ministers with a minister for each member and the Court of Justice enforcing decisions and litigation.

Senegal, Mauritania, Gabon, the Congo (Brazzaville), the Central African Republic, Chad, the Gold Coast, Dahomey, Upper Volta, Niger, Togo, Mali, and Madagascar were associated under the leadership of France, which considers its relations with those African states that have their origin in its Community special, and is firmly convinced that they should be economically integrated into the system of highly-developed countries represented by the Common Market by the abolition of tariffs and expansion of aid and investment. The Common Market, associated with the Africans and discriminatory against all outsiders, has expanded rapidly and become one of the major economic powers because of its superiority in absolute numbers and percentage increases over all other blocs, especially in foreign trade.[40] The volume of African trade is directed chiefly to the former metropolitan countries, which means that western Europe continues to dominate it. In recent years, particularly between 1958 and 1959, the six members of the European Economic Community have gained ground economically at the expense of the other western European countries, especially the United Kingdom,[41] although the French zone contained only 57,000,000 inhabitants and the English about 80,000,000.

The trade dispute has divided and not integrated Europe; it has excluded other regions from European trade and not made it more liberal. Basically, the communities are rooted in the capitalistic system, are concerned with the big and dominant economic interests, notwithstanding treaty articles to the contrary, and there is a chronic conflict

---

[39] J. R. Lambert, "The European Economic Community and the Associated African States," *The World Today* (August, 1961) 344–355.
[40] *Economic Survey of Europe in 1961*, United Nations, 17 and 19.
[41] *Economic Bulletin for Africa*, United Nations, Addis-Ababa, January, 1961, I, 1, pp. 12–13.

among them between the apostles of free enterprise and the hard facts of economic reality, as E. Strauss has observed.[42]

The formation of a new economic bloc showed this policy clearly, irritated the struggle, bought time in the European trade dispute, and further divided Europe and the world.[43] On November 20, 1950, Great Britain, Sweden, Norway, Denmark, Switzerland, Austria, and Portugal formed the European Free Trade Association which from July 1, 1960, began to remove trade barriers among them. Like the Common Market, this second group of nations obligated itself not to extend concessions to non-members, European or otherwise. Economic relations between the two blocs affected not only Europe but the whole world, which was practically excluded by the severe discrimination. The creation of the group of Seven aimed not at reconciling the Common Market with the rest of Europe but at forcing its acceptance by that Market.

In the meeting of the Council of Ministers of the Six, May 11–13, 1960, it was decided that this bloc would be prepared to enter into negotiations with the Seven in order to settle trade problems and "attempt to maintain the present trade currents in Europe and expand them if possible." [44] But the agriculture question [45] always made any agreement difficult, and so relations have not been satisfactory and obstacles to harmony and multilateral association have grown, while the success of the first group has gradually been consolidated. The success has been so great that Great Britain and other members of the Seven have tried to join the Common Market.

The Rome Treaty permitted the other European countries to participate in the Common Market either by accession or association. Great Britain's decision to apply for entry into the Common Market in October, 1961, when the negotiations began, first brought a reaction from the British Community, which accepted this step only with

---

[42] E. Strauss, *European Reckoning, The Six and Britain's Future,* London, 1962.
[43] M. G., "The Outer Seven. Buying Time in the European Trade Dispute," *The World Today* (January, 1960), 15–23.
[44] Marianne Gellner, "Relations Between the Six and the Seven. A Survey of Recent Developments," *The World Today* (July, 1960) 278–287.
[45] On the position of the Common Market with respect to agriculture, see *The Economic Survey of Europe in 1961,* United Nations, 1961, 40–42.

restrictions, and then the desire to follow suit by requesting membership on the part of some of the members of the E.F.T.A., such as Denmark, Norway, and Ireland,[46] while Austria, Sweden, Switzerland, and Spain wanted to be associates.

The chief consequence was not only the possibility of dissolution of the group of Seven but also the rejection of the British Community, which saw its leader obliged to submit to the supervisory and fiscal directives of the Continent. Furthermore, Great Britain acted without consultation when it began its formal negotiations.[47] It is certain that by its entry into the Common Market it expected to obtain special treatment for its colonies or ex-colonies, as France had requested and obtained in 1957. In the Conference of the Ministers of Finance of the Community held in Acra certain African states, especially Ghana, replied hostilely to the British suggestion to ask for associate status. The plan was considered a despicable neo-colonialist maneuver.[48] Even so Great Britain hoped to persuade the African states of the British Community to be associated with the overseas territories of the Common Market. For the latter integration is the natural course for the Africans, although some of them think that it is an instrument to keep the backward countries underdeveloped. In the French group Guinea has preferred to follow its own course, and the African states belonging to the British Community have remained subject to the discriminations of the Common Market.

The division of Europe between the Six and the Seven, forming groups of favored and unfavored countries, was used as an argument in behalf of Great Britain's entry into the Common Market and with it that of the African countries in the British Community, thus ending discrimination in Europe and Africa. But the Africans themselves hesitate and show contempt for the idea because they think that, as their trade in the past has been closely linked with Great Britain's and Europe's, to institutionalize it would mean restricting its liberty to develop in other areas such as the Communist bloc, the United States,

---

[46] J. R. Lambert, "The Neutrals and the Common Market," *The World Today* (October, 1962) 444–452.

[47] Andrew Shonfield, "The Commonwealth and the Common Market," *The World Today* (December, 1961) 532–537.

[48] *Ibid.*, 533.

and Japan, and retarding the growth of inter-African trade. It was thus quite possible for some of the African members of the Community to refuse to become associated on the basis of political objections. Ghana and Nigeria manifested their doubts on the advantages of association, especially because despite suggestions made during the conference its terms and conditions have to date not been established. Hence their objection to Great Britain's entry into the Common Market, for in addition to offering no remedy for the present discrimination between different parts of Africa, it would menace them with the possibility that their chief customer might move to the discriminatory side.[49]

Despite the reaction of the entire Community, including Canada and New Zealand, against its intention to enter the Common Market, Great Britain would still prefer the chance to participate in the economic recuperation promoted by the Common Market to the threat of losing its traditional markets. If it does not yet place Great Britain among the chorus of universal protests, the French veto to British admission in January, 1963, obliges it to reformulate its economic policy.

The opposition to Great Britain's entry into the Common Market was really world-wide, for it would have meant the creation of a vast discriminatory system against some unfortunates—Africans, Arabs, Asians, or Latin Americans, and even against some Europeans, for example, Yugoslavians—or against such important countries as Japan, which western Europe cannot have go over to the other side and which its powerful protector, the United States, would like to see among the more favored nations. All this would be put aside in the economic cold war between blocs.

Because of their underdevelopment and dependence on exports of primary materials, Africa and Latin America should suffer most from the consequences of European discrimination. The evolution being taken by world trade policy has great influence on the economic development of Latin America, which alone cannot influence its course. For its part, the Common Market shows that it prefers financial and technical coöperation to tariff agreements as a means of attending to its

---

[49] Kenneth Younger, "Reflections on Africa and the Commonwealth," *The World Today* (March, 1962) 121–129.

direct or indirect restrictive effects on Latin American economy.[50]

In view of this, leading circles in Latin America have a very pessimistic opinion on the possibility of indemnification or compensation of the Latin American economy for harmful effects of the common foreign tariff.

In an interview granted on January 8, 1962,[51] upon his return from a ministerial-level meeting held on the occasion of the Nineteenth Session of G.A.T.T., Ambassador Dias Carneiro explained that the common foreign tariff, which had resulted from the transformation of individual tariffs negotiated bilaterally between the Six and the participant nations of that organization,

was higher, equal, or lower to those concessions given Brazil by the members of the European Common Market when they negotiated with Brazil bilaterally. This obliged the Common Market to renegotiate the common foreign tariff with us in relation to the products on our export tariff list. The bilateral negotiations with the Common Market were held from December, 1960, to July, 1961, when they were interrupted unilaterally by the Common Market due to an impasse that arose in fixing tariffs on the following Brazilian products: coffee, cacao, cocoa butter, and Brazil nuts, for which the tariffs of 16, 9, 22, and 5 per cent respectively had been fixed. These tariffs were considered unacceptable by Brazil, especially as these products enter Common Market countries without any tariff when they come from associated overseas countries and territories, which include two-thirds of the African countries: Senegal, Sudan, Guinea, Ivory Coast and others. The prejudice caused to Brazilian trade is therefore flagrant.

The Brazilian delegation pointed out to the Nineteenth Session the various retaliatory measures that it could take. The first would be not to send to the National Congress the protocols relative to the agreements with France and Benelux, thus showing Brazil's dissatisfaction with the interruption of negotiations with the Common Market; the

---

[50] Esteban Ivovich, "Latin America's Position in Relation to World Changes in Trade Policy," *Economic Bulletin for Latin America,* Santiago, Chile (February, 1962), VII, 1, pp. 53–60.

[51] Interview granted by Ambassador Otávio Dias Carneiro, Adjunct Secretary-General for Economic Affairs, on the activities of G.A.T.T. and on the Common Market. Mimeographed and distributed by the Ministry of Foreign Affairs, January 8, 1962. We summarize the following passage from this interview.

second would consist of using discriminatory measures, unilaterally raising our tariffs and reducing concessions with regard to certain countries; the third, already provided for in Article 3 of the Tariff Law, would permit raising tariffs unilaterally on products from several countries that are in competition with Brazilian exports. In addition to this, by legislative authorization to the executive branch Brazil could further suspend the clause of most favored nation, so long as this does not affect other countries that do not discriminate and are also favored.

In the same meeting there was debate on a proposal from Nigeria that tropical products have duty-free entry to industrialized countries. Brazil supported the Nigerian proposal, for its adoption would abolish tariffs on cacao and coffee in the Common Market and would benefit Brazil, but "Senegal, supported by France, declared itself against the proposal in an extremely violent manner." France then stated that if it were obliged to withdraw the preference granted to associated territories it would compensate them with capital and technical aid. "For Brazil the matter is very important," concluded Ambassador Dias Carneiro, "as the preferences granted by the Common Market to its associated territories could prejudice our exports by $100,000,000 to $130,000,000. We do not wish abolition of the preference. We want it to be extended to Brazil and to other countries prejudiced by it, thus reëstablishing the system of most favored nation violated by the Common Market."

Two months later, while on a mission to Europe in the name of the Brazilian government during the Quadros administration, Ambassador Roberto Campos stated that Brazil intended to reduce its imports from Common Market countries if they did not maintain a substantial exchange of trade. The Common Market agreement had already altered the exchange between Brazil and the European Six, and with its agricultural program, it will continue gradually to reduce and eliminate all South American imports, as in the case of sugar.[52]

When Sr. San Tiago Dantas was in Rome in May of 1962 he explained Brazil's position on the problems and difficulty imposed by the European Economic Community on Latin American economies to

---

[52] *Correio da Manhã,* Rio de Janeiro, March 23, 1961.

the chiefs of the Latin American diplomatic missions. He then alluded to the specific situation of Brazil vis-à-vis the European Economic Community as an exporter of tropical products in competition with similar African products. He declared that Brazil did not wish to prejudice the development of those African nations that deserved the support and special coöperation given by the Community to its overseas associates. Brazil was combatting discrimination and unacceptable preferences and had requested their immediate elimination, but although it recognized the "duties" of former colonial governments toward the underdeveloped or developing economies of their former colonies on the African continent, such duties could not "engender unjustified prejudices to the Brazilian economy and the economies of the Latin American countries." He suggested the need to adopt a concerted action on the part of the Latin American countries in meetings of the E.C.F.L.A., G.A.T.T., Economic and Social Council of the United Nations, International Commission for Basic Commodities, the Council and Commissions for the Organization of Agriculture and Food, and the International Coffee Conference. He recalled, moreover, the articulated action of the Latin American countries and the United States with the Italian government for the reduction of rates on coffee, and as a member of the Community the latter had proved to be understanding and receptive to Latin American claims and had even offered its collaboration as mediator between Latin America and the E.E.C.[53]

It was not only Brazil that took this position; all America shared it, as well as the non-associated African nations.

Frontal attacks on the Common Market were made by Latin American figures and even the O.A.S. sought an understanding. When on July 6, 1962, a luncheon was held in the Latin American House for French Prime Minister Georges Pompidou, the dean of the Diplomatic

---

[53] "Posição dos Países Latin-Americanos em face do Mercado Comum Europeu." (Memorandum sent to the Latin-American diplomatic missions and United States Embassy in Rome, the Italian Ministry of Foreign Affairs and accredited Brazilian diplomatic missions in Paris, Bonn, Brussels, The Hague, and London, and the Brazilian mission with the European Economic Community in Brussels) "Noticiário" of the Ministério de Relações Exteriores, May 14, 1962.

Corps, Ambassador Abelardo Saenz, revealed the Latin American concern with Common Market protectionism. The Prime Minister attempted to dissipate Latin America's fears by stating that this was not "an instrument of protectionism but of liberalism within Europe and that the stabilization of prices of raw materials constituted an essential problem for the stabilization of the West itself." [54]

The voyage of José A. Mora, Secretary-General of the O.A.S., to Europe in July of 1962 had as its goal the examination of trade problems affected by the Common Market, and at the same time a regional office of the O.A.S. was created to serve as an information and liaison center with such European organizations as the Common Market and European Free Trade Association. Mora and the regional director, Uruguayan Daniel Rodrigues Larreta, were unsuccessful although they heard much advice and many promises about the regrettable privileges, which did not resolve the imbalance of trade relations between the Common Market and Latin America. The unfavorable balance was revealed by Latin American imports of European products from the Six to the amount of $1,700 billion compared with exports of $1.5 billion.

A traditional market for European products, Latin America once had the second largest customer in the world for its coffee in the countries of the Community, but this trade is now reduced because of a tariff from which African coffee is exempt.

The inattentiveness of the Executive Secretary of the Common Market, Walter Hallstein, to the Mora Mission and the indifferent treatment given Latin American claims show that the South American continent must unite in order to be able to negotiate, if necessary on hard terms, with the European Economic Community. The promise to lower the customs duty on coffee by 40 per cent [55] coincided with the program presented by the Executive Commission of the E.E.C. in which it was stated that "the Latin American market is as important to the European Economic Community as the African countries affiliated with it, in view of the fact that statistics demonstrate that this region, together with the countries on the Dark Continent, is the part of the

---

[54] *Correio da Manhã* and *Jornal do Brasil*, July 7, 1962.
[55] The decision to reduce the common foreign tariff on coffee and cacao was adopted in the meeting of the Council of Ministers of June 1962. See "Noticiário" of the Ministério de Relações Exteriores, June 25, 1962.

world whose sales to the Common Market are increasing at the lowest rate, while those of the Common Market to this region are growing normally." [56]

The program promised the following: 1) the Market's disposition to conclude trade agreements on a world scale with the Latin American countries producing coffee, sugar, cacao, meat, bananas, and nonferrous metals; 2) reduction up to 40 per cent of E.E.C. customs duties on tropical farm products; 3) reductions in consumer taxes in E.E.C. countries on products like coffee and bananas; 4) an appeal to Latin America to provide guarantees for credits and investments from E.E.C. countries; 5) the E.E.C. would coördinate its Latin American policy and would propose to all Latin American countries the installation of diplomatic missions in Brussels, which had already been done by Argentina, Brazil, Columbia, and Mexico.

This program of June 1962 showed that the Common Market was softening, willing to compromise because it saw the possibility of a hard line from Latin American countries. In November, 1961, Brazil, for example, had denounced air agreements with certain European countries. By this it aimed not only to defend national aeronautical interests but also to obtain an advantageous position that would enable Brazil to secure the suspension of restrictions imposed by the European Common Market.[57] This measure was in line with the reprisals that Brazil had stated could be adopted at the time of the Nineteenth Session of G.A.T.T. in 1961.

To resolve a problem without reprisals has always been the course of Brazilian diplomacy, but there are signs that our national psychology is beginning to adapt to world changes. We have traditionally held belief that traditional markets are more important than opening trade to new areas, although political and emotional considerations can momentarily cloud the issue. The fact is that Brazil and Latin America today are trying to expand their trade by extending it to every area. The Free Trade Zone instituted by the Montevideo Treaty [58] involving seven countries (Argentina, Brazil, Chile, Mexico, Paraguay, Peru, and Uruguay) on February 18, 1960, went into effect on January 1, 1962; but

---

[56] Wire reports from Brussels and Bonn, *Jornal do Brasil,* June 10 and 20, 1962.
[57] *Jornal do Brasil,* November 28, 1961.
[58] Treaty in *Diário do Congresso,* January 13, 1961, 127–130.

it operates on such restricted bases that, on his visit to Chile in April 1963, President João Goulart appealed for greater economic integration on the continent to resolve the difficult problem of stagnated production and per capita export profits and thus increase per capita income and our capacity to import. He proposed a joint note from the governments of Chile and Brazil strengthening the process of economic integration in order "to promote the harmonious economic and social development of the countries in the region" and acquire "the pace demanded for solutions to the great and serious problems afflicting the people of Latin America." Toward these ends the governments declared their decision to sponsor a meeting of the foreign ministers of the member states of the L.A.F.T.A. (Latin American Free Trade Association) in order to "a) establish a mechanism for permanent consultation among the foreign ministers of the contracting parties, who are to examine progress in the execution of the Montevideo Treaty and grant and orient a policy tending to accelerate the growth of the economic independence of Latin America by means of the rapid establishment of the Latin American Common Market; b) promote the coördination and harmonization of the policies and program of economic development of the member countries, as well as various other measures." [59] To unite efforts and form a determined bloc without the radical ideologies that existed at the Cairo Conference can facilitate negotiations with the other blocs, including and especially those with the European Common Market, which discriminates against Latin America.

In April of 1963 Ambassador Roberto Campos further accused the European nations of limiting Latin American exports. France, West Germany, and other European countries give excessive preference to imports from Africa and raised customs barriers against imports from Latin America, said the Ambassador, adding that "the tariff charges imposed by the three principal European consumers raise the retail sale price to more than 200 per cent of the unit value of the product at the port of entry." Furthermore, "the harsh restrictions on coffee imports generally, and in some cases on Latin American coffee, will aggravate the problem by generalizing a discrimination that at the moment is not

[59] "Boletim Informativo," Ministry of Foreign Affairs, April 25, 1963.

collective." The statistical data of the O.A.S., added the Ambassador, demonstrated that exports of Latin American coffee to the European Common Market can be increased by some $130,000,000 annually by the simple elimination of present barriers. Latin American exporters send 20 per cent of their total exports to the European Common Market and Latin America imports 20 per cent of the production of the European Common Market.[60]

Thus Ambassador Roberto Campos showed how the Europe of the Six is slowing the economic development of Latin America and especially that of Brazil. Between 1953 and 1960 exports of basic commodities originating in the industrial countries increased 57 per cent, while the non-industrialized traditional exporters added only 14 per cent to their sales; in total world trade the volume of primary exports was raised by 50 per cent, but prices declined 7 per cent.[61] From the Brazilian point of view it is sufficient to point out that between 1953 and 1960 the volume of Brazilian trade increased by 20 per cent while prices went down 37 per cent.

The bonds historically uniting Latin America to Europe have not been sufficient to lead to greater economic and commercial understanding between the two regions. But reasons of a pragmatic nature justify the reduction of barriers by the E.E.C. to allow the free competition of Latin American coffees. Twenty to twenty-five per cent of Latin American foreign trade is conducted with the Community and the coffee imported from Latin America is valued at about $300,000,000 annually. However, for the period 1957–1960 alone, the accumulated deficit of Latin American trade with the Community amounted to $856,000,000.[62]

The Europeans are thinking of giving financial and technical assistance to Latin American plans for development, as they are doing

---

[60] Wired story in *Jornal do Brasil*, Rio de Janeiro, April 18, 1963.

[61] Wired story by Isaac Piltcher, *O Globo*, Rio de Janeiro, April 18, 1963. In the meeting of ministers of the G.A.T.T., May, 1963, the Brazilian delegate again stressed the continued relative impoverishment of the underdeveloped nations, and despite the American plan to increase the world market, coldly received by France, no practical decision was reached.

[62] *Jornal do Brasil*, July 19, 1962. Total Brazilian exports to the E.C.M. in 1961 reached $313,000,000. *Jornal do Brasil*, June 12, 1962.

for the Africans,[63] but the truth is that the solution of trade problems is more important, for decapitalization has occurred as a result of the fall in export prices. The future Trade and Development Conference of the United Nations will be able to find solutions to this problem, especially when it begins to have the American support that was reaffirmed in the Senate Foreign Affairs Committee.[64]

The Latin American reaction to the privileges of the Common Market has its allies in Africa too. Like all Africans, those Africans who are English-speaking wish to share in the aid and trade agreements given by the European Economic Community to French-speaking Africans. But the Africans of the British Community are suspicious of the beautiful trimmings in which the presents of assistance are wrapped. By signing treaties of association with Europe, they say, we commit ourselves to the West, and our policy is to be neutral. When Great Britain applied for entry into the Common Market, the majority of the English-speaking African countries (except Sierra Leone) rejected the offer to be associated, alleging that they would try instead to obtain separate trade agreements with the E.E.C. When France vetoed Great Britain's admission to the Common Market, the policy of the Africans in the British Community remained unaltered: they still wanted to sell their cacao, cotton, and coffee to the Europe of the Six on the same terms as the associates, without becoming associated. With this objective Nigeria named a minister to Brussels, and a delegation from east Africa is on its way to that city. It is certain that these missions will soon be in conflict with France's purposes in regard to its own African customers: any diminution of the advantages of association by granting its privileges to non-associates would weaken the French political position in the French-speaking African states.

The other side of the question is found in the refusal of the Dutch and Italians at the last meeting of the Council of Ministers of the Common Market to sign the agreement for the association of eighteen African states belonging to the French Community. At the moment all of the Six have economic and political interests that make negotiations

[63] The Council of Ministers of the E.C.M. granted $780,000,000 in aid to sixteen African states associated in a five-year coöperative agreement. *Manchester Guardian Weekly,* June 28, 1962.
[64] *Jornal do Brasil,* June 7, 1962.

difficult and they have agreed only on a grant of $800,000,000 to the African states.

The agenda of the next meeting of twelve French-speaking African states in Ouagadougou, Alto Volta, includes debate on ratification of the new constitution, which may lead them to reëxamine the whole idea of association and to attempt to liberalize the concept of association of all of Africa and the Common Market. Some are against the association for ideological reasons, for example, Sékou Touré, President of Guinea. "At the moment," he has said, "Europe is hastily organizing the Common Market and anxious to include Africa in it. We say no. At present we constitute a very small market. We must first expand our own free market. We have nothing against anyone, but prefer to negotiate agreements freely and believe that it is more honest to say so. We are underdeveloped and backward economically. It is better for us to exploit what we have and coöperate with anyone who wishes to work with us." [65] Many others are afraid that the French plan has as its objective only to maintain French influence in France's former colonies. Fear of neo-colonialism can bring the African states together; rather than succumbing to De Gaulle's blandishments they are diversifying their economies and reducing their dependence on the Common Market. "By neo-colonialism," has said Mr. Quaison-Sackey, representative of Ghana to the United Nations, "we understand the practice of granting formal independence with the hidden intention of making the liberated country a customer-state and actually controlling it, or rather, teleguiding it by means other than political." [66]

In order to confront this threat the organization of a kind of African Common Market is being considered, an idea supported by President Olimpio Sylvanus, now deceased, in a speech to the National Assembly on Independence Day.[67] Whether favored or not by the Common Market, the idea is making progress. The Casablanca group took the initiative and announced several economic plans with a view to African unity. It decided to create an African Development Bank and an

---

[65] "The Republic of Guinea," *International Affairs* (April, 1960), 168–173.
[66] United States Assembly, Sixteenth Session, 1057 Plenary Meeting, November 17, 1961, 687.
[67] J. J. van der Lee, "The European Common Market and Africa," *The World Today* (September, 1960), 373.

African Council for Economic Unity. The belief that an African Economic Market would be an alternative to the European Common Market is beginning to gain ground among rebels in the French group and among the British Community.

The relations of the European Common Market with Latin America and Africa have thus prompted varied reactions and their evolution does not yet permit prognosis. It is certain that the French denial of Great Britain's admission will have considerable political and economic repercussions in several regions, especially in those that have suffered from the discrimination of the Six. The first British reaction consisted of reviving the E.F.T.A. (European Free Trade Association), which will naturally lead to its reformulation on new terms. Its transformation into a non-regional Common Market, including all the members of the British Community within a more flexible and adaptable system, would make its reappearance very attractive to those not associated with the E.C.M. But so far no such step has been taken.

In the meeting of the Council of Ministers of the E.F.T.A. of February, 1963, it was decided that the reduction of customs duties on industrial products should be effected in 1966 and not on January 1, 1960, as stipulated by the Stockholm Agreement. Moreover, Great Britain and Switzerland, the two principal leaders of the E.F.T.A., seem determined to preserve the essentially industrial character of free trade, making only marginal concessions with respect to agriculture,[68] which does not open the doors to primary materials, and this is Latin America's and Africa's chief difficulty. The alternatives of reactivating trade with the British Community, starting a British movement for world agreements on basic commodities, and promoting new negotiations with the United States, the Community, the E.F.T.A., and the Six[69] do not represent any radical change nor satisfy the desires of the underdeveloped and developing nations.

President Kennedy's program of world trade expansion is not limited to facilitating negotiations with the Common Market in view of

---

[68] "Seven Seek Earlier End to Tariffs," in *Manchester Guardian Weekly* (February 21, 1963), 3.
[69] R. H. S. Crossman, "Alternatives to EEC," *Manchester Guardian Weekly* (February 7, 1963) 6.

deterioration in the American balance of payments in order to enable the United States still to compete freely in an expanding world that it no longer dominates; [70] it further suggests a plan for growth of 5 per cent over a decade; it permits the reduction or elimination of tariffs on imports of tropical agricultural products from friendly countries in the process of developing, and pools resources for programs of assistance; and above all, it has the intention of shaping an Atlantic alliance between western Europe and the United States [71] in which the participating nations would attempt to reduce to a minimum the existing obstacles to trade among them. The Atlantic Community, which is badly defined and is more North Atlantic than Atlantic, seems to be an expansion of the idea of NATO, and although not so exclusive, would require greater political ties. It would continue the anomalies of NATO, and perhaps create greater ones through the possible inclusion of Australia and New Zealand, political domination by the industrial nations of the Atlantic, and the anxiety of the developing nations. The Community promises equality and interdependence, but policy would be dominated by the greater nations, the lesser would be subjugated, and community would be an idle dream. An Atlantic without barriers, broad, free, equal in opportunities, in which restricted interests and monopolistic or oligopolistic corporations that are deeply attached to the status quo are not hidden in order to maintain control and subjugation, none of this can prevail at present.

More modestly, Brazil can and must think in terms of a policy based not on military strategy but on coöperation, world trade without limitations, and development. As the Secretary of the Latin American Free Trade Association, Rômulo de Almeida, has said, Brazil wishes "to see the prosperity of its African brothers, but there is no reason why these two auspicious projects—European unity and African prosperity—may be realized only by sacrificing Latin America." [72]

---

[70] Nancy Balfour, "President Kennedy's Programme for Expanding Trade," *The World Today* (March, 1962), 95–102.
[71] Henry A. Kissinger, "Strains on the Alliance," *Foreign Affairs* (January, 1963), 281.
[72] *Jornal do Brasil*, May 12, 1962.

AFRICAN COMPETITION WITH BRAZIL

In the words of Estanislau Fischlowitz,[73] the increasingly keen competition between Africa and America with respect to the application of investment capital, public and private, foreign and international, with results that are not always favorable to the flow of capital to Latin America, cannot escape the attention of those responsible for our development policy. In Afro-Brazilian relations, adds the same author, the possibility of absorption by the growing consumer market in Africa of the manufactured and semi-manufactured products of Brazilian industry must receive a detailed examination. An increase in these relations offers great possibilities, especially considering that our products are the work of mestizo races, white and black, living together in the best of human relationships, free of colonialism. Psychological affinities and multi-racial tolerance can facilitate the successful penetration of our products.

The problem of African coffee, recently referred to by Professor Felisberto Camargo,[74] with its production of 11,000,000 sacks threatening our position in the world market and our chief source of revenue abroad, must not act as a bugbear to prevent our seeking an economic adjustment for Brazilian and African interests. The loans granted by the World Bank to African territories producing cotton and coffee, however, especially the $6,000,000 to develop coffee in Kenya, have naturally provoked the most vehement protests from Brazil and Latin America. American financing violated the International Agreement, and as an English dependency, Kenya should rely on English capital. But this is not a hindrance to economic understanding, especially with the new nations of west Africa. Our strong competitor in basic commodities, west Africa can become a large potential market for Brazilian products.

Our exports to Africa are just beginning, for from the years 1959 to 1962 they totalled only CR$1,583,733, CR$1,714,616, and CR$3,186,271, or $16,344, $12,067, and $15,697, of a total foreign trade amounting to CR$109,449,699, CR$147,122,627, and CR$245,150,739, or $1,281,969,

---

[73] "Subsídios para a Doutrina Africana do Brasil," *Revista Brasileira de Política Internacional* (March, 1960), 82–93.

[74] *Correio da Manhã,* June 26 and 29, 1960.

$1,268,803 and $1,402,970.[75] In 1961 Morocco gave up first place in our foreign trade to the Union of South Africa, followed by Algeria, ex-French West Africa, Tunisia, with the Sudan falling and Egypt climbing. Except for the Sudan, we really have no trade with Dark Africa. The Portuguese overseas provinces have played a still more insignificant role in our trade relations, as we shall see below. The principal products acquired by the African states from Brazil in 1960 [76] were raw cotton, textiles, butter, sugar, coffee, tobacco, and sisal, with the chief purchaser being the Union of South Africa, followed by Morocco, Algeria, and Egypt, all from white Africa.

Clearly this is nothing or almost nothing when compared with our total foreign trade generally between 1958 and 1961 or even with relative figures for each importing or exporting country. In 1961 Brazilian foreign trade reach $1,460,000,000 in imports and $1,403,000,000 in exports. The United States was in first place with 40.1 per cent of our sales and 35.3 per cent of our purchases, West Germany in second place with 8.11 per cent and 9.6 per cent, respectively, then France, Italy, Japan, and the United Kingdom; the most favorable balances were with the Low Countries and the United States with $50,000,000 and $48,000,000.[77]

Coffee

African competition with us in coffee has been very harmful to our foreign trade interests and has been stimulated by the European Common Market, as we saw in the preceding chapter. Its history is summarized in the first part of this book. In recent years our coffee policy has moved toward long-range international negotiation to defend production, exports, and prices.

Africa has become a serious competitor in coffee markets and in less than five years its exports have reached 8,000,000 sacks per year. The former French territories of Madagascar and West Africa, especially the Ivory Coast, are the chief producers, now supplying 40 per cent of

[75] *Anuário Estatístico do Brasil.* Instituto Brasileiro de Geografia e Estatística, 1962, 159–162.

[76] *Estatística do Comércio Exterior do Brasil por Mercadorias, segundo os países,* Rio de Janeiro, 1960 (January–June).

[77] See Tables 3.2 and 3.2A of the *Boletim da Superintendência da Moeda e do Crédito,* December 1962, VIII.

African production. The Ivory Coast is now the third producer in the world. Production has been increasing also in the former British territories, for example Kenya and Tanganyika. The possibility that the E.E.C. may favor the development of "Arabic" rather than "robust" coffees is another threat to Brazilian production. Angola, which has always been one of the main African producers, doubled its production between 1950 and 1959, most of this owing to non-Africans.[78]

In the period from 1950 to 1960 world production rose from 32.6 to 56.3 million sacks, while exports during the same period went from 32.4 to 40.5 million sacks. Brazil and Africa doubled their production, and Asia's tripled.

It would not be easy for Brazil, if this were its objective, to defeat the competition of African coffees in a price war in the international market. Compensating prices have encouraged the production of "robust" and a price war would not destroy the African threat, not only because the United States would not adopt a policy unfavorable to Africa but also because the American palate is already accustomed to the mixture of Brazilian or Latin American coffee with African "robust." The fact is that Brazil, which in 1959 had participated with 45.58 per cent (10,560,211 sacks) of the imports in the American market, in 1960 furnished only 41.85 per cent (9,261,926 sacks), while United States imports from the chief producers in Africa, which in 1959 amounted to 12.61 per cent (2,291,982 sacks), reached 16.72 per cent (3,700,591 sacks) in 1960.

According to official information, "from 1959 to 1960 the average value of the export sack was more or less stable, reflecting the balance of international quotations on the product. This was possible only through regulation of supply obtained by the International Coffee Agreement, an instrument that controls approximately 93 per cent of the world's production. Only Ruanda, Urandi, the Congolese Republic, Ethiopia, and Indonesia have not signed the agreement."[79] But the policy of long-term agreement attentive only to exports without regulation of

---

[78] *Étude sur la Situation Economique de l'Afrique depuis 1950,* Economic and Social Council of the United Nations, 1959, Ch. 2, p. 8.
[79] *A Situação Econômica Brasileira em 1960 e a atuação da Superintendência da Moeda e do Crédito como Banco Central.* Report for the 1960 Period. Rio de Janeiro, 1960, 55.

production is not wise. African producers find any plan precarious that does not affect production, while Brazil in accordance with its traditional position resists sacrificing production and favors storing surpluses. Only recently has policy of rational, selective production, eliminating uneconomical coffee growers, been undertaken. In 1961 the volume of United States imports from all sources further increased by about 350,000 sacks, with an additional growth of 20.3 per cent registered for African coffees.[80]

The International Coffee Agreement, negotiated under the auspices of the United Nations, represents the dominant fact of world coffee policy. The negotiation brought together twenty-nine exporters, embracing 94.6 per cent of world exports, and twenty importers, representing 91.8 per cent of the imports. Its repercussion was decisive throughout the market and it begins a new stage in this trade. "This agreement, considered by the Economic Commission of the United Nations General Assembly as the most perfect of those already made for basic commodities, was born of the objective realization that the tendency toward imbalance between production and consumption, marked by accumulation of stock piles and reflected in appreciable price fluctuations prejudicial both to producers and consumers, could no longer be corrected purely and simply by the normal controls of the market, and therefore demanded a high-level, world-wide understanding."[81]

It was the responsibility of Brazil, whose control of prices had encouraged production and whose exports are still the greatest, to contribute decisively to a solution of the problems of the coffee trade. At first it sought agreement of the producer-exporter countries of Latin America on the same political line. Initial discussions directed by the Foreign Ministry were concluded by Foreign Minister San Tiago Dantas' statement to the representatives of the Latin American countries on Brazil's position regarding the meeting to celebrate the world agreement on coffee. "I believe," said the Minister, "that today all our governments are following the evolution of the coffee market with

---

[80] *A Economia Brasileira em 1961 e a atuação da Superintendência da Moeda e do Crédito como Banco Central.* Relatório do Exercício de 1961, Rio de Janeiro, 1961, 65.

[81] Omer Mont'Alegre, "Assinado por 49 países, Acôrdo Internacional do Café está apto a entrar em pleno vigor," *Jornal do Brasil,* December 2, 1962.

great concern, fully certain that it depends in large part on our capacity to coördinate our action in order to rebalance the market as quickly as possible, and secondly, to restore prices gradually." He then stressed that it was paradoxical that the Latin American economy should depend so substantially on coffee prices and that we should find it difficult to maintain those prices, it being natural, therefore, that we should seek a firm agreement among the coffee-producing countries of Latin America. "We are not nor have we ever been moved by a desire to discriminate against other producing areas; on the contrary, we greet with sympathy and solidarity the appearance of other great centers of production such as those in Africa. But we cannot fail to view with some apprehension and to consider harmful to a market such as coffee—which is capable of developing only under the control of economic laws—the appearance of certain discriminatory measures in the form of customs and regulation taken by large consumer centers that alter the natural conditions in which the balance between supply and demand in the coffee market must be realized." And he concluded by stating that "because of its basic importance not only for the maintenance of our economies but for the solution of all problems of economic development, the problem of coffee cannot be circumscribed on the technical level; it must be considered also on the political level as a problem of the general policy of the American governments." [82]

Brazil appeared at the conference very conscious and sure of its position, and in the Foreign Ministry's promotion of the agreements necessary for joint action, the Brazilian delegation, led by Ambassador Sérgio Frazão, played a leading role and contributed to successful stabilization of the coffee market by international coöperation. In the meeting Brazil fought for an agreement on export quotas, striving in this way for a balance between supply and demand. Pre-negotiations had been conducted since 1958. An agreement that would not consider the volume of our production did not suit Brazil, nor did a price war with extremely hazardous results. "Brazil's fundamental objective should be, then, to obtain approval of a disciplinary instrument to restrain countries that pour their total production into the market.

---

[82] "Boletim Informativo no. 231," Ministério das Relações Exteriores, April 26, 1962.

Indirectly the agreement would aim at restoring gold prices, without provoking the customary reactions against price cartels in large consumer centers. For this very reason Brazil preferred the solution of quotas to the artificial rigidity of a price agreement, which could suit us only if it included an effective correction of the differentials prevailing at the time between Brazilian and African coffees on the one hand and Central American and Colombian coffees on the other." [83]

The conference was not an easy meeting, for in the words of Ambassador Sérgio Frazão, "it embodied the final hopes for an ordering of the world coffee market to which is so closely linked the economic and social stability of the producer countries, all of which are still faced with underdevelopment." In his speech he made clear that the producer nations desired "stability promptly, and that restoration of prices is to come gradually as the producer countries proceed to control their production. This increase in international prices must not be borne by the American consumer exclusively, but must be obtained also by means of a legitimate increase in world consumption through the removal of artificial barriers to coffee imports in many European countries." [84]

The resistance of the Common Market made negotiations very difficult, for they defended the thesis of regionalization of trade in basic commodities in order to safeguard the precarious conditions of the African economy. As our delegate said, this thesis was an excuse for the discriminatory treatment used by the E.E.C. against Latin American coffees; and he further pointed out that: 1) the Latin American countries attributed primary importance to negotiation for the purpose of eliminating the preferential systems in effect in Western Europe and reducing internal taxes; 2) the Coffee Conference could not be used as an instrument to consolidate regional discriminatory systems, for it had been called as a means of developing trade on a world basis; 3) Brazil agreed that frequently the region must be the point of departure, but in the case of coffee the moment had arrived to move in the direction of a real world agreement; 4) the Common Market, which was conceived by the French, could not be used to impede progress in certain areas; 5)

---

[83] "Política Internacional do Café: O Convênio a Longo Prazo," *Jornal do Brasil,* January 25, 1963.
[84] "Brasil: prejuízo dos produtores de café compromete planejamento e combate à inflação," *Jornal do Brasil,* July 13, 1962.

if, as the French delegate alleged, the Common Market was prospering
notably and if this regional grouping would tend to have a growing
share in total world trade and in the coffee trade, nothing would be
more fair than to give Latin America access to this trade on a
competitive basis; 6) it was up to the European Community to make
the first proposal to negotiate a program of reduction and eventual
elimination of barriers, without which there would be no possibility of
arriving at an agreement acceptable to the Latin Americans. Sérgio
Frazão further rejected the attempt to set Africans against Latin
Americans, recalling that the Brazilian point of view was shared by
Nigeria, Ghana, Morocco, Mali, and Liberia.[85]

The Latin American statement against obstacles to the expansion of
the coffee trade was supported by the United States, the Soviet Union,
Portugal, and Norway. The Brazilian delegate then reaffirmed our
country's constructive and conciliatory position, spoke of our efforts for
world understanding in the coffee market, and tried to demonstrate the
coherence of our policy in favor of world trade and against the
colonialist orientation in international exchange of primary materials.
He recalled the decisive role played by Brazil in the formation of the
"Economic Commission for Africa" and showed that the Brazilian and
Latin American position has been identical to that of different African
countries. "This is not," he stressed, "an isolated phenomenon, but is
part of a collective action on the part of countries producing raw
materials and basic commodities seeking a fair return on their labor and
growing expansion of their trade with highly industrialized areas." [86]

The Brazilian argument presented two different points: first, the low
consumption of coffee in European Common Market countries, where
there is increasing predominance of African coffees that benefit from
tariff exemptions; second, the high internal taxation of coffee.[87] The
Brazilian theses, all successful, defended a rigid system of export quotas
capable of stabilizing the market and assuring the immediate maintenance of and a subsequent gradual rise in prices, the recognition of new

---

[85] "O Brasil lidera a resistência ao Mercado Comum," *Jornal do Brasil,* July 21,
1962.
[86] "O Brasil na Conferência Mundial do Café," *Jornal do Brasil,* July 26, 1962.
[87] Omer Mont'Alegre, "Vitória do Brasil sôbre o Mercado Comum em Nova
Iorque," *Brasil em Marcha,* August 1962.

markets, the possibility of exporting for industrial purposes, the recognition of the necessity to remove obstacles to trade (defined as high tariffs and taxes), discriminatory tariffs, restrictions on quantity and subsidies, the obligation of importing member countries to limit their purchases of coffee from exporting non-member countries, and the right of Brazil to a guaranteed deliberative vote and a suspensive vote.[88]

Brazil made it very clear that it was not against Africa but desired equitable treatment for coffees from both regions. Brazil's victory over the Common Market set a precedent for solutions of other problems of basic commodities, and it is already recognized that the International Coffee Agreement, obtained thanks to the efforts of the Brazilian delegation, has served to focus upon agreements for basic commodities on which the Trade and Development Conference must concentrate.[89]

As to volume of total production, the International Agreement [90] allowed Brazil 39.2 per cent (18,000,000 sacks),[91] Colombia 13.1 per cent (6,011,280 sacks), the Ivory Coast 6.0 per cent (2,324,278 sacks), Portugal 4.5 per cent (2,188,648 sacks), Uganda 4.2 per cent (1,887,737 sacks), and Mexico 2.5 per cent (3,509,000 sacks).[92]

Cacao

The problem of competition, although keener in the case of coffee, does not exist only with regard to this product. In cacao Brazil, which is one of its major exporters, has its chief competitors in Africa, especially Ghana. A native of Amazonia and of other American regions such as Mexico, exploited since the colonial period and spread throughout Africa, cacao has never attained the position of coffee and rubber in Brazilian foreign trade. During the period of greatest world consumption the chocolate industry did not satisfy its demands in Brazil only, for there were many competitors, especially the cacao-producing regions of

---

[88] "Política Internacional do Café. O Convênio a Longo Prazo," *Jornal do Brasil,* January 25, 1963.
[89] William Butler, "Trade and the Less-Developed Areas," *Foreign Affairs* (January, 1963), 379–380.
[90] Presidential Message submitting the Agreement to Congressional approval in *Diário do Congresso,* January 25, 1963.
[91] In the first half of 1962 coffee exports represented 55% of the total value of exports and almost all of this was purchased by the United States.
[92] Omer Mont'Alegre, *Jornal do Brasil,* December 2, 1962.

Africa where its development was more rapid. At the beginning of this
century the Gold Coast, now Ghana, dominated the world market. The
English were repeating on the Gold Coast what they had done in the
case of rubber, which they took to Ceylon and Malaya from the
Amazon and then surpassed Brazilian production. It is sufficient to
recall that in 1895 the Gold Coast contributed only thirteen tons to
international trade; ten years later there was an increase of 5,620 tons
and in another ten years the Gold Coast surpassed its competitors by
exporting 78,574 tons; a short time later it dominated the world market
with 40 per cent of total world production.[93] Between 1950 and 1959
Ghana's production, which represents from 45 per cent to 50 per cent of
total African production, seems not to have developed, owing in part to
a disease (swollen-shoot) the eradication of which required massive
destruction of cacao plants.[94] It was with the introduction of plants from
the Upper Amazon—by December, 1959, 10,000,000 sets and slips of
Brazilian varieties had already been distributed—that production was
restored in Ghana.[95] In Ghana as in Nigeria, the second African
producer, and other cacao-producing countries, production is in the
hands of Africans, except in the former Belgian Congo, the Island of
Fernando Po, and São Tomé, where the plantations are operated by
non-Africans. From 1950 to 1959 Africa produced two-thirds of the
world's supply.

From 1950 to 1960 international prices of cacao were in general high
and stable. The high price of the product prevented the popularization
of chocolate, was consumed only by a small elite.[96]

The international cacao trade has been undergoing important
changes since 1954. The first is the continuous decline in imports of
cacao beans by the United States, the largest world consumer ($\frac{1}{3}$ of the

[93] Caio Prado Jr., *História Econômica do Brasil,* Brasiliense, 1945, 253–256.
[94] *Étude sur la Situation Économique de l'Afrique depuis 1950,* Economic and
Social Council of the United Nations, 1959, Ch. II, 6–7.
[95] Carlos Berenhauser, Jr., "Aspectos de Gana. O Aproveitamento do Rio Volta,"
Carta Mensal do Conselho Técnico da Confederação Nacional do Comércio,
June, 1961, 19–31, esp. 25.
[96] See indices showing cacao production for the world and Africa between 1953
and 1961, in *Economic Bulletin for Africa,* Addis-Ababa, Ethiopia, United Nations, January 1961, I, 38. For statistics on the chief producing countries in 1960,
see *Conjuntura Econômica* (April, 1961), 59, table III. Brazil was in second place
with 178,000 tons; Ghana was in first place with 318,000 tons.

world total), which is compensated in part by greater importation of cacao products (chocolate and ground cacao). In the second place, Western European imports have fallen by about 10 per cent. On the other hand, Asian and Eastern imports have increased relatively; the increase in the Soviet Union between 1950 and 1957 was followed by a decline in 1958 and 1959.[97] Falling imports, more rapid increase in production than in consumption, and the imposition of a preferential tariff by the European Economic Community have promoted unity in defense of prices among the non-associated countries. The unfavorable international position of the product statistically, the fall in prices and the loss of approximately 30 per cent of the harvest of the principal Brazilian crop in 1960–61 [98] constituted the bases for Brazilian diplomatic negotiation with Ghana, as well as negotiations between the authorities of Ghana and Nigeria. These were three chief producers suffering from E.E.C. discriminatory practices.

During the Cacao Conference promoted by the F.A.O. (Food and Agriculture Organization) in April, 1961, in which twenty-two producer and consumer countries took part, Brazil acted to promote meetings between representatives with a view to better understanding in the defense of common interests. The Director of the Foreign Trade Funds of the Banco do Brasil, Antônio Arnaldo Gomes Taveira, stated to President Nkrumah Brazil's purpose in greater rapprochement with the new African countries whose economy is in many ways parallel to ours, as in the case of cacao, and received from him a statement of identical intention. The way to an Alliance of Cacao Producers was open, and progress was made during the new F.A.O. Conference in Rome when it was decided that there would be another meeting in Abidjan on the Ivory Coast. In January, 1961, with the participation of Ghana, Nigeria, Ivory Coast, Cameroons, and Brazil, the greatest producers, having a total of 80 per cent of world production, the Alliance of Cacao Producers was founded and its statutes were debated and approved *ad referendum* by the respective governments. In Brazil

[97] *Economic Bulletin for Africa,* I, 38–39; and "Cacau, Reduz-se o consumo mundial," *Conjuntura Econômica,* April 1961, pp. 55–62.

[98] *A Economia Brasileira em 1960 e a atuação da Superintendência da Moeda e do Crédito como Banco Central.* Reports of the Proceedings of 1960 and 1961. Rio de Janeiro, 1960 and 1961, 56–57 and 68–69, respectively.

the document was approved by the Currency and Credit Control Council and will probably soon be ratified. Ghana was the first to ratify the document, with Nigeria second. Ghana's approval has overcome the difficulty that arose in Rome when Brazil proposed that internal consumption not be included in the export quota and Ghana, Nigeria, Ivory Coast, and Cameroons did not agree.

The founding of the Alliance is the first concrete act toward a formal union of cacao-exporting countries for protection of the product and stabilization of prices.[99] With its suggestion of the Alliance Brazil again demonstrated its desire for coöperation and understanding, as it had in connection with coffee, showing that parallel economies must have a common, constructive plan and not act competitively and destructively. This international body—initiated by the Banco do Brasil through its Director of Foreign Trade Funds and not by the Foreign Ministry—is a powerful instrument of defense and an example of the coördination of common Afro-Brazilian interests. The last meeting, on March 13, 1963, in Port of Spain (Trinidad), gave definite direction to the plan for the protection of prices. All that remains, declared our representative, A. Arnaldo Taveira, is to fix price levels and export quotas.[100]

The example of the International Coffee Agreement and the agreement on cacao in the near future show that understanding and coöperation are possible even when there is competition, as is the case in all of Latin America with respect to basic commodities. The International Trade and Development Conference also set out to solve these problems, as we saw in the last chapter. Latin America depends on United States Government support for the stabilization of basic-commodity prices. A report of the Senate Foreign Affairs Committee, "recognizing the importance of stabilizing the income of less developed countries having as its source the sale of primary materials," stated that "the United States is now taking the initiative in promoting agreements on basic products wherever feasible, for the purpose of establishing organized trade and achieving minimum prices for these products by means of balanced supply and demand in international markets."[101]

---

[99] *Jornal do Brasil*, May 10, 1962.
[100] *Jornal do Brasil*, April 30, 1963.
[101] Wire news story from Washington, *Jornal do Brasil*, June 7, 1962.

Brazilian diplomacy aims not to create discriminatory regional systems but to develop international agreements regulating world trade without continental distinctions, as has already been done on other occasions, overcoming through unity the dominant position attained by European powers in organizations like G.A.T.T. and the International Currency Fund. The understanding that we must seek with Europe, especially the Six, does not mean discarding Africans but uniting them with Latin Americans in the struggle against all discrimination and restrictions. Nigeria's proposal in G.A.T.T. that tropical products have free entry into industrial countries, supported by Brazil and strongly opposed by the countries of the Common Market, as well as Ghana's ratification of the Statutes of the Alliance of Cacao Producers, reveal that progress has already been made toward understanding and economic coöperation. It is true that it was an African country, Senegal, that most violently opposed the Nigerian-Brazilian proposal in G.A.T.T.[102] Senegal, intimately associated with France, voted against the Afro-Asian motion on Algeria in the United Nations and took sides with Kasavubu at the time of Lumumba's assassination, but by way of compensation it received the only Brazilian Foreign Minister ever to visit Africa. In April, 1961 Afonso Arinos de Melo Franco conversed with the poet Léopold Senghor, establishing literary contacts and cultural agreements, but nothing was said or learned concerning Senegal's position in support of the Common Market discriminations that are so prejudicial to non-associated Africans and Latin Americans. The alienation of the latter was counterbalanced in African eyes, according to Senghor,[103] by the breaking of diplomatic relations with Portugal in July, 1961, as well as the present difficulties that Senegal is creating for Portugal by alleging violation of its territory by Portuguese forces.

Free competition joins more than it separates, but privileges and discrimination destroy unity and hold the threat of subjugation. But

---

[102] "Entrevista concedida pelo Embaixador Otávio Dias Carneiro, Secretário-Geral Adjunto para Assuntos Econômicos, sobre as atividades do G.A.T.T. e do Mercado Comun," mimeographed copy distributed by the Ministerio de Relações Exteriores, January 8, 1963.

[103] On L. Senghor's Francophilia, see Moacyr Werneck de Castro, *Dois Caminhos da Revolução Africana*, Instituto Brasileiro de Estudos Afro-Ásiaticos, 1962, 55–65.

just as the Common Market removes Brazilian competition through discrimination and restrictions, so too balances favorable to Brazil in the socialist countries, amounting to more than $30,000,000, in addition to creating internal sources of inflation, cause a serious decline in purchases by socialist countries from Brazil. Unable to expand their trade with Brazil, especially with respect to coffee, these nations are being forced to resort increasingly to other markets supplying the product (Colombia, Ghana, Guinea), with perhaps irreparable damage to our present position in the markets of Eastern Europe.[104] If it is true that immediate liquidation of these balances has depended on Brazil more than on the East, the fact is that this type of competition is extremely harmful.

On the contrary, the proposal of the Algerian government to sell Brazil 600,000 tons of petroleum is a first step toward the conclusion of a Trade and Payment Agreement that our government plans to suggest to the Algerian government, thus freeing us of heavy payments in dollars and pounds on imports of petroleum from Venezuela and Saudi Arabia.[105]

Brazilian interest in strengthening economic relations with Africa in order to discover instruments of international coöperation, especially in areas of underdevelopment, instability of the world market for similar basic commodities, and technical and economic assistance, has been demonstrated in preceding chapters and in this one. The strengthening of trade relations, the examination of possibilities in the African market for Brazilian products and vice versa, economic associations, transportation problems, and difficulties imposed by the Common Market, these are goals for the near future.

In May, 1960 the Nigerian diplomat Godwin Alaoma Onyegbula suggested the possibility of Brazil's exporting electrical appliances and machinery to Africa. Brazil's modest industrial exports can and must be expanded in the vast region of western Africa, where our manufactured products would arrive free of colonialist, imperialist, and racist imputations. A drive to export chemical and pharmaceutical products, machinery, vehicles and accessories, rubber, wood and mineral products,

---

[104] Reunião Plenária do COLESTE (Comissão do Comércio com o Leste [Eastern Trade Commission]): Plano Para Aumentar Intercâmbio Comercial," Boletim Informativo do Ministério das Relacões Exteriores, April 18, 1953.
[105] "Noticiário do Itamarati," No. 353, April 10, 1963.

textiles and metals, sanitary articles of porcelain, and especially sewing machines and motor vehicles can help free us of dependency upon the export of primary products and accelerate our process of industrialization. In a recently circulated study the Brazilian trade office in Great Britain revealed great opportunities for our pharmaceutical products, sewing machines, motor vehicles, and novelties in British East Africa (Kenya, Tanganyika, and Uganda).[106] After his return from Cairo in August, 1962 Ambassador Dias Carneiro stated that Brazil could export railroad equipment, all types of vehicles, mechanical parts, lathes, butane gas, electrical equipment of all kinds, and other manufactured products to Africa. Moreover, there is the possibility of Brazilian soft drinks entering into competition with alcoholic beverages from any country, for consumption is enormous in Moslem countries where the Koran prohibits the use of alcohol.[107]

The opinion that there are possibilities of greater trade has been spreading. In a lecture Flávio Maranhão stated[108] that the African market can be won by Brazilian manufactured products, which are less subject to fluctuations in price than agricultural products. Declaring that nothing objective has been done to gain this extraordinary consumer who is right next door and will pay for our manufactured products at sight, in pounds or dollars, Flávio Maranhão argued for practical measures facilitating trade, such as simplification of export procedures and establishment of permanent sea and air lines linking us with the countries on the Gulf of Guinea, where we can offer products that in quality and price are capable of competing with those traditionally in control of the markets there. In 1951 Ghana imported a number of products, totaling CR$826,000,000, paid in pounds, that we could export at competitive prices.

The industrialist Newton Pereira, Executive Secretary of the National Confederation of Industry, who was one of the Brazilian delegation at the Conference on Problems of Economic Development in

---

[106] See Antonio Marinho, *Possibilidades Comerciais do Brasil na África Oriental Britânica,* London, 1960 (mimeographed).
[107] "Boletim Informativo da Embaixada do Brasil em Washington," August 2, 1962.
[108] Lecture delivered at the Instituto Brasileiro de Estudos Afro-Ásiaticos, April 27, 1962, summarized in *Jornal do Brasil,* April 29, 1962.

Cairo, also stated that it is indispensable to reëxamine the question of forms and possibilities of a closer collaboration between the Latin American bloc and the African and Asian blocs, and accused the L.A.F.T.A. (Latin American Free Trade Association) of negligence in this connection.[109]

It was the Jânio Quadros administration that took interest in this trade and in linking Brazil and Africa. In June 1962 it was decided that the Brazilian Lloyd's should establish a direct line to Africa.[110] Since then Brazil has slowly and gradually been exporting its products to the African countries by Lloyd's ships going directly to Lagos, whereas formerly the trade was conducted through the ports of New Orleans and Durban. Brazilian trade organizations are already functioning in Africa and believe that the west coast of Africa is a potential market for which Brazil can compete.[111]

The thesis that Africa must be considered a new market, without fear of competition from African tropical products, is thus becoming general and gaining ground in the national consciousness despite the opposition of economic groups interested in maintaining traditional markets, who hold that it is in Europe and the United States that we must seek agreements in order to modify our foreign trade situation. "We must court Europe instead of African chiefs," these sectors say. They forget that it is difficult to be limited to traditional markets, and everywhere there is an effort to expand trade freely, as for example Canada today, which is trying to increase its trade relations with Japan in view of the surprising decline of its traditional markets in the United States and Great Britain. The statements cited here on the possibilities for our industry in African markets reflect the conviction in advanced quarters in industry, the press, and academic circles that Brazilian manufactured products can compete today in price and quality with those of other industrial countries.

Changes in our economy created this conviction. The following conclusions, offered by Professor Inácio Moura Rangel in his lecture of

---

[109] "América do Sul necessita examinar sua atitude para com africanos e asiáticos," *Jornal do Brasil,* August 17, 1962.

[110] Panair also inaugurated a direct Rio de Janeiro–Cairo line.

[111] "Major penetração de productos brasileiros no mercado africano," *Jornal do Brasil,* October 25, 1962.

April, 1962 at the First Debate Session on Afro-Brazilian Economic Relations, correspond to a new national economic consciousness:

1. The tendency to exaggerate the danger of African competition for our traditional export products is lacking in basis. The world market is sufficiently broad to accommodate everyone, and after all, our capacity to sell is limited by our capacity to buy, which is much more restricted than is generally supposed.

2. Only under the conditions of planned, bilateral trade between states can Brazil enable itself to take advantage of the African and other new markets.

3. The legal form for structuring such trade, under Brazilian conditions, is to grant a concession as a public service to an economically mixed body, with interested organs of the state predominating but with indispensable representation from the corporate bodies of private enterprise.

4. As a new market the African countries constitute a special case because they are underdeveloped markets, although in the processs of development. They will compete with Brazil in the world market in raw materials but will constitute markets for refined products.

5. The African revolution in progress is a vigorous, irreversible process, which in a few years will give rise to some of the most dynamic national economies in the world.[112]

---

[112] "A África e outros novos mercados," *Tempo Brasileiro* (December, 1962), 81–102.

Brazil's African Policy

No Afro-Asian people freed from colonialism or in a struggle for liberty can forget that Portugal inaugurated European hegemony in the African and Asian world. European domination in Africa and Asia dates from 1482, when Diogo do Cão discovered the Congo estuary, and from 1492, when Vasco da Gama arrived in Calcutta. We know this history according to the Western version. For Orientals this dominance, designated the "Vasco da Gama period in Asian history" by the Indian historian K. M. Panikkar,[1] means the beginning of terrorism, piracy, and barbarism. It affected relations between East and West, crushing the former by gross, profit-greedy mercantilism and by the immorality of European conduct, which made war in order to sell opium illegally and with the greatest vandalism destroyed oriental palaces to strike fear into the hearts and spirits of Asian peoples. Ambition for riches and the might of the cannon were accompanied by Christian evangelization, a partnership that not only joined God and Mammon but also meant spiritual aggression upon the established oriental religions. And the idea of European superiority, always immanent in conquest, must not be forgotten.

At the height of its expansion, the Portuguese Empire extended from the coasts of Brazil and western Africa, dominating the South Atlantic, to Sofala in eastern Africa, and thence to Nagasaki in Japan, commanding the Indian Ocean, controlling the Persian Gulf and Red Sea, and

[1] *Asia and Western Dominance,* London, Allen & Unwin, 1961.

navigating in lordly fashion the Chinese and Japanese seas, where the Portuguese were the first Europeans to arrive. It does not matter that by the beginning of the seventeenth century, between 1605 and 1665, the Portuguese Empire in Asia was reduced to toeholds in India, the island of Macao, and half of Timor, although with the aid of Great Britain it managed to keep other possessions in Asia and with Brazil, those in Africa that today really constitute its only colonies. Despite its obstinacy, the Indian possessions were lost, less violently than they were conquered; Macao survives through the benevolence of the Chinese, and Timor continues to be menaced. The Portuguese were the first to arrive and will be the last to leave, for they are impenitent colonialists; their attack on the financial prosperity of the Moslem nations is now reversed in the threat to their economy represented by the possible loss of their extra-European resources. All those who have succeeded the Portuguese since the beginning of the seventeenth century, the Dutch, English, and French, with their conquests and empires have all one by one withdrawn from Asia and are withdrawing from Africa; only Portugal insists on its historical right, as if the fact of having arrived one century earlier, during five centuries of European domination, gave it greater authority or, further, as if its achievement, at first so vast and ultimately so slight, were greater than that of British imperialism.

It is true that the Portuguese policy that tolerated Hindus and persecuted Mohammedans has had more lasting effects than that of the Dutch, above all linguistically, for a Portuguese "patois" has survived down to the twentieth century and still persists in a few places. It is true, also, that methods of religious propagation were more coercive than persuasive but, if they were unsuccessful against Islam and made little impression in India and China, where Catholicism was established it put down roots, as for example in Ceylon.[2] But cultural influences and repercussions between Orientals and Occidentals made themselves felt only after the imperialism of the middle of the past century. It would take too long to list the elements of the cultural graft made by the Orient on European civilization; Oriental influences have even been

---

[2] Charles Boxer, *Four Centuries of Portuguese Expansion, 1415–1825: A Succinct Survey,* Johannesburg, Witwatersrand University Press, 1961. See K. W. Gunarwardena, "A New Netherlands in Ceylon," *The Ceylon Journal of Historical and Social Studies* (July, 1959), 203–244.

pointed out in Brazil. The essential Western influence consisted of creating the native leadership that eventually dislodged European supremacy from Asia. It must not however be forgotten that the nationalist idea and Asianism were born as a reaction to European preponderance. Considering their cultures superior, Orientals recognized that European social and economic organization was stronger and more powerful and, finally, in cultural and political contacts they found Asia's role in the world and European limitations.

What did Portugal do in this connection? As one of the most backward areas in Western culture, one of the most underdeveloped countries in Europe, it neither formed native leadership nor advanced the peoples under its domination with technology or social organization. It was unable to give because it had nothing to give. The Portuguese government believes in its colonial potency, whereas it is colonially impotent. Yet it retained more than it could have hoped for, due in large part to its old ally, Great Britain, which demanded so much and forced so many concessions.

The crisis in Angola suddenly changed the picture, overthrew the oldest dictatorship in Europe, and frightened one of the most oblivious oligarchies in the world. Portugal may believe that it will once again weather the storm that has broken out over its colonies. No other European nation has so long been accustomed to having a colonial empire, and the majority of its people finds it comforting to think that this small state possesses as much African territory as all Western Europe. The feeling experienced by the Portuguese soul for this dominion is not only sentimental; it is also economic, for the two colonies have occupied an important position in the Portuguese economy, although they are not so prosperous as the Congo, the Rhodesias, and South Africa.

Portugal would not disappear if it lost these colonies, but it would have to reformulate its economic policy and reduce its already modest national aspirations. For this very reason, since the Salazar administration began in 1926 there have been attempts to create solidarity between the metropolis and its colonies. This is a modern enterprise, for the Portuguese really began to give their attention to Africa at the end of the last century. I do not believe that it serves Portugal's interests to persist in asserting its five-hundred-year-old historical rights, because the world judges its accomplishment not by the real and serious effort of the last eighty years in Africa but by the alleged five centuries of its modest activity.

At the beginning of the past century (1835–1836), a Portuguese who lived in Africa for nineteen years and later joined the struggle for independence in Brazil wrote that "the Portuguese government has lost the spirit of discovery for almost two centuries, and the few discoveries that have been made in east and west Africa indicate that there is a certain lack of confidence in the enterprises of the industrial nations." After recalling the causes of Portuguese decline in eastern India, he said that "other and similar reasons have caused the discredit and discouragement of the Portuguese in Angola." He further noted "an almost complete indifference, relaxation, an incomprehensible negligence, or something of the sort, has presided over the destiny of Angola, owing as much to the dominant whites as to the dominated Negroes. . . . The government of Mozambique is a shadow of the rich provinces of this name, for old Mozambique was the land of gold and modern Mozambique is the land of poverty. . . . The Portuguese should thank the Almighty that the neighboring Arab chiefs are continually involved in internal disorders and that the natives are becoming more brutish, so that they [the Portuguese] are not expelled from lands where for centuries they have ruled without strength, policy, or morality."[3] This is a simple and objective portrait of the centuries-long domination that today constitutes an historical right of occupation, a portrait that is forever repeated, even by Salazar.[4]

The beginning of the Portuguese attention to Africa, during the monarchy (1885–1910), was contradictory and equivocal, not only because of the critical position of Portuguese economy but also because of the evils of slave labor, as denounced by Nevinson in his book *A Modern Slavery* (1906). The republican period (1910–1926) brought

---

[3] *Compêndio Histórico das Possessões Portuguêsas na África Oriental e Ocidental*, Rio de Janeiro, Arquivo Nacional, with Preliminary Note by José Honório Rodrigues, pars. 591, 601, 643, 685, and 692.
[4] See interview in *U.S. News and World Report* (June 9, 1962), reproduced in *Notícias de Portugal*, Sup. No. 793, July 14, 1962.

much instability and frustrated hopes for development despite the dynamism of Norton de Matos.[5] With Salazar Portugal is balancing its finances and lowering its international debt, with a prudence that excites the greatest admiration of housewives, and satisfying the aspirations of a rural, underdeveloped, devout, diligent, semi-literate, and politically conservative society. It is a policy that delights the Portuguese oligarchy and all anti-progressive currents in the world, including the well-placed "colony" in Brazil and its allies or employees.

The principles of this colonialism are: first, *the unity of the empire;* hence, the title of "provinces" by which the shrewd expect to deceive the simple people of this world. Historically they have always been colonies, whether they were called overseas provinces as in the nineteenth century, or colonies at the beginning of the Salazar phase, or overseas provinces again by 1951 legislation. "Portugal and its colonies form a complete and indivisible unit. Portugal extends from Minho to Timor." It is not the separation or contiguity of the colonies in relation to the metropolis that validates or invalidates colonialism, but whether or not the interests of the former are subordinated to those of the metropolis. The second principle is that of *assimilation of the population,* which has meant the attempt to make Africans over into Portuguese, with no respect for their African individuality. If it has not been possible in three centuries to transform them into Portuguese, however, what may be expected now of an attempt that ignores the fundamental fact that Africans are essentially Africans, and not Europeans or sub-Europeans.

Assimilation is an unsuccessful policy, for only 35,000 have been assimilated in Angola (with a population of 4,500,000) and 4,349 in Mozambique (with a population of 5,700,000). Not to mention the failure of miscegenation, which has resulted in the extremely low figures of 30,000 and 25,000 mestizos, respectively, for these "provinces." At this rate, with 1 per cent assimilated in Angola and ½ per cent in Mozambique, it will take 50,000 years for Portugal to accomplish its "civilizing mission."

These figures are not pamphleteer propaganda against Portugal but the statistical result of the policy of assimilation in Africa. It is sufficient to say that in the whole overseas area there is only one institution of

---

[5] On the evolution of colonialism, see J. M. da Silva Cunha, *Questões Ultramarinas e Internacionais,* Lisbon, 1960, esp. 87–123.

higher learning, with one hundred and thirty-five students, a hundred and fifteen in the Faculty of Medicine and twenty in Pharmacy. There are only five high schools in Angola, three in Mozambique, and one each in Cape Verde, São Tomé and Príncipe islands, India, Macao, and Timor. There is only one normal school in Angola and India; in Mozambique there are six, and there are none in the other colonies.

In an interview granted by Minister Oliveira Salazar to the *New York Times*,[6] the reporter, after recalling that according to official data the population of Angola was 4,583,833 natives (Negroes), under "tribal administration," and 277,386 whites, plus "assimilated" mulattoes and natives,[7] asked "how much longer can a situation be maintained in which 6 per cent of the population enjoys the rights of citizenship and 94 per cent does not?" Salazar replied sophistically that possession of the rights of citizenship is valid only "in those cases where such rights may be exercised effectively and that, along with the privileges they guarantee, there must be a clear notion of the responsibilities and duties they impose." Thus, he is willing to grant the right of citizenship to the Negro when he is prepared to exercise it, or rather, when he has become a Portuguese citizen. Until then, he will be considered a native, subject to a complex of juridical and administrative controls.

Native status has been sharply criticized by Marvin Harris.[8] The Portuguese policy is based on the system of assimilation, which requires that the African speak Portuguese and satisfy fixed official norms so as to become virtually a Portuguese citizen. Thus, in order to be a citizen with full rights in Portuguese Africa, the African must first become a Portuguese.

Sithole has observed that the goal of Portuguese policy is to hold African nationalism in embryonic form. The African is taught to see himself as Portuguese and not African. The aim of Portuguese policy seems to be to obtain a black-skinned Portuguese. And if the African wishes to be himself, not to lose his identity or become the caricature of a Portuguese? Sithole relates that an African from Lourenço Marques

---

[6] March 31, 1961. Reproduced in *Notícias de Portugal,* June 10, 1961.

[7] According to the 1950 census, the number assimilated in Angola was 30,089.

[8] *Portugal's African "Wards." A firsthand report on Labor and Education in Moçambique;* Portuguese trans. "Trabalho e Educação em Moçambique," *Educação e Ciência Sociais* (September, 1960), 99–141.

told him: the Portuguese believe that God made a mistake when he made the Africans African. Their policy of assimilation is an effort to correct this divine error. But people like to be what they are and must be accepted as such.[9]

In the aforementioned interview, the reporter raised the question: "Portugal is proud of its five centuries of civilizing rule in Angola; how does one explain then, the relatively low number of about 2 per cent assimilated?"[10] Oliveira Salazar confesses his discontent with the results of the policy of assimilation but points out that, if Portuguese contacts with Africa go back for five centuries, they were organized only during the nineteenth century. "It was at that time, therefore, that the policy of assimilation began to be applied, but it had already proved itself: Brazil was by that time, and continues to be, the most vigorous example of the multi-racial society that is now recognized by everyone as the ideal to be attained in human relations."

This statement contains many inaccuracies and contradictions. After all, Luanda was founded in 1575 and, therefore, at the beginning of the nineteenth century four centuries of control had already elapsed, proving Portugal unable to do in Africa what it says it did in Brazil. Furthermore, the policy of assimilation was not initiated at the beginning of the nineteenth century, for until the fourth decade of that century Angola existed more for Brazil's than for Portugal's benefit. Only after 1870 did Portugal begin to be interested in Africa, and even then it did not immediately apply the policy of assimilation, for which the first legislation dates from 1917. Native or African policy existed only incidentally; from 1895 to 1930 a policy was formulated concerned only with problems of education and alcoholism.

The new era in Africa was more a result of the European colonialist threat than of concern for the African or the African colonies. Moreover, the allusions to Brazil beg the issue, as Brazil is not a good example in this case. First, slavery here made miscegenation and, in turn, assimilation possible. Without both it would have been impossible

---

[9] N. Sithole, *El Reto de Africa,* trans. of *African Nationalism,* Spanish ed., 1961, 42.

[10] The calculation of 2% is made on the basis of a population of 4,855,219 in Angola, when this number does not even constitute the total of the two "provinces."

to create a Brazil whose experience is unique and original. Miscegenation, which accounts for 26 per cent of Brazil's population, is still insignificant in Portuguese Africa today and equivalent to the pitifully small number of those assimilated. Secondly, it was no more possible in Brazil to manufacture a Portuguese-American than it is possible to manufacture a Portuguese African. When between 1758 and 1777 the use of the general language was forbidden in Amazonas and São Paulo, Brazil was already Brazilian and not Portuguese; and we were on the eve of the conspiracy in Minas, not to mention the many previous rebel movements revealing that Brazilians did not wish to be Portuguese but Brazilian.

There are no abstractions or subterfuges to hide the fundamental incoherence of comparison of different historical processes, or the supposition that they can give similar results. Portuguese Africa will not be a new Brazil. The rare examples of a few assimilated persons and mulattoes occupying certain relatively high positions in the administrative scale cannot hide the brutal statistics. The mechanism of assimilation and objection to miscegenation are used as a disguise to reject the political and cultural aspirations of the Africans and to maintain European domination. Nor does paternalism obscure the negation of African rights on which the Portuguese oligarchy insists. The Africans are kept in a world of ignorance, isolation, and obscurantism.

Sithole expressed to a Portuguese African the opinion that the Portuguese policy of acceptance was better than that of non-acceptance of South Africa, and he replied that there was no policy of accepting the African. "In Portuguese Africa today there are 11,000,000 persons who are neither citizens of Portugal nor of Africa." But, said Sithole, there were several thousand accepted and assimilated Africans, and he replied: "No; when they accept the thousands of Africans, the Portuguese are pretending to accept the African, but actually they are refusing, definitely, to accept him. When they accept the assimilated African, the Portuguese are doing no more than reclaiming the Portuguese they put in him. In other words, they are really accepting themselves and not the African." [11]

This idea of assimilation is so entrenched and obscured in the

---

[11] Sithole, *op. cit.,* 43.

Portuguese mind, which also thought that it was manufacturing a neo-Portuguese in Brazil, that when the Overseas Council was adjourned in 1962, Adriano Moreira declared that "the Portuguese spirit has gained in vigor in the territories precisely during periods of great suffering." [12]

Education, including primary instruction, is reserved for the "civilized." Before elementary school, natives are obliged to undergo a pre-apprenticeship in schools of rudimentary training, which are reserved for them, from the age of seven to fifteen in order to become "civilized." This rudimentary education, along with the literary part and physical education, trains young Negroes for agricultural work, crafts, and the care of livestock. It is entrusted to the Catholic Missions and is administered in 3,833 schools to 409,445 children.

Once this obstacle is hurdled, the elementary course is begun, including the elementary and the complementary, the first being obligatory (for the civilized) and the second optional. There are already 658 official institutes and 263 subsidiary ones, with 56,000 and 19,500 students, respectively, who may continue with technical-professional training in 34 official institutes plus 3 recognized subsidiary ones and 252 belonging to the Catholic Missions, or a total of 289 with 10,487 students in the whole overseas area. The upper and intermediate technical levels exist only in Portugal, and the system for granting scholarships is open to all, theoretically, in the Higher Institute of Economics and Finance, the Faculty of Economics in Pôrto, the Institutes of Commerce and Industry, and the Higher Technical Institute. For training on the administrative technical level there is the Higher Institute of Overseas Studies, which during the school year of 1959–1960 had 54 registered students from overseas of a total student body of 264, or one-fifth. According to the 1950 census, 99 per cent of the African population was illiterate, no African had ever completed the seven years of the Mozambique High School, and there was only one African with a university degree among the 6,000,000 Negroes in Mozambique.[13]

The integration policy is designed to form European elites, upon

---

[12] *Notícias de Portugal,* No. 810, November 10, 1962, 4.
[13] M. Harris, *op. cit.,* 104 and 117.

whom consolidation of the Portuguese position throughout the overseas area will be incumbent.[14] It aims at forming cadres on the European model and, although declaredly without racial discrimination, it does not wish the Africanization of leadership in Africa. The failure of miscegenation and assimilation is notorious, and of the latter James Duffy has written that such a selective system, which during a twenty-five year period has affected the legal status of less than 0.5 per cent of the African population, has little to recommend it as an instrument of native policy—unless the goal of the policy is to maintain the degrading status of the majority of the population.[15]

Division of the population into the categories of *indigenous,* obliged to undergo rudimentary instruction, and *non-indigenous,* colonists and their children, immediately discriminates between natives and Europeans or their descendants, and the lack of coincidence between the categories of Christian and Portuguese reveals the failures of native policy. It is true that the final objective is the establishment of Lusitanian civilization in the territory and, for this reason, the autochthonous population plays an insignificant role on the local scene. For this reason, too, B. T. G. Chidzero speaks of the illusion of the assimilated person, for the road to assimilation is painfully slow and time has become a decisive factor in Africa. Sooner or later it will be rejected by the Africans in Angola, as the French policy of assimilation was elsewhere, especially in view of economic stagnation and educational deficiencies.[16] The British, too, are quite skeptical about the future of the Portuguese Empire.[17]

In comparison with the atrocities committed in the Belgian Congo at the turn of the century, or with the repressions of the Germans in east and west South Africa, Portuguese conduct in its colonies has been tolerant. Portugal would never adopt a policy of drastic subjugation of indigenous peoples, as South Africa does. But even with tolerance, "the

---

[14] José Júlio Gonçalves, *Alguns Aspectos do Problema dos Quadros no Ultramar Português,* Lisbon, 1960.

[15] *Portuguese Africa,* Harvard University Press, 1959, 295.

[16] "African Nationalism in East and Central Africa," *International Affairs* (October, 1960), 468.

[17] *Ibid.,* 436.

obstacle of citizenship is difficult to overcome," [18] which is equivalent to saying that Euro-Lusitanian, and not Luso-African or simply African, interests prevail.

Another grave problem is that of the forced labor by the natives, denounced by Basil Davidson in 1955 as real slavery.[19] Although the Colonial Act declares in its first article that native labor must be remunerated, and Article LXXXVI of the Organic Law of the Portuguese Overseas Territories [20] restates the same principle and prohibits the state from supplying native workers for enterprises involving economic exploitation, the truth is that the state can compel natives to work "on projects of general interest to the community" or can "direct them to methods of work in private enterprises that will improve their condition individually and socially."

In the practice of labor recruitment the following abuses occur: inadequate wages, illegal extension of contracts, the labor of minors and women in an advanced state of pregnancy and, finally, the illegal requisitioning of *volunteers,* that is, of those contracting directly with the employer, as opposed to *contractees,* whose recruitment is inspected by the administration. The number of contractees surpasses that of natives exported as labor to Rhodesia, the Congo, and the Union of South Africa. In 1956, for example, more than 600,000 natives were contracted in Angola and 160,000 were exported.[21] The immigration is continuous, regulated by agreements between the Portuguese government and South Africa and Rhodesia. Suffice it to say that the present number of Negro workers from Mozambique contracted to work in the Transvaal mines varies between eighty and one hundred thousand and those that go to Rhodesia number one hundred thousand; from fifteen to twenty thousand Angolan workers are contracted to work in Northern Rhodesia and South-West Africa. Harris shows that one of the reasons behind indigenous status is the exploitation of African labor, the greatest of Mozambique's natural resources. In 1893 High Commissioner Antônio Enes affirmed: "We need native labor, we need it in

---

[18] João Tendeiro, "Aspectos Marginais da Literatura na Guiné Portuguêsa," *Estudos Ultramarinos,* 1959, No. 3, 118.

[19] *The African Awakening,* London, 1955.

[20] *Leis de 1953 e 1955,* Lisbon, 1959.

[21] Antônio S. Labiza, "Alguns Problemas da Produção e Mão-de-Obra Indígenas em Angola," *Estudos Ultramarinos,* 1959, No. 4, 97.

order to improve the condition of the workers themselves; we need it for the economy of Europe and African progress." [22]

A declared racist, as Duffy has called him, Enes is considered to have been one of the most prominent Portuguese colonial politicians, and his attitude favoring forced labor was decisive in the Labor Code of 1899 and in labor legislation reforms thereafter. And the net result, says Harris, "of the legal definition of vagrancy and the *shibalo* system, which always accompanies it, is to force not only 100,000 workers but the overwhelming majority of African males in Mozambique to participate in the European economy, on terms that are profoundly damaging to native well-being but greatly lucrative to Europeans, especially in the neighboring territories." [23]

Today there is great concern over this "voluntary" immigration of Portuguese Africans because, if those transferred to Southwest Africa usually return, those who go to the Congo (ex-Belgian) do not always come back because wages are higher beyond the frontier, thus causing a permanent loss of cheap labor. Moreover, there is always the danger of political contamination.

Clandestine emigration also assumes great proportions. The movement is to the Congo, Malawi, Rhodesia, and South Africa, in search of better wages and a higher standard of living.[24] The total amount of all emigration varies greatly, but Marcelo Caetano calculates at 500,000 the number of Portuguese Africans from each province displaced from their territories,[25] again revealing the weaknesses and deficiencies of Portuguese native policy, which after all, as Davidson has written, is the fruit of pre-industrial imperialism. Otherwise one would find it difficult to believe that 10 per cent of all adult African males in Mozambique are employed outside the territory. The exportation of labor is one of the principal "industries" of Mozambique.[26]

---

[22] The evolution of these agreements may be followed in Vítor Hugo Vélez Grilo, "Aspectos Sociais resultantes do trabalho migratório em Moçambique," *Actas do Congresso Internacional de História dos Descobrimentos,* Lisbon, 1961, 121–127. The 1928 agreement, modified in 1934, is going to be newly revised. See *Notícias de Portugal,* No. 805, October 6, 1962, p. 2.

[23] Harris, *op. cit.,* 127.

[24] James Duffy, *op. cit.,* 325.

[25] *Os Nativos na Economia Africana,* Coimbra, 1954, 34–35.

[26] C. F. Spence, *The Portuguese Colony of Mozambique. An Economic Survey,* Cabo, 1951, 81.

The imposed processes of assimilation and exportation of workers attend not to African aspirations but exclusively to Portuguese interests, which frequently crush nationalists or nationalist organizations with a merciless iron hand. Above this repression floats the cream of African leadership, precisely men who heed the imperatives of the New State. The crisis in the Congo, which is Angola's longest frontier, independence in Tanganyika, Mozambique's northern border, the influence of Abako groups, to which Joseph Kasavubu belongs and which desire the restoration of the ancient Congolese empire of the sixteenth century, and the return of workers from other African territories where African aspirations are being decided threaten a nationalist rebellion in the near future similar to that of the Congo (ex-Belgian), where representational and educational rights were long denied as they are still in the Portuguese African provinces. Only racial tolerance can diminish the tension of the future clash, yet in the "Provinces," as formerly in Brazil and in the Belgian Congo,[27] European small businessmen provoke the animosity of the natives by certain habits so well known here.

Any comparison between these methods of colonization in Africa, originating in the nineteenth and twentieth centuries, and those initiated in Brazil in the sixteenth would be foolish. Although many virtues are the same, such as essential racial tolerance, Christianity, and humanism, and many of the defects are similar, too, such as inefficiency, corruption, and lack of interest in education, what is lacking above all is miscegenation.

The truth is that Portuguese colonization in Africa is completely alienated from the African people in its system of education, its policy, and its economics. Politically the Portuguese have little to offer, for they themselves are subject to a repressive regime. This does not prevent Rear-Admiral Sarmento Rodrigues from criticizing the regime in Ghana, "which would be cause for condemnation in any European country," [28] as if dictatorship were not a European creation, common to its ancient, modern, and contemporary history, but rather a Latin-American or African contribution to the political evolution of nations. If

---

[27] C. F. (Spence?), "The Odds in the Belgian Congo," *The World Today* (July, 1960), 277.

[28] "Evolução Recente da Política Africana," *Boletim Geral do Ultramar*, March 1960, 139.

democracy and universal suffrage are not general in Africa, neither are they on other continents, least of all Europe.

For all these reasons Harris thinks that in the system of indigenous status is concealed the intention to create a politically inert and servile native mass and—here showing his unfamiliarity with Sithole, whose thought on this is similar—that the system is no more than one of many varieties of apartheid found throughout Africa. The discrimination may not be accompanied by an institutionalized racist ideology, but oddly enough the latter can exist in a country professing a tradition of anti-racism. Harris further shows the prejudicial and defamatory stereotypes that are prevalent in Mozambique with respect to the intellectual, physical, and spiritual qualities of the Negro race. It must be added, moreover, that the theoretical principle of racial equality is not upheld in practice because of the Africans' lack of access to civilization, the subordination of native to Portuguese interests, and, above all, the vain desire to transform an African from Angola or Mozambique into a Portuguese. The Portuguese are in the habit of talking about their lack of racial prejudice, but they piously believe in European superiority. Has Salazar not said that "all of Africa will move toward forced labor as the white man's influence disappears"? [29]

In 1957 Chester Bowles wrote that "Portuguese Africa is one of the most backward regions in the world," and that only the poverty and ignorance of its inhabitants constitute a barrier to the penetration of nationalist ideas.[30] The truth is that only the poorest of the European nations continues to this day to cling to its right to maintain a colonial empire, as the same author later wrote.[31] This is not an isolated opinion. R. J. Harrison states also that "the Portuguese and Spanish empires of today are relics of empires preserved more for traditional than economic reasons." [32] In a recent study James Duffy is not less critical: "Portugal is determined to remain in Africa and to convince Africans, and perhaps the rest of the world, that it has the right to remain. Yet, one cannot tell how long the artificial colonial mystique of the New State or traditional racial tolerance will serve the cause of Portuguese Africa. The present

---

[29] *Notícias de Portugal*, No. 803, September 22, 1962, 4.

[30] *Africa's Challenge to America*, Berkeley, 1957, 28–29.

[31] Chester Bowles, "O Declínio do Comunismo como fôrça ideológica," *Jornal do Brasil*, July 20, 1962.

[32] *Modern Colonization*, London, 1951.

tranquility in Angola and Mozambique is not a sure indication of future harmony." [33]

In contrast with this accurate prognosis are the fatuousness and stupidity with which Silva Cunha writes: "Enjoying historical prestige and viewed with interest [and, we may add, also with some envy] because of the results obtained by its present policy, which has in its favor the magnificent arguments of peace throughout its provinces, absence of racial hatreds, and a common feeling of national unity, Portugal is availing itself of a special moral authority to intervene in African politics." [34]

The empire, which serves the oligarchy and powerful economic groups, not the Portuguese people, and certainly not the overseas territories as claimed by Adriano Moreira,[35] even after the Angolan revolt still functions on the basis of the Overseas Council. This is the archaic, obsolete institution created in 1642 that controlled Brazil and that has always subordinated the interests of the colonies to those of the metropolis despite its constant revisions. With consultative rather than executive functions, and without authentic representation based on universal suffrage, the councilors from overseas are subalterns of the metropolis. In the extraordinary meeting of the Overseas Council in October, 1962, after affirming "the national unity of the Portuguese fatherland in its multi-racial and multicontinental structure," they advised "administrative decentralization in everything concerning purely provincial interests," recommended "council chambers eventually to be called Corporative Councils," the appointment of independent provincial secretaries, "the expansion of provincial representation in the National Assembly, that the governors-general be part of an Overseas Council of Ministers, and that in national advisory bodies there be adequate representation from the Overseas Provinces." [36]

---

[33] *Portuguese Africa,* Harvard University Press, 1959, 342–343.
[34] J. M. da Silva Cunha, "Universalismo e Regionalismo em África." *Colóquios da Política Internacional,* Lisbon, 1957, 135.
[35] *Notícias de Portugal,* No. 792, July 7, 1962, p. 2.
[36] *Notícias de Portugal,* No. 809, November 3, 1962, 3–4. See "Comunicação do Ministro do Ultramar Adriano Moreira, de 22 de setembro de 1962, na Sessão Pública do Conselho Ultramarino," in *Notícias de Portugal,* Sup. to No. 804, September 29, 1962, and "Discurso" of October 15, 1962, in *Notícias de Portugal,* Sup. to No. 807, October 20, 1962.

So now facing total loss and dissolution of the empire the overseas councilors dare to present such simple, modest remedial suggestions. The following is a model of submissiveness: "recommend that national services, insofar as *possible,* be under the authority of the provincial government, and on the national level, under that of the Overseas Minister, in matters related to the overseas territories." These pale and shabby aspirations, born of colonial subjection, conceived in the Portuguese settler's head and not in the African's heart, reveal the falsity of then-Overseas Secretary Adriano Moreira's statement that "if we are not the first, we are never the last in the scale of accomplishments." [37] They represent the sunset of Portuguese dominance in Africa, despite new attempts at economic integration of the Portuguese area—which favor the metropolis more than the colonies. The policy of economic integration will further stifle the regional liberty that has dared cautiously to support its slight advisory function in the Overseas Council.[38]

The plans encouraging the development of a national economy in the Portuguese area obviously give greater importance to metropolitan projects when they list aspirations and define tasks, especially as they will be presided over by that mentality which excludes initiative and expected a 3.3 per cent rate of growth in the national product between 1950 and 1958 and a 0.7 per cent net increase in population annually. The second plan hoped to increase the annual average rate of growth from 3.3 per cent to 4.2 per cent.[39] This general development is subject to restrictions in Africa, for "the economy of Angola, as well as that of Mozambique and our other remaining provinces in Africa, depends and will long depend on foreign investments (through its exports or imports

[37] Speech in Cape Verde, September 5, 1962, *Notícias de Portugal,* Sup. No. 802.
[38] The economic integration of the Portuguese area, determined by Law-Decree No. 44,016, November 8, 1961, began on August 15, 1962, *Notícias de Portugal,* No. 799, August 25, 1962, 3–4. See "Comunicação do Ministro de Estado: Hora Certa de Portugal. A Integração Econômica do Espaço Português," in *Notícias de Portugal,* Sup. to No. 801, September 8, 1962, and *Notícias de Portugal,* No. 828, March 16, 1963.
[39] Fernando Meireles Guerra, "A planificação do fomento do Ultramar Português nos séculos XIX e XX." *Actas do Congresso Internacional de História dos Descobrimentos,* VI, 1961, 129–184.

of money) as the only means capable of maintaining or raising the standard of living." [40] Furthermore, it must be considered that "although for the Portuguese, by their nature, education, and even predestination [!], the racial question does not exist [they always play the same tune, as if they had a guilt complex], the African environment always means a socio-economic dualism. Not the racial dualism between Negroes and whites, but the 'natural' dualism between civilized and non-civilized."

Here, first of all, is an economy based on color, black and white, without reflection that black can become blood red and demand different treatment. In the second place, we see the hackneyed oppressive notion that the non-civilized must become civilized through the blessings of the Portuguese; and it does not matter to the Portuguese how many centuries it takes for those blessings to diffuse among the people. The oligarchy has other ideas. It believes that "the simple fixing of a rate of economic growth could not express a synthesis of their objectives for Western nations, if this did not involve an increase in other moral and cultural values, incapable of translation into percentages, but constituting nevertheless [the nations'] reason for being and the strength of the civilization represented and defended by them." [41]

One must never forget that the cost of these moral and cultural values is to be borne by Africans, and that oppression is practiced in their name. The oppression has evidently increased, for during the war Angola and Mozambique produced much more, that the metropolis might be paid for the values it transmitted with such missionary spirituality over the long centuries, and might at the same time bar its people's access to liberty. But the metropolis, so rich in these moral, Western values and so poor in resources, cedes the exploitation of colonial wealth to foreign capital. It is known that the basic industries, Moatize's coal mines and Mozambique's cotton and tea, are controlled by British capital; Tete's uranium deposits belong to the "British South Africa Company" and Angola's Mexican coal to the Krupp group; Benguela's roads are the property of a British, American, and Belgian

---

[40] *Op. cit.*, 67.
[41] Statements of Minister Corrêa d'Oliveira, in *Notícias de Portugal*, No. 813, December 1, 1962, 3.

company; Angola's diamond mines are in the hands of American groups, and the bauxite is in French hands.[42]

But to Salazar's financial way of thinking, the truth is that the empire is the way to keep in the black, although the balanced budget is not the system practiced in the United States and Great Britain today.[43] "Long live the balance and let the people suffer" is the motto of Salazar's imperial dictatorship.

ANGOLA'S STRUGGLE FOR FREEDOM

A short time ago Portugal still thought a general Portuguese intervention in Africa possible, and exhibited a desire for leadership rather strange in view of its own underdevelopment and small size. In a lecture given at the Institute for Advanced Military Science in 1960, Admiral Sarmento Rodrigues, who had just been named Governor-General of Mozambique, declared that by strengthening Africa "it will be possible for us to become accepted as arbiters and a model for African evolution." [44] The "provinces" were at peace from Trás os Montes to Timor, and no opportunity was lost clearly to assert inalienable rights to the Afro-Asian territories. And even in the face of the explosion in Africa Portugal's attitude remains the same, a mixture of exaggerated independence. No concession, no extension of rights, no advance; on the contrary, the old reaffirmation, pure and simple, of Portuguese rights to territories discovered or conquered five centuries ago.

Foreign Minister Franco Nogueira, former head of the Portuguese Delegation to the United Nations, has written that "the nineteenth century was a European century par excellence. Two distinct realities

---

[42] The statements on control of Angolan economy by foreign economic groups were made at several meetings of the United Nations. See Ghana Delegate Quaison-Sackey (Security Council, meeting No. 953, June 8, 1961, p. 6), Mali Delegate Be Ousman (Plenary Session No. 1,100 of the General Assembly, January 29, 1961, pp. 1316–1317) and Roumanian Delegate Brucan (Plenary Session No. 1,052, November 13, 1961, p. 628). See also "O que é o colonialismo. Angola sob a pata do capitalismo internacional," *Semanário* (Rio de Janeiro) (December 6, 1962).

[43] The budgetary deficit of the United States for 1963–1964 is greater than the total national income of Chile. See Dudley Seers, "The Great Debate on Inflation in Latin America," *The World Today* (April, 1963) 139–145.

[44] "Evolução recente da Política Africana," *Boletim Geral do Ultramar,* March 1960, 143.

existed then: Europe and, subordinate to it, the other continents." His study, *A Luta pelo Oriente*,[45] conforms to the usual ideas of racial supremacy, with the white European race at the top, and considers the Atlantic the vehicle for white expansionism.

The International Congress of the History of the Discoveries in 1960 was no more than a new attempt to demonstrate Portuguese superiority, interpret modern history by divine grace, defend universal European preponderance, and restate that Portugal was not renouncing its mission, its sacred duty, its destiny in the world. For Professor Adriano Moreira, then Undersecretary for Overseas Territories, the greatest modern application of Prince Henry's thought was to be found in his rejection of "the regional idea of European greatness, thus opening the way to expansion abroad." Nevertheless, "Europe did not follow the Prince's decision until much later, and is returning to a purely regional idea of greatness, which has led it to withdraw to its original frontiers. Since the last war it has adopted a spirit of renunciation with regard to its mission in the world, and is nervously trying out a scheme for unity that limits it to the frontiers it had before Henry's time." Thus all its recent efforts, such as the Common Market and the European Zone of Free Trade, abandon extension overseas and limit themselves to European regionalism, "devoid of any broader conception of its role, and therefore poorly equipped to intervene in the struggle for power that we are witnessing." "The ideological demobilization of Europe goes with its loss of importance in international life, as well as the transformation of former zones of confluence of the European power into marginal zones into which new political powers animated by dynamic ideologies expand." As the people are the same, as the Christian mission persists, Portugal, fully conscious of what it is contributing, is determined to continue the Prince's program for the better understanding of nations and the greatness of Europe, refusing to subscribe to ideological demobilization—which explains Europe's series of failures—and assuming the task of restoring the West's confidence in itself.[46]

---

[45] Lisbon, 1957, esp. 11-12 and 103.
[46] Adriano Moreira, *O Pensamento do Infante D. Henrique e a Atual Política Ultramarina de Portugal.* Lisbon, 1960. Communication presented on September 10, 1960.

The piousness of this mission, which is no longer purely national but above all European, shows how Portugal and its most lucid interpreters are satisfied with their fifteenth and sixteenth-century history and forget today's realities. Portugal in the glowing image of its leaders is the firmest, most determined, safest, and most confident stronghold of Western civilization, and explains to Europe that the latter risks death when it withdraws from the Afro-Asian conquests that are its natural extension and its Calvary, for the moral and spiritual pacification, improvement, and perfection of which it has suffered so greatly. If Europe persists in its withdrawal, in returning to its original frontiers, the world in general and especially the Afro-Asian world will fall into nihilism, annihilation, and perdition. The Portuguese, as pure Europeans and the legitimate creators of overseas expansion, as trustees of the sacred mission to favor other peoples with their presence till the end of time, and as founders of a world state, warn Europe of the dangers run by Africans and Asians because they lack the protection of the Old World, but only Spain and South Africa still listen sanctimoniously to the advice and reproval of Portuguese leaders. If Portugal explains to France and Great Britain, for example, that what is at stake is the very destiny of the West, nevertheless France and Great Britain heretically insist on promoting new adjustments between nations in a community of mutual interests. Portugal remains alone and takes its own way, believing in the restoration of the past, hoping to escape the march of time, forgetting that to exist on the basis of the past is to be anti-historical, and thinking, when it hears Lord Home say that Africa and Europe are indispensable to one another, that this means the subordination of Africa to Europe.

As the African proverb says, "What the child ate yesterday does not soothe him today." Heroic imagination lives today not in relived feats of oceanic conquest but in dreams of interplanetary adventure. As Theodor Schieder writes, when the great task of history consists of "leaping from a national past to an interplanetary future and acquiring consciousness of the multidimensional character of history," imagination and heroism in the face of tremendous changes must seek and inspire new paths and not believe that Prince Henry's solution is the solution today.

The world mission of protecting Afro-Asians is not opposed, official

Portuguese thinking makes clear, to the myths of European and Western superiority. Portuguese arguments reveal the belief that Portugal is the only sure bulwark of European culture, but they confuse the survival of that culture with the passing of its world dominance.

All that Ludwig Dehio, Oscar Halecki, and Geoffrey Barraclough have written concerning the passing of European dominance is theoretical and abstract and insulting, in Portuguese eyes, and Portugal, now the most European of European nations, would never, as Alfred Weber does, consent to say farewell to European history,[47] although it may recognize that the end of that history would mean the conquest of nihilism. Only Portugal can reconcile its admitted European spirit with its professed Afro-Asianism and consider itself "the only country with conditions appropriate for the restoration not of institutions but of man, specifically the white man, whose resurrection in Lusitanian molds will guarantee a world of justice for all, regardless of color." [48]

So it is that some Portuguese consider themselves—capable of saving the white man (in his Portuguese type) for the benefit of colored men, Afro-Asians. The African or Asian minds that created a feeling of solidarity in the common struggle against European imperialism, the several ideologies that assert Asian unity, Pan-Africanism, and Afro-Asian coöperation find no future in the face of the determination, pious vocation, and humble fervor of a nation that wishes to save them from the illusions of heresy, from anarchy, annihilation, and profanation.

For the Portuguese settle for no less. They proclaim that their intention is purely and simply to impose Western culture. They do not recognize the existence of African societies that had deep roots before the arrival of European culture. They think, or pretend to think, that when they reached Africa they found a barbaric chaos without norms, instead of the integrated, organized society brought to mind by the words Ghana, Mali, and Benin. They insist on denying Negroes the pride of being Africans and think that only themselves, as Europeans,

---

[47] Ludwig Dehio, *Deutschland und die Weltpolitik im 20. Jahrhundert,* Munich, 1955; Oscar Halecki, *The Limits and Division of European History,* London, 1950; Geoffrey Barraclough, *History in a Changing World,* Oxford, 1955. See also Alfred Weber, *Farewell to European History,* trans. from German, London, 1947.
[48] Henrique de Souza e Melo, *Missão Nacional,* Lisbon, 1960.

are right. They consider Africa still in its minority and forget that European culture proved insufficient in America, which was civilized by Africans too. The reduced educational opportunities and barriers to citizenship they impose seem designed to maintain white European dominance. The theory of gradualism—progress is a slow process—[49] suits the spirit of official Portuguese bureaucracy, keeps the Negro masses subordinated to the "small whites" who emigrate unwillingly, and takes care of poverty in Portugal, which finds it difficult to master its own problems of illiteracy and economic and social progress.

To strengthen Portuguese civilization and to inject European blood into Africa, the number of whites has been increased in recent years: from 45,000 to 160,000 in Angola, and from 27,000 to 70,000 in Mozambique. This immigration is not for purely economic but also for racial motives, and new white communities are being created to reaffirm European superiority. "We intend," said Secretary Adriano Moreira on August 28, 1961,[50] "that our population in Africa be supplemented by European elements." Thus stated, the declaration may seem to have no other intention, yet it reveals a desire to Europeanize Africa, or, simply, to make it Portuguese, "a great national and civilizing mission" without which "the vast territories and millions of persons for whom we intend the benefits of Portuguese nationality would not have awakened to history; and we know that without continuation of this process they would again be lost by an accelerated regression."

The Africans must therefore be merely grateful for the favors of the Portuguese, who have awakened them to history; without them, they would regress to the barbarism of the pre-European era. They must learn Portuguese history, the holy story of Portuguese imperial expansion, and accept the centuries-old European view on African feebleness. Only European culture (in its Portuguese form) is deserving of

---

[49] See statements of Ambassador Teotônio Pereira to *U.S. News and World Report,* reproduced in *Notícias de Portugal* (October 28, 1961). "We are not trying to turn back the clock, as many people seem to believe. But the Portuguese way of proceeding is by gradual assimilation, and there is no reason to hurry this process."

[50] *Notícias de Portugal,* No. 747, date cited. The United Nations report calculates that in Angola alone the European population increased from 79,000 in 1950 to 209,000 in 1959. *Report of the Sub-Committee on the Situation in Angola,* New York, 1962, 37.

attention. *Tabula rasa* is made of the great African empires, the African contribution to American civilization, Negro esthetics, and Africa's past. One should proceed as the French history professors did in Africa when they distributed Lavisse's brief manual to the natives, with the first lesson beginning: "We, the descendants of the Gauls. . . ." The Africans will thus be revealed as descendants of the first Lusitanians, and their history to be that of Portugal. But then, and this can already be seen in the exaggerated courtesy with which the Portuguese address them, the only path left is that of South Africa and Rhodesia: rejection of the African, maintenance of the European. The whole intent of Portuguese colonial policy is to hold the status quo by converting a land of 11,000,000 Africans into a simple, patriotic extension of the mother country and by resisting the nationalist waves disturbing the peace that existed before the war. For this reason Portugal is satisfied with and believes in the statements of its new ally, Sir Roy Wallensky, Prime Minister of Rhodesia and North Nyasaland, according to whom the light of civilization will be extinguished if Europeans should withdraw from Africa; [51] furthermore, the future of Africa, whether the Africans know it or not, is in the hands of the Portuguese and the Federation itself.[52] But Africans are no different from other races and, like Asians, can see not only the benefits of European culture but also the brutality and inhumanity that have accompanied its dominance, the materialism hidden in its Christian missionary spirit.

The accumulating threats hanging over Portuguese Africa and the demands made by Afro-Asian solidarity in the United Nations were seen by the Portuguese as the diabolical fruits of world-wide Communist subversion. Confronted by African independence, the old Holy Alliance dating back to the time of Brazil's emancipation arose now with Communism as its pretext. The divine privilege of governing the poor Africans was not thus to be menaced, nor would Portugal abdicate it; no, Portugal would have the courage and strength lacked by Great Britain, France, and Belgium. It would react, it would not allow what

---

[51] *Notícias de Portugal,* No. 772, February 17, 1962. The Portuguese educational policy with regard to natives seems, according to the United Nations report, to have as its goal the preparation of African natives for the "status" of Europeans, or at least "Europeans" as idealized by the Portuguese. *Report,* 32.

[52] *Notícias de Portugal,* No. 801, September 8, 1962, 20–21.

the West, by an intolerable pressure, was suggesting concerning the self-determination of Angola. Such a suggestion constituted intervention in the domestic affairs of Portugal, and Portugal would not submit because, after all, the African people would themselves be the victims if Portuguese protection should abandon them. No. Portugal was different from all other colonial powers because it was neither colonial nor a power, but rather an upright underdeveloped country with overseas responsibilities (possessions).

Peace and confidence still reigned in November of 1960 throughout Portuguese territory, despite the imprisonment of more than fifty-two persons for sedition in July of that same year.[53] Forgotten were the insurrections of 1910 in northern Angola, the deportation and disappearance of entire families around Luanda in 1915, and rebellions in Pôrto Amboim in 1924 and Ambuz in 1925. A reign of silence had been imposed in Portugal and in the "provinces." Riots in Luanda in February, 1961, "an abominable and suspicious act of pure banditry" offensive to the historical rights of Portugal, did not suggest to Portuguese leaders the consideration, equally historical, that Angola has had a tradition of liberty since 1822, when it sympathized with the Brazilian movement for independence; it suited them to think that the whole business was merely the work of international Communism. To the Portuguese, the African heart must not, cannot give birth to African nationalism; that is born only in Moscow, and Africa is threatening world peace, not the West or the Soviet Union. The incidents in Luanda in February, 1961 were no more than "a gross exploitation by which the internal affairs of a sovereign state were to be turned into an international dispute." This was also the view taken of United Nations protests against Portuguese violence in Africa, the imprisonment of freedom-seeking Angolans such as Agostinho Neto, and the panic-stricken, "frenzied mob of Portuguese armed with clubs and stones in the suburbs of Luanda."[54]

The centuries-long dream of remaining in Africa indefinitely, was suddenly interrupted. The February riots became a revolt on March 15,

---

[53] See wire news story from London in *Jornal do Brasil*, July 3, 1960, and *Notícias de Portugal*, November 26, 1960.
[54] Wire story from Johannesburg, February 8, 1961, in *O Jornal*, Rio de Janeiro, February 9, 1961, and *Notícias de Portugal*, March 18, 1961.

1961, in the jungles of northern Angola and Cabinda. Armed bands launched a campaign of terror and reprisals, and many Portuguese were sacrificed or suffered in excesses which, although regrettable, could not have been surprising, for the dictatorial Portuguese government had refused to make any concession or, despite complete turmoil in the Congo, to reform its African policy. The greatest atrocities were committed on both sides, and the response to African terrorism was Portuguese counter-terrorism. The large reinforcements sent by Salazar were guilty of the worst violence and the colony underwent a crisis bloodier than that in Kenya at the time of the Mau-Mau or even that in the Congo, according to the English-language press in South Africa.[55] Compared with the blood bath in Angola, the horrors of the Congo seem mere child's play.[56] In April even the Vicar-General of Angola, Monseigneur Mendes das Neves, was imprisoned,[57] and soon it was announced that eight Methodist ministers and several African catechists had been shot or executed after quick trials.[58] The extreme violence of the repression, admitted even by the Portuguese authorities, and the use of NATO weapons put down the revolt quickly and bloodily. The Angolan rebels had no arms, or very rudimentary ones, except those stolen from the Portuguese themselves.

In July representatives of the Labor Party challenged Prime Minister Macmillan on the use of NATO weapons in Angola and requested that exportation of these armaments to Portugal be prevented. "At this moment armaments supplied by NATO, including napalm (incen-

---

[55] News stories published in Johannesburg, taken from *Cape Town Times* and *Rhodesia Herald,* in *O Globo,* April 29, 1961.

[56] See summaries from the world press in Brasil Davidson, "Angola 1961. Le Dossier des Faits," in *Présence Africaine* (3d trimester of 1961), 20–44.

[57] Wire news stories for Luanda, *O Globo,* April 10, 1961.

[58] Wire story from New York, in *Última Hora,* April 20 and 25, 1961. A succinct and objective description of the disturbances and conflicts in Angola, especially in Luanda, district of Malange, in February 1961, the March events and their evolution, and the repressive measures, is found in *Report of the Situation in Angola, General Assembly. Official Records: Sixteenth Session,* New York, 1962, 11–17, in Davidson, *op. cit.;* for the Portuguese viewpoint, see *Boletim Geral do Ultramar,* starting with May, 1961. See also Clifford J. Parsons, "Background to the Angola Crisis," *The World Today* (July, 1961, 278–288; Marion Way, *The War in Angola,* New York, 1961; Antoine Matumona, *Angola: Views of a Revolt,* London, 1962; George Hauser, *Report on a Journey through Rebel Angola,* New York, 1962.

diary) bombs, are being used by the Portuguese government in Angola," declared A. Fenner Brockway, while his colleague Stanley Awberry referred to the great indignation felt in England because arms were being supplied, directly or through NATO, to crush the people of Angola. The Prime Minister replied that no permission had been given to export arms or munitions to Angola and Mozambique, but that this did not affect deliveries of fixed quantities of equipment due Portugal as a NATO ally.[59]

The United States also was accused in the United Nations of delivering NATO arms for the massacre of Angolans,[60] although according to a report made to Congress the American government had warned Portugal not to use them in Angola. It is believed that with or without authorization Salazar used NATO weapons to combat Angolan aspirations for independence. A short time later he himself stated that NATO had won the first battle when it stopped the Russian threat hanging over Europe after 1945, but that the menace had been transferred to other zones of the globe, "and with the very same objective, which is that of weakening what is customarily referred to as the West. It seems to me, for this reason, that either the alliance extends its defense mechanism to the new sensitive nerve spots and makes its sense of solidarity and its strength felt there, or else it will eventually allow itself to be beaten by the same enemy, although in a different field of operations. If this is so, the fact of having won the first battle will fail to have meaning or even usefulness."[61]

The struggle that, according to Holden Roberto, had resulted from a conflict between a Portuguese employer and his African workers and had spread over an area of more than a hundred square kilometers, was interpreted differently by the Portuguese authorities; it had been inspired from abroad by the Communists, and the rebels, only the rebels, had used terrorism. This version was long exploited and

---

[59] Wire news story in *Jornal do Brasil,* July 5, 1961.
[60] See statement of the delegate from Cyprus, Rossides, in Plenary Session No. 1,055ᵃ, November 15, 1961, *United Nations General Assembly, Official Records: Sixteenth Session,* 661; and that of the Bulgarian delegate, in Session No. 1,058, November 20, 1961, *ibid.,* 707.
[61] Interview with President Salazar granted to the newspaper *Il Tempo* (Rome), *Notícias de Portugal,* Sup. to No. 795, July 28, 1962, 8.

repeated, but it convinced no country in the United Nations except Portugal's faithful allies, Spain and South Africa, which make use of the same arguments.

The truth is that for a long time there had been growing dissatisfaction among Angolans. Open resistance came not only from the accumulation of suffering and injustice, but also from news of other African territories winning their independence. The fiasco of the policy of assimilation, the non-participation of Africans in public affairs, the denial of human rights, the abuse of authority, the basic distinction between Europeans and non-Europeans leading to discrimination, the gap between the goals proclaimed by the Portuguese government and its practice in the territory, the compulsory labor programs, especially those on cotton plantations, the deficiencies in education and sanitation, the abuses generated by white Portuguese immigrants' invasion of native territory (four-fifths of the coffee plantations are in Portuguese hands), the economic subordination of Angola to metropolitan interests and, finally, the lack of recognition of the legitimacy of any nationalistic aspiration to self-determination and independence; all these led the people of Angola to direct action or to flight from the territory. About half a million Angolans live outside Angola, and since the beginning of the struggle 140,000 have taken refuge in the Congo (Leopoldville) or in the Republic of the Congo (Brazzaville).

In June, 1961 the Portuguese government applied for $17,000,000 additional credit for the purchase of arms, planes, and ships and the training of an army to maintain control over its colony. Troops and more troops, supplied with arms from NATO, imposed anarchic terror [62] that pitilessly killed thirty thousand "African animals." In view of the scandal in Angola, the official Danish newspaper suggested that it would be better for Portugal to withdraw from NATO.[63]

The Portuguese government, impassive in the face of world criticism, has continued to declare that there was no insurrection, but only bands of adventurers paid from abroad and oriented by the Communists, a dark plot that, although it affected only one per cent of the Angolan population, justified drastic measures.[64] Thus Portugal refused to recog-

---

[62] The definition is that of *Time* (Latin American edition) (May 19, 1961, 26).
[63] See *Jornal do Brasil*, June 13, 1961.
[64] Interview with Adriano Moreira by *The New Bedford Standard Times*, in *O Globo*, July 30, 1961.

nize the existence of organized political groups whose leaders were leaving the territory to escape harsh repression.

Despite Portuguese victories in Angola, African nationalism will not lack the courage to attempt national liberation again and again. The Union of the People of Angola (U.P.A.), the Angolan Democratic Party (A.D.P.), and the Popular Movement for the Liberation of Angola (P.M.L.A.) cannot be classified as merely terrorists or Communists. The Union, organized since 1957, requested independence for 1960 in leaflets distributed throughout northern Angola. The repressive measures taken by the P.I.D.E. (International Police for the Defense of the State) since 1958, the beatings, collective punishment, imprisonment, and violence, exacerbated relations between the state and Negro communities. The present campaign, initiated by the U.P.A., has the support of the Bacongo and Quimbundo tribal groups, whose combined population according to the 1950 census was more than 1,500,000. Portuguese authorities hold that the Ovimbundo group, the largest tribe in Angola, is loyal to the regime, but information as to persons imprisoned in the south does not seem to confirm this. The P.M.L.A., with its seat in Conakry, seems to have no direct participation in the present movement, but attempts have been made to unify the two organizations. The rivalry between these political groups has favored Portuguese action and repression. In April, 1962 the Angolan National Liberation Front (A.N.L.F.) was formed; by uniting the U.P.A. and the A.D.P., the Provisory Government of the Angolan Republic was constituted under the leadership of Holden Roberto.

The merger of the U.P.A. and the A.D.P. at Leopoldville in the Congo represents an important stage in the Angolan revolution. As he forms his government in exile and organizes the National Liberation Army, which is being trained in the neighboring republic, Holden Roberto, whose politics are moderate, encounters the opposition of the P.M.L.A., which does not hide its leftist sympathies.[65] Holden seeks Western support, condemns the aid that some Western nations are giving Portugal, and helps the work of the United Nations commission examining the Angolan case with his information. His leadership, which seems determined to obtain Angola's complete independence, declares that it is not dominated by a spirit of hatred against the whites,

[65] Wire news story from Leopoldville, *Jornal do Brasil*, April 6, 1962.

and trusts in the possibility of reconciliation between Angolans and Portuguese as soon as the former are freed of colonialism and Portuguese fascism.[66]

Meanwhile, the conciliation of the U.P.A. and the P.M.L.A. has not been accomplished. The latter, which has its chief leaders in Agostinho Neto, recently escaped from prison in Lisbon, and Mário de Andrade,[67] was founded in December, 1953; it is linked to the militant Pan-Africanism group in Casablanca. Both organizations include representatives from the independence parties of Guinea and the Cape Verde Islands, as well as delegates from Mozambique, São Tomé and Príncipe.

Internal party rivalries, even between the two most powerful groups, hinder the struggle against Portuguese colonialism. In September, 1962, through the insistence of African leaders, negotiations were conducted in Leopoldville between the two principal groups. If the U.P.A. army, trained in the Congo, and that of the P.M.L.A., trained in Algeria, were united, the days of Portuguese colonialism would be numbered. The independent African countries are aiding the Angolans; in the Congo Foreign Minister Justin Bomboko has rejected Portugal's protest against the training of Angolan troops in that territory, declaring that he had decided "to support the efforts of our sister nations in their constant struggle to obtain independence from the colonialist."[68] The choice of Algeria for training P.M.L.A. soldiers is justified by the fact that, except for South Africa, it is the African country having the most and best military equipment and leaders trained for combat. This gives Angolans the hope of acquiring the arms and munitions needed to fight for their nation's independence more easily in Algeria than in other African countries. Moreover, it was in the clandestine camps of the Algerian National Liberation Front that the first Angolan guerillas were trained for combat. Ben Bela, Prime Minister of the Algerian Provisory Council, firmly supports the P.M.L.A. elements, thus confirming his words that "there would be no logic in Algerian politics

---

[66] John Marcum, "The Revolt in Angola," *The New Leader* (April 30, 1962).
[67] See his interview in Moacir Werneck de Castro, *Dois Caminhos da Revolução Angolana,* Instituto Brasileiro de Estudos Afro-Asiáticos, 1962, 95-101.
[68] Wire story from Leopoldville, *Jornal do Brasil,* August 30, 1962.

if it did not demonstrate complete solidarity with movements for African liberation." The war in Angola, which has not ended as Portuguese authorities claim, will enter a more advanced stage in the near future, especially if the forces trained in Thysville (Congo) and Algeria unite.

With its dictatorial obscurantism, Portugal thinks that it can liquidate the fight for freedom by means of napalm bombs, violence, and accusations. For Salazar no liberation movement exists. His policy is the genocide of free Africans who dare to affirm their hope for liberty. According to him in principle there is almost complete autonomy in Angola and Mozambique, and the government serves the interests of these regions. In no case will he consider setting a date for the liberation of Angola, for again he declares that administrative cadres are lacking and the people have not yet reached the necessary social and cultural level.[69] The required human resources take a long time to prepare, he said on another occasion.[70] Thus another five hundred years will have to elapse before further limited results are attained.

For Salazar, "subversive elements today are stimulating action against those countries defending the two positions in the world that are considered fundamental: anti-Communism and the progress of African peoples through the mediation of Europe." The subversive plan against the Iberian Peninsula aims at destroying "the obstacle represented today by the Portuguese and Spanish provinces in Africa to Communism's complete domination of that continent." In addition to the declared indispensability of the presence of Portuguese whites, and in addition to the confusing of independence and Communism—similar to what was done at the time of Latin American independence when the Holy Alliance indulged in sophistry on liberalism—one must further consider that "no desire for independence on a territorial scale exists in Angola or Mozambique, or in any other Portuguese overseas province"; if in Angola "daily life is not yet completely normalized, it is not because the people aspire to independence but because certain elements, the over-

[69] "Problemas Portuguêses em África," *Notícias de Portugal,* Sup. to No. 783, May 5, 1962.
[70] Interview with President Salazar by *U.S. News and World Report,* in *Notícias de Portugal,* Sup. to No. 793, July 14, 1962.

whelming majority of which are foreign, have set out to control them." [71] Foreign elements of all kinds are used to prove the movement's lack of authenticity. Salazar himself has officially claimed information that Portuguese-speaking Poles are being recruited to fight in Angola,[72] and a Brazilian journalist, ex-director of a Brazilian government enterprise with an office in Lisbon who works for the Portuguese dictatorship and its colonialism, reported that Brazilians from Santa Catarina were being recruited for the same purpose.[73]

When by a vote of ninety-nine to two (Spain and South Africa) the United Nations General Assembly reaffirmed Angola's solemn right to liberty and independence and disapproved of repressive measures and armed action against the Angolan people, Salazar declared that "no one in the province, whatever his race or condition, can understand this verdict." For were the Portuguese not "civilizing the savage land" and "defending wealth accumulated through the course of generations for the good of all?" [74] A "savage land" that has been developed, as we know, for five hundred years, and a wealth accumulated for the benefit of a small oligarchy in Lisbon; do the urbanization of Luanda, its clean streets, trains running on schedule, a few children's shelters and hospitals, and several schools justify total suppression of liberty, and do they by any chance crush the hope of independence?

What will the outcome be? It is difficult to prognosticate, but it is difficult also to believe that Salazar's totalitarianism is prepared to negotiate with dissident groups. Only recently, in an interview granted to a Brazilian newspaperman associated with the Portuguese colony, Salazar replied to a question regarding concessions that he would be willing to make to opposition parties in order to organize a nationally-unified government by saying: "My dear fellow, national unity already exists. That is what does exist. As to those on the outside, it behooves them to meet us halfway and adapt themselves to our ideas and principles, because we are the majority and indeed almost the whole of

---

[71] Interview with President Salazar by the *Ottawa Citizen,* in *Notícias de Portugal,* Sup. to No. 815, December 15, 1962, 6.
[72] *Ibid.*
[73] Alves Pinheiro, "Lisboa todos os dias," *O Globo,* March 9, 1963.
[74] "Mensagem ao Povo de Angola," *Notícias de Portugal,* No. 781, April 21, 1962, 8.

the nation." [75] The Portuguese Ambassador to Washington, Pedro Teotônio Pereira, has said: "We shall proceed with our mission in Africa, believing firmly that we shall meet there again when all this dust raised by anticolonialism has settled." [76]

The African nationalists will certainly not enter into an agreement with those whom they consider their oppressors. If in military terms the possibility of a nationalist victory is still remote, in economic terms the effects of a long campaign will be seriously depressive upon Portugal and, day by day, the Portuguese people may reduce their support.

It is difficult, then, to foresee an area of compromise; the Portuguese oligarchy does not wish to follow the example of the English, it has contempt for the action of the French, and daily it draws closer to the "Afrikaner" policy of South Africa: white European supremacy, historical right. The tragedy is that there is no party in Portugal to defend a policy of progress and lead to concessions that might perhaps still save the relic of empire and avoid a colonial war. Popular uprisings, disturbances of the peace in Portugal, and international pressures may persuade the government to change its course in Africa. Answering the challenge is not easy, especially because, like all dictatorships, it hates all challenge.

Thus the future of Portugal's African colonies depends on several factors. In the first place, it would be childish to think that the revolutionary movement has already been defeated and strangled. For Salazar the war ended on "the very terms on which it was launched, that is, for exclusive domination by a restricted part of the territory where Portuguese authority could not assert itself"; but "this is a trickle of water, originating beyond and protected to the frontier, which infiltrates through the trackless jungle and reappears within our territory. Strange as it may seem, that small trickle originating in the Congo, in Conakry, or Acra, or farther away still, can nevertheless be checked or dried up in a few great capitals such as Washington or London. But politics there are not practiced in that way." [77] But the trickle has not

---

[75] *O Globo,* August 24, 1961, 5. See an excellent summary of the political situation in Ronald H. Chilcote, "Politics in Portugal and Her Empire," *The World Today* (September, 1961), 376–387.

[76] *Notícias de Portugal,* Sup. No. 808, October 27, 1962.

[77] *Ibid.,* No. 814, December 8, 1962, 3–4.

ended yet, and the settlement of the Algerian case may increase assistance to the fighters in Angola.

As James Duffy has said, "there is no easy solution to the problems of Portuguese Africa. Independence cannot be an answer in itself, but without it there will be no answer." [78] But what answer can there be if Portugal is unable to face the challenge of winning by its own development and that of its colonies? It is possible that patriotism can inspire the Portuguese briefly to support a leader who for thirty-seven years has given them an autocratic and uneventful administration and has left the country underdeveloped. But although they are struggling with domestic problems and perplexed by deficiencies in education and sanitation, that the people are awakening to the reality of present difficulties is revealed by internal disturbances in 1961 and 1962. [79]

The many years of autocracy have not succeeded in ending the paradox of low wages and high production costs, nor in coördinating uneconomical industries responsible for annual losses in trade. At present these losses are compensated by favorable balances of escudos in the African zone. But the situation in agriculture is worse, because although half of the population of Portugal is employed in farm work, they produce only one-quarter of the national income. This is not therefore an "affluent society" that could attract Angola and Mozambique to remain associated with it. It is this situation that makes the average Portuguese apathetic concerning Africa's political future. As Angola and Mozambique are the principal bases of the Portuguese economy, the present regime hates the very idea of self-government, and for this reason it has prepared no African elite capable of governing itself. [80] If there are elementary schools and a few secondary and technical schools, no university has been created and even permission to study abroad was withdrawn because, when the Africans returned, they expressed "anti-national" opinions.

Without Angola and Mozambique the escudo would go under, for those possessions contribute about 35,000,000 pounds to the balance of payments. A large part of Portuguese exports, especially wine and cotton goods, goes to Africa and growing percentages of Luso-African

---

[78] *Portugal in Africa,* London, 1962.

[79] Ronald H. Chilcot, *op. cit.*

[80] See *The Economist* (January 17, 1962), 605.

products—coffee, tea, sisal, coconut, diamonds—are offered to the world market. Angola's coffee alone produces approximately $19,000,000 annually and is Portugal's best money-maker. Angola's diamonds, Mozambique's tea, Angola's cotton, which supplies Pôrto's textile industry, and sugar from both colonies support the metropolis. Politically and economically Angola is united with Lisbon, and about a dozen powerful companies control its trade. Many of their directors are political appointees, and a recent foreign minister was the owner of one of the largest sugar enterprises in Angola. The Portuguese oligarchy's dependence on Africa [81] has become more conscious and prudent, but it continues to ignore African nationalism.

A government that considers itself a "colonial power" never refers to its underdevelopment, although it was obliged to hear Ludwig Erhard, when he visited Lisbon in May 1961, declare himself "at your disposal for the economic development of your country" and that he had no doubt that less developed nations can be developed, so long as there is solidarity and more prosperous nations are willing to help them.[82] A year later, in June 1962, German, French, and American loans totaling CR$4,500,000,000 were negotiated, statedly for economic progress, perhaps secretly for the colonial war.[83]

In his counter-attack on India at the time of the invasion of Goa, Salazar accused it of being overpopulated and poverty-stricken.[84] His Foreign Minister again criticized the West for surrendering to the theory of the "winds of history" and declared that "the wealth of Goa, especially the iron mines, which had been exploited for the benefit of the people of Goa, had now been seized by the Indians for the exclusive advantage of the Indian government and Indian industry." [85] Now, Portugal is possibly one of the most underdeveloped countries in

---

[81] "Portuguese Dependence on Africa," *Manchester Guardian Weekly,* February 15, 1962.

[82] *Notícias de Portugal,* No. 733, May 20, 1961, 3.

[83] *Ibid.,* No. 787, June 2, 1962, pp. 6–7 and 12.

[84] "A invasão e ocupação de Goa pela União Indiana," *Notícias de Portugal,* January 6, 1962, No. 766, 19, and interview by "Le Figaro," in *Notícias,* December 30, 1961, No. 765, 5.

[85] *Notícias de Portugal,* January 13, 1961, No. 767, p. 5. The government of Goa has just scheduled direct elections for the legislature and it will also have a council of ministers. The legislative assembly will select an official language. See *Goan Tribune,* Bombay, March 2, 1963.

western Europe, having a per capita income of $244 per year and a high rate of illiteracy. A large part of its people lives at a level of mere subsistence with high indices of infant mortality and tuberculosis. The oligarchy, which has grown fat at the expense of its people and the Africans, has done nothing to raise the standard of living but rather has bled them and made them impotent.

Therefore, as Andrew Marshall rightly says, African nationalism is a process threatening the tightly ordered Portuguese economic and social structure. Portugal is the last world empire in the strict sense of the word, and rules Africa with nineteenth-century methods. Incredible as it may seem, the minority that is out of step sees itself menaced by the African liberation campaign, which may come to be also the liberation campaign of the Portuguese masses. The African historical process emphasizes the profound contrast between Portugal's grandiose programs of world leadership and dominance in Africa and the poverty of the majority of its people and their legitimate aspirations to economic well-being, education, and health.[86]

THE LUSO-BRAZILIAN COMMUNITY AND AFRICA

The history of Luso-Brazilian relations is a chapter in the history of Brazilian international politics and as such does not fall within the province of this book. There is space here only for the development of the idea of the Luso-Brazilian Community, which involves the African problem whether the Portuguese like it or not.

The idea of community is recent, but opposition to Brazilian association with Africa dates from the time of our independence. Portugal denied us authorization to open a consulate in Angola, and only after much insistence was Brazil able to open one, just as only between 1892 and 1897 was it possible to install Brazilian consulates in Goa, Quelimane, and Mozambique.

Our relations with Portugal constitute a history of claims, protests, and difficulties that seem more like a list of grievances than a community of interests. Two breaks mark and characterize the phase of deterioration in our relations that lasted until the first attempts to relocate the Luso-Brazilian problem. It was in 1921 that the Portuguese

---

[86] See Andrew Marshall, "Portugal: A Determined Empire," *The World Today* (March, 1961), 95–101.

colony in Brazil published the *História da Colonização Portuguêsa no Brasil* [87] "for the greater glory of Portugal in all ages" and "apotheosis of the Lusitanian race that has already ruled the world." The criticism of Raul Pompéia, Jackson de Figueiredo, and Antônio Tôrres, a frank criticism of the Portuguese colonization and defense of the thesis that Brazil and Portugal constitute different entities, revealed that the time was not ripe to speak of a Luso-Brazilian community as the *História* had suggested.[88]

The creation of such an atmosphere in Brazil is owing especially to two men: Otávio Mangabeira and Gilberto Freyre. It was the former who, when Minister of Foreign Affairs, gave Luso-Brazilian relations their formal, academic, affected character in the name of linguistic purity, pointing to "the pride with which we defend the language in Brazil as the best heritage from our ancestors, to whom we owe the founding of our nation and its commitment to culture." [89] Later we were to sign the orthographical agreements of 1943 and 1945; the last was so subservient, so full of concessions that it was rejected in favor of the 1943 agreement. Brazilian Portuguese was considered "an overseas dialect" and the speech of approximately 50,000,000 Brazilians at that time was made subject to and modeled after that of 7,000,000 Portuguese.

But it was actually *Casa Grande & Senzala* (*The Masters and the Slaves*) in 1934 that brought about a reconsideration of the work of the Portuguese in Brazil, giving it value and importance and freeing it of those depressing prejudices that still appeared at the peak of Antônio Tôrres' campaign. Since then a new attitude and interest and great esteem have characterized the analysis of Portuguese activity in Brazil. Indeed, it was Gilberto Freyre who, with his revision of history, made a somebody of the Portuguese John Doe. If there is no black legend about the work of colonization, as in Hispanic America, that is owing to *The Masters and the Slaves,* which isolated and ennobled the good qualities of the Portuguese. This is not to say, of course, that one should forget

---

[87] Pôrto, Lithografia Nacional, 1921, 3 vols.
[88] See respectively, "Introdução" to *Festas Nacionais* by Rodrigo Otávio, Rio de Janeiro, 1893; *Do Nacionalismo na hora presente,* Rio de Janeiro, 1921; and *As Razoens da Inconfydencia,* Rio de Janeiro, 1925.
[89] *Relatório do Ministério das Relações Exteriores,* Rio de Janeiro, 1928, 69–71.

João de Barros on the Portuguese side, or accept the campaign of João do Rio (Paulo Barreto). If extreme attacks, like Antônio Tôrres', had formerly occurred only on rare occasions, the vogue now was to accentuate the advantages, benefits, and excellence of Portuguese accomplishments in Brazil.

Thus, the ground was prepared for future subjection, so that "the most demanding province in Brazil," to quote Paulo Barreto, might seek to derive from these advantages the benefits that it considered rightful. First, by means of the orthographical agreements to which we have referred; secondly, through the new regulations in 1944 facilitating Portuguese immigration,[90] which was judged suited "to the ethnic or social composition of the Brazilian people" and capable of substituting for Brazilians themselves in settlements of foreigners;[91] and, finally, crowning Luso-Brazilianism, by means of the 1953 Treaty of Friendship and Consultation.

The honeymoon phase of the literary-orthographical discussions and validation of the Portuguese past in Brazil led to generous concessions to the Portuguese, who took advantage of this "passionate attachment of one nation for another," so similar to the one severely criticized by George Washington in the earliest days of United States history.

Not even the enormous favors granted Portugal, with no reciprocity whatever, increased the number of immigrants, which had fallen from 380,325 in 1940 (0.92% of the total Brazilian population) to 336,856 in 1950 (0.65% of the total Brazilian population), distributed especially in urban areas, with the greatest concentration in São Paulo (44.92% of the total in Brazil) and the former Federal District (39.75% of the total in Brazil).[92]

To the idea of community, stated explicitly in the 1953 Treaty of Friendship and Consultation, was linked that of Portuguese superiority, which was much proclaimed in *O Mundo que o Português criou* by Gilberto Freyre.[93] Since then Portuguese propaganda has aimed to

---

[90] *Relatório do Ministério das Relações Exteriores,* Rio de Janeiro, 1944, 89.
[91] See Law-Decree No. 406, May 1, 1938, Art. 40, and Law-Decree No. 7,967, September 18, 1945.
[92] *A Distribuição Territorial dos Estrangeiros no Brasil,* I.B.G.E., Conselho Nacional de Estatística, 1958, 7–10.
[93] Rio de Janeiro, 1940.

harness us to its objectives. Anyone examining the modern political literature of Portugal will see that we are used as means to its ends, whether these are in our interest or not. Antônio Tôrres complained of this and recalled the words of Dom Carlos at the time of the break in diplomatic relations: "The Portuguese government must not forget that we can be on bad terms with everyone except Brazil and England." [94] But our diplomacy has reversed the situation and Portugal is using Brazil in the United Nations for its sole and exclusive purposes.

We have already stressed the concept of leadership revealed by the present Portuguese authorities who gamble with Brazilian support in conducting affairs in their "provinces." For some Portuguese "Portugal and Brazil, Africa and Portuguese India, Madeira, the Azores, Cape Verde, Macau, and Timor today constitute a unity of sentiment and culture," and the "South Atlantic (Africa and Brazil) is a Lusitanian sea." The United States of Portugal would then have its day as a new and powerful nation.[95] "Brazil," says another author, "is and will be increasingly the keystone of our Atlantic policy, notably, in our development in Africa." [96]

As may be seen, the grandiose plans of the Portuguese to press us into service are not purely the product of megalomaniac imagination; they are the result of that anachronistic thinking in support of the Community which gives first importance to Portugal and considers the Community indestructible because it is founded on a blood relationship reënforced by four centuries of affection and communion. They are the result, too, of the thinking that holds we must never assume attitudes that are contrary to the old country or restrict the liberty with which it confuses its interests and ours.

During the First World War Theodore Roosevelt replied to a group of Americans who had appealed to him to approve the idea of being considered Anglo-Americans by lamenting and reproving it. "England is not my mother country, nor am I German in origin. The United States is my mother country, my country of origin, my only country."

Brazilian thought was different. "Our policy with Portugal is not

---

[94] *Op. cit.,* ciii.
[95] Henrique de Souza e Melo, *Missão Nacional,* p. 9.
[96] Almerindo Lessa, *Meridianos Brasileiros,* Lisbon, Junta de Investigações do Ultramar, 1960.

really a policy. It is a family affair. No one plays politics with his parents and brothers. He lives with them in the intimacy created by bonds of blood and sentiment. In difficult times everyone looks to his own for support and advice. Without regulations. Without treaties. Without compensation. Because they have the same blood."[97] This was the opinion of João Neves da Fontoura, who was chiefly responsible for the 1953 Treaty of Friendship and Consultation, for which he had fought from the time of his voyage to Lisbon as ambassador from Brazil. His goal was to stress the spirit of Luso-Brazilian Community, convinced as he was that in principle our policy with Portugal had never changed, despite the separation in 1822 and although until 1914 there had been no more than affective, historical, and cultural ties. João Neves da Fontoura considered it indispensable for the two nations to have a Luso-Brazilian policy, a community, "dedicated to maximum extension and depth." He based this, moreover, on the conviction that "there are two main constants in Brazilian foreign policy: the cult of Pan-Americanism and closest association with Portugal."

I have always been informed that our foreign policy has been based on two principles: balance in the Rio de la Plata, which is indispensable to our security, and rapprochement with the United States, so that we should not remain isolated in the midst of a unified Spanish America. Today I do not believe that such tendencies have existed or that they have been systematically followed. Rather I believe that there has been an admirable capacity for improvisation and that some of those who constructed this policy were extraordinarily intelligent. Until around 1848–1850, and we have already stressed this, the primary objective of our foreign policy was a balance between Great Britain, despite all its enormous pressure and privileges, and Africa in order to defend our agricultural interests. After Africa was removed from our deliberations through the dictates of the English, it was only about 1848–1850 that the Rio de la Plata began to concern us, and Europe, represented by Great Britain and France, did not cease to take precedence over Latin America and the United States, with which our increased trade became pronounced around 1870. Portugal has nothing, absolutely nothing to do with this whole period, except for a string of small incidents and

---

[97] João Neves da Fontoura, "Por uma Política Luso-Brasileira," *O Globo*, June 10, 1957.

prejudicial relations frequently marked by dishonesty and degradation.

The Treaty of Friendship and Consultation, signed in Rio de Janeiro on November 16, 1953,[98] was celebrated in view of the "spiritual, moral, ethnic, and linguistic affinities that after more than three centuries of common history continue to link the Brazilian and Portuguese nations, which results in a most special situation for the reciprocal interests of the two peoples." Seeking to reaffirm and consolidate the perfect friendship existing between the two sister nations, "the two parties agreed that in the future they would always consult on international problems manifestly in their common interest"; each granted "special treatment to the nationals of the other, making them equal to their own"; in the field of commerce and finance, taking each country's circumstances of the moment into account, each conceded all "possible facilities to attend to the particular interests of the other's nationals"; they provided for free entry and exit, establishment of residence and unrestricted movement in Portugal and Brazil, and obligated themselves "to study, whenever opportune and necessary, means of developing the progress, harmony and prestige of the Luso-Brazilian Community in the world."

The concessions that were made were mutual only on paper, there being no reciprocity because there are practically no Brazilians in Portugal. When attention was given to "the particular interests of the other's nationals" in the commercial and financial area, this clearly meant the Portuguese in Brazil. This was protection for the money in the pockets of Portuguese, who with the new "facilities" would continue to send their hoarded funds back to Portugal, an income that until recently was always one of the means of balancing the Portuguese budget. Few went against the tide and there was the highest praise on the occasion of each presidential visit in preparation of greater concessions to Portugal.[99] Extended by the Kubitschek administration, these concessions became so inconceivable that the Quadros administration

---

[98] Getúlio Vargar Government. Legislative Decree No. 59, October 25, 1954, *Diário do Congresso Nacional,* October 30, 1954, and *Coleção de Atos Internacionais,* No. 357, Ministério das Relações Exteriores, 1955.

[99] See, for example, the homage paid to President-General Higino Craveiro Lopes, in *Diário do Congresso,* June 9, 1957.

placed a quarantine on them.[100] Actually, there was something carica-
tural about the concept of community under the treaty, for we were
thereby associated with territories subordinate to the Lisbon government and involved in its future international complications.

The treaty is a victory by Portugal that pulls Brazil into its orbit in
accordance with the aforementioned pretensions and for the purpose of
disposing of our support in international difficulties. By it we obligate
ourselves to consult with Portugal and its colonial dependencies on
international matters, thus removing or at least hindering our diplomatic free play. Imagine the United States consulting Great Britain on
what it must or must not do, or not acting in this or that manner
without hearing Australia and New Zealand, just because all speak
English. I have already referred to the indignation with which John
Adams rejected the British proposal regarding the slave trade. The
United States was born very alert and independent because of the early
warnings given by George Washington: "There can be no greater error
than calculating or counting on real favors between nations."

In Brazil, however, we soon forgot the warnings of José Bonifácio,
Cunha Matos and Senator Vergueiro (both Portuguese by birth), the
Marquis de Abrantes, and Bernardo Pereira de Vasconcelos against the
indignity of the treaties that were forced from us by the European
powers. We did not have the strength to resist pressures and injunctions
in former times. But to surrender today because of friendship, blood, or
language is inconceivable in international affairs where, as Palmerston
always recommended, the national interest is foremost.

If we examine relations between countries united by similar bonds,
such as the United States and Great Britain, we shall see that difficulties
predominate and both maintain their freedom to maneuver internationally.[101] They would never allow themselves to be guided, as were
those who drew up the Treaty of Friendship and Consultation, by blood
ties and sentimental attachments without compensation, and we must

---

[100] Recently Nuno Simões spoke against nonratification of Kubitschek agreements.
See "Acôrdos e Tratados Luso-Brasileiros," summarized in *Correio da Manhã*,
January 30, 1962, and "Temas da Comunidade Luso-Brasileira," in *O Jornal*,
April 28, 1961.
[101] See C. M. Woodhouse, *British Foreign Policy since the Second World War*,
London, 1961, 123–124; and H. C. Allen, *The Anglo-American Predicament*,
New York, 1960.

especially not forget that Portugal, unmoved by our Portuguese blood, which is African also, was not our ally in the Second World War.

We are not depreciating the Portuguese; as Gilberto Amado has written, "We should be very honored to be Portuguese, but the fact is that we no longer are Portuguese, for many reasons such as environment, climate, education, and socio-political system. Moreover, even the Portuguese who returns to Portugal after having lived here in Brazil for a long time is not the same. He has bathed and been transformed in the American atmosphere." Gilberto Amado further stresses "that the circumstance of our speaking the same language is not sufficient to identify us and that, because of diverse circumstances, we find ourselves increasingly more removed in character, individually and nationally, from our brothers overseas." [102] Later Gilberto Amado resumed the thesis, so out of tune with the many Luso-Brazilian courtesies then prevalent, and reaffirmed: "The dissimilarity will tend to become increasingly more profound. Population, commerce, exchange, social and political regime, agricultural production and industrial development, ways of thinking from one generation to another, everything will separate us from Portugal and draw us closer to peoples having similar racial mixtures, ideas, and political and economic system. Our relations with Portugal will be reduced to recollections of the past and the exploitation of common memories." [103]

What remains, then, of a community that exists only for the other partner, who alone derives benefits from the association? A climate favorable to community has been created also, independently of the intellectual influences and political thought mentioned, by the strong pressure group, especially of commercial interests, represented by the Portuguese colony in the two large centers of Rio de Janeiro and São Paulo.[104] It is sufficient to recall that the Portuguese centers, associations, clubs, houses, and so on, in Brazil number a hundred and five with thirty in São Paulo and twenty-eight in the State of Guanabara; they engage in great political activity in their country's favor, as auxiliaries to the Embassy, which no other foreign group has done, unless it was the

---

[102] *A Dança sôbre o Abismo,* Rio de Janeiro, 1952, 124–125.
[103] *Depois da Política,* Rio de Janeiro, 1960, 79.
[104] For an evaluation of interest and pressure groups, see Lêda Boechat Rodrigues, *Os Grupos de Pressão no Govêrno Representativo,* Fortaleza, 1960.

pre-war subversive German and Japanese groups that were soon re-
pressed.

The economic pressure exercised by the colony in Brazil is well
known.[105] Further, and this should cause no surprise, one of the colony's
most fruitful activities in Rio de Janeiro is conducted through the Vasco
da Gama Regatta Club. Serious things, said Huizinga, may be denied,
but not games; by cultural and ethnic diffusion the club glorifies the
nation's Portuguese origins with the name of a Portuguese
discoverer—the only case among sports clubs here, there, or
anywhere—and inculcates in the popular collective mind the ideology of
the cultural heritage through the symbolism of competition and the
dramatization of victory. As in any game, there is no doubt; victory
represents and signifies a whole set of values that it suits Portugal to
keep alive in Brazil.[106]

But most important of all is the much-publicized community's lack of
an economic basis. Brazilian exports to Portugal as a rule occupy a
greatly inferior position, I will not say in relation to our large buyers
and sellers, such as the United States, West Germany, the United
Kingdom, the Low Countries, Argentina, France, Sweden, Japan, Italy,
Denmark, Spain, Venezuela, and Finland, but in relation to Czechoslo-
vakia, Chile, Poland, Hungary, Ceylon, the Dutch West Indies,
Morocco, South Africa, Tunisia, Yugoslavia, the Soviet Union, Hong
Kong, and Algeria.[107]

The "provinces," too, have almost no trade with Brazil, as Portugal,
so much an ally and friend of ours, prefers to encourage exchange with

---

[105] There is no specific study on this, but it is a subject worth investigating.
Portuguese political activity in Rio de Janeiro has already been very important
and the colony used to control the local press by its economic power. Even
today there are deputies who court the colony and are its candidates. The colony
issues political manifestos and replies in paid newspaper announcements to stands
taken by politicians opposing directives of the Portuguese government. See
manifesto in *O Jornal*, May 10, 1961, and letter on "Movimento dos Portuguêses
no Brasil" to Deputy Afonso Arinos Filho, in *O Globo*, July 10, 1961.

[106] The club is always much feted in Portugal, and on its visit in April, 1963, took
a message from the Governor of Guanabara defending Portugal's Atlantic alliance
with Brazil; recently it has almost ceased to travel to Africa for political reasons:
in order not to displease the colony. See *O Globo*, April 27, 1963.

[107] See *Anuário Estatístico do Brasil*, I.B.G.E., Conselho Nacional de Estatística,
1955–1960.

Great Britain, the United States, and West Germany. Here are some figures:

Brazilian Exports (in units of CR$1,000)

	1938	1948	1954	1956	1957	1958	1959	1960	1961
ANGOLA	6	808	2,121	1	5,936	3,421	318	717	269
MOZAMBIQUE	1,007	12,877	2,752	2,056	2,760	3,094	3,743	4,201	44,872

Great Britain, the United States, and West Germany are the great suppliers of the "provinces." In return, West Germany occupies third place among Guinea's customers, after Portugal and France; it is Angola's fifth largest customer, right after Portugal, Great Britain, the Low Countries, and the United States, and its fourth largest supplier, right after Portugal, Great Britain, and South Africa.[108]

In the period 1953–1957 Angola's chief suppliers were Portugal and the United States, Europe (Common Market and E.F.T.A.) supplying 47 per cent in 1948 and 46 per cent in 1957 with no great fluctuation in the period generally (1953–1957); the United States declined from 20.2 per cent in 1948 to 15.1 per cent in 1953 and 13.5 per cent in 1957. Great Britain, West Germany, Belgium-Luxembourg, and France occupy the next places.

The "provinces" of Angola and Mozambique conduct much of their trade with Portugal, but the latter occupies a much less important place in the imports and exports of these colonies than did any other metropolis in those of its African territories. Between 1950 and 1957 Portugal furnished only 39 per cent of imports and received only 27 per cent of exports.[109] The United States is the chief purchaser of Angolan coffee, absorbing on the average 48 per cent of the total coffee exported, which in turn represents 48 per cent of the total value of exports. Great Britain is the principal customer for diamonds. Angolan imports are basically composed of non-edible consumer goods (22%); its exports

---

[108] Paul Gache and Robert Mercier, *L'Allemagne et l'Afrique*, Paris, 1960, 159–160.

[109] The statistical charts on trade distribution for Angola and Mozambique are found in *L'Étude sur la Situation économique de l'Afrique depuis 1950*, Economic and Social Council, United Nations, 1950, Ch. 3, 25; exports for Angola and Mozambique may be seen in *Economic Bulletin for Africa*, Addis-Ababa, Ethiopia, United Nations, January 1961, I, No. 1.

are foodstuffs (71%) and raw materials for industry (29%); about 53 per cent of its imports come from abroad, 47 per cent supplied by Portugal and 50 per cent by the United States and the United Kingdom.

But our soul mate and great friend prefers to buy from countries in the E.O.E.C. (68.4% of industrial tools and machines), or the European Economic Coöperation Commission, of which it is a member, or the Common Market (34% of industrial tools and machines) in which West Germany is predominant (22.1%). In imports of heavy vehicles also the E.F.T.A. supplies 47.8 per cent and the Common Market 14.4 per cent.[110] As for Brazil, we live on future promises, like the one made in the conference of the European Free Trade Association in 1960 by the then Portuguese Secretary of Commerce, who alleged that "the fact that in our African territories we have products similar to those of Brazil has until now constituted the principal obstacle to increasing our imports from Brazil," and that regarding manufactured goods Portugal purchased them more cheaply in Europe because of the shorter distance.

Now it was obvious that without the overseas territories, the Luso-Brazilian agreements and any spirit of community were doomed to failure. But the Community as the Portuguese understand it aimed only at defending the interests to which we have referred, for the advantages that we may or may not obtain matter little to them. Instead of the Common Market or E.F.T.A., Brazilian industry might already have been supplying the "provinces" with a number of manufactured products, as we have already indicated. All of the commissions established, however, particularly during presidential visits, have had negative results due to the difficulties created by the Portuguese. In 1960 the Luso-Brazilian balance of trade still made patent the fragility of our relations and the economic insignificance of our trade.[111]

The logical conclusion is this: Portugal belongs to a different zone of international trade and our economic relations are precarious and unimportant. It is sufficient to recall further than in the balance of payments [112] from 1955 to 1959 commercial transactions between Brazil

---

[110] Data based on Augusto L. Ferreira dos Santos and V. M. Rabaça Gaspar, *Estrutura do Comércio Externo de Angola,* Lisbon, 1959. See also João Dias Rosa, *A Luta pelos Mercados Africanos,* Lisbon, 1958.
[111] See note in *O Globo,* August 15, 1960.
[112] Data supplied by the Superintendência da Moeda e do Crédito (SUMOC).

and Portugal are of no consequence. Our few exports to Portugal are constantly decreasing. The figures, stated in thousands of dollars, have been the following: 1955—3,413; 1956—3,392; 1957—3,886; 1958—2,668; 1959—2,683. Our few imports also are increasingly on the decline: 1955—7,595; 1956—3,136; 1957—3,513; 1958—3,861; 1959—2,318. In 1959 alone, Portugal exported more than $4,000,000 in services, and Brazil imported only $1,300,000. The most negative aspect is that of gifts, because the Portuguese here sent home about $6,000,000, while we received only $800,000 from Portugal. Thus the old process of remitting funds to Portugal continues, about $10,000,000 in gifts having been sent in 1957. Furthermore, in 1960 the Luso-Brazilian balance of trade showed a credit of 8,000,000 escudos; in 1962 the amount in Brazil's favor was 27,888 escudos.

Recent modest investigations show how poor these relations are, although Aventino Lage, President of the Federation of Portuguese Associations, stated that Prime Minister Oliveira Salazar had expressed to him his surprise that Brazil had not yet taken steps to gain Portugal's overseas markets, which are so lacking in industrial products, white (sic) immigrants, capital, and technicians. Salazar would be willing to provide necessary legislation.[113] Willing now, after the war, perhaps in order to control our vote in the United Nations. Meat to Mozambique and iron ore and Brazilian jeeps and trucks to Portugal, that is the extent of attempts made between 1961 and 1963.[114]

In all areas and from every aspect the Luso-Brazilian Community is a mere rumor. In the cultural field, for example, during the past five years Brazil has spent more than CR$260,000,000 on the acquisition of Portuguese books. In 1959 alone, of a total of CR$439,000,000 expended on foreign books, CR$71,000,000, or 16 per cent, were applied to imports from Portugal, which were second in value only to books imported from the United States (CR$102,000,000). According to Portuguese statistics, in 1959 Portugal exported books totaling 17,419,494 escudos in value, and of this total 16,051,724 (92.1%) went to Brazil. On the other

---

[113] "Portugal abre ao Brasil seus mercados no Ultamar africano," *O Globo,* March 28, 1962.
[114] *Boletim Informativo do Ministério das Relações Exteriores,* No. 698, September 18, 1961, and No. 389, April 24, 1963.

hand, Brazil was in an extremely disadvantageous position, having furnished Portugal books only to the amount of 12,400 escudos, seventeenth in place among foreign suppliers, below the United Kingdom (2,157,889 escudos), France (1,225,066 escudos), Germany (748,936 escudos), the United States, Spain, Switzerland (all with more than 400,000 escudos), Belgium-Luxembourg, Italy, Holland (all with more than 100,000 escudos), South Africa, Sweden, Argentina, Norway, Austria, the Portuguese territories, and Canada.[115] In 1960, 1961, and 1962 the figures are still more impressive. We purchased books valued at $1,122,001, $690,250 and $618,275, respectively, and they bought only $1,149 in 1960 and nothing in following years.

There is no need to comment on these facts; the surprise is that there are people who defend the Community, including of course prominent figures in politics and journalism who have received Portuguese honors and decorations, sometimes in groups.

Moreover, Portugal belongs also to a different zone of international politics. Its chief problem is the defense of its colonies, and in this we cannot join. For this very reason, at the peak of official Luso-Brazilian courtesies in 1957, Minister Paulo Cunha said that "concrete proof of the Luso-Brazilian reality has been seen recently in two cases affecting Portugal. The first was Goa, where Brazil supported the Portuguese position; the second was when the euphemism of colony and province was discussed in the United Nations, and Brazil gave its vote in favor of Portugal."

The Community seemed to flourish, but despite the rot of colonialism, sticky and difficult to eliminate, Brazil was changing daily and escaping the domination of Lusitanian traditions that existed not in modern Brasília but in the mind of its creator. With the administration of Jânio Quadros came a new policy toward the Portuguese and the beginning of difficulties and resentment because they no longer enjoyed a special situation that was no longer justifiable. One did not have to be clairvoyant to foresee that the movement for development would necessarily bring about a review of relations between the two countries, in spite of Juscelino Kubitschek's formulation of a regressive foreign policy that was opposed to a progressive domestic policy. His agree-

---

[115] *Boletim de Serviço,* I.B.G.E., Rio de Janeiro, December 16, 1960, p. 4.

ments were destined to fail; they shouted for revision and reformulation; Portuguese international problems, with its colonial territories and membership in NATO, were not the same as those of Brazil.

There was no point more sensitive to Portugal than its colonies. The hardest heads in the world are found in Portugal, wrote *The New York Times*.[116] We shall not succeed in convincing them, nor shall we follow them. The area of friction was immediately created and continues to disturb political relations, although it is less serious than the episode of the "Santa Maria" or the incident with the director of the Companhia Colonial de Navigação[117] or, finally, the case of the political refugees in the Brazilian Embassy in Lisbon. Politicians interested in "colonial" or "crypto-colonial" votes, senators, and one governor all identified themselves with traditional lines in Luso-Brazilian relations. They forgot that Brazil could not approve a colonialist policy and that, in order to preserve the common heritage, the noblest and most profound historical, psychological, biological, affective, cultural, and spiritual bonds that link us to the old practice of our ancestors, "we must do everything to avoid any political alliance sweeping us where we do not wish and ought not to go," to quote Tristão de Athayde.[118] From an international point of view there is nothing more important affecting Brazil's future at this time than a coherent policy in favor of self-determination, peace, and development, and against colonialism. We cannot approach Africa arm in arm with Salazar. This would compromise us irremediably, not only with Portuguese Africa but with all the new African nations, and our legitimate interest lies in seeing them free and prosperous; for if present economic European preponderance continues, so will greater competition for our products, without the industrial exchange that we are able to initiate free of colonialist, imperialist, and racist restrictions.

Our industrial penetration in Africa depends on the sympathies of the African peoples, Arab or Negro. If Guinea does not offer the same prospect as Angola because of the latter's proximity to us, Mozambique

---

[116] Editorial transcribed in a wire-service story published in *O Jornal*, Rio de Janeiro, February 12, 1961.

[117] José M. D'Orey is reported to have expressed himself crudely with respect to President Jânio Quadros at the time of the "Santa Maria" affair.

[118] "Laços mais altos," *Jornal do Brasil*, February 8, 1962.

presents even greater difficulties because of its heavy Moslem influence. We must not therefore agree with the Portuguese point of view expressed in the National Assembly on April 20, 1961, by Deputy Armando Cândido:[119] "If contrary to all expectations Brazil should prefer to deny that it is the best example of Portuguese colonization, then it is Brazil that would be untrue to itself." He hoped "that Brazilian foreign policy does not allow itself to be seduced by any easy policy of immediacy, when certainly now and in the future it can count on the friendship of Portugal on points vital to Brazil's own security, such as Angola, which the ambition of elements foreign to the Luso-Brazilian Community is at this moment attempting to assault and take over." And, as usual, he trusted that Brazil would understand that its experience in the tropics was based on that of the Lusitanian race.

We have not contributed to the reduction of Portuguese territory and population; Portugal itself has not been able to face the challenge of African liberty. Let the Portuguese remember the somber refrain by Tom Lehrer and so popular today in Great Britain:

> We'll all go together when we go,
> We'll all burn together when we burn,
> We'll all char together when we char.[120]

The Portuguese did not leave Africa when they should have, as the others did; now let them pull the chestnuts out of the fire all by themselves. Not with our help, because we cannot compromise ourselves in Africa and still hope in the future to find any but enemy, or at least unfriendly, peoples on the other side of this Atlantic.

We repeat, the much publicized Luso-Brazilian Community does not really exist. There is, indeed, a community of friendship; but Portugal has taught us that this means nothing when its national interests are at stake. In 1962 Salazar himself was evidently very skeptical with regard to the Community when he stated that "its outline, which is broad and at the same time vague, may be the foundation of an international structure on the grandest of scales or be limited merely to timidly-inspired sentimental messages."[121]

---

[119] *Diário das Sessões,* Lisbon, pp. 598–601.
[120] Not we, but all Europeans, especially they who are so European, should follow their example rather than wish to instruct them.
[121] Speech of January 3, 1962, *Notícias de Portugal,* No. 766, January 6, 1962, p. 25.

There remains the sentimental aspect. I do not believe it necessary to declare to Brazilians that our greatest moral obligation is to our own country, or rather, to our country alone. This lesson comes down to us from the first days of our independence. There is no earthly sentiment that supersedes the interests of the fatherland. It must not be forgotten that Limpo de Abreu, Viscount de Abaeté, who was Portuguese by birth, served as Foreign Minister four times from 1836 to 1853, and it was between 1825 and 1857 that the Mixed Commission of Brazil and Portugal discussed Portugal's insatiable claims relative to our independence.

The stereotyped image that Brazilians had of the Portuguese has undergone a moderating influence, but this is no reason for us to serve their interests rather than ours. In the eyes of the Portuguese we are independent but have a duty to assist them, to identify ourselves with their causes, unquestioningly and without considering our own problems, because sentiment and moral obligation to the mother country are transcendent. And so, as an ethnic pressure group, the Colony conducts its political demonstrations, parades, and protests, supported by some newspapers and by public figures who do not even investigate whether or not there is a conflict between Portuguese interests and ours that would oblige us to fulfill our patriotic duty first. This is what politicians and intellectuals who unconcernedly identify themselves with the Portuguese government should examine above all. The United States, which on the day it declared its independence learned that there is only one native country, did not vacillate, wrongly or not, but immediately after the Second World War gave massive aid to Germany and put England in second place.

Finally, it is fitting to ask what these our special relations with Portugal are? The feminine disdain with which the Portuguese government views Brazilian policy and the air of grandfatherly wisdom with which it thinks it is civilizing us [122] do not favor the Community, which

---

[122] Portuguese professors scattered throughout the colleges in the interior or writers seeking refuge in Rio de Janeiro or São Paulo always assume this patronizing air. See Mauritônio Meira, "Tese de Casais: brasileiro patriota defende Portugal," *Jornal do Brasil,* April 19, 1961, and "Memória do Ensino da Literatura Portuguêsa," *Tempo Brasileiro,* March 1963, pp. 276–292, on the case created by Professor Rodrigues Lapa and the reactions of Eduardo Portela, Celso Cunha, Afrânio Coutinho, Cassiano Ricardo, Heron de Alencar, and Jorge Amado.

should be based on solid economic interests and political solidarity, and not on family or domestic sentiments. Even the language is becoming more differentiated in usage and idiom, and in more than one instance Brazilian books, especially works of fiction, have had to be adapted to Portuguese style. As to the spoken language, the fact is that in the movies or on the radio we find it difficult to understand one another. On the international level, Brazil's and Portugal's national objectives have not coincided since 1822. The zone of attrition is greater than the Community, which has become no more than propaganda and a series of difficulties.

BRAZILIAN INTERNATIONAL POLITICS AND AFRICA

The Second World War restored our link with Africa and served us as a warning. Without the cession of our bases in the Northeast, the victory of El Alamein, the invasion of Europe, and later events of consequence, the destiny of the African nations would not have been possible. Since then, a number of Brazilian scholars have been calling attention to the strategic importance of Africa.

Colonel Golbery do Couto e Silva has warned that "we must take it upon ourselves to observe vigilantly what takes place along the whole west coast of Africa, for it is incumbent upon us by self-interest and even tradition to collaborate effectively in whatever manner is eventually decided best to preserve it from domination by aggressive imperialist forces." And when he defends a creative and positive geopolitics of peace, he maintains that "in view of a planet torn apart today still more by poverty and hunger than by ambitions of expansion and domination—which do in fact exist and are in no way negligible or remote—[Brazil] cannot refuse its proper role in the concert of nations to favor redemption of the socio-economic periphery to which it still belongs and which extends tragically from the Andes throughout Africa, the Middle Orient, India and Southeast Asia, to Indonesia." [123] The strategic importance of the west coast of Africa—where Dakar represents the key point in air connections with Northeast Brazil—is not purely military, as Colonel Golbery do Couto e Silva stressed. It is for peace and in peace that we should coördinate our coöperative efforts.

---

[123] *Aspectos Geopolíticos Brasileiros*, 1959, 27–28.

We are indeed a nation that must think intercontinentally, and the South Atlantic leads us to Africa with which we are linked in all ways, from geographical similarities (climate, soil, vegetation) to ethnic forces, historical precedents, and economic interests. The South Atlantic unites us with almost all of western Africa and suggests a broad, intercontinental policy, the improvement not only of our defense and security conditions, but also of our friendly economic alliances. By our extension and position in the South Atlantic we are an intercontinental nation and a protagonist in international relations with the African world. Perhaps many believe this a world of no importance or one that carries no weight. But this is not the case today in the United Nations or in alliances for world security. Because of our position with respect to Atlantic routes we enjoy a privileged situation for an intercontinental-ism favoring our commercial and political relations.

If we play a geopolitics of peace with these trumps, our possibilities are even greater. Consider all the moral forces that we have on our side, such as miscegenation, racial tolerance, anticolonialism, our pacificism, and our respect for all nations. For all these reasons, public opinion has been most sympathetically and enthusiastically supporting all action in favor of African claims and Afro-Brazilian rapprochement, and diplomatic and scholarly opinion has been maintaining the need to formulate a policy, not merely for the African market but for Afro-Brazilian friendship.

This explains the failure of the policy that Brazil had adopted which was concerned exclusively with the United States, Europe, and Latin America, and the Pan-American Operation, and which was formulated during the administration of Juscelino Kubitschek as a system of continental regionalism. The P.A.O. overshadowed the most important phenomenon in world history between 1958 and 1960: the liberation of Africa. It removed us from the world historical process and if it was not completely a diversion—because it did represent a part of our national interests—it served to screen our indefensible accompaniment of the colonial powers and submission to their greater clairvoyance or blind-ness. We voted with the colonial powers in the United Nations, gave in to all Portuguese pressures, those from Salazar's oligarchy and those from the Colony here, and occasionally disguised our colonial align-ment with abstentions. We had not a word of sympathy for African freedom and did not evaluate the dangers to national security that an unfriendly west Africa could represent. Whether in its own field of action or in the United Nations, Juscelino Kubitschek's government ignored African progress toward freedom and, after the African states had achieved independence, limited itself to *de jure* recognition. Nothing more; no encouraging message, no solidarity, no gesture, not to mention coöperation, as though we were ashamed of the springtime of African power, as though we were humiliated by our alter ego, as though we were embarrassed by our common identity, as though it were possible to continue this dichotomy between an international policy directed by a Europeanized elite working to preserve the status quo and the Brazilian people, whose entry into the area of decision has just begun. The failure of Juscelino Kubitschek's foreign policy was due to the one-sidedness of its regionalistic vision. With regard to the other horizon it was an act of self-liquidation, although we could not expect its articulators to commit harakiri.

As was known and has been demonstrated, the problem of underdevelopment could be overcome only by avoiding the fall in prices of products for export. Because of this it was recognized that competition among underdeveloped countries was less a reason to fight than to unite in defense of common interests. The P.A.O. was therefore too one-sided and narrow; it was ignorant of Afro-Asian reality and, rather than uniting in defense of basic products, divided into regions and gave rise to competition and political selection by the Common Market. In the directives and speeches of President Kubitschek, the debates in Congress, the orientation of the Brazilian Foreign Office, and among the followers and even the opponents of the government there was no preoccupation, no concern, no attention to the African problems that during this time were beginning to absorb public opinion and the press through the world.[124] It was maintained that Brazilian foreign policy was inalterable, and criticism had to grant United States leadership in Latin America; and there were some who were more disturbed by possible United States preferences for Asia or Africa than by the world struggle against underdevelopment. But setting our sights on regional

---

[124] The documentation published on the Kubitschek administration is perhaps the most complete on any of the Brazilian heads of state.

goals was no more than to reactivate the fraternity of the American continent, reciprocal assistance, and Western solidarity, said the opposition, and to avoid criticizing United States negligence and redefining principles to provide greater economic coördination between Brazil and Africa.

It was surprising that from the beginning of his presidential campaign Mr. Jânio Quadros should have expressed a decided intention to reform our foreign policy by rapprochement with the Afro-Asian countries. In his meeting with the Republican Party on May 12, 1960, after speaking of the experience that he had acquired on his trip to the Far East and Africa, he said that Brazil could not continue in its current timid position, for the way was clear in Asia and in Africa. Expansion of international relations and advantageous shifts in trade will increase our authority among nations, for we already are a country with a definite future and cannot remain simply a member of the South American community. Provided there is a national interest served in each case, we must maintain diplomatic relations with all countries.[125] This seems to have been the then presidential candidate's first expression favoring our relations with African peoples.

A short time later, on May 31, he stated: "The general lines of Brazilian diplomacy are set in Victorian molds. I believe it indispensable to bring the orientation and procedures of our international politics up to date. We must be more objective, more practical, more dynamic." As to Brazil's participation in conferences promoted by Afro-Asian countries, he said that "because of its economic characteristics, racial origins, and the sentiments of its people Brazil merits an outstanding role in the awakening of the immense Afro-Asian world. Unfortunately, in this solemn, fleeting hour Brazilian diplomacy is wasting opportunities, some through omission. The great states of the future in Africa and Asia should be able to find in Brazil's international maturity the courage they lack to shorten the period until inevitable emancipation." [126]

In his understanding of international events candidate Jânio Quadros revealed himself to be much better prepared and shrewder than his

---

[125] *O Globo,* Rio de Janeiro, May 12, 1960.
[126] *Ibid.,* May 31, 1960, 7.

competitor. He was not afraid to visit Cuba and on various occasions reaffirmed his independent line of rapprochement with all nations and solidarity with the African peoples. The victory in October gave him his opportunity. Addressing himself to the Brazilian people through the "Voice of Brazil" on January 31, 1961, the new President declared: "We are going through some of the most trying days that humanity has ever known. Colonialism is breathing its last, ashamed of itself, incapable of resolving the dramas and contradictions that it has engendered." In addition, he repeated his commitment, sanctioned by the people, to an independent policy of relations with all countries: "We open our arms to all nations on the continent. We are a communion without political and philosophical prejudices. Our ports will welcome all who wish to trade with us. We are a communion without rancor or fear. We are sufficiently conscious of our power not to be timid about dealing with anyone at all."

This affirmation of "a sovereign policy, sovereign in a real and full sense, before any and all powers," was a notice of our maturity that came as no surprise to anyone at home or abroad because it had been announced throughout the entire campaign. No time was wasted in initiating the policy of rapprochement with all countries, and consequently with those in Africa to which we are bound by a destiny of influence for peace that cannot be postponed. It was a policy that freed us from those classifications so common in international political literature, so-called Latin- or South-Americanization, that is, making the continent a satellite of United States interests or of European imperialism. It was above all the foreign policy that the President, in the enjoyment of his special constitutional powers and supported by a decisive majority, decided to formulate. President Jânio Quadros promoted the about-face in Brazilian foreign policy, an about-face not only in the sense of independence but also in that of broader horizons. He preserved liberty of action that had been restricted by external pressures and coerced by oligarchic interests, and those of other economic groups, and even by voices in Congress or in the press, frequently confused with those of public opinion; it was the last that elected Quadros and later applauded the independence of his conduct, his broadening of international relations, his new directions, his anticolonialism, his solidarity and coöperation with redeemed Africa. The historical process had changed and our position in that process; therefore, the objectives and methods of our foreign policy had to change. Because this was the first Brazilian president who knew the other world, who had not, as usual, visited only Europe and the United States—where it was always the same old story about our destiny on the brink—it was possible to think his vision broad and universal, as demanded by our situation as a middle power, one of the key countries in the so-called free world.

On his side were his Foreign Minister, Afonso Arinos de Melo Franco, who had affirmed and reaffirmed his anticolonialist position before, as in his speech to the Chamber of Deputies on August 13, 1958, or his approval of rapprochement with Afro-Asian peoples in the Senate on July 30, 1960. When he took office as Foreign Minister on February 1, 1961, Afonso Arinos said:

Brazil is in an especially favorable situation to serve as a link between the Afro-Asian world and the great Western powers. A democratic, Christian people whose Latin culture was enriched by indigenous, African, and Asian influences, we are ethnically half-breeds and culturally a mixture of elements originating in immense geographical and demographic areas that are making their appearance in international life in this century. Furthermore, the processes of miscegenation introduced by the Portuguese Metropolis to mold us have facilitated our racial democracy, which if not as perfect as we should like is nevertheless the most advanced in the world. We have no such prejudice against the colored races as is found in so many white or predominantly white populations; nor prejudice against whites as happens in predominantly colored populations.

And he concluded: "Therefore, the legitimate exercise of our sovereignty in international politics will lead us to give sincere support to the efforts of the Afro-Asian world to attain democracy and liberty." [127] As in July, 1960, he recognized that we resemble the underdeveloped countries of Africa and the Middle and Far East, although we are more mature in the juridical and political field, and he interpreted Jânio Quadros' overwhelming victory as expressing rejection of any sort of dictatorship. An anticolonial and antiracist country, Brazil is convinced of the necessity of development as a basis for democracy.

All of these directives were in keeping with the pre- and post-election statements of the President and his Minister, who in his first press

---

[127] *Discursos,* Ministério das Relações Exteriores, 11–12.

conference restated the totally independent character of our foreign
policy and our sympathy for nations emerging or yet to emerge from
colonial oppression. Free of prejudice, he then said that mestizo races
like that of Brazil have not stained history as have the so-called pure or
white races; Brazilian anticolonialism was not limited to recognition
and support of the nations that had just become liberated, but involved
colonialism's over-all liquidation, encouraged and favored by our unconditional support, although this would be modified when it required
interference in the internal affairs of other countries. He declared also
his decision to seek the collaboration of Congress in developing foreign
policy, as he had stated when he left the Senate.

President Quadros was very authoritarian, however, and would not
abdicate total direction of foreign policy. There was a repetition of what
had happened in the Kubitschek administration when there were two
foreign offices: one in the Itamarati (Foreign Office Palace), devoted to
routine tasks, and another in the Catete (Presidential Palace in Rio de
Janeiro) creating the P.A.O. and other developments. Now, while
bureaucratic affairs were the responsibility of the Itamarati, decisions
were made in Alvorada Palace (Brasília). The President directed the
Itamarati without discretion, issuing instructions in little notes previously circulated by the press and radio. One of the first, dated
February 24, 1961, requested that provision be made: "(a) to constitute
a work group for the purpose of preparing Brazilian diplomatic
representation in the new African states; (b) for the foreign ministry to
review Brazil's African policy, which must be examined in all its
aspects, especially political, economic, and cultural." On the same day
President Quadros decided to create scholarships for Africans through a
20 per cent reduction in diplomatic salaries equal to or higher than $400
per month, half of the savings from the cut to be applied to the
scholarships.

In March, 1961, Minister Afonso Arinos delivered the requested
review based, as always, naturally, on the self-sufficient wisdom of the
diplomatic corps, which although competent is obliged because of the
needs of the service and its own interests often to break the continuity
that is necessary for research. Furthermore, the policy of secrecy
inherited from Portuguese colonialism makes it inadvisable for the
foreign office to make use of the services of outside consultants as do the

well-organized cabinets of great powers. On this occasion the Foreign Minister declared that "it is not we who are looking to Africa; rather it is the young nations of that continent that are looking to Brazil." A surprising statement, for Brazil was a country practically unknown in Africa,[128] with little or no place in African declarations, books, or references, and could not therefore be sought out "to serve as a natural link between the African nations and democracy."

The plan approved by Quadros included cultural agreements between Brazil and Morocco, Senegal, Ghana, Tunisia, and Nigeria to be celebrated by the Ministry in due time, and offers of scholarships. There would be twenty of these in 1962, forty in 1963, and one hundred in 1965, at first only for students of medicine, pharmacy, odontology, architecture, agronomy, and veterinary medicine.[129]

Aside from the creation of new embassies, finally limited to Ghana, Nigeria, and Senegal, on the economic level the "Declaration of Rio de Janeiro" established a new policy for Brazilian and African coffee. It was understood that although Brazil and some of the African countries were competitors in a certain segment of the international coffee market, it was in their common interest to regulate competition, making it possible not only to obtain relative stabilization of prices in the world market but also to provide a fair wage for their rural populations. The "Declaration of Rio de Janeiro" was a natural outcome of efforts toward international coöperation, especially concerning the Afro-Brazilian plan to stabilize prices. Signed in July, 1961, by Brazil and the Inter-African Coffee Organization, it established the bases of a consultive system for commercialization of the product, adoption of similar criteria and policies to control production, and strengthening of agriculture in the individual economies.[130] This step accelerating the process of international understanding and integration was in a sense a complement to the Acra Conference, which in April, 1961, had estab-

---

[128] Statement made in Brazil by the Nigerian Labor Minister, Mr. Joseph Medupe Johnson. See *O Globo,* July 18, 1961.

[129] The scholarships proved unsuccessful. Fourteen African students from several countries first took courses in Bahia and were later distributed among several colleges in the country. This limited initial move was not pursued. See *Boletim No. 10* of the Ministério de Relações Exteriores, January 3, 1962.

[130] "Também o Café une o Brasil e a África. Nova Política Firmada na 'Declaração do Rio de Janeiro,'" *O Globo,* July 29, 1961.

lished the bases of the Cacao Agreement. Coöperation in the economic sphere seemed easier than in the cultural and political.

The decisions concerning circumnavigation of Africa by the Coast Guard, the traveling exhibit of Brazilian products on the ship *Custodio de Melo,* and the decoration of the Order of the Southern Cross conferred on the President of Ghana and the Heads of the Councils of Ministers of Senegal and Tanganyika are innovations of little significance, especially when compared with President Quadros' instructions to the Director of Brazilian Lloyd's to conduct studies for the purpose of creating a shipping service between Brazil and Indonesia with stops in Africa. It was only in June, 1962, that this last provision finally began to take form with Congressional approval of the resolution establishing a direct line between Brazil and Africa.

The vacillations of President Quadros and his Foreign Minister are more apparent in the political field. First, one must not forget that a Cabinet aide, later an ambassador, was chosen because he was a Negro. The error here was obvious: it was racism in reverse.[131] The presidential decision to provide incentives for trade relations with South Africa, at the very moment of the Sharpeville massacre, seemed equally inopportune. The same was true of the arrival of Belgian settlers from the Congo and of whites from Kenya dominated by prejudice, negotiated at the beginning of the Quadros administration in March, 1961, and expedited by Minister Hermes Lima in May, 1963.

But the really important matter was political. Attention to Africa could have been accepted without criticism, but there were those who claimed that Brazil should restrict its activity in the international sphere and not turn to the East and Africa. Brazil's "new look" was beginning to displease the conservative classes and their allies in the press undertook one of the most vigorous campaigns that Brazil has ever seen. This is not the place to study the various developments to which the attacks of the conservative press and established reactionary figures gave rise. In short, the plans of reëstablishing relations with the Soviet Union and of sending an observer to the meeting in Bucharest, the possibility of movement toward neutrality, and our position with respect to Cuba

---

[131] José Honório Rodrigues, "O racismo às avessas do Presidente Jânio Quadros," *O Jornal,* March 2, 1961.

were reasons to believe a complete about-face had occurred despite financial understandings with the United States and Europe. The administration was accused of wanting to flirt with Asia and Africa, and even of being concerned primarily with Africa and Eastern Europe.

One of the most serious questions heatedly discussed in the press was the case of Angola and the attitude that Brazil should take in the United Nations. From the start it was expected that the President's and Foreign Minister's first anticolonial declarations would be put to the test. The opportunity would arise when the Foreign Ministry formulated instructions for our delegation in the United Nations. But when the time came for a decision, hesitation began. There was a treaty, that of the Community, which as we have seen provided for consultation on international problems of manifest common interest. Actually, these problems were manifestly only of Portuguese interest and consultations compromised our relations with countries on the African continent. On March 30, 1961, after a conference with Ambassador Manoel Rocheta, the Itamarati issued an official note declaring that with respect to Angola the President was aware that "our country's orientation derives, on the one hand, from the government's firm anticolonial position and, on the other, from international engagements and bonds of a very special nature uniting Brazil and Portugal"; and consequently that instructions had been sent to our delegation in the United Nations to abstain from voting on the matter.

The retreat was made between March 27 and 29, 1961, even before Afonso Arinos' trip to Lisbon in April, 1961, to consult with the Portuguese government. The Minister's visit—the President and Minister having forgotten that, if there was a Community, its seat was here, not there, and that it behooved Mr. Salazar to consult us, not us him—represented one of the greatest weaknesses and contradictions of Jânio Quadros' policy. Upon his return the Minister declared, after highly praising Salazar, that Brazil reserved the right to act freely on the African situation, condemned colonialism, reaffirmed the two government's unified action in other matters of interest to the Community, and supported self-determination for "peoples capable of aspiring to independence." In the words of a commentator at the time, there was no greater "imbroglio," since it was suggested that to give an opinion on

Angola was to intervene in Portugal's internal affairs and it was supposed that Angola was incapable of aspiring to independence.

The withdrawal was accomplished and, in spite of the Minister's declarations that Brazil would not decide until September, the truth is that it abstained from voting on the resolution creating a commission to examine the case of Angola. Our international policy vacillated in its anticolonialism, and the Minister referred to the North-South economic conflict.[132] This geographical conception of wealth and poverty in the world was such a significant discovery that it was circulated in the Presidential Message.

In Congress opinion was divided, reflecting not only partisan ideological tendencies but also the indecision that marks Brazilian political parties. The hesitations of the President and Minister also influenced parliamentary indecisiveness; yet many senators and deputies indicated their preferences in supporting speeches without regard for party distinctions, and a few, committed to their old integralist convictions, reproached the government vehemently. Not a few others visited Dictator Salazar in Lisbon to express solidarity on the Angolan question and support for the Luso-Brazilian Community.[133] Indiscreet, with always the same old story of our "being descended from Portuguese," they censured the Brazilian government abroad precisely on points of divergence. The major parties had expressed their support for the government's foreign policy,[134] but the government felt pressure from the Portuguese Colony, which had made public its repudiation of the

---

[132] Interview in Lisbon, transcribed in *O Jornal,* April 9, 1961. It is Sir Oliver Franks' well-known idea that "the chief problem of international affairs is not that of East versus West, of which one hears so much, but that of North versus South: whether the southern nations, in Africa, Asia, and Latin America, follow along the lines of the industrialized nations of the North, or the methods of state control of the two great Communist nations of the North, the Soviet Union and China." East is East and West is West, but a large part of humanity is beginning to consider them North, wrote the London *Economist.* See "Os Africanos preocupam-se antes de tudo com a África," special from the London *Economist* for the *Estado de São Paulo,* June 11, 1961.

[133] See esp. *Notícias de Portugal,* Nos. 751, September 23, 1961; 782, April 28, 1962; and 784, May 12, 1962. Other numbers of the same publication record expressions of solidarity from state deputies.

[134] Statements of the Presidents of the P.S.D. (Social Democratic Party) in *Correio de Manhã,* March 24, 1961, and the U.D.N. (National Democratic Union) in *Jornal do Brasil,* August 24, 1961. (The P.T.B. is the Brazilian Labor Party.)

official orientation through manifestos and letters to deputies and sharp attacks in the press associated with the Colony. The pressure groups were not yet acting as vigorously as they would on the Cuba question later, either in official quarters, the press, or in public.

Senator Nogueira da Gama declared before the Congress: "The world no longer admits of the tutelage of one nation over another, and Africa has already run through its historical cycle as the continent of slavery. It is facing enlightenment and progress in the world and needs to arise and emancipate itself, becoming free in order to be integrated in the concept of the free world." [135] More precise and more firm was the speech of the head of the P.T.B., Deputy Almino Afonso: "It is to be hoped, therefore, that the anticolonial line proclaimed by the President now has a practical consequence. We wish Brazil to give its vote in the U.N. in favor of the anticolonial movement, in defense of the Angolan people, for the liberation of Angola, and for absolute condemnation of the savage attitude of the Portuguese authorities." Deputy Adauto Lúcio Cardoso expressed himself along the same lines for the U.D.N., saying that it was through Minister Afonso Arinos "that we collaborate in this anticolonial policy for which we have clamored in this House; that we collaborate in this policy of justice toward underdeveloped peoples." One of the leaders of the P.S.D. also proclaimed his support for the President's foreign policy, "which rips away old prejudices and signifies Brazil's diplomatic and commercial expansion," although he expressed the suspicion that there was a lack of perfect understanding between the President's and the Minister's objectives.[136]

Called before Congress on several occasions, Minister Afonso Arinos gave explanations and replied to the questioning of senators and deputies. In May, 1961, Ambassador Negrão de Lima went to Angola to observe the "overseas" territory in conflagration. His mission, dictated by the President according to the newspaper version at the time, or requested by the Portuguese government itself, as the Foreign Minister later said in the Senate, was not well received by Brazilian public opinion. Was this not interfering in the affairs of Portugal? asked a

---

[135] *Diário do Congresso Nacional*, April 7, 1961, 453. This did not prevent him from also going to Salazar to express his support. *Notícias de Portugal*, No. 751, September 23, 1961.

[136] Statement in *Diário do Congresso Nacional,* March 10, 1961, 1379–1380.

senator, and the Minister replied that the Ambassador had been invited by the Portuguese Prime Minister, Foreign Minister, and Ambassador, and that it was therefore not "an impertinent initiative on the part of our government," but corresponded to a request from the Portuguese government.[137]

One of the chief organs of the press in São Paulo commented, under the headline "A Strange Ambassador," that he was "a compromised man, whose opinions on the Portuguese situation are suspect and indeed reflect faithfully the official viewpoints of the Portuguese government."[138] This, then, was one more service lent the Portuguese dictatorship and its colonialism, and on his visit to the "Province" the Ambassador did not see the bloody drama and so returned satisfied, because he had noted "the many indices of progress represented by the excellent highways and large cities in addition to the beautiful capital." He further appreciated important and extremely interesting achievements, both public and private.[139] "I am at home. This is our very soul, our blood," adding for the enlightenment of historians that "Brazil, created by us with Portuguese from Angola and all parts of the Portuguese empire, is today a nation that is still honored by and proud of the principles of liberty, genuine liberty and equality, which the Portuguese implanted here."[140] The strangely partial Brazilian representative sent to Angola presented a report to the Itamarati, which it filed and has kept from the public to this day because of its policy of secrecy, a heritage from Portuguese colonialism. Less satisfaction is given the public today than in the days of the Empire and First Republic; reports are tranquilizing expositions published without official documentation. The only exception was *Brasil em Punta del Este*,[141] published at the peak of the hysteria against San Tiago Dantas.

The Luso-Brazilian Treaty had this peculiar effect: it converted our foreign ministers into honorary Portuguese dignitaries, always visiting

---

[137] *Ibid.*, June 8, 1961, 948.

[138] "Um estranho Embaixador," *Estado de São Paulo*, May 19, 1961.

[139] Wire service story published in *Jornal do Brasil*, June 9, 1961.

[140] "O Embaixador do Brasil visita Angola," *Notícias de Portugal*, No. 735, June 3, 1961.

[141] Ministério de Relações Exteriores, 1962.

Lisbon, consulting their Chief, running to the old Metropolis. Why not wait, with the Greek virtue of moderation, for Sr. Salazar and Sr. Franco Nogueira to come to us? If they believe in the Community, its seat is here. It is not possible to subject a great nation of 76,000,000 inhabitants to consultations with the autocratic leader of 9,500,000 people. Minister Afonso Arinos was not of this opinion, however, when he went to Lisbon; nor when he allowed Sr. Negrão de Lima, Ambassador to Portugal, to be the Brazilian observer in Angola.

Afonso Arinos' trip to Lisbon was concomitant with a voyage to Senegal, we do not know whether because of the Minister's francophile tendencies, or Senegal's conciliatory position in African politics, or its opposition to the Brazilian-Nigerian proposal in G.A.T.T. against Common Market discrimination, or, finally, its radical stand against Portuguese colonialism, a stand carried to the point that it broke relations with and denounced Portugal in the United Nations. So many contradictions might well have shocked common sense generally, but not the Minister. The academic conversations and poetic flourishes brought no practical result, except the limited cultural agreement. The mission to Africa and the mission to Salazar, thesis and antithesis, were without synthesis.

Deputy Coelho de Souza's mission, with visits to Ghana, Guinea, Nigeria, Ivory Coast, the Republic of the Cameroons, and Sierra Leone, to offer the last-named state Brazil's congratulations on independence, departed and returned in silence. According to the news dispatches, the Deputy went through the continent promising Brazil's support for Africa in the United Nations, but upon his arrival here he declared that he had merely discharged "my duties faithfully, engaging in acts of protocol and gathering copious material, filling eight thick volumes that will complete the report to the Minister." [142] Once again the Foreign Ministry's policy of secrecy removed any obligation upon public figures on official missions to give the public satisfaction.

As may be seen, there was an initial impulse toward, a passionate interest in, Africa, but no African policy properly speaking was ever formulated. The two ambassadors appointed to Senegal and Ghana, who were to begin execution of the Brazilian policy, were uninformed,

---

[142] *O Globo,* June 12, 1961.

and although one of them was one of the most famous Brazilian commentators and a great writer, he had never shown any interest in Africa or in the studies of history, foreign policy, international law, and economics that might orient him. During its seven months of gestation, the Quadros government's African policy gave birth to nothing but abstention in the United Nations in votes against Algeria and Angola that were protested by some deputies, such as Fernando Santana and Seixas Dória.[143]

The 1961 Presidential Message to Congress on foreign policy generally opposed the North-South economic struggle, already discussed, to the East-West ideological conflict, reaffirmed support for the United Nations, and declared Brazilians to be brothers of the African peoples "in the struggle for economic development, defense of basic products, industrialization, and the integration into national life of all levels of the population." Now with greater humility it was recognized that "our effort in Africa, however intense it may become, can constitute only a modest compensation, a small payment of the immense debt owed by Brazil to the African people. This moral consideration would alone justify the importance given by this government to its policy of rapprochement with Africa. Moreover, we wish to help create a climate in the Southern Hemisphere of perfect understanding and comprehension in all areas, political and cultural, a true spiritual identity. . . . A prosperous and stable Africa is an essential condition for the security and development of Brazil." Lamenting the Congolese situation, the Message supported the United Nations in its task of creating conditions making it possible for the Congo to belong to the Congolese and stated that "the government would take no greater satisfaction in the world scene than to see the day draw near when a nation of such importance in the world should, like Algeria, achieve its independence." [144]

Here was a program that deserved the unanimous support of the country, that recognized our duty to be on the side of the Africans, although as a developing nation we might be able to offer little beyond unity in the struggle for economic defense and especially friendship and

---

[143] Regarding the former, see *Diário do Congresso,* January 6, 1961, before Jânio Quadros came to power; for the latter, see *Diário,* March 8, 1961. The Brazilian position in the United Nations will be treated in the next section.
[144] *Mensagem ao Congresso Nacional,* 91–92 and 96–98.

coöperation. But it failed in one essential, cautiously avoided point, the obligations we had assumed contrary to our thesis of anticolonialism; there was not a single word on Angola. Later, on the eve of the Jânio Quadros affair, August 16, 1961, the Foreign Minister, questioned by Deputy Fernando Santana concerning the decision to abstain on the Angolan question in the United Nations, said that with regard to Africa our position had been taken because of, and abstention conditioned by, a combination of political agreements, past and present. As always it was necessary to point out that the person speaking was "a man profoundly Portuguese in blood, culture, and love of the Portuguese nation, people, and soil," desirous not of emancipation but of Portugal's acceptance of a solution favoring autonomy. When the time came that he could reveal the tenor of his conversations with the Portuguese government, he added in the most dignified and correct manner, it would be seen how foolish the attacks against the Minister of State had been. "You shall see that we will not betray our position. We will do everything possible to coöperate with Portugal, so that the nation to which we are bound by so many ties suffers as little as possible in this process of separation and emancipation that we consider historically inevitable. But I can tell you what I said before: as I arrive in New York my conscience is clear." [145]

Abstention during the Fifteenth Session of the General Assembly had been the result of a transaction, said the Minister. What transaction? is the question that comes to mind as one is befogged by secret diplomacy and disturbed by the grave accusation made in the United Nations, and never denied, concerning "the shameful offer of the Prime Minister of Portugal to give Brazil and other Western nations a share of the spoils from the Portuguese colonies in exchange for support favoring maintenance of the Portuguese Empire." [146] The statement in the Fifteenth Session of the General Assembly made April 20, 1961, by Secretary Carvalho Silos corresponded to the fluctuation in our policy and to commitments negotiated under the Treaty of Friendship: "I am obliged to abstain from voting on the proposed resolution. This does not mean, however, that Brazil will not continue to follow its decision to fight

---

[145] *Diário do Congresso,* August 16, 1961, 316.
[146] Mr. Dadet of the Congo Republic (Brazzaville), in the 990th Plenary Session of the General Assembly, April 20, 1961, *United Nations General Assembly, Official Records: Fifteenth Session,* 387.

colonialism." [147] In the Sixteenth Session, attended by Mr. Afonso Arinos, no longer as Minister but as head of the Brazilian delegation and representative of the Goulart administration, Brazil abandoned its position of abstention, although with a reservation concerning the expression of the resolution, as we shall see below.

Jânio Quadros' Foreign Minister had indeed been vacillating, but most important was his attitude in facing the problem, an attitude out of harmony with Brazil's traditional position. He showed himself a man profoundly Brazilian in blood, culture, and love of the Brazilian nation and people. The attacks in the press, coming especially from crypto-colonists who considered Brazil's obligation to Portugal indisputable, could not sway his democratic convictions, which is noteworthy in view of the hysteria and unrest that were to take hold of certain sectors of public opinion later during the agitated campaign waged against Jânio Quadros' foreign policy on the eve of his resignation.

Intolerant conservative groups, led by a governor who heads reactionary Brazilian thought and projects his own defects on others, could not or would not understand the innovations in foreign policy, or that that policy should be free of prejudice and fear. The government was only beginning to bring foreign policy up to date, insisting on greater liberty of action and greater imagination, taking it out of the gray zone of unconditional support for the policies of the great powers to a vanguard position. Brazil had become an ally, and was no longer a satellite; it was not traveling a new path, but attempting to establish new, broader bases of international coöperation without ideological limitations, without provincialism.

In its difference with Portugal Brazil's attitude had been one of abstention, while the United States voted in favor of examining the Angolan situation despite its vital bases in the Azores; [148] on the question of Algeria, Argentina preceded us, as did several other Latin American countries on almost all colonial issues. The new Brazilian foreign policy apparently excluded only these colonial questions and offered a spirit more nationalist and progressive, rejected the secondary

---

[147] *Ibid.*, 992nd Plenary Session, April 20, 1961, 433–435.

[148] The defense of colonialism cost the United States dearly, said Senator Wayne L. Morse to the Senate Foreign Relations Committee after having been United States delegate to the United Nations. Wire services story from Washington, Rio de Janeiro, February 20, 1961, *Última Hora.*

role assigned to it by American policy, and desired greater freedom to act internationally, expand political and economic relations, acquire the right to an independent orientation, yet not have its understanding with the United States lose significance as a legitimate affiliation.[149]

Brazil's independent position with regard to the Cuban problem and resumption of relations with the Soviet Union were the chief factors engendering the anti-Quadros hysteria. At that time Walter Lippman wrote that there would be no reason for hysteria should Brazil boldly abandon the line established by the United States, and another commentator observed that the United States would do better to treat Brazil as it did Great Britain and France.[150] President Quadros' message was clear, for it declared: "We were born members of the free world and shall always be aware of this fact," and then said that when Brazil assumed a more positive and independent international position, it was not changing its ideological position, which was basically Western. Although linked to the West, Brazil was not committed to the West, but neither was it neutral; it did not wish to be a part of military blocs nor to participate in the cold war, and on the international front, whether in the United Nations or bilaterally, it was merely defending its interests.

The President's resignation, for reasons that are still obscure, set off a new wave of unrest against the Vice-President, who constitutionally was to assume the presidency, as well as against the foreign policy. Once Goulart had taken office, and the ephemeral Parliamentary Government was formed after he was deprived of his constitutional powers, the rightist conservative forces directed their greatest offensive upon our foreign policy.[151] Criticism and censure increased and became personal attacks and insults, yet immediately after the new President's inauguration it was decided to retain the previous foreign policy, with some of its methods altered, such as its lack of discretion, the presidential notes to which we have referred, and excesses in word and deed resembling threats more than understandings.

But if discretion is indispensable, the right to information is a

---

[149] José Honório Rodrigues, "Uma Política Externa própria e independente," *Jornal do Brasil,* June 10 and 17, 1962.
[150] Robert J. Alexander, "New Look in Brazil," *The New Leader* (March 20, 1961).
[151] The questions of Jânio Quadros' resignation and João Goulart's inauguration lie outside the scope of this work.

fundamental democratic liberty and international politics, because it concerns the people, must be known to and involve them. It must not shut them out as it did when it was the expression of an elite, a social group working to conserve the status quo, subject to decisions by the great powers and contented to obtain small concessions in exchange for compromises and obligations that were often extremely grave. The innocence of the people and the pretensions of the elite should never permit the latter to think of us as a nation of lambs, always losing our battles, always deceived, always easily maneuvered by the attorneys of great international economic interests. Love of peace and devotion to universal understanding without prejudice and discrimination came from our hearts; but from our hearts, too, came the courage to initiate our great struggle for development—not for a few but for all—and for our high aspirations.

Despite the Parliamentary Government, Minister San Tiago Dantas acted freely in initiating his development diplomacy. He was bold and imaginative, and with extraordinary courage entered the battle against reactionaries of all types. In his first statements he reaffirmed the principles of nonintervention, self-determination and anticolonialism. His policy was firmly executed along these lines, including its implementation in the United Nations when for the first time there was a vote on proposed resolution No. 1742, dated January 30, 1962, creating a commission to gather information on the situation of territories under Portuguese administration, inasmuch as Portugal was not prepared to supply the information referred to in resolution No. 1542 of the Fifteenth Assembly; the Brazilian delegation had reservations not only regarding the word "condemns" in the expression "condemns Portugal's persistent refusal to comply with the obligation to supply information," but also about the last paragraph, which reflected the concern of the sponsors of the proposal for the improper use by Portugal of NATO weapons.[152] The then–Foreign Minister's instructions to our delegation

---

[152] Actually it was the American delegate, Mr. Bingham, who requested amendment of the word "condemns" to "laments." The great American interest in renewing leases for bases justified courtesy to Portugal. The amendment, however, was rejected 56–16 with 22 abstentions. See *United Nations General Assembly, Official Records: Sixteenth Session,* 1083rd Plenary Session, December 19, 1961, 1101 and 1105.

were definite, less subject to the pressure of crypto-colonialists, and we did not go to Lisbon to consult the Portuguese head of state.

Meanwhile, nothing more was said about the African policy, which had begun with such lofty aspirations. In his inaugural speech in the Ministry of Foreign Affairs, San Tiago Dantas, who made his office solely responsible for foreign policy, making rather than letting both the Itamarati and the Catete divide the task, referred only to abolition of colonial vestiges; he uttered not a word in regard to African policy. Colonialism was condemned and support for aspirations to independence expressed on the so-called bases of the program for government by a Council of Ministers.[153] Nothing more. The Presidential Message [154] stated quite vaguely that we were "most attentive to the campaign for emancipation of the African and Asian peoples begun at the end of World War II." Again, nothing on African policy. Revealing, however, was the speech by the Foreign Minister upon the appointment of the Under-Secretary for Western European, African, and Near Eastern Affairs, an odd office that itself exhibits the still dominant colonialist spirit that unites in a group Western Europe and Africa and the Near East. With respect to Africa he said that the Brazilian government's anticolonialist policy had reached its peak with the historic vote on the Angolan question. "Our anticolonial policy is free of hesitation and doubt, and our position alongside those countries fighting for their freedom is today a combat position. We play a great role as an American nation in the effort to build a new Africa upon the principle of self-determination."

These words generally repeated previous statements that had been reënforced, it is true, by the vote given in the United Nations, but in addition to fusing Africa and Europe the Minister declared that the affairs of Western Europe, the area that had been decisive in shaping Brazil, requires the adoption of an alert policy in view of the European effort at integration. The European Common Market bloc, which discriminates against everyone with no respect for the interests of others and creates great difficulties, demands more ministerial attention. The Europe of the Six, faced with the dilemma of defending their domestic

---

[153] *Programa de Govêrno. Bases.* Conselho de Ministros, Brasília, 1961, 192–193.
[154] *Mensagem ao Congresso Nacional*, Rio de Janeiro, 1962, 45–47.

interests or becoming an economic satellite, also preferred the way of discrimination. Brazil, too, will no longer accept the modest, unrealistic role formerly assigned it by Europeans and Americans.

The outcome of our foreign policy depends on free participation in a world community and on the success of our international trade. We are threatened with isolation by the European Common Market and, regarding Latin American integration and our important bilateral trade with the United States, we still have the possibility of uniting the Latin American Common Market and the African Market and all countries that are not part of economic blocs, in a struggle against all forms of world domination or disguised subjection to regional interests, in a progressive march toward a world policy, a universal civilization respecting the strength of every region and the interests, aspirations, and expectations of all peoples.

Our foreign policy was limited to the one vote in the United Nations, to regular shipping between Africa and Brazil (at Jânio Quadros' initiative), to recognition of the independence of new African nations such as Algeria, Rwanda, and Burundi, and to President João Goulart's unfulfilled promise of a trip to Africa to affirm the policy of solidarity announced in April, 1962. Some of the opposition immediately saw a "pretext for anti-American treachery" in our diplomacy's new racial considerations, and the Foreign Minister was criticized for his proposals when actually he had not executed *any* African policy and in a speech examining the results of Brazil's foreign policy declared "the making uniform of our orientation toward colonialism, especially with respect to Africa, the emancipation of which Brazil defends although it is working to preserve foci of Portuguese civilization." [155]

We doubt that Angola has a civilization that is only Portuguese and not also Angolan, or at least Luso-Angolan. [156] Secondly, it is not Brazil's role to defend the remnants of Portuguese culture in Malabar, Goa, Ceylon, and China. Either that culture has strength and will survive, or it will die, with or without the aid of our Ministry of Foreign Affairs.

---

[155] *Boletim No. 302,* Ministério de Relações Exteriores, April 18, 1962.
[156] Examination of the work of Castro Soromenho, an Angolan novelist, will prove the falsity of the thesis. See Alfredo Margarido's study, "Castro Soromenho," in *Estudos Ultramarinos,* No. 3, 1959, 125–139.

On his trip to Europe in May, 1962, perhaps with such defense in mind, perhaps only with the thought of helping Portugal undo the Gordian knot of its foreign policy, Foreign Minister San Tiago Dantas during his stop in Lisbon held conversations with Minister Franco Nogueira at the special invitation of the Portuguese government. This beginning was "a demonstration of Portugal's interest in creating new perspectives on its relations with Brazil" and had as its objective the examination of "points of discord between positions assumed by Brazil and Portugal on the international level and in relations between the two countries." [157]

Luso-Brazilian relations are indeed creating difficulties in the formulation of our African policy. Our international politics of a multilateral nature in the United Nations and our bilateral Luso-Brazilian diplomacy are not creatively inspired, but rather are stagnated by archaism and lack of conformity on the part of the Portuguese elite, which is to this day exhausted by its efforts in the sixteenth century. What does Portugal do? It threatens to break with everyone, to withdraw from international organizations, the United Nations, NATO. Yet what it sought for in the last was Atlantic solidarity that would permit it to impose its order and rule in Angola without consulting the South Atlantic nations and without respect for the Treaty of Consultation, with which we, according to the Itamarati's traditional internationalists, must comply when Angola is concerned. It has threatened not to renew the lease for the base in the Azores expiring in 1963 and is beginning to flirt with Red China,[158] with the hope that in an eventual conflict over border questions India may return Goa, just as Great Britain did on another occasion.

How can Brazil help Portugal? Certainly it will not influence the solution of Portuguese problems with sentimental or academic demonstrations, nor with the declarations of a handful of Brazilians, some of them seduced by the votes of Portuguese descendants or the financial support of the Colony, others enamored of decorations, and still others

---

[157] *Jornal do Brasil,* March 24, 1962.
[158] In the NATO conference of November, 1962, Portugal did not vote against Chinese aggression in India. See Agência Nacional de Informação report in *Notícias de Portugal,* Rio de Janeiro, November 22, 1962.

attached, as are the upper classes in Portugal, to oligarchies that do not want change here and therefore prefer to remain forever archaic internationally.

As *The New York Times* has said in connection with the Anglo-Portuguese Pact,[159] one must distinguish between harmonious mutual interests in Western Europe and interests in other parts of the world where the two countries are taking different courses of action. We must say clearly that Brazil cannot support Portugal everywhere in the world. Luso-Brazilian relations will not be improved for our mutual benefit by imprudent declarations, on the part of Brazilian legislators here or passing through Lisbon, of Brazilian sympathy with Portuguese colonialism. These visits succeed one another with unaccustomed frequency and without the discretion advisable under present Brazilian policy and demanded by the historical process; this reveals the lack of harmony between these men and the country's socio-political reality. Similarly, and with the approval of the President of the Federação das Associações Portuguêsas no Brasil, Mr. Aventino Lage has on his repeated visits to Portugal stated again and again that "Brazil is unhesitatingly on the side of Portugal."[160]

How so, and to what extent? These are the questions raised by such declarations contradicting the present line of our foreign policy. The Portuguese government is aware of our anticolonial position. In his speech to the National Assembly on January 3, 1962, Salazar himself said that "Anticolonialism is a constant in Brazilian policy." He recognizes, too, that the Community cannot be limited to the timid inspiration of sentimental messages alone. It should be directed toward the broadest kind of international organization.

Although Portuguese leadership considers itself internationally inclined because of Portuguese possessions on several continents, it has always defended European supremacy because this represented its own supremacy over colonies and former colonies. At this moment of crisis in the inescapable and inevitable trial of colonialism, the Portuguese government continues to declare itself the defender of the West and of European supremacy, "a unique example in Europe of resistance to the

---

[159] Transcribed in *Jornal do Brasil,* January 5, 1962.
[160] *Notícias de Portugal,* Nos. 752 and 770, September 30, 1961, and February 3, 1962.

so-called tides of history." Recently, the academician Augusto de Castro greeted his colleague, Elmano Cardim, by naming "Brazil, which is more Atlantic than American, the Europe of the New Continent." There is no more select example of academic barbarism.

Portugal's new direction is that of integration into the economy of Europe by means of the Common Market, which has triumphed over the European Free Trade Association. No one questions its right to do so, but in that case, the Portuguese government really does not seek to forge a Luso-Brazilian economic community, and the Treaty of Friendship obliges Brazil to consult Portugal only when the latter's interests are at stake, as in its colonies, and not when its own are threatened, as by the Common Market discrimination against Brazil, or when Portugal calls upon NATO forces to take action off our beaches in the South Atlantic.

From the political point of view the two countries are divided by their common language. First, as I have already said, because self-determination and anticolonialism are principles of our foreign policy that we cannot put aside when dealing with Portugal merely through sentimentality, which should never have any influence in this area. Second, because if the Community has served Portuguese interests only, and clashes internally in its own bilateral politics, how can it create policy with respect to the world? Portuguese obstinacy has accepted no Brazilian suggestion in problems that arise in the United Nations.

I do not believe that the Portuguese people resent the stronger position held by Brazil today in the Portuguese-speaking world. But I do believe that the haughty upper classes in Portugal will not swallow this pill. I recall that on my last trip to Portugal in 1960 a prominent lawyer told me that Brazilian politicians did not deserve the confidence of the Portuguese government, and for this reason no progress was being made in the formation of the Community. We were at that time under the complete domination of Juscelino Kubitschek and Horácio Láfer, precisely those who made the greatest concessions to Portuguese colonialism and its autocratic regime. President Kubitschek wanted to grant still more than he did, and his plans, which seemed in opposition to the Itamarati itself, were suspended during the Quadros administration. After leaving his post, where he supervised routine matters, in contrast to the Catete which handled important affairs, Horácio Láfer wrote: "I noted how wise and just was the Itamarati's traditional foreign policy with respect to [Portugal]." [161]

Later, on a trip to Portugal in January, 1963, ex-President Kubitschek went further and stated, according to the news services, that the best foreign policy for Brazil would be to favor Portugal. "Personally I feel that Brazil can have only one foreign policy: whatever best suits Portuguese interests." Still more clearly and precisely, he added, "even when I was President of the Republic, I never differentiated between Brazilian and Portuguese foreign policy." "The distinctions between Brazil and Portugal will eventually be wiped out," he concluded. I do not know if the ex-President was not overstepping himself and contemplating the future association of Portugal with our Federation as a twenty-third state.

When Juscelino Kubitschek arrived in Brazil he belittled these statements, attributing them to moments of gallantry when, more Oliveira than Kubitschek,[162] he felt himself glow in sympathy with Portugal. It would have been preferable to have spoken seriously. Moreover he was often disloyal to his country's history, forgetting, for example, the blood of Tiradentes and of many patriots of 1817 and the War of Independence when he said that freedom "cost us no sacrifice, but rather was a gift of the Portuguese Crown. This gift was the most powerful link uniting the two nations." But the height of madness was reached in this statement: "As there is so much talk internationally about self-determination, it is opportune to recall that Brazilian self-determination clearly and significantly includes the right to be a nation of Portuguese. We are not Portuguese through choice, but because we are the product and glory of the creative genius of Portugal." [163] No, Sr. Kubitschek, we are not Portuguese; rather we are Brazilians, exclusively.

The unreality, fantasy, and false rhetoric of such declarations prove, once again, how Brazil's African policy is hamstrung by the persistence of certain factions in our public life in thinking that to help Portugal is to collaborate in its archaic vision of the world and to strengthen

---

[161] "Suplemento especial dedicado a Portugal," *O Globo,* Rio de Janeiro, December 9, 1961, 30.
[162] In Portugal the ex-President is called Juscelino de Oliveira or Kubitschek de Oliveira, never simply Juscelino Kubitschek.
[163] *Notícias de Portugal,* No. 820, January 19, 1963.

Salazar's colonialist position, instead of saying clearly and objectively that in order to be able to count on Brazil Portugal must review its international policy and make it more flexible. Furthermore, because truth and frankness are a virtue, we must say that economic and political reasons and Portugal's identification with Europe have created an area of friction that will not be removed by mere appeals to sentiment. The economic dependence of Portugal on Africa is making its problems more desperate. We are sorry, but we did not create them. They were the making of the dominant, oligarchic Portuguese groups that had no sense of history. A large empire, wrote Edward Gibbon, must be supported by an elaborate, oppressive police system. In view of Afro-Asian nationalism, the Mandarins of colonialism cannot discipline such a force. Without its Afro-Asian colonies [164] Portugal (92,150 sq. km., 9,500,000 pop.) will survive, as Holland (32,449 sq. km., 12,000,000 pop.) and Belgium (30,507 sq. km., 9,000,000 pop.) have survived. All that is needed is a popular progressive movement to shape and follow a progressive policy.

While Juscelino Kubitschek was speaking in Lisbon, Brazil was already deciding by popular vote to return to presidentialism, and the New Foreign Minister, Sr. Hermes Lima, who took office on September 24, 1962 during Parliamentarism, and was confirmed in the Presidential regime on January 25, 1963, having been a Socialist and Laborite, was executing a moderate policy, vigorously trying to avoid radicalism while stimulating somewhat less vigorously a left of center policy. This position, which may not please either extreme Rightists or Leftists and which causes deep fears and suspicions among rigid conservatives because of the Minister's former ideological affiliations, is extremely important today. This is owing not only to Brazil's conciliatory role in the field of disarmament negotiations but also to its recent behavior in international organizations, offering bold proposals with a view to removing the last international privileges that make rich countries richer and poor countries poorer. Moreover, moderation will facilitate negotiations to improve socio-economic conditions in the

---

[164] Not included are the Madeira archipelago (740 sq. km., 270,000 plus pop.) and the Azores (2,388 sq. km., 300,000 plus pop.), which even in the United Nations classification are not considered colonies, as per Resolution No. 1,542 of the Fifteenth General Assembly.

underdeveloped world. Combating political colonialism is not enough, for Portugal is the only country to resist and its resistance cannot long persist, the modern enemy is economic colonialism, which continues to suck the people's blood on several continents, especially those of the South in Sir Oliver Frank's classification.

Brazil has carried on a vigorous struggle in the field of economic development, and radicalism will not make it easier to find solutions that will be supported by capitalism as well as socialism. This policy has been maintained independent of successive changes of ministers. Minister Hermes Lima, much criticized on all sides, because of either the paralysis from which our Foreign Office suffered under his management, when it was occupied with purely routine matters, or his lack of the imagination required to overcome accumulated difficulties, does not seem interested in making it more dynamic. The presidential message, which expresses his thought also, limits itself to reaffirming our anticolonial ideas. "We have recognized and shall continue to recognize the right of independence for all colonial peoples and the obligation of colonial and administrative powers to accelerate preparations for their independence, *including Angola and other Portuguese overseas territories, as well as South-West Africa.* Brazil however considers it most important that the new states be able to count on the collaboration of the powers that formerly administered them, and that this collaboration be done in orderly fashion so as to preserve their unity and the authority of the central government, and to give them guarantees that will permit them to defend themselves from insidious forms of economic or ideological neo-colonialism." [165]

Several newspapers stated that the reference to Angola was made against the wishes of the Minister, who, quite annoyed and attributing it to presidential aides, cut it from a later edition of the same message, in which there is indeed no reference to Angola and Portuguese overseas territories. The weakness of the Minister, who is much influenced by Ambassador Negrão de Lima and by ties with Portugal (?), gave rise to great enthusiasm in Portugal, where headlines proclaimed that the

---

[165] *Mensagem ao Congresso Nacional*, Brasília, 1963, p. 161. Omission of the words "including Angola and other Portuguese overseas territories, as well as South-West Africa" in the second printing of the same message merely required widening the spaces between lines slightly without otherwise altering the page.

hostile remark, introduced inadvertently, had brought forth an explanation from the Brazilian government. A case such as this is extremely rare in our diplomatic affairs. First, because of the contradiction in documents; second, because the second printing created an embarrassing situation; third, because the deletion represented an enormous setback in Brazilian foreign policy, which had recently freed itself from the sentimental pressures of the Colony and the political pressures of reactionary national groups and requests from Portuguese government; fourth, because the blunder actually exposed itself, or at least, explained officially what had happened. I do not believe that in Brazilian diplomatic history there is any more blatant example of tepidity and vacillation, considerate of the personal feelings of the Minister but insensitive to the dignity of the country and the anticolonial policy that had been adopted and affirmed by the Minister himself as co-author of the message and in a lecture delivered at the Brazilian War College.[166]

Moreover, the paragraph that was cut suggests that the collaboration of the administrative powers in the process toward independence is indispensable, a strange idea; such collaboration had generally good results in the English colonies but was a failure in the Congo and impossible in Algeria and will hardly be possible in South-West Africa or the Portuguese colonies. Originating in Brazil, this new form of liberation is contrary to American and even Brazilian tradition. Independence now is thought of as an orderly process; that would be contrary to history and an excuse for Portugal and South Africa to postpone indefinitely the aspirations of Angola and South-West Africa. There is little else to add, except to mention the decrees on September 29 and December 3, 1962, decorating a number of Portuguese personalities; it is to our credit that on the first of these dates the embassy in Algeria was created.

It must be said that in his first speech as Secretary-General for Foreign Affairs, Ambassador Henrique Rodrigues Vale made no positive statement on African policy. He limited himself to affirming that "with underdeveloped nations in general our objectives are economic development and social progress, and we must therefore continue to strengthen our relations with them, especially with those whose voice

---

[166] *Boletim No. 308*, Ministério de Relações Exteriores, March 25, 1963.

in international conferences will give our just claims greater weight." [167]
Just as caution and chicken broth hurt no one, so the words of the
Secretary-General both affirm and deplore relations with the underdeveloped world, forgetting or pretending to forget the opposition between seeking Afro-Asian support indispensable to plans for development and refusing to oppose Portuguese colonial policy.

In conclusion, Brazil became passionately interested in freedom for
Africa, felt that it should stand by Africa at this time, conceived a policy
of coöperation and friendship for Africa, and President Jânio Quadros
made the first gestures, spoke the first words, took the first steps.
Minister Afonso Arinos believed that Brazil had a role to play in Africa
that would serve as a link between the West and Africa and placed his
intelligence and combativeness at its disposal; with dignity he confronted violent, unjust, pitiless criticism and with the President helped
to formulate this policy initially. Jânio Quadros' message, on which he
collaborated and which is the first and only statement to outline a plan
of action, recognized that Brazil has an undeniable debt to the African
people and that a prosperous and stable Africa is an essential condition
for the security and development of Brazil. The seven months Quadros
was in office did not provide an opportunity for more. Vacillation in the
case of Angola and consultations with Lisbon were Quadros' weakness.
Minister San Tiago Dantas' strength lay precisely in the stand to
abandon support of Portugal's African policy and not to ask Lisbon's
advice, and it fell to Afonso Arinos, then in the United Nations, to carry
out his instructions, and the vote was truly historical. Minister Hermes
Lima's unjustified withdrawal was illustrated by his insistence on
avoiding so much as a reference to Angolan liberty in an official
document. The backward step will compromise Afro-Brazilian relations, and is another sign that we really do not yet have an African
policy. In this regard Portugal still has us on a leash, and we are torn
and bewildered by its contradictions, its archaism, its decrepitude.
Which means a counterbalancing of Brazil's image upon the international scene today and some of its bold plans and reforms.

The military and anti-communist coup of 1964 was a total repudiation of the foreign policy in effect since 1960. That independent policy

---

[167] *Boletim No. 476, ibid.*, May 21, 1963.

was considered subversive, and so Brazil returned to the uncondi-
tional support of Western policy under the leadership of the United
States. The government manifested a disinterest in the African policy
Quadros proclaimed and contrary to recent practice gave full support to
Portuguese policies in Africa.

BRAZILIAN POLICY IN THE UNITED NATIONS:
COLONIAL QUESTIONS [168]

Having participated in the Conference of the International Organization of United Nations, held in San Francisco between April and June
of 1945, Brazil is a founding member of the United Nations. In that
meeting the Brazilian delegation limited itself to the support of general
principles, such as the universality of the organization, expansion of the
General Assembly's powers, extension of the jurisdiction and competence of the World Court of Justice, creation of a Social and Economic
Council, retention of the regional system for solution of inter-American
controversies, and Latin American representation on the Security
Council. It supported also the principle of nonintervention and, by
means of the revision including the world "health" in Article 55,
collaborated in founding the World Health Organization. It did not
participate, however, in the debates on colonial questions that were the
basis of Chapters XI, XII, and XIII of the United Nations Charter [169]
dealing with colonial territories, the international tutelage system, and
tutelage council.

At that time there was no Brazilian public awareness regarding
colonial problems, removed as we were from the Afro-Asian world; our
upper class, very much oriented toward Europe and the United States,
had lost interest in these questions, especially after we were led by President Bernardes' nationalism to withdraw in 1926 from the League of
Nations, where we had done the bidding of the great powers. Not
having followed the evolution of the mandate system, nor the important

[168] This study is based especially on reports of the Brazilian delegations to the
United Nations and United Nations documents.
[169] The Charter was signed on June 26, 1945, by fifty nations, among which twenty
were Latin American and five Arab. Ratification by Brazil took place on September 12, 1945. Brazil had already signed the Declaration of the United Nations on
January 8, 1943.

changes being accomplished in the colonial world by the Second World War, the ruling minority in Brazil, with their very continental vision of the world and excessively juridical minds, did not demonstrate the least interest in the aspirations of colonial peoples. The "Declaration Relative to Colonial Territories" (Ch. XI, Arts. 73 and 74), a document of the greatest significance which proclaimed the importance of the interests of the inhabitants of these territories and affirmed the obligation of the administrators to assure their political, economic, social, and educational progress and to develop their capacity for self-government, was made without participation on the part of Brazil. In San Francisco as in the First Session in London (1946), Brazil remained aloof, indifferent to the problem, as it proposed the adoption of French and English as the official languages. The general principles of Article 73 of the United Nations Charter did not clash with the instructions to our delegates, who did not see that sooner or later Brazil either would be opposed to some of its traditional allies in Western Europe and obliged to declare itself anticolonial, in keeping with the aspirations of its people, or would vote in favor of the colonial and administrative powers, in accordance with its "elitist" diplomacy. This ambivalence, favoring colonialism because of the interests of Brazil's ruling classes and opposing it because of popular idealism and realism, has led us to compromise solutions, the most characteristic instrument of domestic politics in times of crisis since we became independent.[170] At that level Brazil and Latin America were already resentful of United States preference for reconstruction of Europe, to the detriment of underdeveloped countries dependent on exports of raw materials.

Not a word regarding colonialism, or rather, there was a clear conviction that favoring liberation would mean aggravating relations with the colonial powers, which were daily becoming more sensitive, especially France and Belgium. The fact that the Soviet Union and certain other members of the extreme wing had become the champions of anticolonialism, and the establishment of the cold war between the Western and Soviet blocs made adoption of a line critical of colonial administrative methods difficult. Such a line could lead to complexities unbefitting a conservative country which, although poor, underde-

---

[170] See José Honório Rodrigues, *Aspirações Nacionais,* São Paulo, 1963.

veloped, and with a population that had suffered long, was a defender of the status quo and through the insistence of a minority had always stood on the side of the "protectors," which rather than collaborate to overcome colonial difficulties were assisting in the reconstruction of nations proven to be insatiable instigators of destruction and world-wide slaughter. This respected and honorable position was an ideal in keeping with the traditions not of Brazil but of its elite. The latter would always play it safe on the familiar ground where privileges obtained through the support of colonial powers might be retained. Whether or not some of the members of the Brazilian delegation had a more liberal philosophy, a broader interpretation of the United Nations Charter regarding colonial territories, they had to remain faithful to instructions worked out here in secret conferences within the government and the Itamarati.

If domestic policy influences foreign policy, and vice versa, at that time our diplomacy was unquestionably controlled by ultra-conservatives led since 1947 by Minister Raul Fernandes, who behaved as though he were a viceroy dominated by legalism and alienated from national reality. When, for example, the treatment given Hindus in the Union of South Africa was being discussed, Brazil supported the South African government's suggestion to submit the case to the World Court of Justice and joined Belgium in attempting to find a conciliatory juridical solution, which was opposed by India; and as we saw earlier the question is still unresolved. In accordance with the thought that juridical solutions are always best, even when adopted in a political institution, Brazil supported also the Arab proposal to submit the question of Palestine to the World Court.

In the Third Assembly in 1948, Sr. Raul Fernandes, who at the Paris Conference in 1950 would again prove to be more concerned with Italian damages than with ours, decided that Brazil should oppose the British proposal for studies on the future of Italy's former colonies in Africa. The question was postponed, and in 1949 France, Brazil, and the Latin American nations (except Haiti) advocated return of the former colonies to Rome, thus again opposing the British plan and the Arab-Asian bloc. It was India that defeated the proposal of Italian tutelage for Tripolitania and Libya.

The proposal for a resolution giving the members of the United

Nations a free hand in their diplomatic relations with Spain—authored by Minister Raul Fernandes, again, in opposition to the Polish proposal that imposed greater restrictions—does not fall within the province of this study, but it is another milestone in his career of making Brazil serve interests that are not its own. Mexico opposed the Brazilian proposal, characterizing it as an attempt to oblige the United Nations to adjust their conduct to that of a small number of states, whereas the correct thing would be to compel those states to follow the recommendations of the United Nations. Furthermore, in the question of the treatment of Hindus in South Africa, Brazil supported the French proposal asking that the two governments discuss the matter, but it did not approve inclusion of a reference to the Declaration of the Rights of Man.

In 1950, when the Itamarati was still under the direction of Minister Raul Fernandes, one of our delegates, Sr. Vicente Rau, who is well known for his Fascist sympathies, congratulated himself and Belgium "for the noble as well as courageous measures that it has just adopted with a view to the general progress of native peoples." We have seen how those noble and courageous measures resulted in the tragedy of the Congo. It was significant that the Brazilian delegate should flatter himself on measures favoring Belgian settlers, yet also praise the enlightened policy of the Colonial Office on the forthcoming concession of dominion status to the Gold Coast (later Ghana) and on progress realized in Nigeria.

Much friction was caused by the interpretation of Article 73e of the Charter, according to which the administrative powers of non-autonomous territories were to transmit regularly to the Secretary-General statistical and other technical information relative to the economic, social, and educational conditions of the territories for which they were responsible. From the beginning the Soviet bloc considered transmission of such information obligatory, and the administrative and colonial powers always considered it voluntary. The problem arose for the first time in 1946 when France, Great Britain, and the United States stopped sending information. At that time it was preferred not to attempt to define "non-autonomous territory" and, in response to the Secretary-General's inquiry, to be content with listing in Resolution 66 (I) those territories so designated by the administrative powers. Although they considered such a demand intervention by the United Nations in affairs within their own exclusive competence, the administrative powers continued to supply the information, trying however to reduce to a minimum the supervisory and regulatory function of the international organization, performed through an Information Committee composed of an equal number of colonial and noncolonial powers. This committee, of which Brazil has always been a member, was at first ad hoc in nature but became permanent in 1949.[171]

Again in 1949, in the Fourth Session of the Assembly, there was an interruption of reports on the part of some powers, and discussion took place concerning what elements should be taken into account to determine whether or not a territory had attained a complete degree of self-government. The tendency of each metropolis was to give its own definition and exempt itself from giving information. The Assembly decided [172] that the United Nations should be kept informed of any constitutional change that might make transmission of reports unnecessary.[173] The 200,000,000 inhabitants of non-autonomous territories, however, required more responsible vigilance by the United Nations, and the Assembly therefore resolved that it should give its opinion on criteria adopted by the member states to define such territories. Following which, again to the protests of the administrative powers, the Information Committee was charged to study what factors should be taken into account to ascertain whether or not a territory had attained self-government.

At that time Minister Raul Fernandes suggested that our guide on the subject of colonialism should be an article by P. O. Lapie published in the *Revue des Deux Mondes*.[174] Lapie said that the colonial problem had acquired capital importance in the last Assembly and that normal exercise of competence by the Fourth Commission (Trusteeship Council) obliged France to take a stand in order to save the French Union. France could not allow the sending of reports to become a means of control over all the non-autonomous territories that it administered,

---

[171] Resolution 332 (IV), December 2, 1949.
[172] Resolution 222 (III), 1948.
[173] Thesis defended when Holland stopped reporting on the Dutch West Indies and Surinam, alleging that constitutional changes had been introduced there.
[174] "L'Union Française devant l'O.N.U.," January 1, 1950, 443–456.

much less its overseas territories or Algeria, which was a French *département*. Lapie went on to say that a hostile atmosphere prevailed in the Fourth Commission, inspired not only by the Soviets but also by the United States and South America; most of these countries, former colonies, voted against those that they called colonizers; he further criticized American diplomacy and said that the countries of South America (always the vague designation, treating us *en masse*, just as for Americans there is only Latin America) "listen to us, like us, pay us compliments, and vote against us." He understood the anticolonial atmosphere dominating South America since the Bogotá Conference, but it was necessary "to make those states aware that if they want our friendship, they must not insist." The thoughts of a Latin civilization on the other side of the Atlantic through extension of the French language and improvement of humanity inspired by French liberty and France's political maturity, should inspire these states to collaborate in a reconciliation between the United Nations and the French Union.

This program was considered intelligent advice on which to formulate the instructions that eventually oriented Brazilian action in the United Nations. Minister Raul Fernandes, still convinced of the superiority of Latin-French thought, with little or no faith in national roots and with no historical vision, and unhesitatingly persuaded that modern political maturity belongs to Europe—which frequently makes use of disguised or undisguised forms of dictatorship, while it accuses Latin America of practicing it—would adopt this colonial position and thus compromise Brazil in the United Nations.

We remained, therefore, on the side of European political maturity, which was well financed ($12,000,000,000 in 1948–1950 alone) and growing stronger through colonial exploitation. But, at the same time, on November 22, 1950, a Brazilian representative took the liberty of disregarding the Minister's views and voting in the face of objections from the colonial powers for a declaration of the suitability of establishing special commissions. He did not fail to make clear that Brazil was not engaging in irresponsible criticism, nor did it wish to introduce sudden and dangerous changes in the political structure of non-autonomous territories. If the objectives of the administrative powers are identical to those of the Charter, he declared, it was difficult to understand their persistent rejection of certain measures of outside supervision. His language of special deference to the colonial powers, despite the stand taken against their interests, was a precaution against possible censure by the Ministry.

One cannot but note the difference separating the international position of Getúlio Vargas' government in 1951–1954 and that of the Café Filho administration in 1955 when one of the greatest regressions in Brazilian domestic and international politics took place. Raul Fernandes' conservatism before and after Getúlio Vargas meant greater coöperation with the colonial powers, while Vargas inspired an anticolonialism that was idealistic but inefficient and hampered, to be sure, by our association with Portugal.

It is true that in the Fifth Session of the General Assembly (1950) Brazil supported the thesis of economic development and full employment, not only invoking the idea of world economic coöperation but also pointing out the risk to the economies of underdeveloped countries resulting from lack of opportunity for new investments. The simple absence of the symbol of Brazilian conservatism in the post of foreign minister permitted the support of such moderate views; but this did not signify defeat—not through deficiencies within the Brazilian diplomatic corps, but because of the conservative orientation of the ministers—of the stubbornly unimaginative and indecisive outlook characteristic of Brazilian policy in the United Nations, especially in colonial questions.

But progress could be noted in 1953 when the important Resolution No. 742 (VIII, November 27) was drawn up defining the factors that should be considered in determining whether or not a territory had attained self-government, and the Brazilian delegation approved it. The precise definition demanded great effort and our delegation gave special attention to the requirement of express desire on the part of territorial peoples to verify whether or not they had acquired the autonomy that would dispense with United Nations supervision. The opinion of the people, freedom of choice, unlimited sovereignty, self-government, ethnic and cultural conditions, and eligibility in the United Nations were some of these factors. And even more important because of its consequences, Brazil would maintain that in economic, social, and educational matters the administrative powers should always act as extra-territorial powers so long as the inhabitants did not participate in choosing the political authority responsible for them.[175]

Even the Trusteeship Council suffered the consequences of antagonism between Western and Soviet groups and between the administrators and the non-administrators, the former always defending their own interests and the latter attacking colonialism. The Western nations, especially the United States, were long in breaking this identification. Although their colonialism was mitigated by an occasional concession or advance, always under the leadership of Great Britain, which demonstrated a proper understanding of contemporary reality, the administrative nations were essentially conservative. They agreed to accept the recommendations of the United Nations but, when it came to carrying them out, they did not wish to relinquish their prerogatives. Abolition of corporal punishment in non-autonomous territories is a case in point. Flogging in British, French, and Belgian zones had been condemned and its immediate abolition recommended in several resolutions (323 of the Fourth Session, November 15, 1949, and 440 of the Fifth Session, December 2, 1950), yet Great Britain, France, Belgium, and Australia, which administered various trust territories as well, continued to apply it and justify it by local conditions. In the Sixth Session the Brazilian delegation offered a proposal for complete abolition of corporal punishment. But as France presented an identical proposal our delegate, Sra. Rosalina Coelho Lisboa, withdrew hers and praised that country and Europe also in the most ridiculous, exaggerated, and pompous terms on behalf of the elite that she represented.

Another example of the administrative powers' conservatism is the case of the recommendations concerning the inadvisability of strengthening administrative ties between the trust territories and the contiguous colonial dependencies. The United Nations Charter placed preparation for self-government and independence among the basic objectives of the trust system. The administrative authorities agreed but continued to govern these territories by the same methods with which they administered colonial territories, apparently preferring to add the former to the latter and considering "dangerous" haste in reaching the

---

[175] *United Nations, General Assembly, A/2556,* November 17, 1953.

objective of self-government and independence. In the Fifth Session in 1950 Sr. Vicente Rau had declared that administrative ties were permissible if they were not incompatible with Article 76 of the Charter,[176] and if the trusteeship agreements did not threaten the territorial integrity of trust territories or contradict the supervisory powers of the United Nations. In accordance with this juridical opinion, in 1952 Brazil proposed that the World Court of Justice should give its opinion on the compatibility of administrative ties and the Charter and trusteeship agreements; it later withdrew this proposal, however—perhaps under pressure from the administrative powers, which were very resentful of criticism in the General Assembly. Dissatisfied with the Trusteeship Council's moderate attitude, the non-administrative countries, including Brazil, voted in turn on a proposed resolution making possible participation in the work of the Council by the native inhabitants of trust territories.

Brazilian coöperation in the affairs of the trust territories was more active, although almost always obeying a juridical formula and soliciting the opinion of the World Court of Justice. For example, the Ewe, an ethnic group imported in large numbers in the seventeenth century whose imprint may be seen in popular Brazilian myths, folklore, and stories,[177] were distributed through French and British administrative zones in Togoland and wished to be united. Brazil supported Resolution No. 555 of the Sixth Session, January 18, 1952, which called for an urgent study and the presentation of a report with specific recommendations embodying the real desires and interests of the people in question.

Brazil has always taken a coherent stand also in the fight for economic development. In 1951, seconded by Greece, it proposed a resolution that an effort be made through international financial institutions to expand the financing of underdeveloped countries, facilitating long-term loans to them at low interest rates for the solution of their basic problems. In 1952, further supporting projects for development, such as the creation of the Special United Nations Fund for Economic Development, the Brazilian delegation received instructions

---

[176] Defining the basic objectives of the Trusteeship System.

[177] See Artur Ramos, *As Culturas Negras no Brasil, O Negro Brasileiro,* São Paulo, 1946, 299–306.

to back Chile and India in the plan to create a special fund for economic development, and to oppose the system of raising funds on the basis of universal participation, "as it is contradictory to link the contribution of countries lacking such funds to that of countries endowed with an excess of funds available for capitalization." In justification of this stand it was said that "the American thesis that the development of underdeveloped countries must be financed by private capital is in part false, as this type of capital does not circulate internationally for application in basic industries that benefit the public, which produce little profit although they are the point of departure for any program of economic development; and this thesis is in part unacceptable to the underdeveloped countries because when private capital moves internationally, it always does so toward the exploitation of raw materials, such as petroleum and mineral products, that affects the national income of the investing country while the country receiving the investment tends to remain in a colonial position"; and, "therefore, only government capital or credit from an international organization can be used to pull underdeveloped economies from the stagnant if not regressive state in which they find themselves"; and, finally, "the World Bank must make loans only for specific projects, on bases still not completely divorced from those on which commercial and investment banks extend credit, there being, then, a place for an international organization."

With these ideas and action favoring the financing of economic development for underdeveloped countries, Brazil led a fight serving the then underdeveloped and those that when freed from trusteeship or colonialism would later swell the ranks of the underdeveloped. This fight always encountered opposition from capital-exporting countries, which would be the first to contribute to the Special United Nations Fund for Economic Development.

The return of Getúlio Vargas in 1951 gave greater liberal and social content to the instructions sent our delegation, leading it to abandon its rigid conservatism. The Moroccan and Tunisian questions began then to dominate the interest of the General Assembly. After 1946 the nationalistic aspirations of these two French protectorates created grave international tension, and in the United Nations the Arab countries made strenuous efforts to have French violations of the principles of the Charter and Declaration of the Rights of Man placed on the Assembly's agenda. The Franco-Moroccan and Franco-Tunisian conflicts became explosive subjects, and in the face of demands from the people and governments of those territories, France declared that it could not discuss such questions and that foreign interference would be disastrous to negotiations.

Indeed, Tunisia had been changing gradually from a protectorate into a French colony. It is enough to cite one example of the method used by the French to take possession of the best lands. Thousands of acres of tillable soil had been classified arbitrarily as forests and placed under state control; a second law reclassified the "forests" as tillable soil and distributed them among the French settlers. The method of "legal forests" was to delight our jurists, supporters of the French status quo and foreign policy. Stimulated by such sleight of hand, the nationalist movement grew so that in 1950 Schuman stated that "independence is the ultimate goal of all territories in the French Union."

In Brazil we had been using the old trick of maintaining that there were two parts to the equation: on the one hand, an interest in preserving the peace and security of North Africa, which could be done only by strengthening the position of France; on the other, a just desire for the emancipation of peoples under foreign sovereignty. Brazil had every sympathy for such desires, but our traditional ties, our interests, were with France. This was the train of thought in the Itamarati under Sr. Raul Fernandes, who always confused the traditions and interests of the nation with his submissiveness and interests as a great international lawyer. It was Lourival Fontes, Head of the Civil House under President Vargas, who solved the equation. "Peace and security in North Africa are permanently threatened so long as France does not adopt effective, concrete measures to satisfy the minimal claims of the Tunisians. Continuation of the present situation can only aggravate conditions of insecurity and agitation in North Africa. Thus Brazil must give its support to any plan tending to move the French government to resolve the situation by means of concessions capable of satisfying the Tunisians and consequently of insuring the return of Africa to the peaceful climate indispensable to the security of the Western world." The same applied to Morocco. The fact is that Brazil really took a firm stand. In the debate Brazil insisted, with Chile and China, that there was an uninterrupted tradition of allowing any item for discussion, and that in view of the nature of the dispute and the importance of the countries involved, discussion was especially needed.

On April 14 five members (Brazil, China, Chile, Pakistan, and the Soviet Union) voted in favor of including the Tunisian question on the Security Council's agenda. Only France and Great Britain were opposed, but with Greece, the Low Countries, Turkey, and the United States abstaining discussion was prevented. France continued to maintain, as Portugal would later maintain, that jurisdiction over the matter was strictly domestic and that the intervention of the United Nations could only contribute to the encouragement of strife in a vital region and weaken the West. It was Brazil's task to promote the necessary understanding to obtain approval of Resolution No. 611, which word for word reproduced the Brazilian proposal (VII, December 17, 1952) expressing confidence that the French government would make an effort to promote real development of free institutions among the people of Tunisia, and the hope that the interested parties would continue negotiations with a view to granting self-government to Tunisia, carry on relations, and compose their differences in accordance with the spirit of the Charter, abstaining from any act that might aggravate the present tension. Despite the discretion of the French, Arabs, and Asians, the political significance of the act was enormous; the first thus avoided the possibility of drastic measures of United Nations intervention, and the Arabs and Asians obtained recognition of United Nations competence and assured discussion of this and similar problems there.

Independence, granted by France in 1956, was promoted more by the nationalists' struggle than by the resolutions of the Assembly, where the case was again discussed in 1953 in a less heated atmosphere.

The French protectorate in Morocco was a result of European bargaining over colonial possessions; it was extremely lucrative for French industry and an important strategic point in providing incentive and vitality to French morale. Using the old imperialistic argument that the Moroccan people were incapable of self-government and that Morocco would fall back into barbarism if France should abandon it, as Portugal continues to affirm with respect to its colonies, the French statesmen had to face the nationalist struggle of which the 1952 conflicts in Casablanca were only one episode. The gravity of the situation brought the case before the Assembly and, as in the case of Tunisia, it was not easy to have the subject placed on the agenda or arrive at a resolution expressing the general opinion. The Egyptian *Memorandum* of October, 1951, after referring to the conflict between France and Morocco and the Moroccan nationalist claims, requested the Secretary-General to bring the question to the knowledge of the Assembly. The debate became heated with the declarations of the Moroccan nationalist leaders and the support given by several Arab countries to the Egyptian proposal. The question was postponed due to French opposition, supported by Canada and the United States.

In September, 1952, thirteen member states of the Arab-Asian group requested inclusion of the "Moroccan Question" in the agenda of the General Assembly. They declared that the negative attitude of the United Nations was jeopardizing the legitimate interests of the Moroccan people, and that the French were not only disregarding their promises but still using old methods and procedures that were not in harmony with the present situation and the nationalist claims. Moreover, the Universal Declaration of Human Rights was being violated. The French delegation adopted the same negative attitude that it had had on the Tunisian question: the matter was under the strict domestic jurisdiction of the member state. The debate, which took place one week after discussion of the Algerian question, was conducted with greater knowledge of political forces, and the parties involved knew that a resolution would be adopted. Again the Brazilian delegation presented the approved resolution, with slight modification in this case for greater emphasis on the aspiration of self-government, in view of the difference established by the French between Tunisia and Morocco.

The Arab-Asian plan was rejected (25–27, with three abstentions) with the support of the United States, which was greatly influenced by French pressure and concerned with the strategic situation in North Africa, and the Brazilian plan was approved 45–3 (Belgium, Luxembourg, and Union of South Africa), with eleven abstentions (Resolution 612, VII, December 19, 1952). The difference between the resolutions on Tunisia and Morocco was that the second did not speak of self-determination or self-government, but only of promoting basic freedoms and developing free institutions.

Again the Brazilian action had great political significance and represented progress in the treatment of colonial questions, not only in relation to Brazil's own foreign policy but in relation to United Nations competence and activity in the future liquidation of colonialism. Morocco obtained its freedom in 1956. There is no doubt that, along with nationalist action and better French comprehension, the United Nations resolution refusing to endorse French policy, yet not wounding its pride, forewarned the government in Paris and gave it the great responsibility of promoting a liberal program of political reforms.

Although moderate, the Brazilian position was really an advance compared with its previous phase and with the future phase when the steadiest and most solid figure in conservatism, inspired by Lapie, should return. Though twice defeated, he had led and would lead us to the lukewarm policy of colonial alliances. Although more liberal because with regard to the Arab countries it aimed at the establishment of self-government, our policy vacillated on the question of trusteeship and colonial territories, especially in Africa. In 1952 the instructions still read that in colonial affairs "the Brazilian representative should dwell preferably on progress made rather than criticize deficiencies," in order "not to offend certain countries that are traditionally friends of Brazil." The directives were not very coherent, not only because of the conflict between the position taken in the case of Tunisia and Morocco and the complacent attitude vis-à-vis the administrative powers in Dark Africa, but because in the Committee on Human Rights Brazil voted in favor of the proposed resolution maintaining the principle of self-determination and recognized that establishment of the right of self-determination should be promoted in non-autonomous territories. Further, we were trying to avoid the issue with the Union of South Africa: we voted in favor of the proposed resolution presented by the Arab countries creating a Committee of Good Offices charged with organizing and facilitating negotiations between the governments of the Union and India and Pakistan, so that they might find a satisfactory solution in the question of the treatment of persons of Hindu origin settled in the Union; and at the same time we dissented to the proposal presented by eighteen countries on the question of racial conflict in the Union because it was drawn up in terms that could be interpreted as undue interference in internal affairs.

It was in the Information Committee for Non-Autonomous Territories, when the report was being discussed and, later, during the debate on the factors to be taken into account to determine whether or not a territory is autonomous, that the Belgian representative wished to include in the interpretation of Chapter XI of the Charter the indigenous population of the member states. For Ryckmans and later Langenhove, this chapter aimed at protection of all underdeveloped ethnic groups, and it was unfair that only eight states submitted reports when "more than half of the United Nations have backward indigenous peoples in their territories." The Belgian thesis maintained that there was internal colonialism where elements or sectors of the native population were kept at an unfavorable political, social, economic, or cultural level. France, Great Britain, and the Low Countries, said Ryckmans, are obliged to furnish reports on their colonies in Guiana because they are territories administered by a metropolis. But "Brazilian Guiana" is administered from Rio and "Venezuelan Guiana" from Caracas, yet the United Nations do not keep informed on the fate of their people. The objective of the Congo "missionaries" was obvious: to invalidate the anticolonial position of the Latin American countries and threaten possible United Nations intervention in the domestic life of these nations populated by indigenous peoples.

The Brazilian reply, which was very juridical, based on the existing distinction between "separate collective groups in public law" by Professor E. Moresco and researched in *Recueil des Cours,* and very badly informed on Brazilian indigenous groups, was made by Senator Georgino Avelino, who stressed the difference between indigenous populations and those colonial populations to whose territories Article 73e of the Charter applied. But the Belgians insisted on their thesis and, during discussion of the question of factors determining whether or not a territory is autonomous, Ryckmans specifically mentioned the Brazilian Indians and our Service for Protection of the Indians, including Brazil, Venezuela, India, Malaya, Ethiopia, Liberia, Indonesia, and the Philippines among those countries that should be obliged to furnish information in accordance with Article 73e. The Brazilian delegation replied immediately, stating that the matter had nothing to do with the work of the Fourth Commission, and that if the proposal were repeated we should be obliged to ask that the intervention be declared out of order. In an attempt to explain his references, the Belgian delegate stated that he had not intended to criticize the states in question, but nevertheless insisted that his words could not be considered out of order. He then expressed his admiration for the work of Rondon, likening him to famous colonialists like Lyautey and Lugard. The Brazilian delegation replied that it was doubtful that General Rondon appreciated being included in a list of colonialists, however famous they might be. "We in Brazil have never thought of Rondon as an empire-builder or as a man who had the burden of taking white civilization to backward peoples on his shoulders." The Brazilian representative, Sérgio Armando Frazão, added that perhaps the Belgian delegate did not know that General Rondon was a famous Brazilian of Indian blood, and asked that he give the name of at least one colonialist linked racially with the people he colonized.

The Belgian thesis wished to equate the obligations of independent countries with regard to their underdeveloped population and those of the colonial powers with respect to their dependent territories, thus ignoring Article 73e of the Charter, which concerning the latter prescribed the basic obligation to stimulate the capacity for self-government and development of free political institutions; by doing so Belgium seemed to negate recognition of its political obligation toward the future of the Belgian Congo. Here the debate was much more solid and it made an essential point when it referred to the distinctions between the underdeveloped peoples of independent countries and those of colonial territories. The latter are subordinated to foreign, extra-national interests, while the underdeveloped peoples, among whom are not only indigenous groups but also those suffering the consequences of archaic economic structures, are being assimilated and integrated into national feeling and culture. It was a pity not to have said that the Brazilian indigenous population was only 0.2 per cent of the total and that, even if it were 55 per cent Indian and 44 per cent mestizo as in Guatemala and Bolivia, or 97, 90, and 86 per cent mestizo as in Paraguay, Honduras, and Nicaragua, its poverty would still reflect class conditions similar to those suffered by oppressed minorities and workers in Europe even at the peak of its imperialistic expansion. This does not signify domination by prejudices of racial superiority for the benefit of a foreign class such as the Europeans in Africa. Belgium's thesis received French and Australian support, although there was no danger that it would be accepted. Its aims were propagandistic and it sought especially to attack what was called the domestic, non-European colonialism practiced by the South Americans, who voted against colonialism yet were more backward in solving their minority problems than the colonial powers. The latter had supposedly done much for their colonial populations, but this was hardly demonstrated in the case of the Congo.[178]

Still attempting to attack the Latin American position, the Belgian representatives returned to the matter in 1953, now comparing Article 23b of the League of Nations Covenant [179] to Chapter XII of the United Nations Charter and inquiring: (1) if the Brazilian Indians were or were not protected by Article 23b of the Covenant; and (2) if when it signed the Charter Brazil "had taken that protection away from the Indians." The fantastic comparison between peoples dependent on a foreign sovereign metropolis and savage tribes that had not yet become integrated into the mass of the populations of sovereign states—made by the representative of a country of such divided peoples as Walloons and Flemish, Catholics and Protestants, bilingual, created in 1830 in the interests of the European balance of power, and pitilessly imperialistic—immediately received the reply that the Brazilian delegation did not recognize the right of any foreign representatives to discuss the legal status of Brazilian peoples.

Ryckmans did not again return to the subject, but Ambassador van Langenhove—author of several studies basic to the thesis and inspired by the colonialistic ideas of the conservative socialist P. O. Lapie, as was Sr. Raul Fernandes—gave the very same argument with which France and then Portugal had been defending retention of their colonies. "It is true," he said in December 1953, "that these peoples are part and parcel of the state possessing the territory where they live, but this is precisely the situation of the population of the Belgian Congo, which is part and parcel of the Belgian state." [180] The United Nations had a basic humanitarian duty not to permit continuation of this state of affairs

---

[178] See some examples of Belgian colonization in Theodore Draper, "Ordeal of the U.N.," *The New Leader* (November, 1960).

[179] "They assume the obligation of insuring equal treatment for indigenous populations in territories under their administration," Claude-Albert Colliard, *Droit International et Histoire Diplomatique,* Paris, 1948, text on 155–166, esp. 164.

[180] Among others, "Continuité de la Mission de Civilization," *Synthèses* (Brussels), VIII, No. 85.

(unprotected native populations), which represented a lamentable regression in international law.

Clearly, this thesis contained quite obvious colonialist implications, not only because of the strategy of attacking those who opposed colonialist interests, but also because it compared different things in order to defend the possession of colonies and negate the constitutionality of the Information Committee that was supervising the state of non-autonomous territories. The Belgian Congo was part and parcel of Belgium, as Algeria was of France and Angola of Portugal. When Ryckmans returned to his post in 1954, he received extremely violent replies from the Latin American delegations and a brief, ironic reply from Ambassador Heitor Lyra stating that the Brazilian Indians still lived under rather primitive conditions, "but it is to be hoped that within a few more years they will be as civilized as the rest of the Brazilian population. Consequently, we hope that in a short time any one of them may be able to take his seat in the United Nations, with citizens of the Belgian Congo as colleagues." [181] Indian and Negro mestizos have already been part of our delegation, but Congolese independence was required before its citizens could participate in the United Nations. The Belgian attack was not echoed, and they did not even succeed in carrying British and French reactionaries.

On August 26, 1954, at the peak of one of the greatest reactionary crises the country has known, which led Getúlio Vargas to commit suicide, Sr. Raul Fernandes returned to the Itamarati and with him Brazilian foreign policy took a different course. It was not recognition of social justice and the right to liberty and national independence that inspired Brazilian anticolonialism, but the conviction that only in this way would Soviet interests not be served: by destroying their pretext to

---

[181] At that time the population was 56,000,000, of which 5,000–6,000 were Indians, an extremely small number. Portuguese Indian policy was essentially one of extermination, and the national policy followed the same direction with slight modifications. The new Indian policy came about in 1910 under the influence of the Positivists (A. Comte), and the chief characteristic of the Service for Protection of the Indians, directed by General C. M. da Silva Rondon, consisted of non-violent intervention in the life, beliefs, and customs of the Indians. Exterminated for centuries and "representing only two per thousand of the Brazilian population, the Indians are today almost without expression in the nation as a whole and their problems cannot be considered national." See Darcy Ribeiro, *A Política Indigenista Brasileira,* Rio de Janeiro, Ministério da Agricultura, 1962.

attack the West's political and economic system. Brazil's stand, thought those who defined it, was moderate, recognized the interests and rights of powers administering non-autonomous territories, and abandoned inopportune anticolonial outbursts as "constitutionally improper and tactically self-defeating."

We were not to attack colonial powers but to give loyal collaboration freely to the member states which before the world community assumed responsibility for the political, economic, and social development of peoples who did not yet enjoy complete autonomy. The collaboration might involve criticism but, our delegation cautiously advised, in this they should see only the constructive aim of wholehearted coöperation. Considering that it said so little, the opening speech was full of embarrassment. Moreover, the Trusteeship Council criticized the attitude of the anticolonialists because it was thought to be dominated by exhibitionism, a desire for publicity, by resentment, although it was recognized that the colonial powers were ostensibly still attached to restrictive and legally contestable interpretations with regard to obligations assumed in the United Nations.

The apparent relief of international tension corresponded to a noticeable retreat on the part of the anticolonialists, not only from the extreme position—which Brazil never espoused as some Latin American nations did—but from the moderate, as in the case of Tunisia and Morocco, when Brazil, after authorizing the two proposed resolutions already mentioned, decided to follow the United States suggestion to approve nothing in view of the negotiations then in progress (completed in 1956).

In 1955, supported by Brazil and sixteen other nations, Portugal was seated in the United Nations. I do not know to what extent our representative was inspired by the new admissions when, speaking on the colonial question, he declared that all the Latin American countries had obtained their independence by insurrection and thus sympathized with those that demanded independence now. But, he warned, the role of the United Nations was to avoid any premature action that, once adopted, might one day be sorrowfully regretted. Real independence resulted from the natural growth of political institutions based on a solid economic and social structure. People had to mature and their institutions develop for independence to be a blessing. This very cautious position was a concession to all colonialists, especially Portugal which claims, as did France and Belgium, that decolonization is not feasible because of its colonies' unpreparedness. But the best means of being responsible is to have responsibility, as Macauley taught: "If men had to wait for liberty until they became wise and good in slavery, they would have to wait forever."

Our Ministry of Foreign Affairs would follow the same course of action in 1956. It was stated that the United Nations and the Economic and Social Council were divided into two groups, one of them "as colonialist as one can be in this age when, thanks precisely to the mechanism created by the San Francisco Charter, so many peoples have already emerged from their former colonial condition into free life. Brazil has been associated with this movement. And now, as in previous Assemblies, it has voted with the colonial powers. The other group "is led by India, and behind India are the Soviet Union and Red China. They lack coördination." Brazil, it was added, should not compromise with either group but become a factor for moderation and common sense. The Bandung group was accused of being based on racial prejudice and intolerance, and it was regretted that many Latin Americans had joined this group, thus introducing the spirit of Bandung into the Western Hemisphere. The Brazilian delegation believed that it was midway between the two and could assume conciliatory, impartial, and discreet attitudes. Thus, the old theory of conciliation and compromise was applied to foreign policy, where it has the same negative aspects as on the national level. It serves the wishes of the privileged and seeks to make the oppressed conform, and if conflict is avoided and the status quo perpetuated, it prevents or delays the victories of those who are dominated. Frequently, all it does is to prolong an extremely pointless checkmate or hurl irreconcilable extremes into war.[182] The result has been hesitancy, Brazilian conduct sometimes condemning South African action, sometimes abstaining in the Trusteeship Council on granting audience to the great defender of the Negro cause in that country, Rev. Michael Scott, and, finally, sometimes expressing perfect cordiality toward South Africa and stating that it wishes to maintain good relations with that nation.

---

[182] Concerning these aspects see José Honório Rodrigues, *Aspirações Nacionais*, São Paulo, 1963, esp. 20–21 and 114–115.

But, actually, Brazilian policy in the United Nations was clearly hindered by agreements with colonial powers and by requests from the diplomatic missions accredited in Brazil made at the last minute and requiring changes in previous instructions. In 1956 anticolonialism "penetrated the work of the Trusteeship Council, for every anticolonial bloc had the clearly stated impression that in each administrative authority there was an imperialism aiming at final absorption of the trust territory," and the Council made few exceptions to the "noble and meritorious work of the administrative authorities." Nothing could diminish praise for this work, "neither Soviet treachery, nor the defeatism and prejudice of Asia and of certain Latin American countries, dangerously associated through demagoguery with models in the Bandung Community." This was the thinking of the Brazilian delegation working in the Trusteeship Council between 1954 and 1957.

In 1958, although greater vigor was felt on the part of the African delegates, with Ghana in the lead and supported always by the United Arab Republic, the Brazilian delegation intervened in the debates to emphasize the several positive aspects of the colonial powers, discourage the establishment of deadlines for independence, and consider innocuous the anticolonial thesis "of the Soviets and their followers." But in that same year, the awareness acquired by the peoples of Africa, united through the negative aspects of colonialism and underdevelopment, and fear of dangerous isolation and dependence in projects of interest to Brazil on the votes of those countries led our delegation to declare to the Secretary of State that "the moment has arrived for us to reconsider the 'middle road policy' that has always oriented us in confronting situations arising out of the nationalist expansion of African peoples." It was thought at that time that, without taking on "Arab-Asian extremism, we could reconcile our line with that continent's tendencies and the obsolete conservative attitude of certain powers." In this way we avoided isolation and reviewed our policy, as several nations had been doing, in order to bring it into line with African reality.

Obviously, there could have been no greater confusion or political fluctuation in the same year; at times we were against anticolonialism and other times we favored a readjustment that would do away with dialectic terms in our interests and those of the great powers, or of the national figures with whom they were closely associated. But the attitude was still clearly sympathetic to the colonial powers, as in the Algerian question where our involvement with France was apparent, although the pill was coated with the customary friendly words. "Brazil sympathizes with the revolt and struggle for independence," said the head of our delegation, "but states have become more or less interdependent. This is the case of Algeria and France, which would certainly have much to gain if they continued together. It is hard to see anyone lose confidence in France, which has decided to cope with the Algerians' needs and help them in their present difficulties."

The Algerian Revolution began in 1954, and in January, 1955, Saudi Arabia called the attention of the Security Council to the situation created in Algeria, where "by means of merciless military operations, the colonialists wish to liquidate Algerian national characteristics." After July, 1955, the United Nations gradually became informed on the Algerian cause and saw the ranks of its partisans swell and an increase in the number of those approving the several resolutions on the question, such as Nos. 909 (X), 1012 (XI) and 1184 (XII). At first the dividing line in debate on the matter separated only the Eastern from the Western group; later, Latin Americans began to join in, and in 1959 the United States attitude moved from opposition to abstention. When he was a senator in 1957, John F. Kennedy himself reproached the American government for the uncritical policy with regard to France that had weakened United States prestige, helped the Communist cause, and denied the American colonial heritage.[183] From the beginning, in July, 1955, France argued that the affair was solely and exclusively one of French national jurisdiction, and it withdrew from the Plenary Session when Resolution No. 909 was adopted on November 25, 1955. Although it was decided to give no further consideration to the item in that session, the Assembly's right to discuss the matter had been recognized. In 1957 the French delegation changed its attitude slightly, no longer refusing to discuss the issue but announcing that it did not feel obliged to act upon United Nations recommendation. The appearance of Minister Christian Pineau in person, however, showed the significance that France placed on the question, although it was still certain that chancellery agreements would prevent any resolution

---

[183] *The New York Times,* July 3, 1957.

contrary to its thesis on the impropriety of United Nations interference and hopeful for a resolution containing even an implicit recognition of United Nations incompetence. Pineau defended his thesis exhaustively in a juridical manner, but cited only one "eminent jurist," Sr. Raul Fernandes. He concluded by saying, in the name of information, that France was ready to cease fire, hold elections, and discuss the future status of Algeria. Dr. Farid Zeineddine of Syria replied by an examination of M. Pineau's insulting attitude and Pineau's and Fernandes' "unilateral legalistic fiction."

The head of our delegation, in statements already referred to, also concluded by citing Sr. Raul Fernandes, who supported France's right and duty to reject United Nations jurisdiction in the Algerian question. Brazil declared itself in support of the French position then, and further proposed a resolution that merely expressed "the hope of finding a peaceful and democratic solution." Brazil was always bound by the idea of not prejudicing France and of voting against proposals allowing United Nations interference. In December, 1959, the Brazilian delegation received instructions from Foreign Minister Horácio Láfer to consult the delegation of the United States with the idea of voting with it, still on the side of the French interests, despite the recommendation made to the Ministry in July of the same year that "without adopting a position in favor of the Afro-Asian bloc, neither must we have a hostile attitude toward them, that is, one of extreme solidarity with France." It is true that the United States had been moving from its traditional stand of opposition toward one of abstention; and most of Latin America was inclined not to vote against the Afro-Asian plan, although it was divided between a favorable vote or abstention. France was daily losing Western support, and if the leader of the Western Alliance was abandoning France, why should this group be more royalist than the king? The dilemma for Brazil now was not whether to be pro or con the Afro-Asian resolution, but whether to be con or abstain. Brazil could not remain conspicuously in the minority, a minority that was annually growing smaller, for in 1958 only eighteen of the eighty-two countries had adopted the extreme position of voting against.

The spirit of Raul Fernandes seemed to persist in the orientation of foreign policy, presided over by Juscelino Kubitschek since 1956. Serve France, even if we should put ourselves in a position of open hostility to the Afro-Asian bloc, whose interests in several other matters coincided with ours. Serve France, even if we were later to be the object of discrimination by the Common Market, or of that depressing negative in 1959 when the head of our delegation solicited French support for the P.A.O. He told Minister Couve de Murville that even "a gesture of sympathy or a word, without the slightest obligation," in his speech to the United Nations on the P.A.O. would help Brazil in its campaign, which we certainly deserved "because we had more than demonstrated our devotion to France," having always voted in accordance with French interests, "frequently isolating ourselves from other nations on the continent, including even Haiti." [184] De Murville's reply was indifference.

Its lack of historical perspective kept the ruling minority from understanding, as to this day it does not understand with regard to Angola, that Algeria was a separate entity on the African continent with obvious national characteristics, and therefore its native population of more than ten millions would fight to form a sovereign state, independent of the one million French and French descendants desiring retention of the status quo or at least autonomy integrated into the French Union. The decision to take up arms would be the way to victory, which would come sooner or later, but blind, paralyzing routine and the knot binding French interests to those of certain dominant Brazilian groups did not admit the possibility of an independent Algerian state. The dominant orientation of Brazilian foreign policy was a disservice to Brazil for it alienated the support and sympathy in the United Nations of a considerable number of Afro-Asian states, knowing that the latter were receiving important reinforcements with the admission of new members. Nor could it be hidden that the presence of petroleum in the Sahara was only aggravating the conflict of interests.

The Algerian tragedy continued to be discussed in the Fifteenth and Sixteenth Sessions of the General Assembly, and Brazil maintained the same compromised position despite the cost of more than 600,000 Moslem and 100,000 non-Moslem lives. The war in Algeria constituted a threat to international peace and security and the United Nations could

---

[184] Augusto Frederico Schmidt, "Negativas Deprimentes," *O Globo*, June 23, 1961.

no longer limit themselves to expressing the hope and desire for mediation based on the principle of self-determination. Resolution No. 1573 (XV), December 19, 1960) [185] was adopted by a vote of sixty-three to eight with twenty-seven abstentions, including Brazil's, and No. 1724 (XVI, December 20, 1961) [186] by sixty-two to zero with thirty-eight abstentions, again including Brazil's. When the work of the Sixteenth Session began in September, 1961, the head of our delegation stated that "our fraternal relations with Portugal and our traditional friendship with France do not prevent us from taking a clear stand in the painful differences that have arisen on the subject of African colonialism between the United Nations and those countries, to whom we owe so much and with whom we still have so much in common. The two European states must, in our opinion, assure the self-determination of Algeria and Angola." [187] Despite this and the affirmations of Minister San Tiago Dantas in favor of self-determination,[188] Brazil abstained from voting on the proposed resolution presented by thirty-three African countries, based as always on formal juridical reasons such as: "(a) the reference to the Provisional Government of the Algerian Republic, which is unrecognized by almost all the members of the United Nations; (b) the reference to the basic principles already accepted by France—self-determination and independence within Algerian unity and integrity—and the lack of reference to guarantees to be granted the European minority in a sovereign Algeria." Without our sympathy, our support, and our understanding, Algeria became inde-

---

[185] The resolution recognized the imperative need for effective guarantees assuring auto-determination, reaffirmed U.N. responsibility, demanded respect for the territorial unity and integrity of Algeria, and proclaimed the inalienable right of peoples to complete freedom. This was the first resolution on Algeria to be approved since 1957.

[186] It recalls the previous resolution; registers the fact that the two parties stated their decision to seek a negotiated, peaceful solution on the basis of the Algerian people's right to auto-determination and independence; laments the suspension of negotiations and requests that the two parties resume them in order to permit the Algerian people to enjoy their right to auto-determination and independence; demands respect for the territorial unity and integrity of Algeria.

[187] Text distributed through the Information Service of the Ministério de Relações Exteriores, September 20, 1962.

[188] Reply to a questionnaire in the *Jornal da Frente de Libertação Nacional, El Moudjaid,* reproduced in the *Jornal do Brasil,* December 16, 1961.

pendent on April 3, 1962, after eight years of bloody strife, and discharging our traditional task by opening the Seventeenth Session in September 1962, our delegate to the United Nations spoke of liquidating colonialism but did not greet the new nation that had been born a few months earlier, supported by the Brazilian people but without the help of the dominant Brazilian minority that had placed itself in the service of France and had received in return the intransigent discrimination of the Common Market.

Our solidarity with France was so broad that even when the question of atomic experiments in the Sahara was discussed, and the French had only the United Kingdom, Italy, Belgium, and the United States on their side, the Brazilian mission to the United Nations received instructions not to associate itself with the Latin American states but to negotiate a plan the terms of which would be acceptable to France. The essence of the plan was to request France to take necessary precautions! We were isolated by voting against the Afro-Asian plan when no fewer than ten countries in the Western political alliances voted in favor of it, including Canada. The latter pointed out that its position was due "to the understandable preoccupation with the risks to humanity inherent in any new increase through human action of levels of radioactivity." The resolution was approved fifty-one to sixteen with fifteen abstentions,[189] opposed by Brazil, Peru, Nicaragua, the Dominican Republic, and Honduras, the only Latin American countries to vote this way.

If there is any coherence in Brazilian policy, it is to be found, as we have stressed above, in the study of plans for economic development in underdeveloped countries. Brazil's orientation in the Economic and Social Council has always been to emphasize the necessity of investigating more deeply and with greater resources the theoretical and practical problems of industrialization in underdeveloped areas and to support the several resolutions, from No. 520A (VI, January 12, 1952) to the most recent ones, especially those of December 19, 1961: No. 1706, "Special United Nations Fund for Finance and Economic Development"; No. 1707, "International Trade as a Chief Instrument of Development"; No. 1708, "Planning for Economic Development"; No. 1709, "Decentralization of United Nations Economic and Social Activities and Strengthen-

---

[189] Resolution No. 1380 (XIV), November 20, 1959.

ing of Regional Economic Commissions"; No. 1710, "Decade of United Nations Development: A Program for International Economic Coöperation"; No. 1712, "Activities of the United Nations in the Field of Industrial Development"; and No. 1713, "The Role of Patents in the Transference of Technology to Underdeveloped Countries." Of all these plans the only one initiated by us was the one dealing with patents, which was presented by the Brazilian delegate, sociologist Guerreiro Ramos. It would be difficult to abandon support of or intervention in favor of plans like these, which are of such economic importance to the nation, despite a Ministry document stating that Brazil's independent line could be illustrated by the fact that plans 1706, 1709, and 1712 had been energetically opposed by the industrialized countries, as was to be expected. Not to join the underdeveloped countries here in order to follow the Western powers would indeed have meant total subservience.

But it has been especially in the problem of the political emancipation of non-autonomous territories, which is the basis of Afro-Asian unity and solidarity, that Brazil has always hesitated in its policy; ever since Jânio Quadros its path has been a zigzag, difficult to follow and to understand.

The question that has most compromised Brazilian policy in the area of colonialism, together with the Angolan problem, has been the obligation on the part of the administrative powers to transmit information on non-autonomous territories. We have already seen the evolution of this problem from 1946 to 1953. When Portugal was admitted into the United Nations, it declared that Article 73e did not apply to its territories, for they were integral parts of the nation. In the Fourth Commission of 1956, the delegate from Iraq raised the problem of Portugal's overseas territories, urging that it was necessary for the new members to collaborate in achieving United Nations goals and showing the need for these territories to come under Article 73e of the Charter. For the Portuguese representative, Franco Nogueira, the article was inapplicable when it conflicted with constitutional norms, and Portugal had only one constitution applied equally in all its provinces. Brazil's position was defined on January 30, 1957, and represented the most extraordinary retreat in Brazilian policy in the United Nations, one that would later be the cause of our vacillation on the Angolan question.

The Brazilian delegate considered that it was exclusively within the province of the interested states to declare if a territory is or is not covered by Article 73e, and as this had been the norm followed by the General Assembly since 1946, he stated, to reform this criterion deserved condemnation on two points, because it ran counter to peacefully accepted practice and constituted a discriminatory act, and because the word of a sovereign state could not be placed in doubt.[190]

Brazilian intervention in a vehement speech that was later supported by the United States, which also maintained that it was up to the member states to declare whether or not they had non-autonomous territories, altered the tone of the debate and brought about the union of those opposing the Portuguese stand and refusing to allow a new system to be inaugurated under which it would be exclusively within the competence of the interested state to declare if a territory came under Article 73e or not. The plan presented by the Afro-Asian group creating an ad hoc committee to examine the replies of the recently admitted states won in the Commission (35-33), but was defeated in the Plenary (35-35) at the conclusion of a frantic struggle in the chancelleries and corridors after all resources had been utilized, including requirement of two-thirds for approval.

Portugal's victory was indecisive, as may be seen from subsequent events; many countries had simply made a concession to Portugal, others were probably not ready for a formal showdown, and others—which had been forced to give in—would not wish to close the door on future questions on the Portuguese overseas territories. Portugal had counted on the collaboration of Brazil, Spain, the United States, and the British Commonwealth for the diplomatic negotiations resulting in this victory, but the Afro-Asian bloc had begun a relentless fight that was to leave Portugal practically isolated. When the plan was defeated the delegate from Iraq stated: "We shall not hesitate to raise the question again next year and, if necessary, year after year."

Thus there was increasingly more articulation, strength, and conviction. Portugal continued to repeat that it was unaware of the existence of non-autonomous territories under its administration, for its entire territory is divided politically and administratively into "provinces," all

---

[190] *United Nations, General Assembly, Official Records: Eleventh Session,* November 12, 1956, to February 22, 1957, New York, 1957, 329–330.

having equal status, including its overseas provinces, and therefore any United Nations interference is contrary to Article 2, No. 7, of the Charter. Later, as its isolation grew, it began to inveigh against the ideological plurality in the United Nations, against anticolonialism, against the West which was making one concession after another, against Latin America which had blind faith in self-determination and believed that African independence would lessen economic competition; finally, it confused issues and rambled on about what colonies and colonialism are. "The open conflict between the United Nations and Portugal could not and cannot be resolved in parliamentary terms so long as the objectives of the majority are opposed as they are to Portuguese national policy," explained Franco Nogueira.[191] And Brazil continued to vote with Portugal, recognizing its arguments and its right not to furnish information, until in the Fifteenth Assembly, in 1960, a huge step was taken with regard to non-autonomous territories.

In the euphoria created by the independence of a large number of African and Asian states, several resolutions were approved to assist various colonial or non-autonomous peoples attain independence. Resolution No. 1514 (XV, December 14, 1960), "Declaration Granting Independence to Colonial Nations and Peoples," which received our vote despite initial hesitation and our delegate's evasive speech, recognized the passionate desire for liberty of dependent peoples and that the nations of the world ardently await the end of colonialism and all its manifestations; it stated that all military action and repression directed against dependent peoples would be ended in order to permit them to exercise their right to complete independence and territorial integrity freely and peacefully. It added that measures would be taken in territories under trusteeship, non-autonomous territories, and all territories that had not yet obtained their independence to transfer all power to the people of those territories, unconditionally and unreservedly, in accordance with their will and freely expressed votes, without distinction of race, creed or color, in order to permit them to enjoy complete independence and liberty.[192]

---

[191] *As Nações Unidas e Portugal*, Lisbon, 1961.
[192] Portuguese text in *Diário do Congresso*, April, 1961, 2519–2520, included in Deputy Bocayuva Cunha's speech when he was a member of the Brazilian delegation.

Approved eighty-nine to zero with nine abstentions (Australia, Belgium, Dominican Republic, France, Portugal, Spain, South Africa, United Kingdom, and United States),[193] the resolution strengthened the anticolonial position in the United Nations and may be considered an about-face, as it is by Senator Wayne Morse, especially if we note that this same Assembly approved Resolution No. 1541 (December 15, 1960), "Guiding Principles for Member States to Determine whether or not the Obligation Exists to Transmit Information according to Article 73e of the Charter." This was a code of twelve principles that were to orient states administering territories in observing the provisions of the Charter and that furnished them with recommendations tending to hasten progress in the dissolution of the colonial system and granting of independence. Moreover—and for this reason, too, 1960 was Africa's year—Resolution No. 1542 (December 15, 1960) was approved, "Transmission of Information according to Article 73e of the Charter," which under this generic title was actually directed to Spain and Portugal, for in view of Resolutions Nos. 742 (VIII) and 1541 (XI) it considered that the following territories were non-autonomous: Cape Verde Archipelago, Portuguese Guinea, São Tomé and Príncipe and their dependencies, São João Batista of Ajudá,[194] Angola, including Cabinda, Mozambique, Goa and dependencies,[195] Macao and dependencies, and Timor and dependencies. The fact that even the Spanish government, although it considered its overseas provinces integral parts of its territory, submitted to the United Nations and supplied the information requested further isolated Portugal in its obstinate insistence that it possessed no colonial or non-autonomous territory. Resolution No. 1514 became the fundamental instrument of United Nations action against colonialism, and Resolution No. 1542 rendered the Portuguese position untenable,

---

[193] When the statement was approved, Mme Zelma Watson George, a substitute delegate, joined in the general applause, later stating to the press that the American delegation was favorable to the Afro-Asian plan and had abstained only because of "orders from Washington"; the American delegate, Senator Wayne Morse, wrote that the United States did not vote in favor of it because of pressure from the British government. See his report to the United States Foreign Relations Committee, *The United States in the United Nations, 1960—A Turning Point,* Washington, 1961.

[194] The Republic of Dahomey removed the Portuguese Resident on August 1, 1961, thus ending Portugal's control.

[195] On December 19, 1961, Goa and its dependencies were occupied by India.

making obvious the slender basis of our attachment to Salazar in 1957 and revealing our total lack of perspective on the historical process of liquidating colonialism.

It was a real about-face for Brazil to vote in favor of Resolution No. 1542 because, with Spain, France, Portugal, and the Union of South Africa only, it had until the Fourteenth Session shown itself in favor of the thesis of exclusive competence of the member states to declare whether or not they possessed autonomous territories.

Since that time several resolutions on colonial questions have received our support and aggravated the Portuguese position, giving rise to strong condemnations of Portuguese colonialism because of the intransigence of Portuguese foreign policy. Year after year, as prophesied by the delegate from Iraq, Mr. Pachachi, the growing strength of the Afro-Asian group is making the debate more fierce and violent, with Portugal even considered on the same level as South Africa as one of the nightmares of colonialism.

Resolution No. 1654 (XVI, November 27, 1961), which had the support of the Brazilian delegation, established a special commission of seventeen members (expanded to twenty-four in the Seventeenth Session) to pursue compliance with the Declaration Granting Independence (Resolution No. 1514), which attended to the aspirations of the anticolonial majority and served as a spearhead for the liquidation of colonialism; Resolution No. 1699 (XV, December 15, 1961) condemned (with a reservation on the part of Brazil) the continuous lack of compliance by Portugal with the obligations of Article 73e of the Charter and with the terms of Resolution No. 1542 (XV), and decided to establish a Committee of Seven to examine any and all information relative to the Portuguese territories and to prepare a report.[196]

The Seventeenth Session of the General Assembly examined this committee's report, which was the result of a trip to Africa between May and June of 1962 and, in addition to arriving at the conclusion that NATO weapons had been used to repress African nationalist movements, recommended that the Assembly set up a unit specifically for the study of development in the territories under Portuguese administration

---

[196] Text of the Charter of the Committee of Seven, New York, March 13, and the Portuguese reply, Lisbon, March 23, in *Boletim Geral do Ultramar,* April, 1962, 20–23. See also *United Nations Review,* May, 1962, 16–18, and June, 1962, 16–17.

and expressed its belief that the most urgent step for Portugal now was to recognize the right of the people in its territories to independence.[197] But Portugal insists obstinately on "not following the current of history and [on] accompanying these territories in the future as a friend and partner." Hence Resolutions No. 1807 (XVII, December 14, 1962), approved eighty-two to seven with thirteen abstentions (including Brazil's), condemning the incompatibility of Portugal's attitude and the United Nations Charter and reaffirming "the inalienable right of territorial peoples under Portuguese administration to self-determination and independence"; No. 1808 (XVII, same date), establishing a training program for territories under Portuguese administration; and No. 1809 (XVII, same date), establishing a Special Commission for the territories under Portuguese administration.

On all these resolutions Brazil's position "has remained inalterable in substance, that is, that such territories are non-autonomous and entitled to self-determination, as an eventual step prior to independence." But in its voting, following the same zigzag path, the Brazilian delegation has abstained, "since, as last year, it could not be a party to the condemnation of Portugal and the recommendation of sanctions approved by the majority of the Latin American and Afro-Asian countries." This was an angle in the broken, vacillating line which alternated with the other angle that approved Resolution No. 1810 (XVII, December 17, 1962) on compliance with the "Declaration Granting Independence to Colonial Nations and Peoples," reinforcing the above-mentioned Resolutions Nos. 1514 (XV) and 1654 (XVI). In this way Brazilian foreign policy supported liberty for all colonial peoples, but held reservations with regard to those peoples subject to the "sacred civilizing mission of Portugal."

This vacillation unites Raul Fernandes and Hermes Lima in the same conservative thought, one of them legitimately reactionary, clear in his logic and the alienation of his viceroy-like attitude, and the other a man who, like P. O. Lapie, illogically combined socialism and colonialism and allowed himself to be dominated by chancellery pressures, corridor and behind-the-scenes politics, and by that sentimentalism which should never inspire a foreign policy dedicated to national interests. Hence the hesitation in the case of Angola—where only San Tiago Dantas

---

[197] "Immediate Independence Asked for All Portuguese Territories," *United Nations Review*, September, 1962, 17–20.

exhibited strength of character—withdrawing, advancing, withdrawing again.

In May, 1961, the Monrovia Conference adopted a resolution calling for all African states to support the Angolan struggle morally and materially. In June, 1961, the delegation from Ghana informed the Security Council that its government had closed its sea and air ports to Portuguese ships and planes, had adopted other restrictive measures in its relations with Portugal, and condemned the latter's policy in Angola; the government of the Congo Republic (Leopoldville) renounced agreements with Portugal made previously by Belgium; the Security Council took note of the great concern in and strong reactions of the entire African continent to the events in Angola; the government of Norway announced that it had refused "permission to export arms to Portugal because of its colonial policy in Angola"; the British government revealed that it had suspended all licenses for the supply of military equipment to Portuguese overseas territories; the government of Senegal broke diplomatic relations with Portugal and, in April, 1963, would denounce to the United Nations Portuguese attacks on its territory. In August, 1961, Dahomey reincorporated Portuguese Cabinda into its territory, justifying itself on the grounds of Portuguese colonial policy, and the foreign ministers signing the African Charter condemned Portuguese policy in Angola. In September, 1961, the conference in Belgrade of the heads of noncommitted states condemned Portuguese methods of repression and demanded an immediate end to the shedding of Angolan blood; and the Conference of the Malagasy African Union condemned Portugal for its action in Angola and proposed the breaking of diplomatic relations with Portugal by member states of the United Nations and assistance to the Angolan nationalists.[198] Later, in April, 1962, an official of the State Department declared in the Senate Foreign Affairs Committee that the government of the United States had sent its protest to Portugal against the use of American military equipment in Angola.[199]

---

[198] See *Report of the Sub-Committee of the Situation in Angola, General Assembly, Official Records, Sixteenth Session,* New York, 1962, 44.
[199] Statements of the Assistant Secretary of State, *The New York Times,* April 11, 1962. Sir Patrick Dean British delegate to the U.N., made similar statements. *United Nations General Assembly, Official Records,* Session 1099, January 26, 1962, 1307.

International reaction was, then, widespread and strong. And what was Brazil doing? Its two-edged policy—generally anticolonialist after 1960, but colonialist with respect to the Portuguese colonies—had no word of friendship for the Angolan nationalists and had reserved its sympathy for the Portuguese alone. Only in Jânio Quadros' message to Congress had mention been made of Brazil's debt of gratitude to the Angolans who had helped to build this country, but never by any act had a foreign minister expressed his feelings to Angolans dying for their country's freedom. Our diplomats heeded the appeal from one side and hardened themselves against appeals from the other. In the United Nations after 1960 the Brazilian delegation supported anticolonialist resolutions and programs for Africa, distinguished itself in the struggle for the freedom of Ruanda and Urundi, but remained inflexible on the Angolan question and looked for legal sophisms as in the case of Algeria.

In February, 1961, Liberia requested an emergency session to deal with the situation in Angola, "the beginning of another colonial war," and on April 20, 1961, the General Assembly approved seventy-three to two (Spain and the Union of South Africa), with nine abstentions (including Brazil's), Resolution No. 1603. This was a request to the government of Portugal to consider as urgent the need to introduce reforms in Angola, with the reminder to comply with Resolution No. 1514 (XV); it was also decided to name a sub-committee of five members to examine the situation and present a report to the Assembly as soon as possible. The debates leading to approval of this resolution greatly stressed not the independence of Angola but the need for Portugal to guarantee the Negro population enjoyment of the fundamental rights of man. Although authorized to vote in favor of the Afro-Asian proposal, the Brazilian delegation abstained because it did not support the work of the sub-committee and preferred that information be requested directly of the Portuguese government.[200]

On June 9 of the same year the Security Council adopted resolutions calling for Portugal to act in accordance with the terms of Resolution No. 1603 and desist in its repressive measures, and expressing the hope

---

[200] Itamarati instructions are dated April, 1961, when Sr. Afonso Arinos de Melo Franco was Minister and Sr. Ciro de Freitas Vale the delegate from Brazil.

that a peaceful solution might be reached. The report of the sub-committee, discussed in the Sixteenth Session of the Assembly, led to the adoption of Resolution No. 1742 of January 30, 1962, by a vote of ninety-nine (including Brazil) to two (Spain and the Union of South Africa), in which Portugal's lack of coöperation in the work of the sub-committee was deplored and regret expressed concerning Portugal's persistent refusal to recognize Angola as an autonomous territory and its failure to take measures to comply with the 1960 declaration on colonialism. This resolution reaffirmed the right of the Angolan people to self-determination and independence, disapproved of repressive measures and the denial of human rights and fundamental liberties to the Angolan people, called for the liberation of political prisoners, stressed the urgent need for political, economic, and social reforms, decided that the sub-committee would continue its work, requested that all member states use their influence to assure compliance with these regulations on Portugal's part and refuse any support to Portugal that might be used to oppress the Angolan people; and, finally, asked the government of Portugal to submit a report on the situation to the Seventeenth Assembly.[201]

Exceptionally, Brazil voted in favor of this resolution—the historic vote referred to by San Tiago Dantas—and this was the first time that we had only one view on colonialism. When he established our line in the Angolan question, our delegate emphasized as usual our centuries-old ties with Portugal (without stressing our ties with Africa) and Brazilian anticolonialism, "a marked trait of our national character, imposed by racial brotherhood, geographical position, economic interests, and sincere conviction, as strong among leading circles as among the popular masses, that believes that anticolonialism and disarmament are the two great causes of this century." He forgot that the source of our anticolonialist conviction was popular and not in the upper classes, and that for this very reason Brazil had never taken a definite and coherent stand on the chief issues discussed by the United Nations. Recognition by Portugal of the right of the Angolan people to self-determination, he added, would facilitate the peaceful solution that

---

[201] *Resolutions Adopted by the General Assembly, Sixteenth Session,* September 19, 1961, to February 23, 1962, New York, 1962, I, 67.

everyone was seeking and would help to safeguard relations between Portugal and Angola. Further, Brazil could not remain indifferent to the preservation of "Portuguese culture in Africa and Asia," by which he probably meant the Portuguese elements in Angolan culture, for he observed that Brazil had always respected elements from the most varied cultures. Despite this, when he exhorted Portugal to assume leadership in the liberation of Angola, the reply that he received was withdrawal of the Portuguese delegation from the Plenary Session, which was exactly the way that France had behaved when the Algerian question was discussed.

In a report to the Itamarati, an important Brazilian delegate wrote:

The opposition of the Portuguese dictatorship to all political progress in the Portuguese colonies makes the question of Angola more difficult. Portugal has defied not only the United Nations but the very logic of the times. The Brazilian position has appeared difficult in this case because of the presence of pressure groups in our government, groups that act in good or bad faith depending on whether they are misinformed or frankly instruments of economic power. They are joined by reactionary elements in our country, such as happens in analogous cases in other countries, including the United States. The reactionaries working against natural evolution of the colonial problem in Angola are the same type as those who support the "rights" of capitalist exploitation in Catanga, and those who support the French "honor" of General Salan's explosive followers. They are the same everywhere in the world.

The stubborn Portuguese resistance that would not hear the appeals of our minister or those of the ministers of the United States and Great Britain further weakens Portugal's stand, especially if we consider that in accordance with Resolution No. 1702 its allies must no longer lend their assistance. Portugal is a member of NATO and as such has received $300,000,000 in military aid and $90,000,000 in economic assistance since World War II; the leasing of bases in the Azores assures it other economic advantages ($100,000,000). The United States and Great Britain have declared officially that NATO arms will not be used in Angola,[202] but the impossibility of inspection, notwithstanding their good faith, makes real prohibition unrealizable. The request for an

---

[202] The gravest accusations on this point were made during debates on proposed Resolution No. 1542 (XV) and in the report of the Special Commission on the Portuguese Territories. See *United Nations Review,* September, 1962, 17–20.

embargo on NATO arms and insinuations concerning secret pacts between Portugal, South Africa, and the Federation of Rhodesia and Nyasaland only make its former allies isolate themselves from Portugal and, in exchange, elicit the applause of two of the most discriminatory countries in the African world, thus further weakening the authenticity of Portugal's announced colonial action.

Portugal cannot escape history nor slow its pace. Portugal is not besieged, nor is it the victim of an unjust world. No nation is hated per se, and none deserves greater friendship than another from Brazil. Rather Portugal is the victim of its superfluous autocracy and the spiritual degeneration of its upper classes, which have become sterile through power and have not responded to popular aspirations nor formed a leadership in the colonies. When a nation sees its policy unanimously rejected by world opinion and the United Nations, it is not the victim of injustice or moral aggression but of the incapacity of its own ruling minority.

The end of bloodshed in Algeria and the Congo will strengthen Angola's march to freedom, and Portugal will face the crisis with the same archaic leadership which, after so much enlightened progress, still repeats the old, worn-out declarations: the attack on Angola, wrote Salazar recently, does not concern Portugal alone but the whole West, and constitutes the chief obstacle to the progress and well-being of the entire African continent.[203] Just how much success Angola and Africa have derived from this leadership over five hundred years is clear. Portuguese leaders do not, therefore, know how to draw all the correct conclusions from the United Nations debates. And one of the greatest errors that may be committed by a statesman is not to keep in step with his times.

Nothing is falser or more tragic than to remain faithful to principles that, although good five hundred years ago, are no longer adapted to our age. Portugal does not unite but divides the world, and the realism and generosity of its people cannot allow it to forget that the prestige of the nation comes precisely from its once having placed itself in the vanguard of the nations of the world. To readjust to new conditions in

---

[203] Antônio de Oliveira Salazar, "Realities and Trends of Portuguese Policies," *International Affairs,* April 1962, pp. 169–183.

the world historical process, and to keep its leadership from continually breaking ties made everywhere by past generations of Portuguese, this is exclusively the task of the Portuguese people, that they be not annually confronted by world-wide censure of their ruling class' reactionary position and confused with an anachronistic leadership.

In the Seventeenth Session Portugal was reproved again by Resolution No. 1819 (December 18, 1962),[204] which deplored and condemned Portugal's colonial war. And again Brazil abstained. The "zig" of approval in some areas was followed by the "zag" of abstention in others, which strengthens the dictatorship and the archaism of the Portuguese ruling minority. If, as an African leader said in May, 1963, at the Conference of African States, it is necessary to "die a little" for Angolan liberty, it is equally true that it is necessary to "die a little" for Portuguese liberty, for only in this way will the irreconcilable become reconciled and the future of Portuguese-speaking peoples be assured.

---

[204] Text in *United Nations Review,* January, 1963, 93–94. The Special Committee of 24 members on April 4, 1963, approved a new resolution condemning Portugal. *United Nations Review* (April, 1963), 9–11 and 30.

Index